Preclinical Speech Science Workbook

Second Edition

Preclinical Speech Science Workbook

Second Edition

Jeannette D. Hoit, PhD
Gary Weismer, PhD

5521 Ruffin Road
San Diego, CA 92123

e-mail: info@pluralpublishing.com
Web site: http://www.pluralpublishing.com

49 Bath Street
Abingdon, Oxfordshire OX14 1EA
United Kingdom

Typeset in 12/14 Palatino by Flanagan's Publishing Services, Inc.
Printed in the United States of America by McNaughton and Gunn

ISBN13: 978-1-59756-521-9

ISBN10: 1-59756-521-0

Contents

Preface

The *Preclinical Speech Science Workbook, Second Edition* is a natural companion to the *Preclinical Speech Science, Second Edition* textbook. It has been carefully designed to help students reinforce, integrate, apply, and go beyond the material presented in the textbook.

The workbook contains a wide variety of activities. These include anatomic labeling, measuring physiologic and acoustic data, interpreting graphs, calculating quantitative problems, answering thought questions about material presented in the textbook, and conducting simple experiments (without the use of special equipment). The solutions to all these activities are provided at the back of the workbook; however, we strongly encourage students to work through each activity independently and refer to the solutions only when completely satisfied with their answers. This will provide the best learning experience and will help students make the transition from passive learners to active participants in their development toward becoming speech-language pathologists and clinical scientists.

Scientists—Humanists—Mentors—Partners—Friends
For Tom Hixon and Sadanand Singh
We hope you are watching and approving.

1

Introduction Questions

1-1. List (in order) the six levels of observation.

1-2. List the four subsystems of speech production and swallowing.

1-3. Define forensics and provide an example of a forensic application of speech production or swallowing data.

2

Breathing and Speech Production Questions

2–1. Label the skeletal structures indicated in the figure.

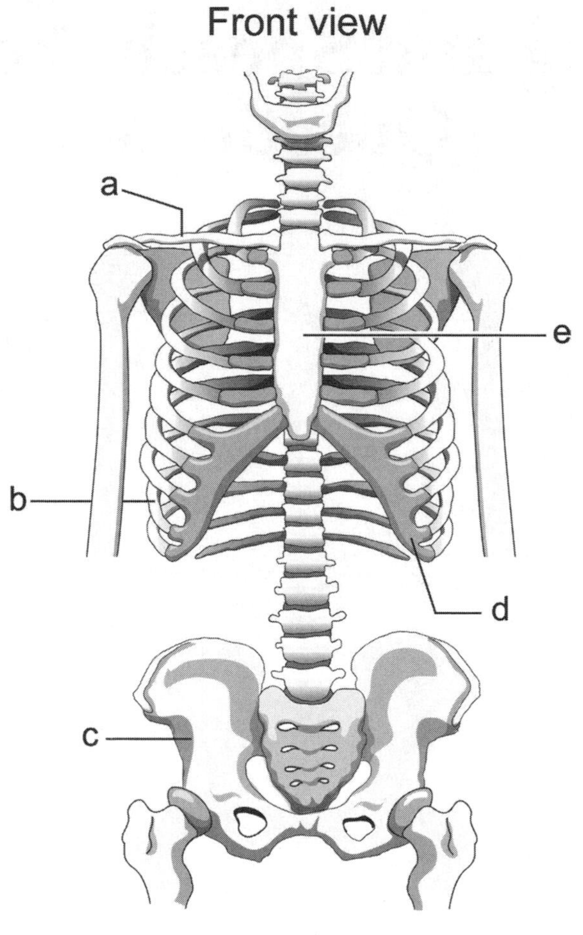

a ______________________________ d ______________________________

b ______________________________ e ______________________________

c ______________________________

2–2. Label the skeletal structures indicated in the figure.

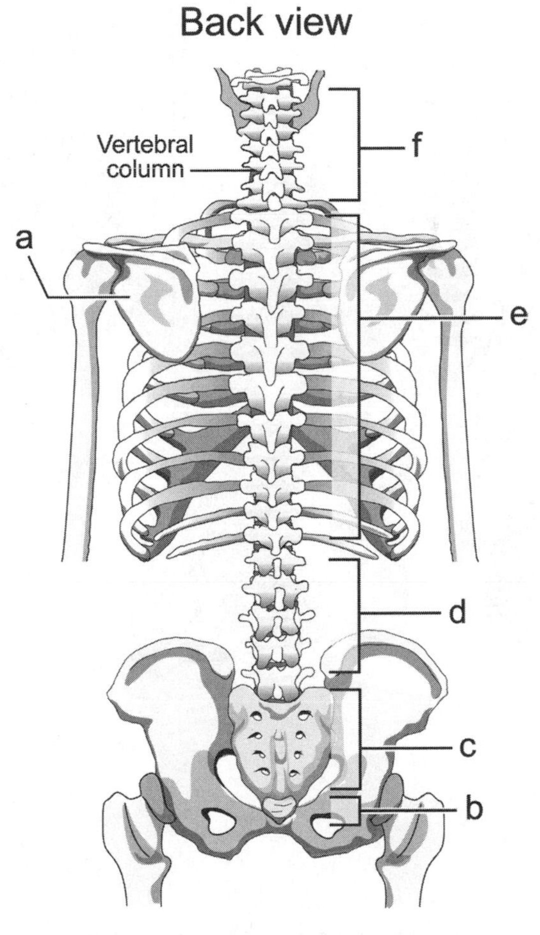

a ______________________ d ______________________

b ______________________ vertebrae e ______________________ vertebrae

c ______________________ vertebrae f ______________________ vertebrae

2–3. Label the pulmonary structures indicated in the figure.

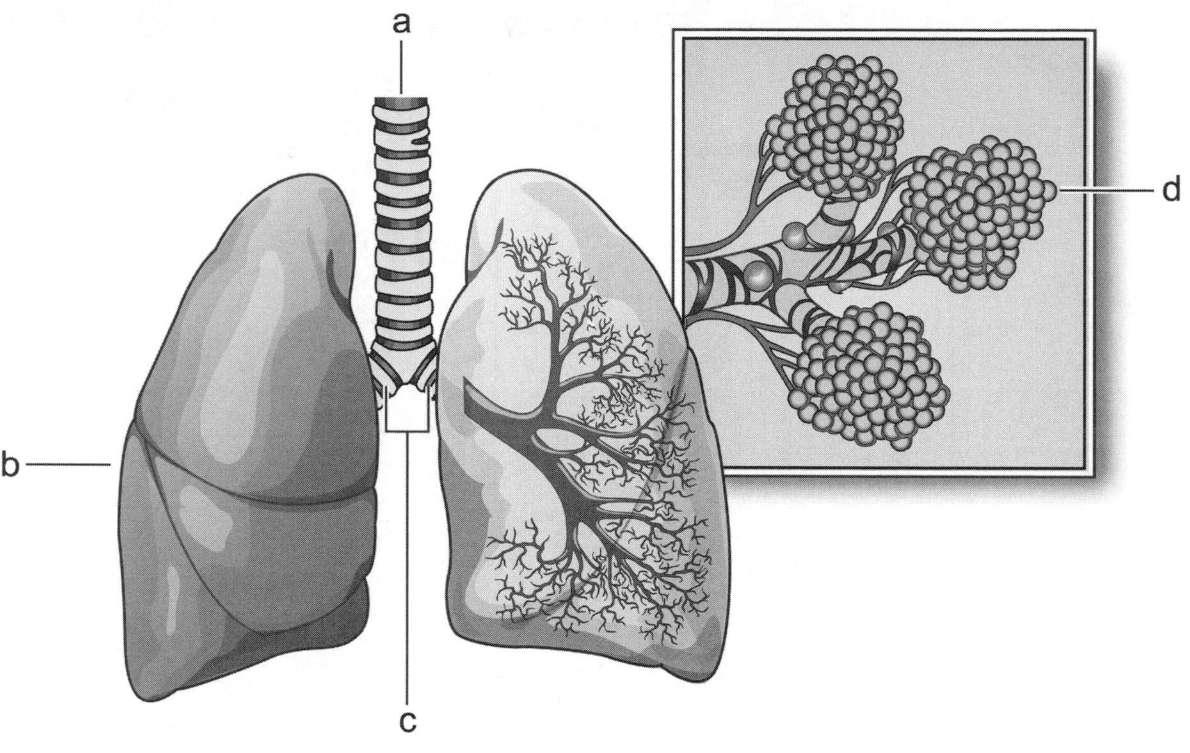

a ________________________________ c ________________________________

b ________________________________ d ________________________________

2–4. Label the muscles indicated in the figures.

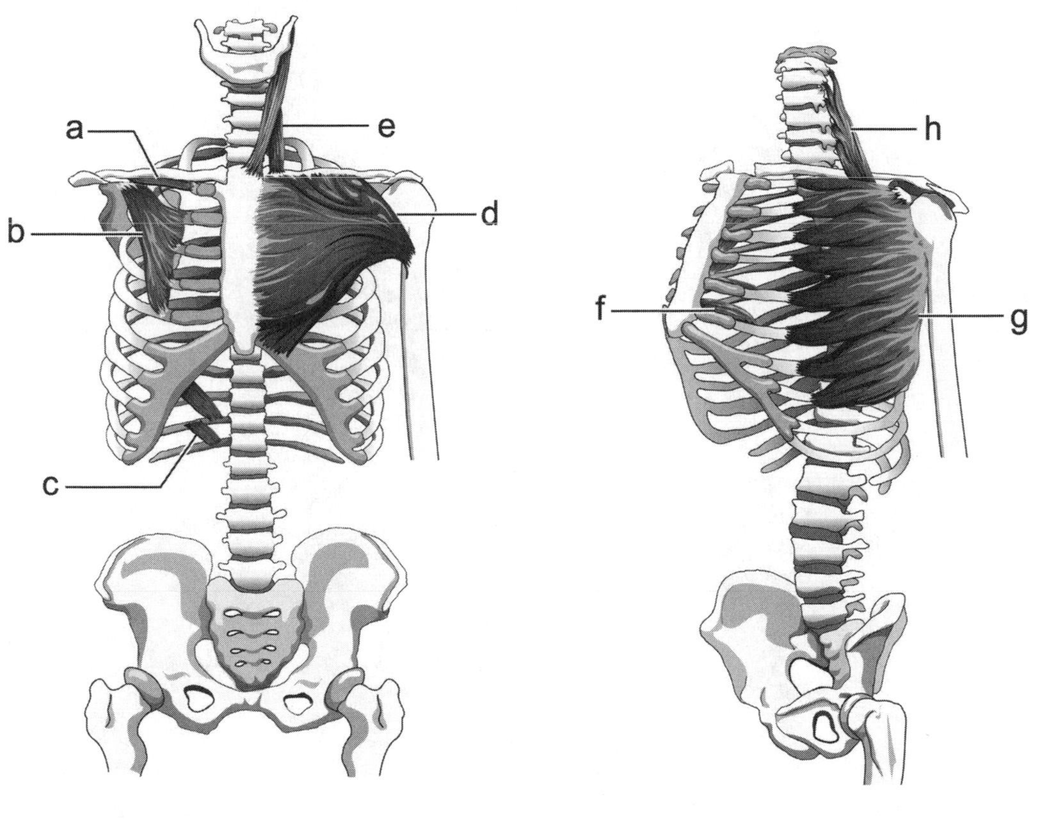

a ______________________________ e ______________________________

b ______________________________ f ______________________________

c ______________________________ g ______________________________

d ______________________________ h ______________________________

2–5. Label the muscles indicated in the figures.

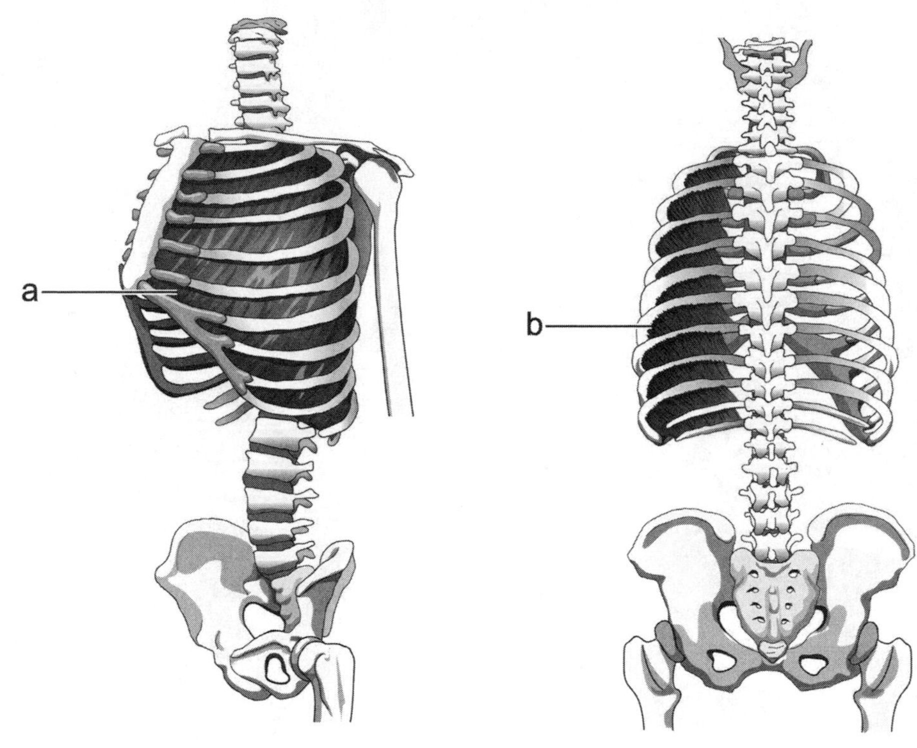

a ________________________ b ________________________

2-6. Label the muscles indicated in the figures.

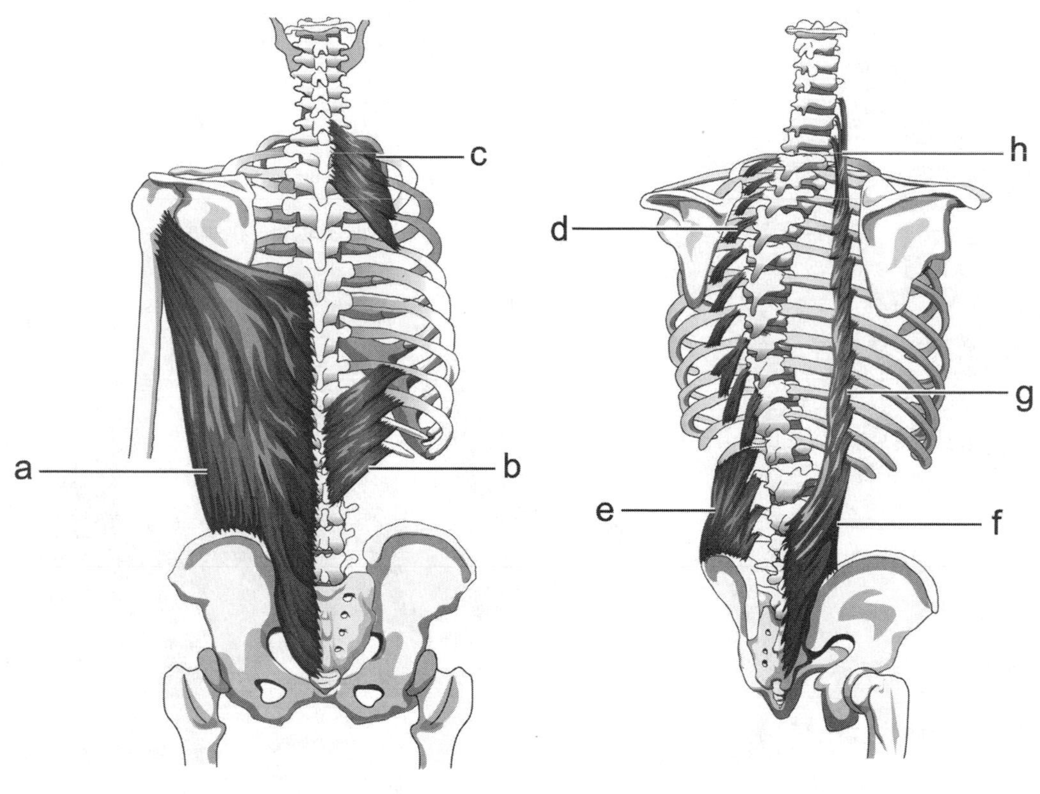

a ______________________________ e ______________________________

b ______________________________ f ______________________________

c ______________________________ g ______________________________

d ______________________________ h ______________________________

2–7. Label the muscle and other structures indicated in the figures.

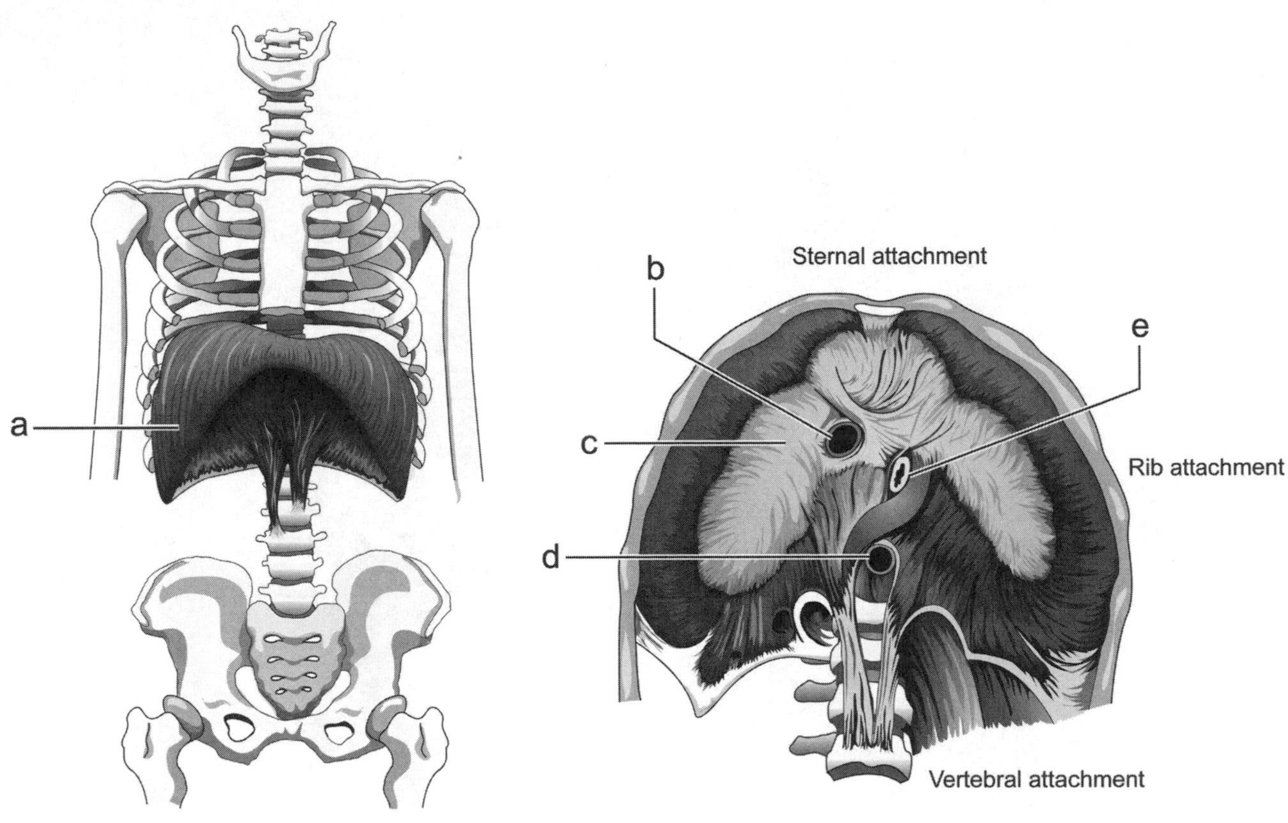

a ______________________

b ______________________

c ______________________

d ______________________

e ______________________

2–8. Label the muscles indicated in the figures.

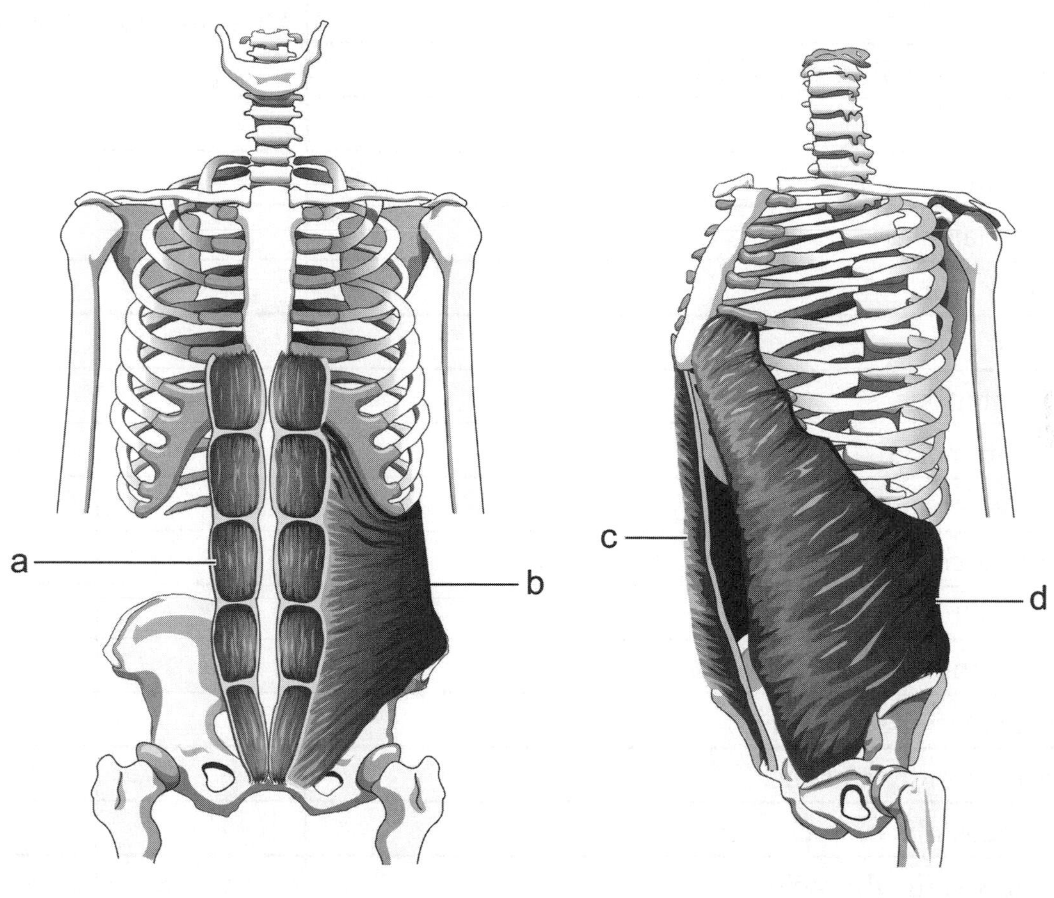

a ______________________ c ______________________

b ______________________ d ______________________

2-9. The muscles of the chest wall are listed below in the order that they are presented in the textbook. Place a check mark indicating whether they have potential to exert inspiratory and/or expiratory force on the breathing apparatus.

	Inspiratory	Expiratory
Muscles of the Rib Cage Wall		
Sternocleidomastoid		
Scalenus anterior, medius, and posterior		
Pectoralis major		
Pectoralis minor		
Subclavius		
Serratus anterior		
External intercostal		
Internal intercostal (between ribs)		
Internal intercostal (between costal cartilages)		
Transversus thoracis		
Latissimus dorsi		
Serratus posterior superior		
Serratus posterior inferior		
Lateral iliocostalis cervicis		
Lateral iliocostalis thoracis		
Lateral iliocostalis lumborum		
Levatores costarum		
Quadratus lumborum		
Subcostal		
Muscle of the Diaphragm		
Diaphragm		
Muscles of the Abdominal Wall		
Rectus abdominis		
External oblique		
Internal oblique		
Transversus abdominis		

2-10. The breathing apparatus can exert both passive and active (muscular) forces. Place a check mark to indicate the passive and/or active force(s) of each component of the breathing apparatus. [*Suggestion:* Do this exercise independently, then go to Figure 2–13 and associated text in your textbook to check your answers.]

	Passive Force		**Active Force**	
Component	**Inspiratory**	**Expiratory**	**Inspiratory**	**Expiratory**
Pulmonary apparatus				
Chest wall				
Rib cage wall				
Diaphragm				
Abdominal wall				

2-11. Active muscular forces exerted by an individual part of the chest wall—rib cage (RC) wall, diaphragm (DI), or abdominal (AB) wall—can cause movement of that part and it can cause movement in other parts of the chest wall. Fill in the table below to summarize the potential effects of contraction of RC (inspiratory and expiratory) muscles, diaphragm (inspiratory), and AB (expiratory) muscles on movements of the different parts of the chest wall. [*Suggestion:* Do this exercise independently, then go to Figure 2–14 and associated text in your textbook to check your answers.]

Muscle(s)	**Move RC outward**	**Move RC inward**	**Move DI footward**	**Move DI headward**	**Move AB outward**	**Move AB inward**
RC inspiratory						
RC expiratory						
DI (with RC fixed)						
DI (with AB fixed)						
AB						

2-12. The amount of air within the pulmonary apparatus can be subdivided into four lung volumes and four lung capacities. Label them as they are shown in the figure.

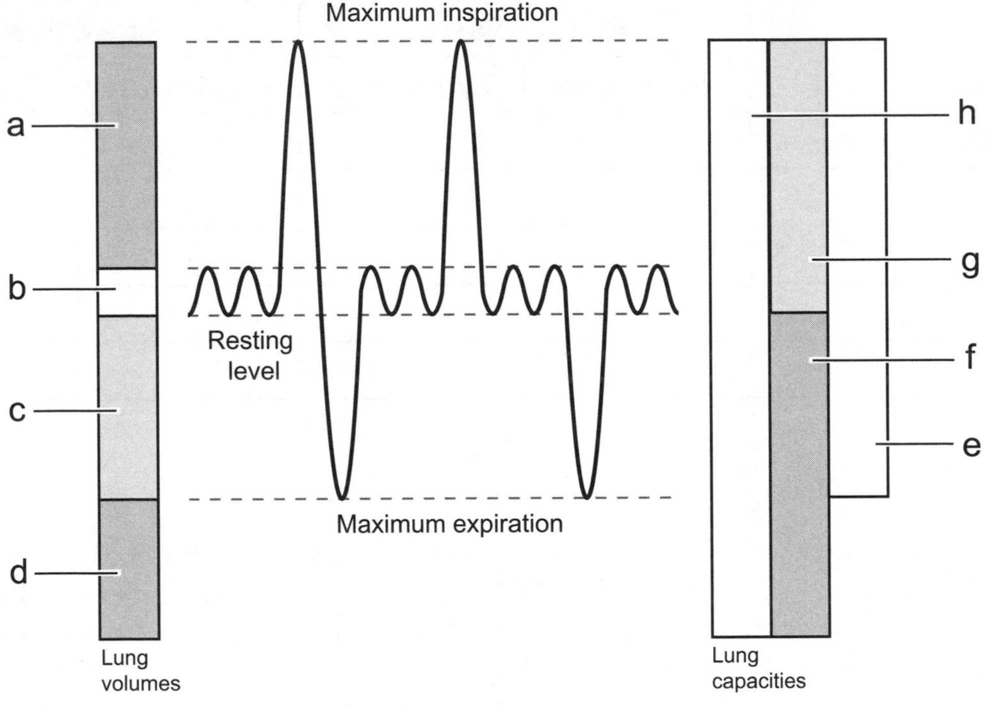

a ______________________ e ______________________

b ______________________ f ______________________

c ______________________ g ______________________

d ______________________ h ______________________

2-13. The table below contains prediction equations for total lung capacity (TLC) and residual volume (RV) in liters (L) (from Quanjer et al., 1993).[1] Ht = height (in meters)[2]; A = age (in years).

	TLC (L)	**RV (L)**
Men	(7.99 × Ht) – 7.08	(1.31 × Ht) + (0.022 × A) – 1.23
Women	(6.60 × Ht) – 5.79	(1.81 × Ht) + (0.016 × A) – 2.00

[1]Note that most prediction equations for lung volumes, including the ones given here, are based on data from both smokers and nonsmokers and people from different races and ethnic groups. Smoking and race/ethnicity (and other variables) can influence lung volumes. For example, if someone is a nonsmoker, the prediction equation above will probably overestimate RV.

[2]Conversion: 1 foot = 0.3048 meter.

(a) Calculate the following:

TLC for a man who is 5 feet, 6 inches tall ____________

TLC for a woman who is 5 feet, 6 inches tall ____________

What does this indicate about sex differences in TLC?

____

____

(b) Calculate the following:

RV for a man who is 5 feet, 6 inches tall and 25 years old ____________

RV for a man who is 5 feet, 6 inches tall and 75 years old ____________

What does this indicate about age differences in RV?

____

____

(c) Calculate the following:

Your TLC ____________

Your RV ____________

What, then, is your vital capacity (VC)? ____________

Would you expect your VC to increase or decrease as you get older? ____________

2–14. The figure below represents lung volume change. Match each letter in the figure with the appropriate item below. Assume that these pertain to the upright body position.

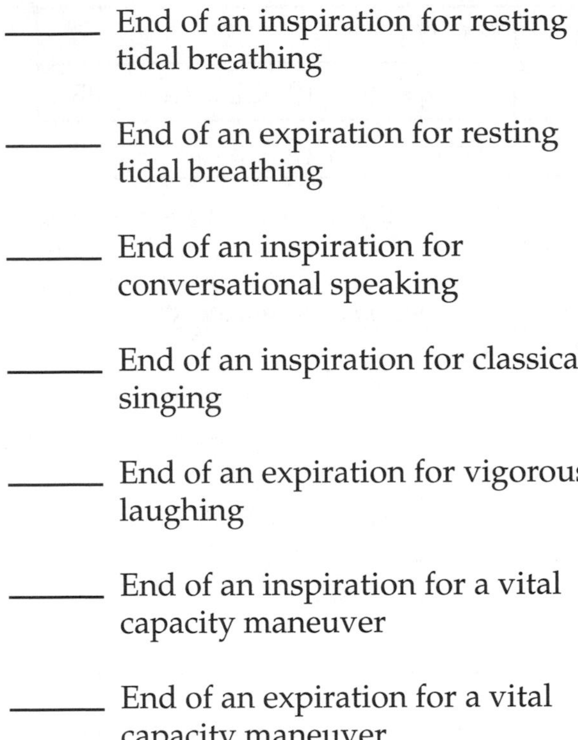

_____ End of an inspiration for resting tidal breathing

_____ End of an expiration for resting tidal breathing

_____ End of an inspiration for conversational speaking

_____ End of an inspiration for classical singing

_____ End of an expiration for vigorous laughing

_____ End of an inspiration for a vital capacity maneuver

_____ End of an expiration for a vital capacity maneuver

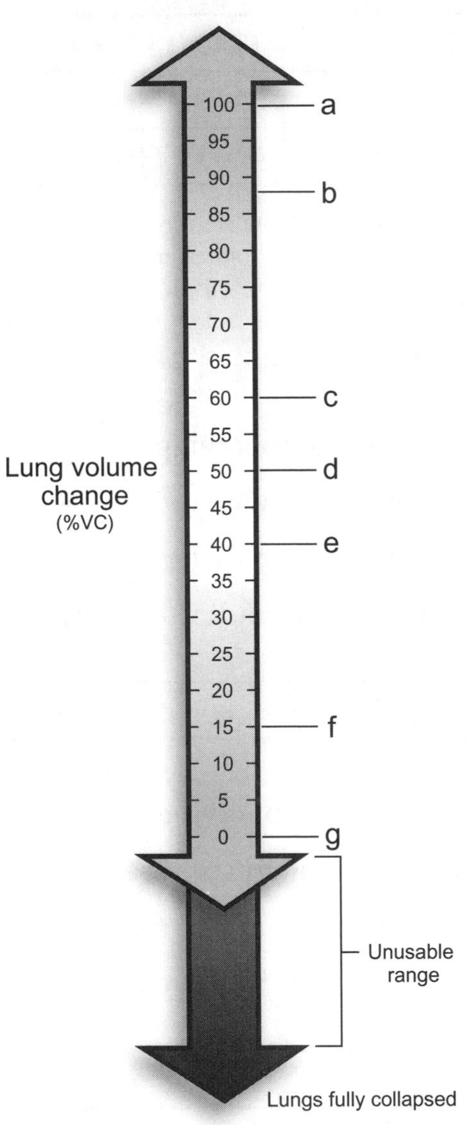

2–15. Use the volume-pressure functions in the diagram below (for upright body positions) to answer the following questions.

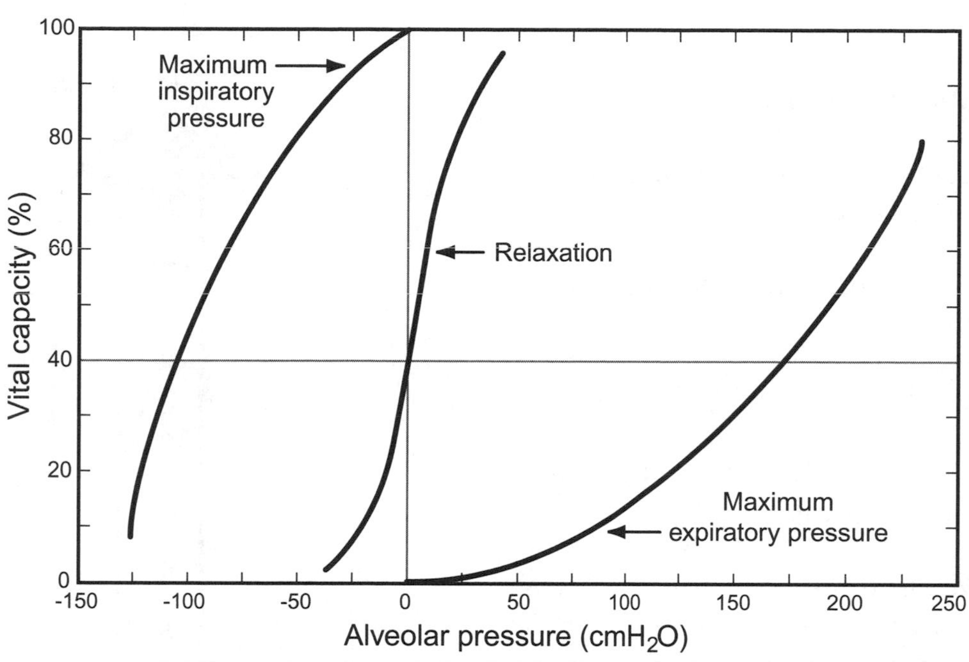

(a) What is the (approximate) maximum expiratory pressure that can be generated? ________

(b) What is the (approximate) maximum inspiratory pressure that can be generated? ________

(c) What is the relaxation pressure at 40% of the vital capacity? ________

(d) What is the (approximate) relaxation pressure at 80% of the vital capacity? ________

(e) Which direction (left or right) would the relaxation pressure move if the graph depicted the supine body position? [*Hint*: If you are uncertain, compare the relaxation characteristics in the upper panels of Figures 2–27 and 2–34 in your textbook] ________

(f) Why does the relaxation characteristic (line) not extend all the way up to 100% VC and down to 0% VC?

____

____

____

2-16. The figure below represents alveolar pressure. Match each letter in the figure with the appropriate item below.

______ Abrupt sniffing

______ Conversing loudly in a noisy restaurant

______ Relaxation at the end of a quiet breath

______ Loud yelling

______ Maximum expiratory effort near total lung capacity

______ Maximum inspiratory effort near residual volume

______ Conversing at usual loudness

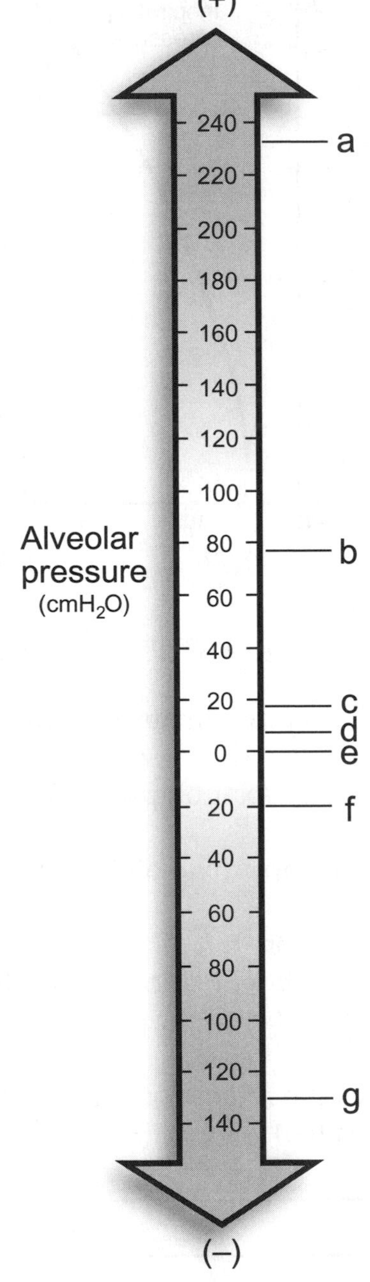

2-17. The figure below represents the shapes that can be assumed by the chest wall (rib cage wall and abdominal wall) throughout the vital capacity.

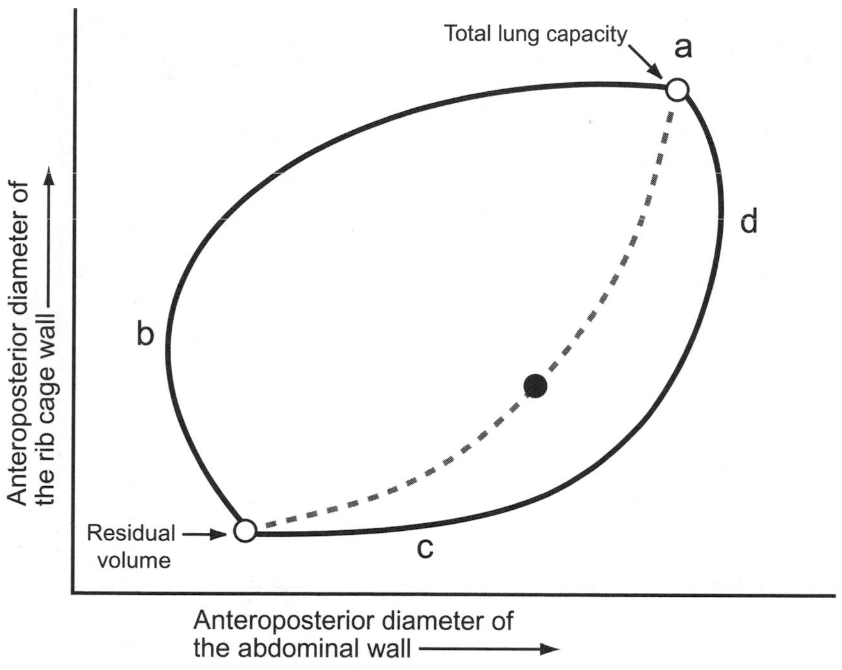

(a) Match each letter in the figure with the appropriate item below.

_______ Largest abdominal wall diameter

_______ Smallest abdominal wall diameter

_______ Largest rib cage wall diameter

_______ Smallest rib cage wall diameter

(b) Use a red pencil to color the area of the figure that represents shapes that could be achieved by using expiratory rib cage wall muscular pressure and abdominal wall muscular pressure, with the latter predominating (+RC < +AB). [*Hint:* The answer can be determined from Figure 2–20 in your textbook.]

(c) Use a green pencil to color the area of the figure that represents shapes that could be achieved by using expiratory rib cage wall muscular pressure and abdominal wall muscular pressure, with the former predominating (+RC > +AB). [*Hint:* The answer can be determined from Figure 2–20 in your textbook.]

2-18. The figure below represents a continuum of chest wall shapes. Match each letter in the figure with the appropriate item below. Assume that these pertain to the upright body position.

_____ Classical singing

_____ Running as fast as possible

_____ Conversational speaking

_____ After eating a large meal

_____ Pulling in the abdominal wall inward to look as thin as possible

_____ Pushing out the abdominal wall to look as fat as possible

_____ Resting tidal breathing

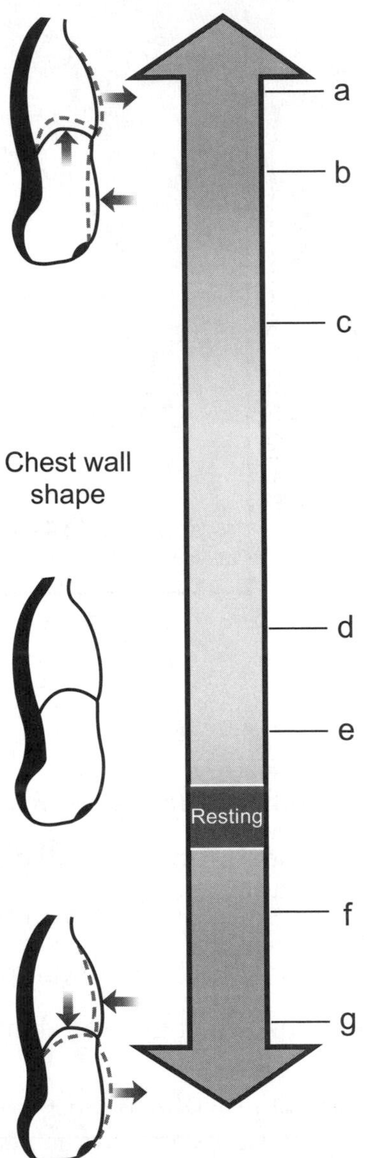

2–19. Complete the following items regarding the neural substrates of breathing.

(a) The motor supply for the diaphragm is called the ______________ and comes from spinal segments ______________.

(b) Nerves supplying the rib cage wall muscles are generally higher (closer to the head) than those supplying the abdominal wall muscles. True or False [Circle one]

(c) A spinal cord injury (which cuts off communication between the brain and the spinal cord at and below the level of the injury) at the C6 level would impair function of [Check all that apply] [*Hint:* See Table 2–2 and the Chapter 2 scenario in your textbook.]

_____ Nearly all of the rib cage wall muscles

_____ Some of the abdominal wall muscles

_____ The diaphragm

_____ All the abdominal wall muscles

(d) Someone with a C6 spinal cord injury (as described above) would have abnormal lung volume subdivisions. Which of the following would be true? [Check all that apply]

_____ Abnormally small vital capacity (VC)

_____ Abnormally small inspiratory reserve volume (IRV)

_____ No expiratory reserve volume (ERV)

_____ Abnormally small total lung capacity (TLC)

(e) Could someone with a C6 spinal cord injury (as described above) breathe on his or her own (without the aid of an external device, such as a mechanical ventilator)? Yes or No [Circle one]

Why or why not? ______________________________

(f) Control of tidal breathing is vested primarily in the cortex or brainstem. [Circle one]

(g) If someone had impairment of the lower brain center for breathing, but the higher brain centers were functioning normally, this person could breathe automatically or voluntarily [Circle one], but not automatically or voluntarily. [Circle one]

(h) Chemoreceptors are sensitive to changes in the amount of oxygen or carbon dioxide or both oxygen and carbon dioxide [Circle one] in blood and cerebral spinal fluid.

(i) If the central chemoreceptors sense a higher than usual concentration of carbon dioxide in the cerebral spinal fluid, ventilation will increase, decrease, or stay the same. [Circle one]

(j) Detection of stretching of the lungs and airways occurs through stimulation of mechanoreceptors or chemoreceptors. [Circle one]

(k) Neural commands for special acts of breathing (such as crying, speaking, or guided breathing) can override neural commands for tidal breathing. True or False [Circle one]

(l) Is it possible for someone who loses function of all spinal motor neurons (from a disease or injury) to stay alive? Explain your answer.

____

____

____

____

2–20. Complete the following items regarding resting tidal breathing. Refer to this figure (and accompanying text) reproduced from your textbook.

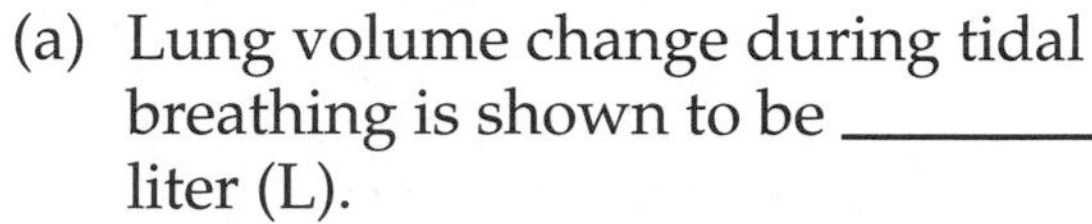

(a) Lung volume change during tidal breathing is shown to be ________ liter (L).

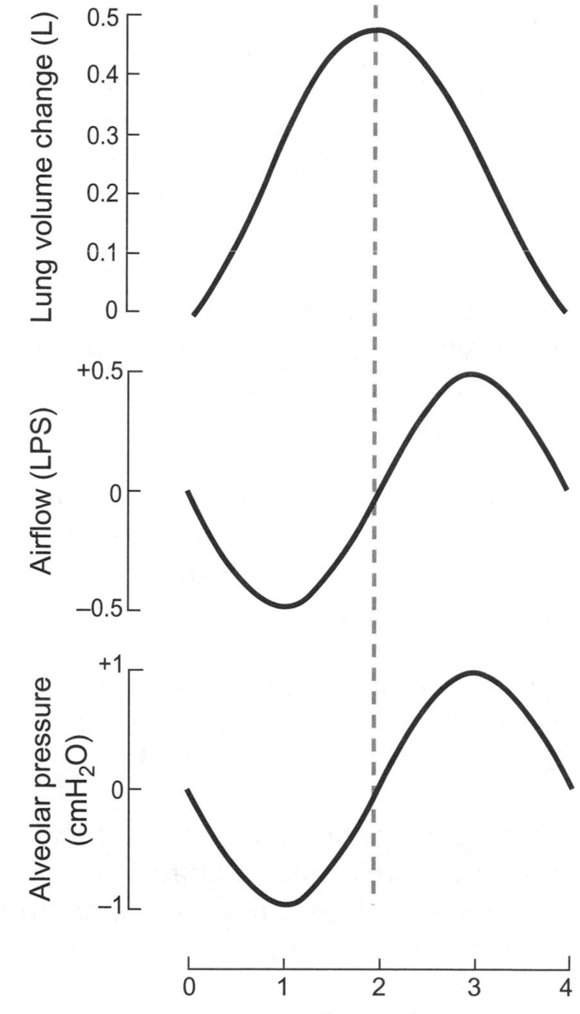

(b) Convert this lung volume change to milliliters (mL): ________ mL [*Hint:* 1 L = 1000 mL]

(c) If tidal breathing typically involves 10% of the vital capacity (VC), what is the best estimate of this person's VC?

____

(d) Estimate how much lung volume change you use during tidal breathing: ________ [*Hint:* Use your predicted VC, which you calculated in Question 2–13c.]

(e) What is the greatest inspiratory airflow generated? ________ liters/second (LPS)

(f) What is the greatest expiratory airflow generated? ________ LPS

(g) What is the greatest inspiratory alveolar pressure generated? ________ cmH_2O

(h) What is the greatest expiratory alveolar pressure generated? ________ cmH_2O

(i) This expiratory alveolar pressure is larger or smaller [Circle one] than that generated during conversational speaking.

(j) During inspiration, oxygen or carbon dioxide [Circle one] leaves the alveoli and enters the blood. During expiration, oxygen or carbon dioxide [Circle one] is released from the blood into the alveoli.

(k) Resting tidal breathing is accomplished by passive force alone. True or false [Circle one] Explain your answer.

____

____

____

2-21. Figure 2–27 from your textbook (reproduced here) represents extended steady utterance produced in an upright body position in response to "Take in the deepest breath you can and say 'ah' for as long and as steady as you can at your usual loudness." Use the figure to complete the following items.

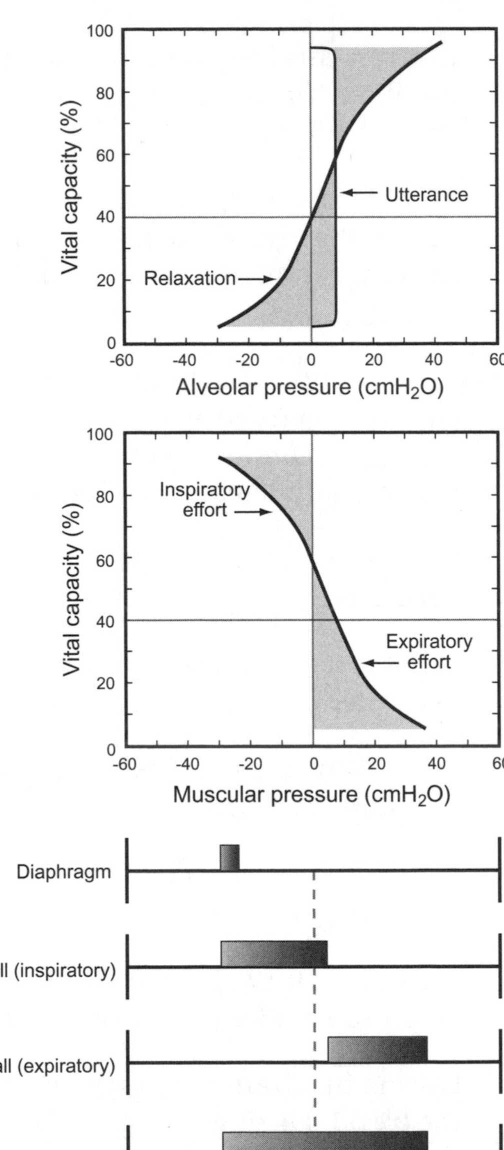

(a) Approximately how much inspiratory muscular pressure is being exerted at the very beginning of the utterance?
________ cmH_2O

(b) At approximately what lung volume does the net inspiratory pressure requirement change to a net expiratory muscular pressure requirement?
________% VC

(c) Approximately how much expiratory muscular pressure is being exerted at the very end of the utterance?
________ cmH_2O

(d) What is the approximate alveolar pressure of the utterance throughout the expiration? ________ cmH_2O

(e) During the period when inspiratory muscular pressure is required to maintain the targeted alveolar pressure, which muscles do the majority of the inspiratory braking?

____

(f) The abdominal wall muscles are active during all, most, or none [Circle one] of the utterance.

(g) The expiratory muscles are most active at large or small [Circle one] lung volumes.

2-22. Complete the following items that pertain to running speech activities, such as reading aloud or conversational speaking in an upright body position.

(a) Lung volume change for running speech production is generally larger or smaller [Circle one] than lung volume change for resting tidal breathing.

(b) Alveolar pressure for running speech production is generally in the range of 50 to 100 cmH_2O or 5 to 10 cmH_2O. [Circle one]

(c) Chest wall shape for running speech production is generally characterized by a more or less [Circle one] inwardly displaced abdominal wall compared to that of relaxation.

(d) Abdominal wall muscles are more or less [Circle one] active during running speech production compared to during resting tidal breathing.

(e) During running speech production, the abdominal wall is displaced inward and the rib cage wall is displaced outward, relative to their respective positions during relaxation. This chest wall configuration has the following consequences. [Check all that apply]

_____ Flattens the diaphragm

_____ Stretches the diaphragm

_____ Stretches the expiratory muscles of the rib cage wall

_____ Causes the abdominal wall muscles to relax

(f) When the fibers of the diaphragm are shorter than their resting length (such as when the diaphragm is flattened), they contract more or less [Circle one] forcefully compared to when they are at their resting length (such as when the diaphragm is more domed).

(g) The muscular pressure(s) used to produce running speech in the upright body position has (have) been shown to be [Check one]

_____ inspiratory rib cage wall muscular pressure alone.

_____ abdominal wall muscular pressure alone.

_____ expiratory rib cage wall muscular pressure and abdominal wall muscular pressure, with the latter predominating.

_____ inspiratory rib cage wall muscular pressure and abdominal wall muscular pressure.

(h) If the abdominal wall muscles were paralyzed, would it be possible to produce speech? Yes or No [Circle one] [*Hint:* Consider the scenario in Chapter 2 of your textbook.]

(i) People often produce loud speech at larger or smaller [Circle one] lung volumes than soft speech. Explain why.

____

____

(j) Is it possible to produce loud speech and soft speech at the same lung volume? Yes or No [Circle one]

2-23. Complete the following items regarding speech breathing in the supine body position and how it contrasts with speech breathing in the upright body position.

(a) In the upright body position, inspiratory braking is accomplished primarily by the inspiratory rib cage wall muscles or diaphragm. [Circle one] In the supine body position, inspiratory braking is accomplished primarily by the inspiratory rib cage wall muscles or diaphragm. [Circle one]

(b) How do muscular activities generated during upright and supine running speech production differ? Fill in the following chart to indicate if selected muscle groups are generally active ("On") or not ("Off").

	Upright Running Speech Production	Supine Running Speech Production
Abdominal wall muscles	________	________
Expiratory rib cage wall muscles	________	________

(c) Sit upright on the floor and breathe quietly. At the end of an expiration, close your airway, either by closing your larynx or by closing your mouth and plugging your nose. Lie back so that you are resting supine on the floor. Open your airway.

What happened?

____

Why did it happen?

____

____

____

(d) Most running speech production occurs at lung volumes that are larger or smaller [Circle one] than the resting level. Does this change with body position? Yes or No [Circle one]

(e) Alveolar pressure for running speech production is usually substantially higher, substantially lower, or generally the same [Circle one] in an upright body position compared to the supine body position.

2-24. Complete the following items regarding ventilation during various activities, including speech production.

(a) Ventilation is often expressed in units of minute ventilation (in liters per minute, LPM). Minute ventilation is the amount of air inspired (or expired) over the course of a minute, calculated as the product of the average tidal volume (in liters, L) and breathing rate (breaths per minute, BPM). Calculate the minute ventilation for each of the following.

Tidal Volume (L)	Breathing Rate (BPM)	Minute Ventilation (LPM)
0.50	12.0	
0.60	10.0	
0.75	10.0	
1.10	7.5	

(b) Rank the following activities according to magnitude of ventilation. Rank the activity you think is associated with the least ventilation as "1" and the activity you think is associated with the most ventilation as "3."

_____ Heavy exercise

_____ Reading aloud continuously (without breaks)

_____ Resting tidal breathing

(c) When people speak under high drive conditions, such as during exercise or while at high elevation, which of the following do they tend to do? [Check all that apply]

_____ They take deeper inspirations.

_____ They reduce airflow while speaking.

_____ They expend more air during speaking.

_____ They take smaller inspirations.

_____ They often blow off air.

_____ They speak at smaller than usual lung volumes (below the resting level).

_____ They speak at larger than usual lung volumes (well above the resting level).

_____ They increase ventilation.

(d) When we speak continuously for several minutes, we tend to hypoventilate or hyperventilate [Circle one] and the amount of carbon dioxide in our blood tends to increase or decrease. [Circle one]

2–25. Complete the following items regarding variables that affect speech breathing, including drive-to-breathe and age and sex of the speaker.

(a) Ask a friend to read aloud the following paragraph (Hoit & Hixon, 1987). While your friend is reading, insert slash marks (/) where inspirations occur.

California is a unique state. It is one of the few states that has all the geographical features found in the rest of the country including deserts, forests, mountain ranges, and beaches. Its beaches draw thousands and thousands of people each year particularly during the summer months when the sun is shining, the skies are blue, and the ocean is warm enough to swim in. Surfers are often in the water by daybreak. Of course, there are many other things to do besides surfing such as sailing, swimming, waterskiing, kite flying, and sun bathing. In the winter, the mountains of California are favorite vacation spots. Here, snow skiing is the sport. There are many places in California to snow ski but the largest and most popular is Mammoth Mountain. Because of its popularity the property surrounding the Mammoth ski resort is extremely expensive. Unfortunately, the threat of earthquakes in this area is very high. In fact, earthquakes are common occurrences in many parts of California. Because of this, there are people who are afraid that someday a large piece of the state will fall into the Pacific Ocean. The possibility of a serious earthquake such as the one that demolished San Francisco in 1906 frightens some people enough that they choose not to visit California just for that reason.

Calculate the average number of syllables produced per breath group (expiration). ______

(b) The number of syllables/breath group would probably increase, decrease, or stay the same [Circle one] if your friend read the paragraph while exercising.

(c) If a 25-year-old man and a 75-year-old man read the same paragraph aloud, which one would inspire more frequently? ______________

(d) If a 25-year-old man and a 25-year-old woman read the same paragraph aloud, would you expect them to have similar speech breathing behavior? Yes or No [Circle one]

(e) Resting tidal breathing is the same in silence as when listening to someone else speak. True or False [Circle one]

(f) Speech breathing is essentially adult like by age 7 years. True or False [Circle one]

(g) Speech breathing becomes more difficult during pregnancy, particularly during the last month. This is primarily because the diaphragm is pulled footward by the abdominal content and is placed at a mechanical disadvantage for generating inspiratory pressure change. True or False [Circle one]

(h) An endomorphic (fat) person tends to move the abdominal wall more or less [Circle one] than an ectomorphic (lean) person.

2-26. The photograph below shows a person performing a vital capacity maneuver in response to the instruction: "Take in all the air you can and then blow out as much as you can into the tube."

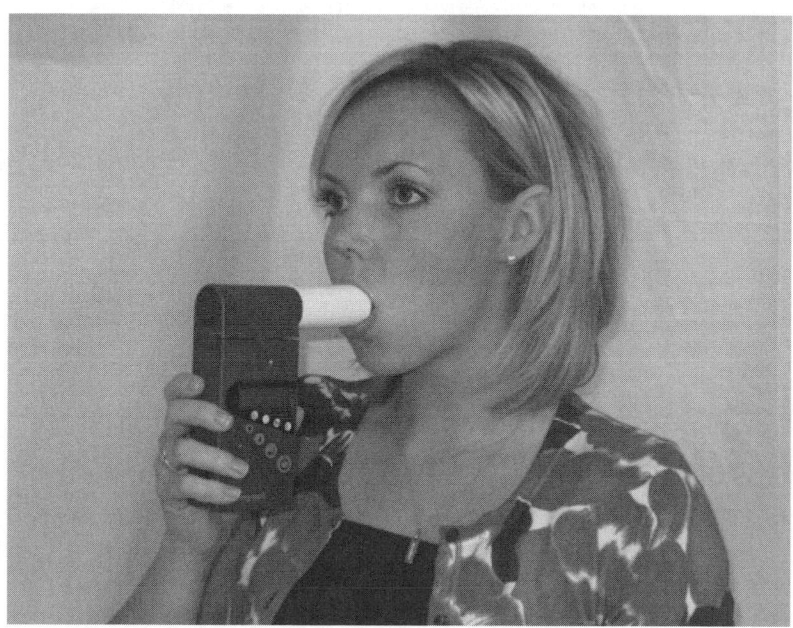

(a) What is wrong with how the measurement is being made?

____

____

____

(b) How might this affect the vital capacity measure?

____

____

____

2-27. The spirometer tracing below shows two resting tidal breaths followed by a vital capacity maneuver (a maximum inspiration from the resting level, followed by a maximum expiration). Use the calibrated lines to calculate the following subdivisions of the lung volume. Be sure to include the unit of measure in your answers.

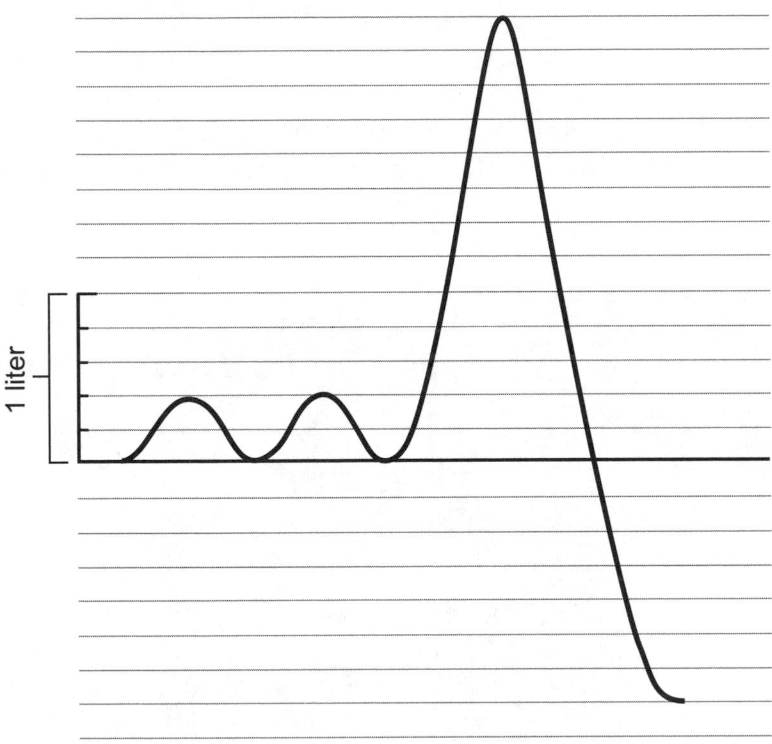

(a) Tidal volume: ________

(b) Inspiratory capacity: ________

(c) Inspiratory reserve volume: ________

(d) Expiratory reserve volume: ________

(e) Vital capacity: ________

(f) What subdivision of the lung volume cannot be measured by a vital capacity maneuver?

____

2-28. The tracing below shows a deep inspiration followed by an expiration during which the person was sustaining an "ah" into a facemask connected to a spirometer.

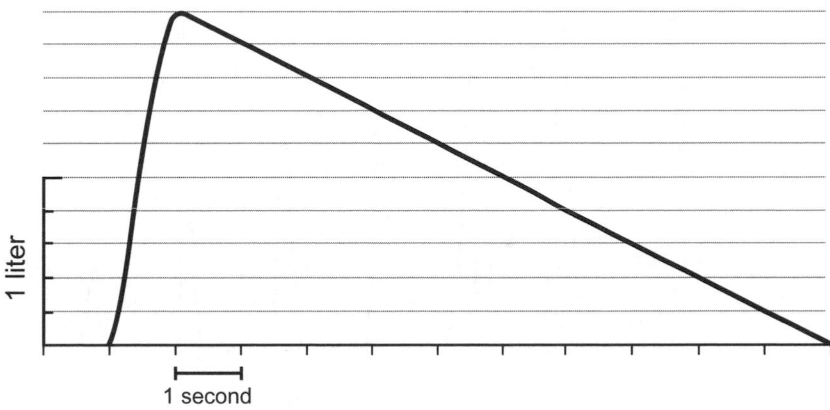

(a) How much volume (in liters) was expired? ________

(b) How much time (in seconds) did the expiration take? ________

(c) What was the average airflow (liters/second, LPS) during the sustained "ah"? ________ [*Hint:* Airflow is calculated as the volume expended divided by time.]

(d) What was the average airflow (LPS) during the inspiration? ________

2-29. The oral air pressure tracing shown below was obtained during repeated productions of "pa" generated during a single breath group (expiration).

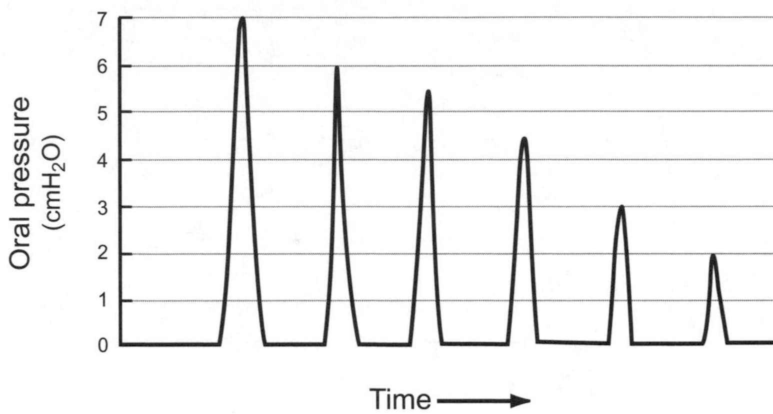

(a) Measure each of the six pressure peaks. Be sure to include the unit of measure.

Peak 1 = ________

Peak 2 = ________

Peak 3 = ________

Peak 4 = ________

Peak 5 = ________

Peak 6 = ________

(b) Connect the pressure peaks with a line. This represents the average (estimated) alveolar pressure across the breath group. What can you conclude about alveolar pressure from this oral pressure tracing?

____

____

(c) Why does the oral pressure drop to zero between the peaks?

____

____

2-30. Collect the following items: (1) large, clear drinking glass; (2) straw; (3) masking tape; and (4) large paper clip. From these construct a "water bubble manometer" such as that shown in the figure below by following these steps:

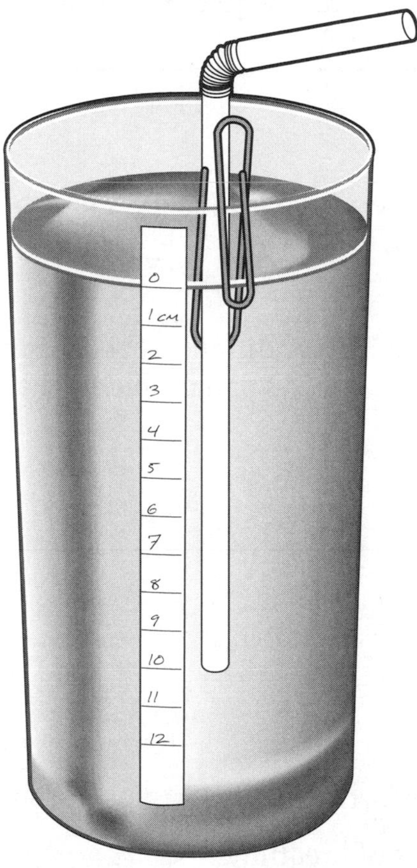

Figure from *Evaluation and Management of Speech Breathing Disorders: Principles and Methods* (p. 174), by Thomas J. Hixon and Jeannette D. Hoit, 2005. Tucson, AZ: Redington Brown. Original figure after Hixon, Hawley, & Wilson, 1982.

- Make tick marks on a strip of masking tape at 1-centimeter (cm) intervals, starting with "0" to "12."
- Fix the tape lengthwise to the glass, with the "0" positioned approximately 2 cm below the rim.
- Fill the glass with water to the "0" level.
- Place the paper clip on the rim of the glass.
- Insert a straw through the paper clip into the glass until the distal end reaches the 10 cm mark (that is, until the tip of the straw is immersed 10 cm below the surface of the water).

(a) With the straw's tip positioned 10 cm below the water's surface, blow into the straw until a bubble appears. How much pressure did you generate?

____

(b) If you wanted to determine if a client could generate an alveolar pressure of at least 5 cmH_2O, where would you place the tip of the straw?

____

2-31. Complete the following items regarding speech breathing disorders and health care professionals.

(a) Categorize each of the following conditions as being functional (F), or as being related to a problem with the chest wall (CW) or a problem with the pulmonary apparatus (PA).

______ Spinal cord injury

______ Asthma

______ Cerebral palsy

______ Malingering

______ Emphysema

______ Misuse

(b) Dyspnea (breathing discomfort or difficulty) can be caused by [Check all that apply]

______ functional disorders of breathing.

______ disorders of the chest wall.

______ disorders of the pulmonary apparatus.

(c) A physician with expertise in breathing disorders is called a ____________________.

(d) Which of the following health care professionals might be responsible for some aspect of evaluation and/or management of a speech breathing disorder? [Check all that apply]

______ Speech-language pathologist

______ Pulmonologist

______ Gastroenterologist

______ Respiratory therapist

______ Neurologist

______ Ophthalmologist

______ Physical therapist

______ Psychologist

3

Laryngeal Function and Speech Production Questions

3–1. Label the cartilages and bone indicated in the figure.

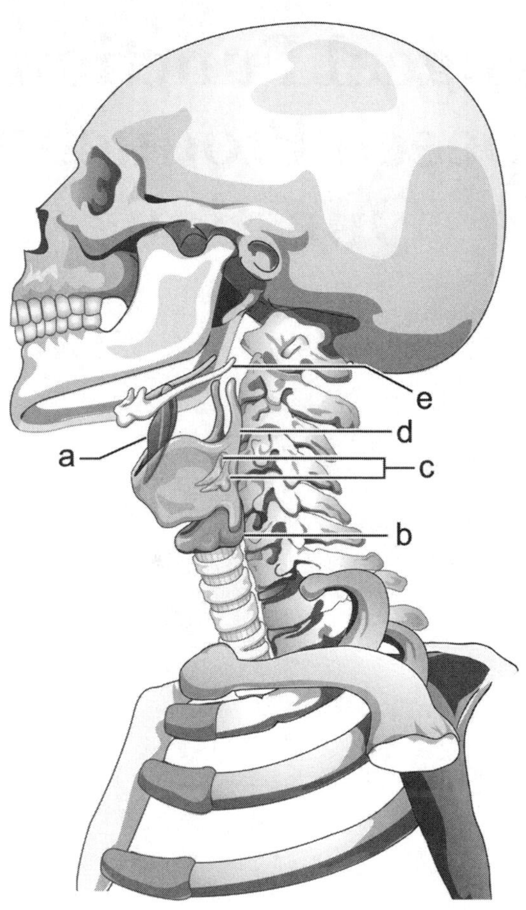

a ______________________ d ______________________

b ______________________ e ______________________

c ______________________

3–2. Label the parts of the thyroid cartilage indicated in the figures.

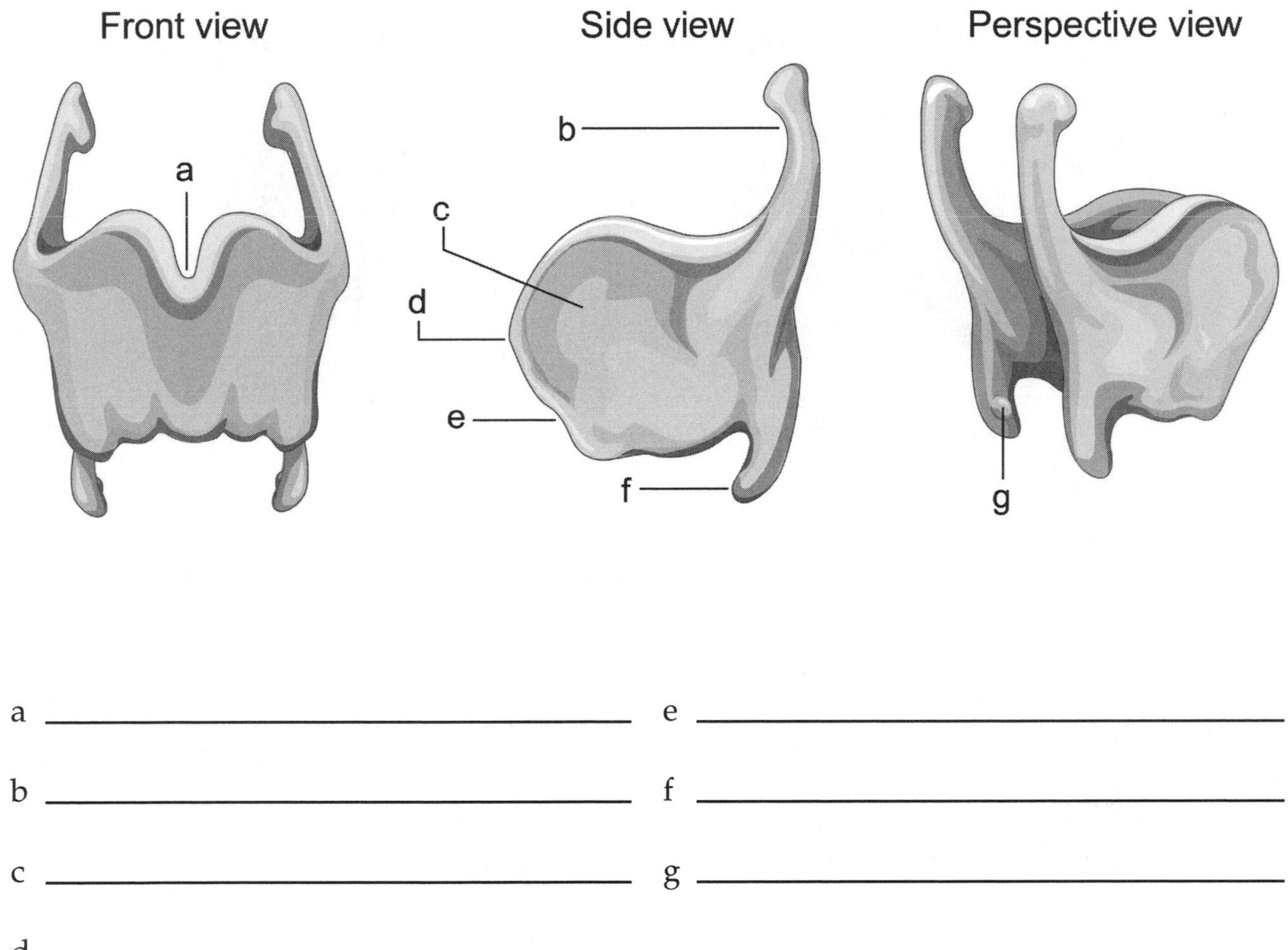

a ______________________

b ______________________

c ______________________

d ______________________

e ______________________

f ______________________

g ______________________

3–3. Label the parts of the cricoid cartilage indicated in the figures.

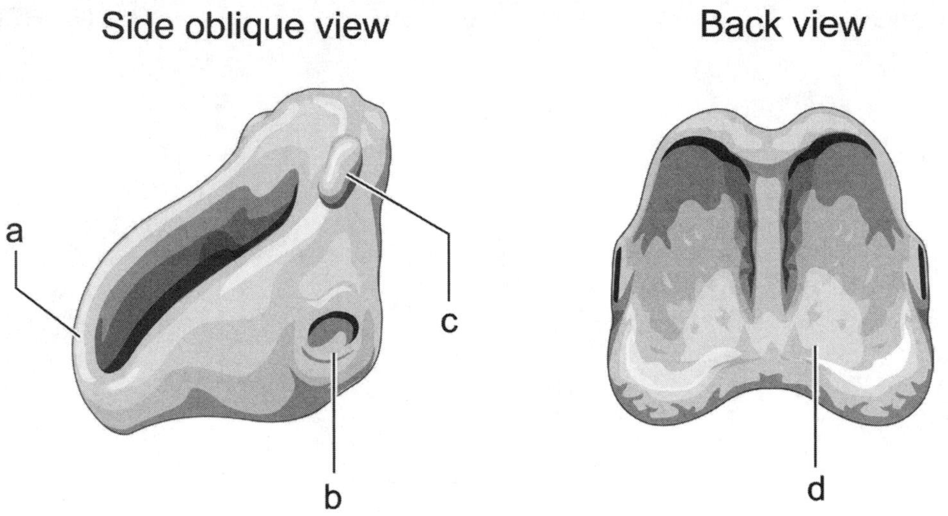

Side oblique view

a

c

b

Back view

d

a ______________________ c ______________________

b ______________________ d ______________________

3–4. Label the parts of the arytenoid cartilages indicated in the figures.

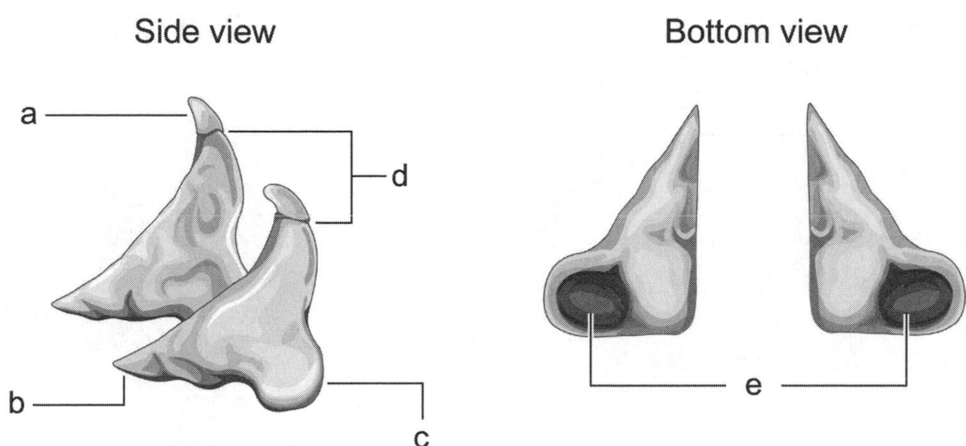

a ______________________________ d ______________________________

b ______________________________ e ______________________________

c ______________________________

3–5. Label the parts of the epiglottis indicated in the figures.

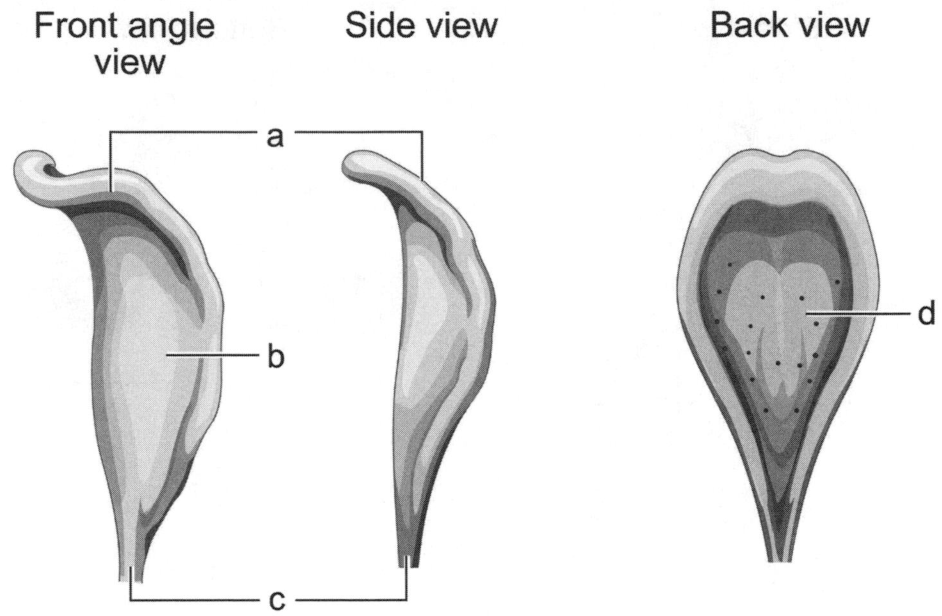

a ______________________ c ______________________

b ______________________ d ______________________

3-6. Label the parts of the hyoid bone indicated in the figure.

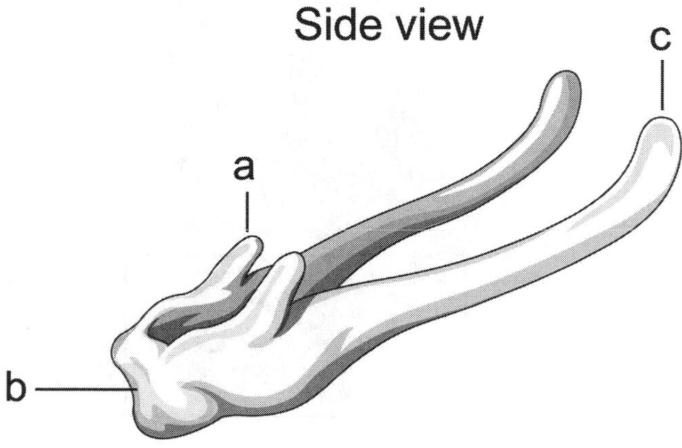

a ______________________ c ______________________

b ______________________

3–7. Label the ligaments indicated in the figure.

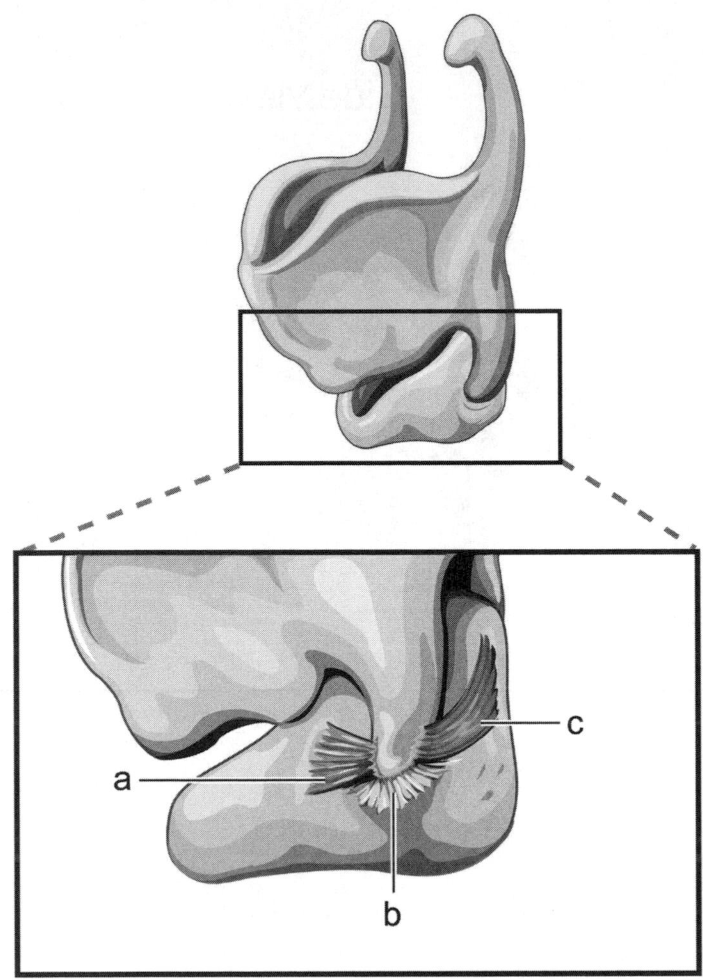

a ______________________ c ______________________

b ______________________

(a) What is the name of the pair of joints formed by these cartilages?

____

(b) What type of movements can these cartilages produce around these joints?

The thyroid cartilage can __________ and __________.

The cricoid cartilage can __________ and __________.

3–8. Label the ligaments indicated in the figure.

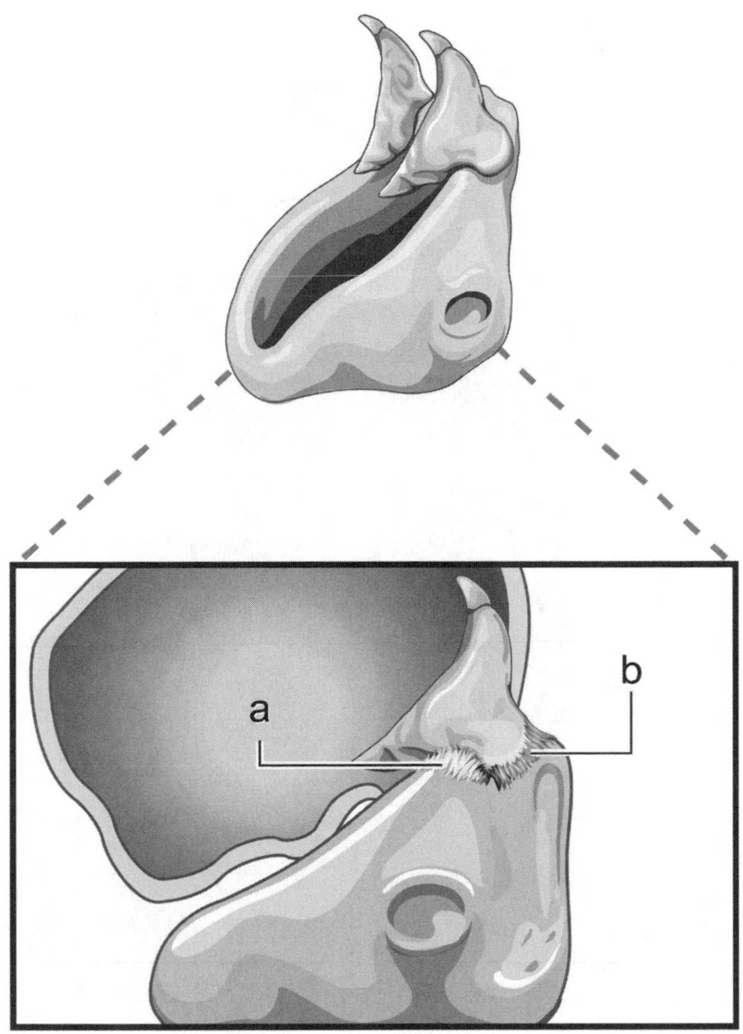

a ______________________ b ______________________

(a) What is the name of the pair of joints formed by these cartilages?

____

(b) What type of movements can these cartilages produce around these joints?

The arytenoid cartilages can ____________ and ____________.

3–9. Label the structures and regions indicated in the figure.

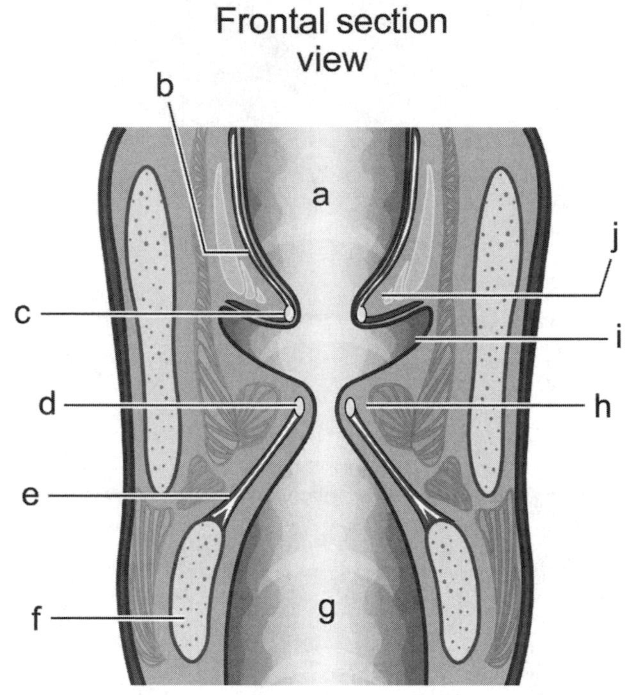

a ______________________ f ______________________

b ______________________ g ______________________

c ______________________ h ______________________

d ______________________ i ______________________

e ______________________ j ______________________

3–10. Complete the following items regarding the vocal folds and glottis.

(a) The vocal folds comprise five layers. Match the name of each layer with its description.

Layer	Description
_____ Epithelium	(a) Elastic fibers, like a bundle of soft rubber bands
_____ Superficial layer of the lamina propria	(b) A thin, stiff capsule that determines the outer shape of the vocal folds
_____ Intermediate layer of the lamina propria	(c) Muscle fibers, like a bundle of stiff rubber bands
_____ Deep layer of the lamina propria	(d) Loose fibrous matrix, akin to soft gelatin
_____ Muscle	(e) Collagen fibers, like a bundle of cotton thread

(b) Of the five layers listed above, which two layers make up the body of the vocal folds?

____

____

(c) Which three layers make up the cover of the vocal folds?

____

____

____

(d) Define *glottis* (as it pertains to the larynx).

____

(e) The membranous or cartilaginous [Circle one] part of the vocal folds make up the anterior _____% of the vocal folds, and the membranous or cartilaginous [Circle one] part of the vocal folds make up the posterior _____% of the vocal folds.

3–11. Label the ligaments and membranes indicated in the figures.

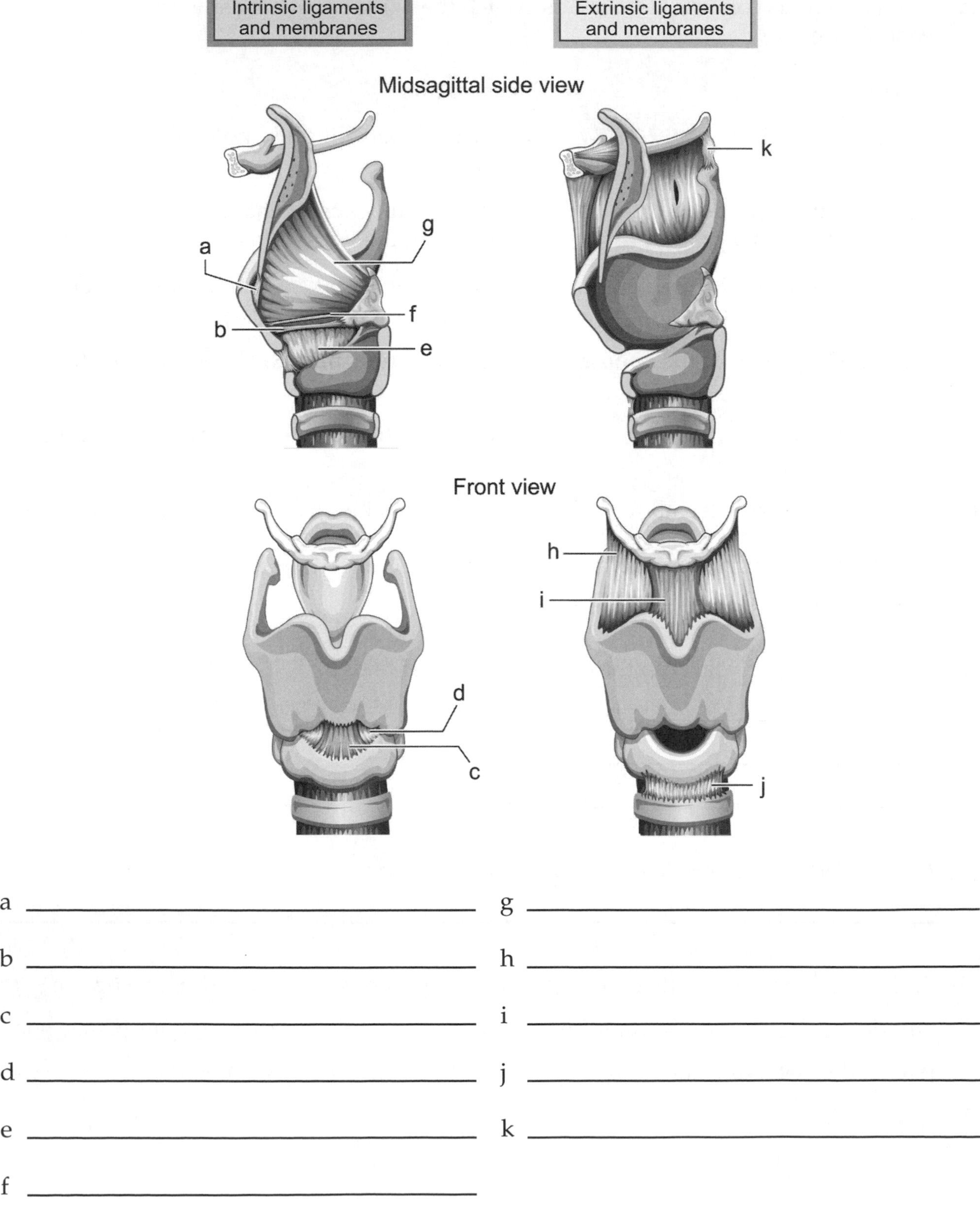

a ______________________________ g ______________________________

b ______________________________ h ______________________________

c ______________________________ i ______________________________

d ______________________________ j ______________________________

e ______________________________ k ______________________________

f ______________________________

3–12. Label the muscles indicated in the figures.

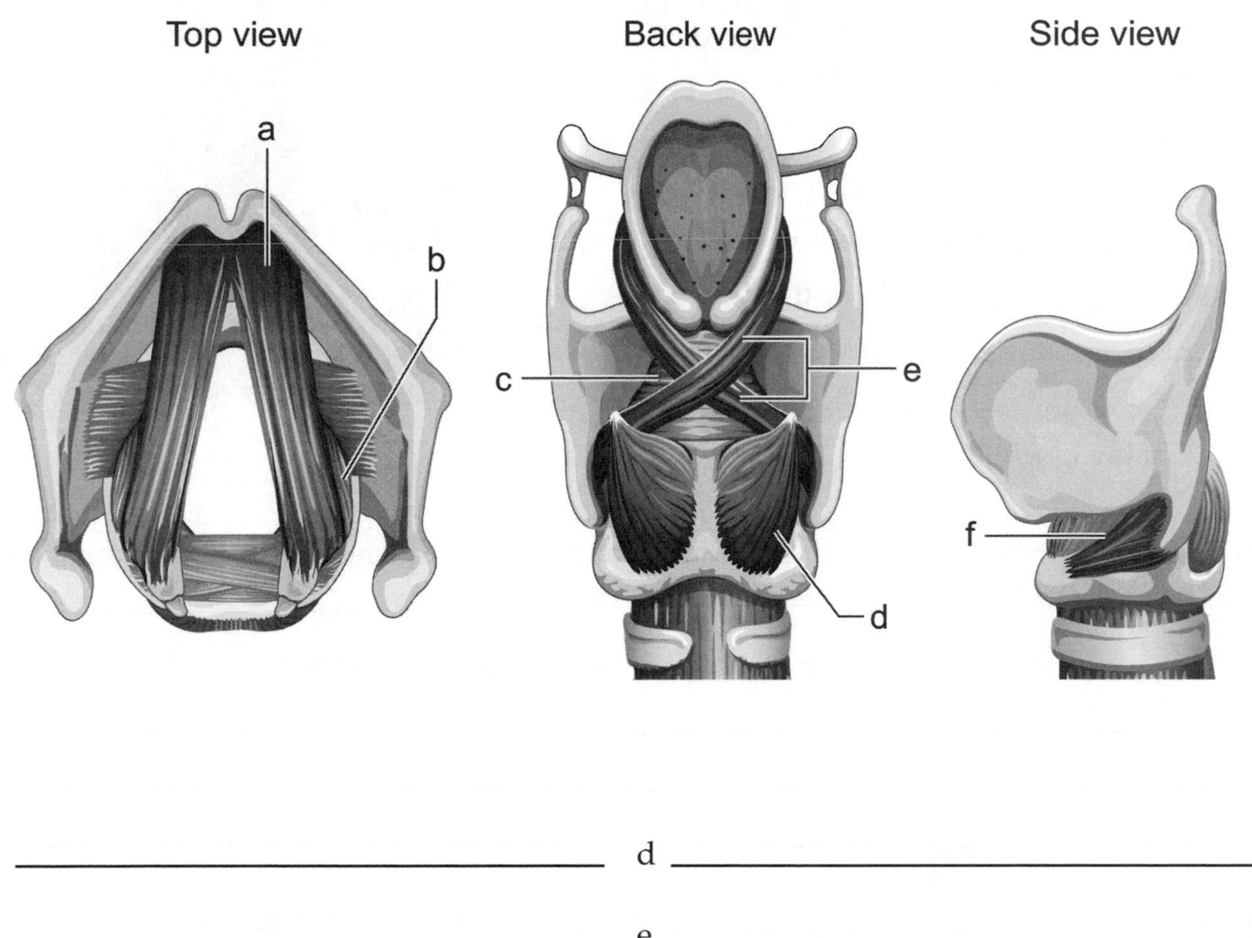

a ______________________ d ______________________

b ______________________ e ______________________

c ______________________ f ______________________

(a) These muscles are called the intrinsic, supplementary, or extrinsic [Circle one] muscles of the larynx.

(b) The reason that these muscles are grouped together is that [Check one]

_____ they do not insert directly into the larynx, but influence its position and stability.

_____ both ends of each muscle have attachments within the larynx.

_____ one end of each muscle attaches within the larynx and one end of each muscle attaches outside the larynx.

3–13. Complete the following items regarding the vocal folds and associated muscles.

(a) The thyroarytenoid muscle is often said to consist of two parts, as depicted in the figure. The part near the laryngeal wall (**a** in the figure) is called the

________________ or the

________________. The part near the midline (**b** in the figure) is called

the ________________ or the

________________, and is bordered by

the ________________ ligament

(**c** in the figure).

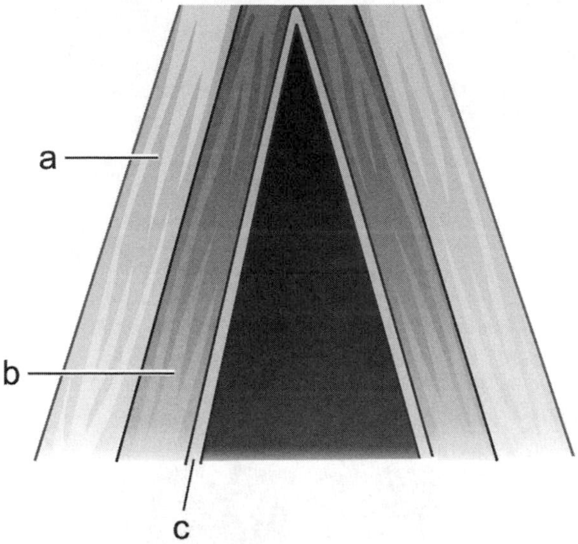

a

b

c

(b) When the thyroarytenoid muscles contract, they increase or decrease [Circle one] the distance between the thryroid and arytenoid cartilages.

(c) What is the difference between a "vocal fold" and a "vocal cord"?

____

____

____

(d) Contraction of the ________________ muscles rocks the arytenoid cartilages away from the midline, contraction of the ________________ muscles rocks the arytenoid cartilages toward the midline, and contractions of the ________________ muscles pulls the arytenoid cartilages toward each other. [Possible answers are: lateral cricoarytenoid, posterior cricoarytenoid, and arytenoid]

(e) The aryepiglottic muscle is part of the transverse or oblique [Circle one] arytenoid muscle. Contraction of the aryepiglottic muscle pulls the ________________ backward and downward to cover the upper opening into the larynx.

(f) The questions in this section refer to concentric (shortening) muscle contractions. Other types of muscle contractions are eccentric (meaning ________________) contractions and isometric (meaning ________________) contractions.

3-14. Label the muscles indicated in the figures.

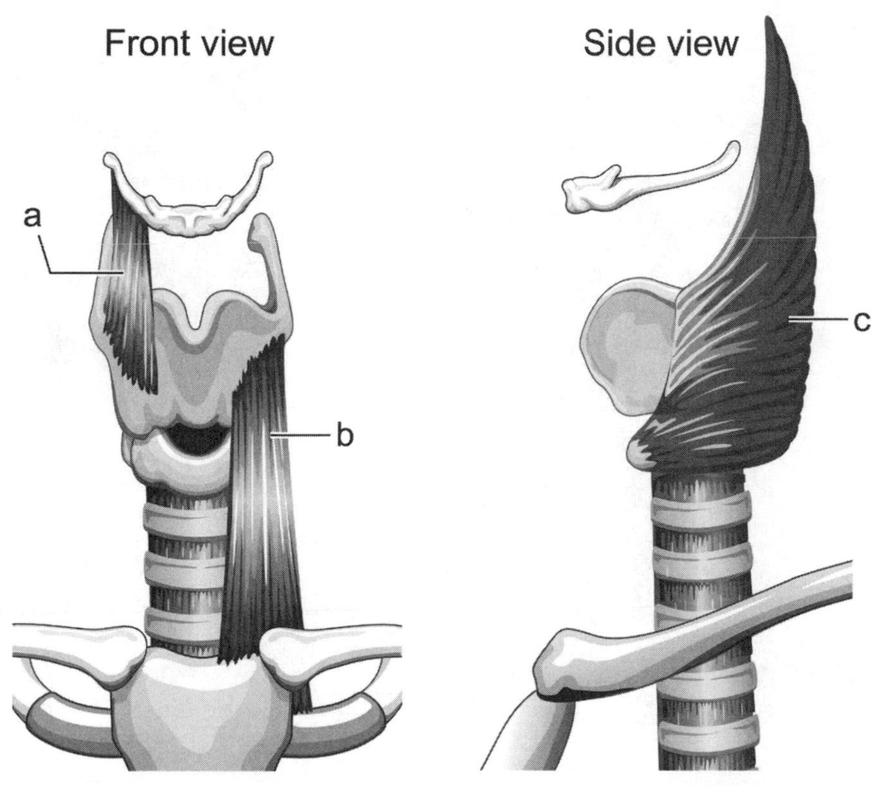

a ______________________ c ______________________

b ______________________

(a) These muscles are called the <u>intrinsic</u> or <u>supplementary</u> or <u>extrinsic</u> [Circle one] muscles of the larynx.

(b) The reason that these muscles are grouped together is that [Check one]

______ they do not insert directly into the larynx, but influence its position and stability.

______ both ends of each muscle have attachments within the larynx.

______ one end of each muscle attaches within the larynx and one end of each muscle attaches outside the larynx.

3–15. Label the muscles indicated in the figures.

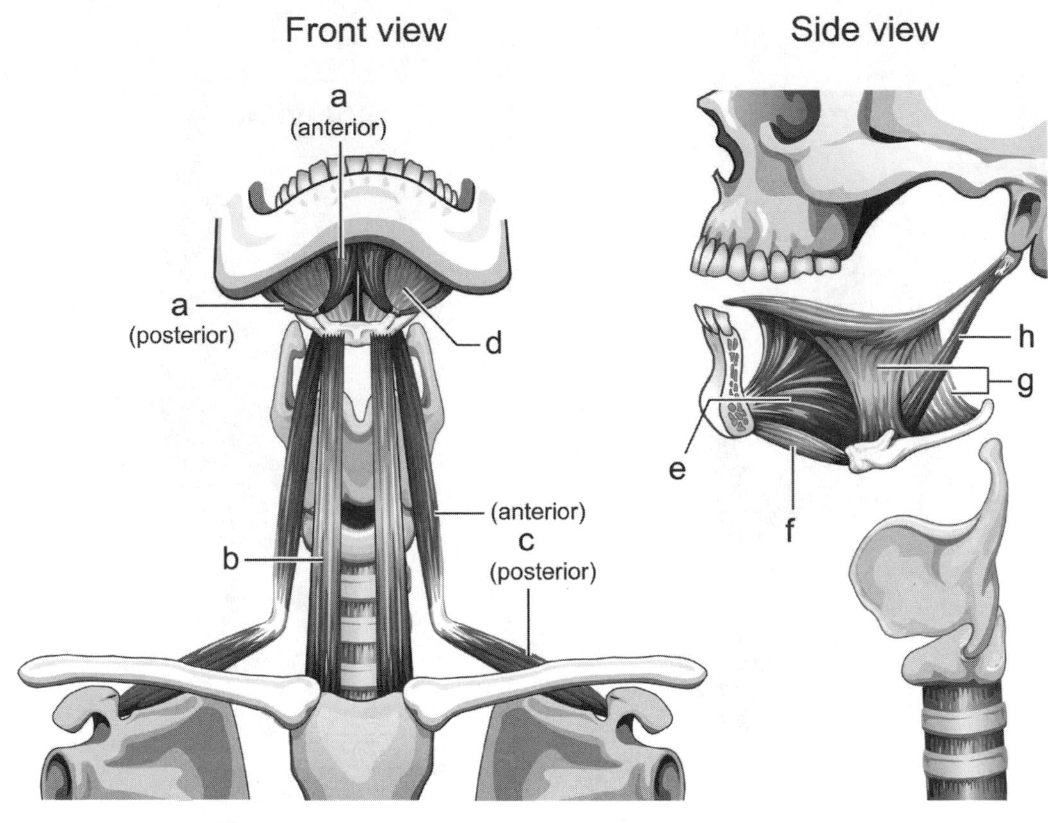

a ______________________________ e ______________________________

b ______________________________ f ______________________________

c ______________________________ g ______________________________

d ______________________________ h ______________________________

(a) These muscles are called the intrinsic, supplementary, or extrinsic [Circle one] muscles of the larynx.

(b) The reason that these muscles are grouped together is that [Check one]

______ they do not insert directly into the larynx, but influence its position and stability.

______ both ends of each muscle have attachments within the larynx.

______ one end of each muscle attaches within the larynx and one end of each muscle attaches outside the larynx.

3-16. Complete the following items regarding the functions of the muscles of the larynx.

(a) The intrinsic muscles of the larynx are listed below. Place a check mark indicating their potential influence(s) on the vocal folds. Note that some muscles may have check marks in more than one column.

	Shortens Vocal Folds	Tenses Vocal Folds	Lengthens Vocal Folds	Abducts Vocal Folds	Adducts/ Compresses Vocal Folds
Thyroarytenoid					
Posterior Cricoarytenoid					
Lateral Cricoarytenoid					
Arytenoid					
Cricothyroid					

(b) Extrinsic and supplementary muscles of the larynx are listed below. Place a check mark indicating their potential influence(s) on the position of the laryngeal housing. Note that some muscles may have check marks in more than one column.

	Moves Housing Upward	Moves Housing Downward	Moves Housing Forward	Moves Housing Backward
Sternothyroid				
Thyrohyoid				
Sternohyoid				
Omohyoid				
Digastric: anterior belly				
Digastric: posterior belly				
Stylohyoid				
Mylohyoid				
Geniohyoid				
Hyoglossus				
Genioglossus				

(c) When the diaphragm contracts, it can exert a downward pull on the larynx through its connections to the trachea. This is called tracheal tug. What is the effect of tracheal tug on the vocal folds?

____

____

(d) The squeezing force exerted between the vocal processes by contraction of the paired lateral cricoarytenoid muscles is called ______________________.

3-17. Complete the following items regarding control variables of laryngeal function.

(a) Indicate the rank order of the following activities according to their probable laryngeal opposing pressure demands. [1 = lowest laryngeal opposing pressure; 4 = highest laryngeal opposing pressure]

_____ Whispering

_____ Coughing vigorously

_____ Singing softly

_____ Speaking loudly

(b) Indicate whether laryngeal airway resistance would probably increase or decrease under the following circumstances (assume that all other variables are held constant).

If the laryngeal airway widened, laryngeal airway resistance would ____________.

If the laryngeal airway narrowed, laryngeal airway resistance would ____________.

If airflow increased, laryngeal airway resistance would ____________.

If airflow decreased, laryngeal airway resistance would ____________.

(c) Match each activity with the probable glottal size.

Activity	Glottal Size
_____ Bearing down while lifting a something heavy	(a) Large glottis
_____ Inspiring	(b) Small/medium glottis
_____ Whispering	(c) No glottis
_____ Producing a voiceless consonant (like /s/)	
_____ Producing breathy voice	

(d) Inspirations during continuous speaking activities (e.g., reading aloud a story) are generally short in duration and involve high airflow. Thus, it is important to inspire using a large glottis so that the laryngeal airway resistance is high or low. [Circle one]

(e) If the vocal folds are stretched, their stiffness increases or decreases. [Circle one]

(f) Contraction of the thyromuscularis muscles can increase the stiffness of medial or lateral [Circle one] parts of the vocal folds, whereas contraction of the thyrovocalis muscles can increase stiffness of the medial or lateral [Circle one] parts of the vocal folds.

(g) An increase in the force exerted between the vocal processes by the lateral cricoarytenoid muscles (causing an increase in medial compression) can increase or decrease [Circle one] the effective mass of the vibrating portions of the vocal folds.

3-18. Complete the following items regarding the neural substrates of laryngeal function.

(a) The two (paired) cranial nerves that provide motor innervation to the intrinsic muscles of the larynx are:

Number	Name
_____	_____________________
_____	_____________________

(b) Motor innervation of the intrinsic laryngeal muscles (except the cricothyroid) is provided by the ____________ branch of the ____________ nerve.

(c) Circle the five cranial nerves and three spinal nerves that innervate extrinsic and supplementary muscles of the larynx.

Cranial Nerves	Spinal Nerves
I	C1
II	C2
III	C3
IV	C4
V	C5
VI	C6
VII	
VIII	
IX	
X	
XI	
XII	

(d) Sensory information from the laryngeal mucosa is transmitted via cranial nerve ______.

3-19. Complete the following items regarding laryngeal function in speech production.

(a) Describe how a glottal stop-plosive is produced.

____

____

____

(b) Describe how a glottal fricative (/h/) is produced.

____

____

____

(c) Which of the glottal configurations shown below would most likely be associated with the production of /h/ or the production of whispered speech? [Choose two]

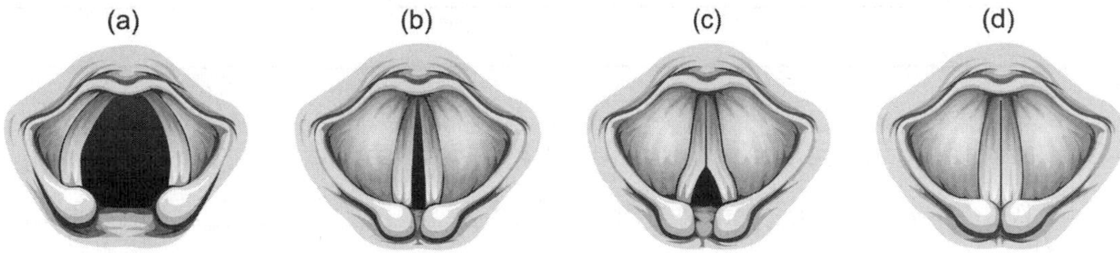

(d) Indicate whether the following statements about vocal fold vibration are True (T) or False (F). If the statement is false, write a revised statement that is true.

_____ The acoustic disturbance that constitutes the voice source corresponds to the part of the vibratory cycle during which the vocal folds move apart and the laryngeal airway opens.

____

____

_____ Vocal fold vibration is usually characterized by a vertical phase difference in which the vocal folds come together at the bottom before they come together at the top.

____

____

_____ The vertical phase difference is caused by different contraction speeds of the inferior and superior thyroarytenoid muscles.

____

____

_____ The average air pressure within the glottis is greater in a converging glottis than in a diverging glottis.

____

____

_____ Vocal fold vibration is always initiated by simultaneous expiratory airflow and vocal fold approximation.

____

____

_____ The minimum tracheal pressure needed to vibrate the vocal folds is approximately 2 to 3 cc/second.

____

____

(e) The vertical phase difference of vocal fold vibration can be thought of as involving two modes of movement, one called ______________ (which means ______________________________) and one is called ______________ (which means ______________________________).

(f) During the closing phase of vocal fold vibration, the vocal folds move back toward the midline (toward each other) because the [Check all that apply]

_____ air pressure in the glottis begins to increase.

_____ recoil force of the vocal fold tissue exceeds the intraglottal air pressure.

_____ neural activation of the thyroarytenoid muscle increases.

_____ intraglottal air pressure begins to decrease.

(g) Hard glottal attack is characterized by high or low [Circle one] laryngeal opposing pressure and gradual or abrupt [Circle one] onset of vocal fold vibration.

3–20. Complete the following items regarding fundamental frequency.

(a) The fundamental frequency (of vocal fold movement) is ______________________________

____.

(b) The strongest auditory-perceptual correlate of fundamental frequency is __________.

(c) As stiffness of the vocal folds increases, fundamental frequency increases or decreases [Circle one]; as effective vibrating mass of the vocal folds increases, fundamental frequency increases or decreases [Circle one]; and as the tautness of the vocal fold covers increases, fundamental frequency increases or decreases [Circle one].

(d) Explain how changes in vocal fold stiffness are caused through actions of the cricothyroid muscles and thyroarytenoid muscles and how they influence fundamental frequency.

____

____

____

____

(e) Is there a single, specific combination of cricothyroid muscle and thyroarytenoid muscle activation that produces a given fundamental frequency? ________________

____

(f) Explain how changes in effective vibrating mass of the vocal folds are caused through actions of the lateral cricoarytenoid muscles and how they influence fundamental frequency.

____

____

____

(g) Explain how changes in the tautness of the vocal fold covers are caused through changes in laryngeal height and how they influence fundamental frequency.

____

____

____

(h) Of the three fundamental frequency changing mechanisms discussed above (vocal fold stiffness, effective vibrating mass of the vocal folds, and tautness of the vocal fold covers), which has the greatest influence on fundamental frequency?

(i) If tracheal pressure increases by 2 cmH_2O (and the activity of laryngeal muscles is held constant), the fundamental frequency will increase or decrease [Circle one] by approximately ____________.

(j) If you wanted to produce the highest fundamental frequency possible, how would you do it?

____

____

____

3-21. Complete the following items regarding sound pressure level.

(a) The strongest auditory-perceptual correlate of sound pressure level is ____________.

(b) Control of speech sound pressure level is vested in the ____________ apparatus, ____________ apparatus, and ____________ apparatus.

(c) An increase in tracheal pressure will generally result in a(n) increase or decrease [Circle one] in sound pressure level, and is generally accompanied by a(n) increase or decrease [Circle one] in laryngeal opposing pressure and laryngeal airway resistance, and a(n) increase or decrease [Circle one] in the size of pharyngeal-oral opening.

(d) Which of the waveforms below (representing change in glottal area over time) is associated with the higher sound pressure level? (a) or (b) [Circle one]

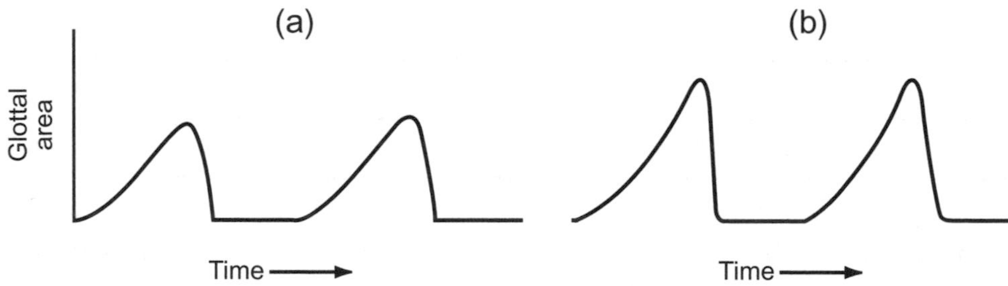

(e) Describe the difference(s) between the two sets of waveforms above.

____

____

(f) The greatest range of fundamental frequencies can be produced in the [Check one]

______ low range of sound pressure levels.

______ mid-range of sound pressure levels.

______ high range of sound pressure levels.

(g) The greatest range of sound pressure levels can be produced in the [Check one]

______ low range of fundamental frequency levels.

______ mid-range of fundamental frequency levels.

______ high range of fundamental frequency levels.

(h) If you wanted to produce the highest sound pressure level possible, how would you do it?

____

____

____

3-22. Complete the following items regarding voice registers.

(a) The lowest speaking voice register is called __________.

The middle speaking voice register is called __________.

The highest speaking voice register is called __________.

(b) Which register is represented by each of the glottal area waveforms below?

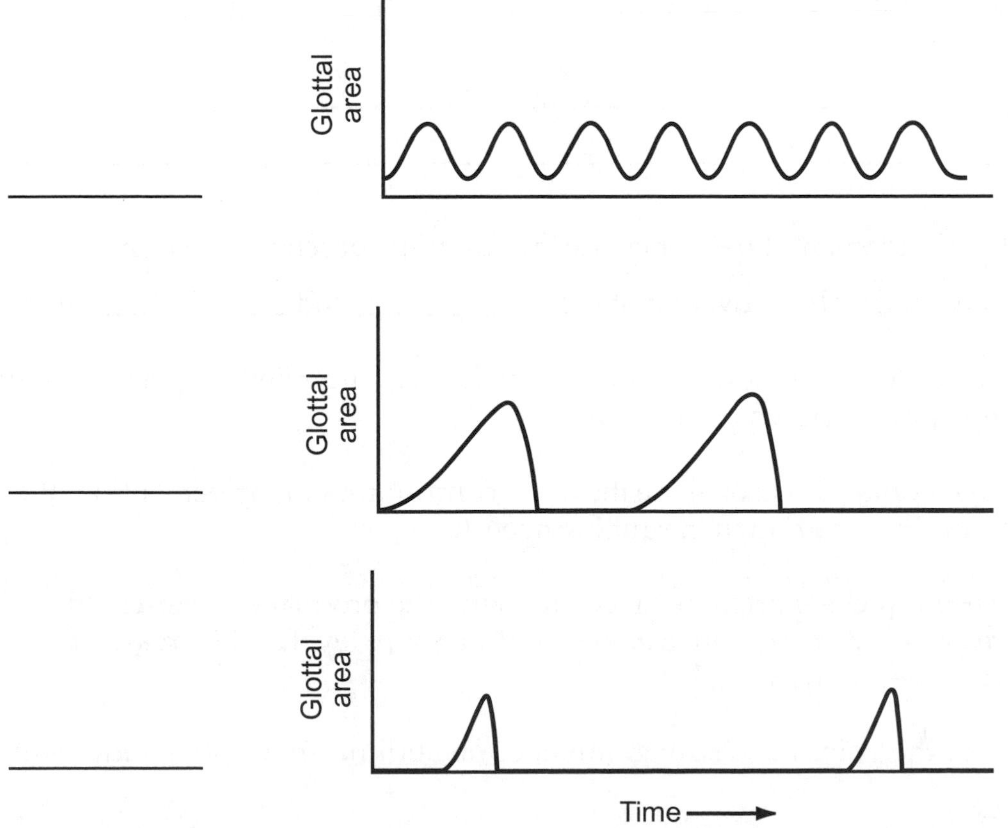

(c) Which register is produced with little or no vertical phase difference? ___________

(d) Which register is often produced at the ends of breath groups when the voice trails off in sound pressure level and fundamental frequency? ___________

(e) The fundamental frequency of the three sets of waveforms above are the same or different. [Circle one] How do you know?

____

____

(f) There is often overlap in fundamental frequency between the modal and loft registers. True or False [Circle one]

3-23. Complete the following items regarding running speech activities.

(a) Give an example of how the vocal folds can act as an articulator during running speech production.

____

____

(b) Adjustments in fundamental frequency during running speech production are accomplished primarily by activation of the ___________ and ___________ muscles.

(c) The intonation contour or loudness contour [Circle one] underlies the perception of the melody of running speech production.

(d) Vowels or Consonants [Circle one] are the main contributors to the perception of loudness and loudness variation in running speech.

(e) Quick increases in tracheal pressure associated with the production of stressed syllables increase or decrease [Circle one] sound pressure level and increase or decrease [Circle one] fundamental frequency.

(f) The spectrum of the voice has a strong influence on auditory-perceptual judgments of ___________.

3-24. Complete the following items regarding the effects of development, age, and sex on laryngeal function during speech production.

(a) Fill in the blanks below with the approximate average fundamental frequency (F0) associated with each age and sex. [*Hint*: Use Figures 3–47 and 3–49 in the textbook to determine the answers.]

Age (years)	Male F0 (Hz)	Female F0 (Hz)
1		
3		
6		
10		
20		
50		
80		
100		

(b) The most important determinant(s) of average fundamental frequency across age and sex is/are the [Check one]

______ length and thickness (mass) of the vocal folds.

______ height of the larynx within the neck.

______ degree of laryngeal ossification.

______ extent of neural innervation.

(c) Why is there a divergence between male and female fundamental frequency after age 10 years?

____

____

(d) It is more common for women, compared to men, to have a gap between the vocal folds during voice production.

Where is the gap typically located in young women?

____

Where is the gap typically located in elderly women?

____

(e) What is the difference between chronological age and physiological age?

____

____

3-25. Complete the following items regarding measurement of laryngeal function.

(a) Give an example of a speech/voice task that can be performed with a rigid endoscope in place.

____

____

____

(b) Give an example of a speech/voice task that can be performed with a flexible endoscope in place.

____

____

____

(c) Explain how a stroboscopic light helps you to see vocal fold vibration when using endoscopy.

____

____

____

____

(d) With electroglottography, the impedance to electrical current flow is higher or lower [Circle one] when the vocal folds are apart and higher or lower [Circle one] when the vocal folds are approximated.

(e) Could you determine fundamental frequency from an electroglottogram? Yes or No [Circle one]

(f) Airflow through the larynx is usually measured with a(n) [Check one]

_____ electroglottograph.

_____ rigid endoscope.

_____ pneumotachometer.

_____ dynamic microphone.

(g) One way to measure changes in laryngeal height is with a(n) [Check one]

_____ spectrogram.

_____ electroglottograph.

_____ pneumotachometer.

_____ sound level meter.

(h) The tracing below depicts airflow through the glottis during vocal fold vibration. The units of measure are milliliters per second (mL/s), which is the same as cubic centimeters per second (cc/s). Examine the tracing below to answer the following questions.

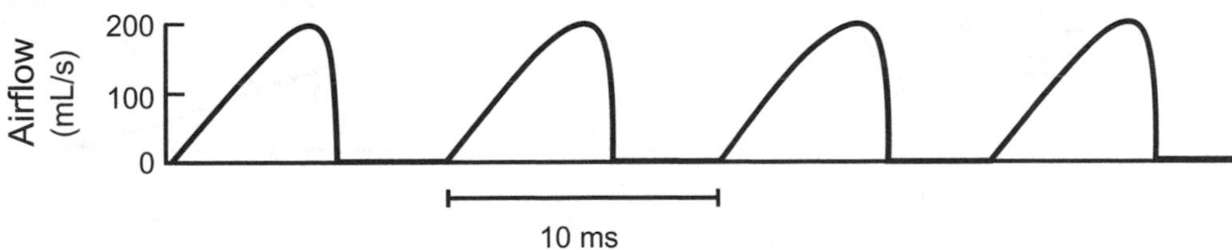

What is the minimum airflow? _______ mL/s

This minimum airflow corresponds to what part of the vocal fold vibratory cycle?

____

What is the maximum airflow? _______ mL/s

This maximum airflow corresponds to what part of the vocal fold vibratory cycle?

____

(i) The tracing below represents average airflow during production of a sustained vowel. [Note that the time scale is substantially compressed compared to the previous tracing.] Examine the tracing to answer the following questions.

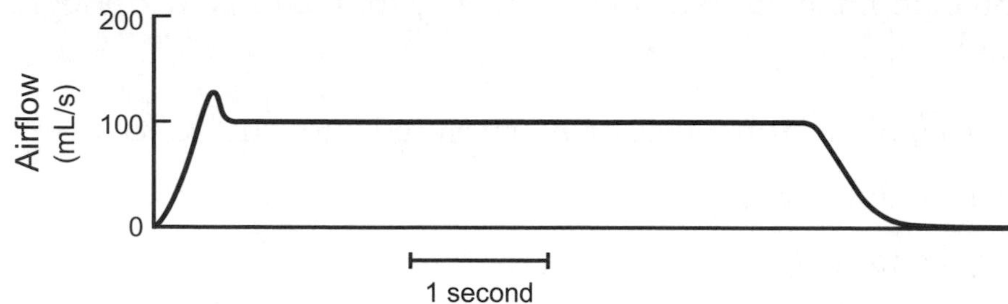

What is the airflow throughout most of the vowel production? ________ mL/s

What is the most likely explanation for the brief period of greater airflow at the beginning of the production?

____

____

(j) The tracing below also represents average airflow during production of a sustained vowel; however, unlike the previous tracing (which depicted a relatively constant airflow), this tracing shows a continually decreasing airflow.

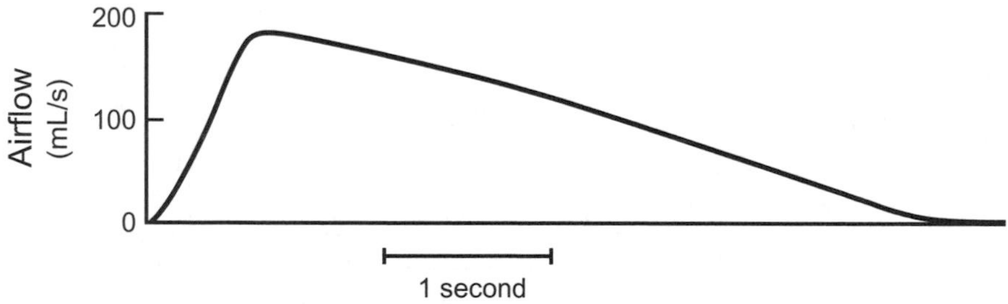

What could cause this decrease in airflow? [*Hint*: There are at least two answers.]

____

____

(k) The lower part of Figure 3–53 from the textbook is reproduced below. It represents tracings of oral air pressure (top tracing) and airway opening airflow (bottom tracing) during the production of "papapapapapapa." The oral pressure is used to estimate tracheal pressure and pharyngeal pressure and the airway opening airflow is used to estimate the airflow through the larynx (translaryngeal airflow). Calculate the laryngeal airway resistance at the midpoint of the fourth vowel production, indicated by the vertical dashed line (at 3.5 seconds) using the formula shown in the figure.

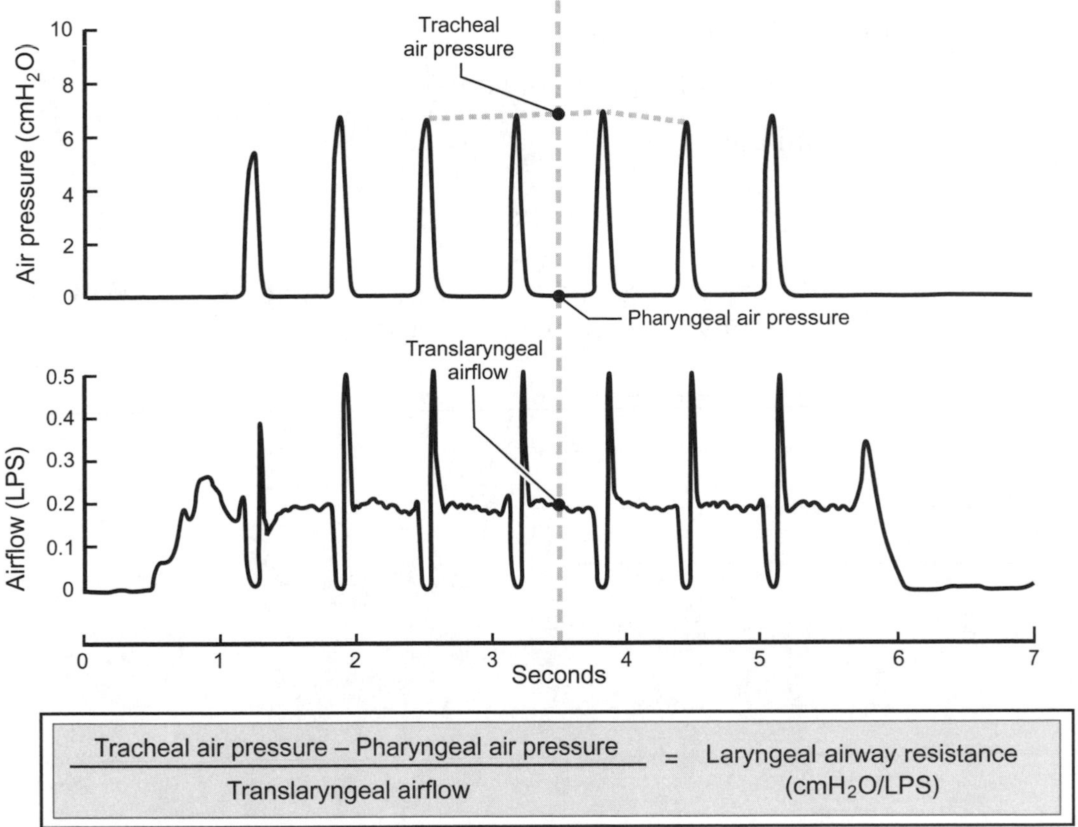

$$\frac{\text{Tracheal air pressure} - \text{Pharyngeal air pressure}}{\text{Translaryngeal airflow}} = \text{Laryngeal airway resistance } (cmH_2O/LPS)$$

Tracheal air pressure = ________ cmH_2O

Pharyngeal air pressure = ________ cmH_2O

Translaryngeal airflow = ________ LPS

Laryngeal airway resistance = ________ cmH_2O/LPS

3–26. Complete the following items regarding laryngeal disorders and clinical professionals.

(a) Identify the following conditions that can cause voice disorders as functional (F), structural (ST), or neuromotor-based (N).

_____ Parkinson disease

_____ Habit of using an abnormally high pitch

_____ Cancerous tumor on the vocal folds

_____ Gunshot wound to the larynx

_____ Pretending to be aphonic (without voice)

_____ Traumatic brain injury

(b) The minister in the chapter's scenario has a _______________ voice disorder.

(c) List at least four health care professionals who might be involved in the evaluation and management of a client with a laryngeal disorder.

____

____

____

____

4

Velopharyngeal-Nasal Function and Speech Production Questions

4–1. Label the bones and other structures indicated in the figures.

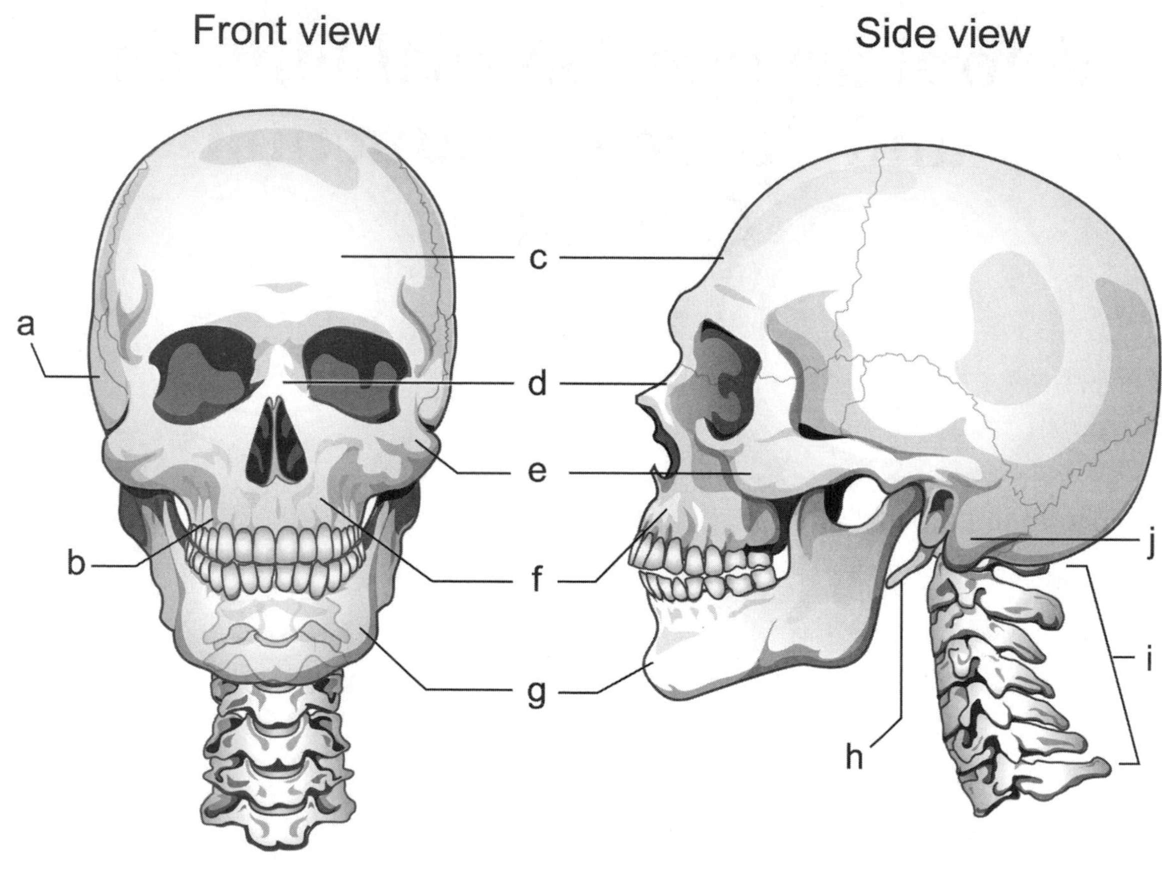

a ______________________ f ______________________

b ______________________ g ______________________

c ______________________ h ______________________

d ______________________ i ______________________

e ______________________ j ______________________

4–2. Label the bones and other structures indicated in the figure.

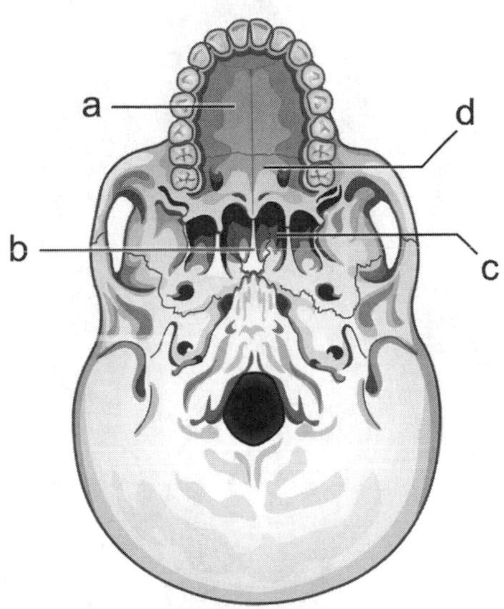

Bottom view
(mandible and vertebrae removed)

a ________________________ c ________________________

b ________________________ d ________________________

4–3. Label the structures indicated in the figure.

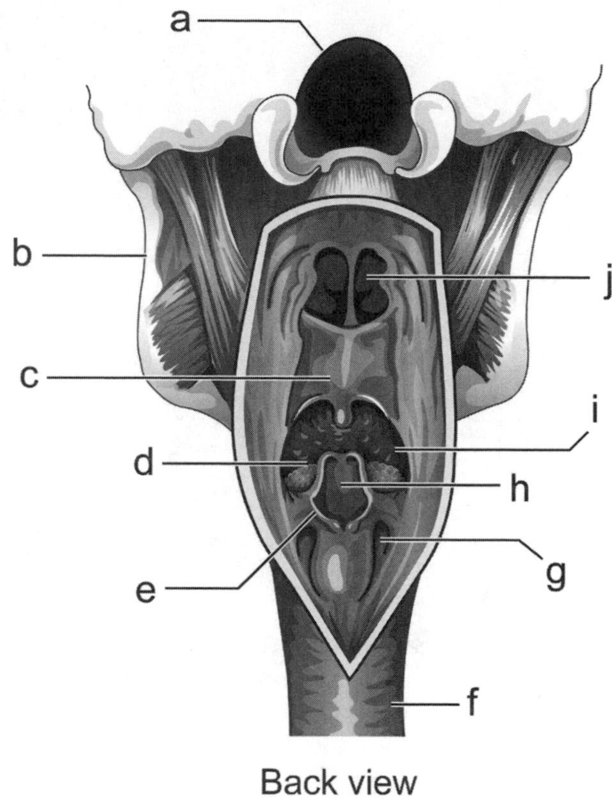

Back view
(opened from behind)

a ______________________ f ______________________

b ______________________ g ______________________

c ______________________ h ______________________

d ______________________ i ______________________

e ______________________ j ______________________

(a) The pharynx becomes increasingly more muscular toward its upper or lower [Circle one] end.

(b) The lower end of the pharynx is continuous with the ________________.

4–4. Label the structures indicated in the figure.

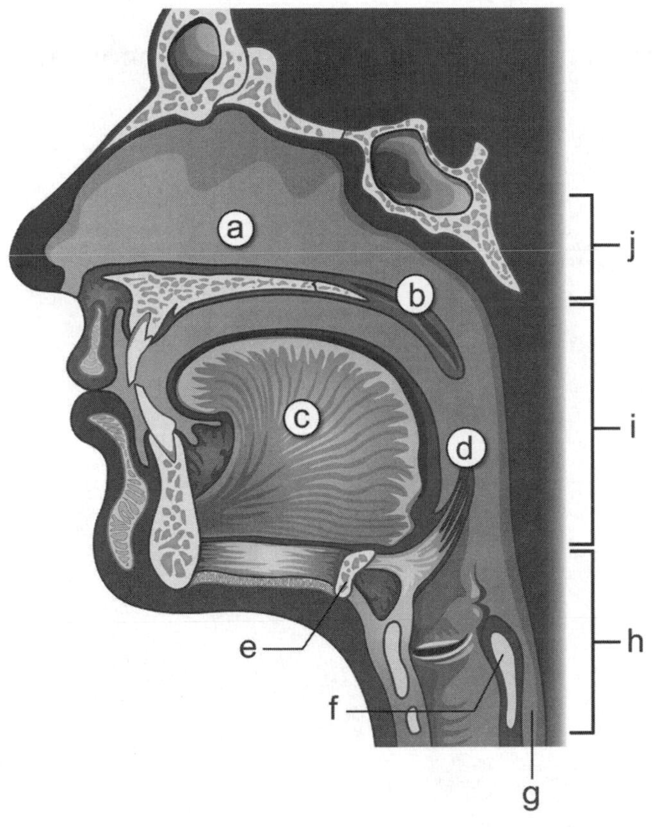

a ______________________ f ______________________

b ______________________ g ______________________

c ______________________ h ______________________

d ______________________ i ______________________

e ______________________ j ______________________

(a) The eustachian tubes extend from the middle ears to the lateral walls of the nasopharynx, oropharynx, or laryngopharynx. [Circle one]

(b) The nasopharynx connects to the nasal cavities via funnel-like openings called the ________________ (also called the posterior nares).

(c) The boundary between the nasopharynx and oropharynx is the ________________.

(d) The boundary between the oropharynx and the laryngopharynx is the ________________.

4-5. Label the structures indicated in the figure.

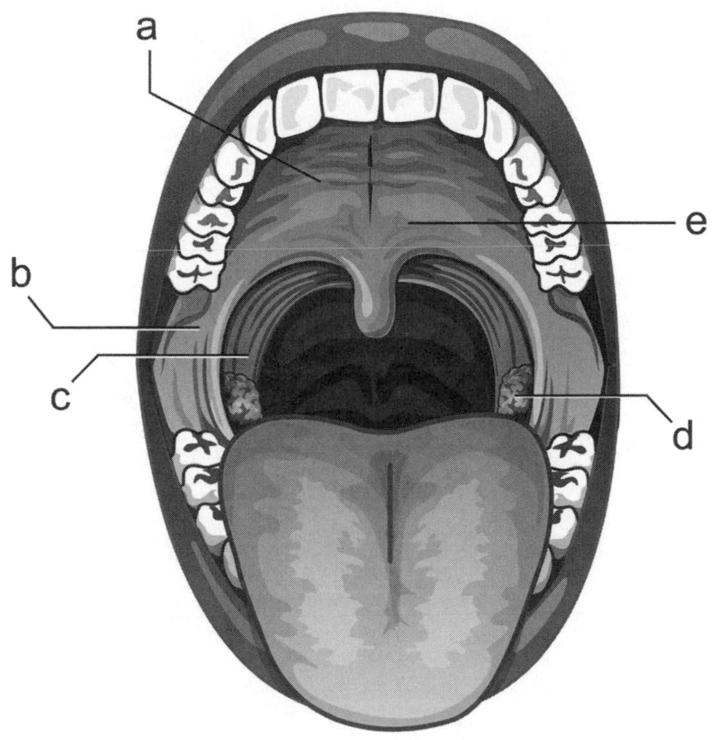

a ______________________ d ______________________

b ______________________ e ______________________

c ______________________

(a) When you open your mouth and say "ah," you can see the back wall of the nasopharynx, oropharynx, or laryngopharynx. [Circle one]

(b) The velum is made up of two parts, the ________________ and the ________________.

(c) Most of the muscle fibers in the velum are located in the front, middle, or back. [Circle one]

4–6. Label the bones indicated in the figure.

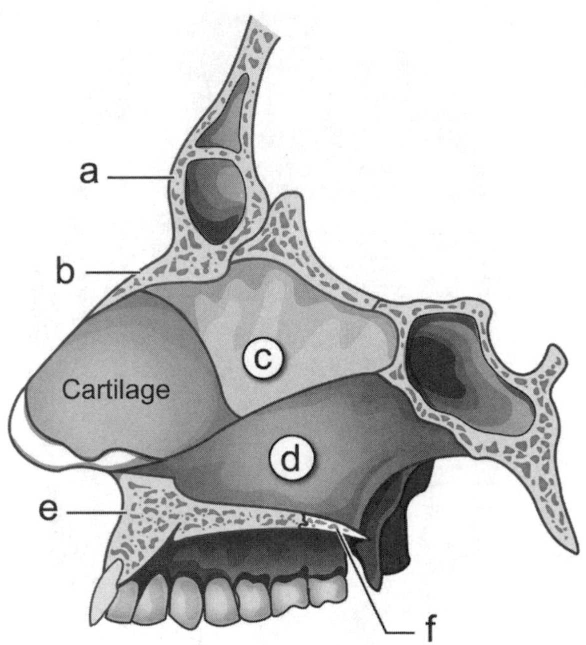

a ______________________ d ______________________

b ______________________ e ______________________

c ______________________ f ______________________

(a) The two nasal cavities are separated from one another by the nasal ______________, which is made up of [Check one]

_____ tendons and ligaments.

_____ a matrix of soft tissue.

_____ muscle.

_____ cartilage and bone.

4-7. Label the structures indicated in the figure.

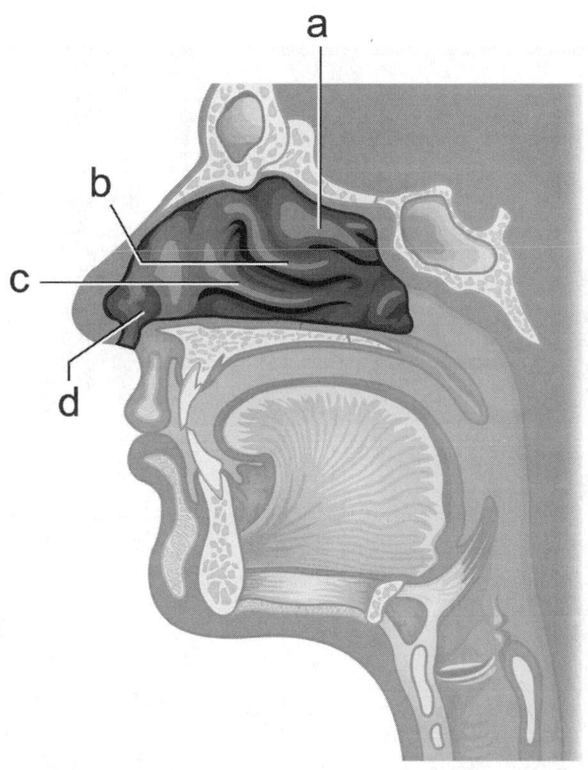

a ______________________ c ______________________

b ______________________ d ______________________

(a) The inner nose has a large or small [Circle one] surface area.

(b) The inner nose has a rich blood supply. True or false [Circle one]

(c) Mucus is moved through the nose by tiny hair cells called ________________.

4–8. Label the parts of the outer nose indicated in the photo.

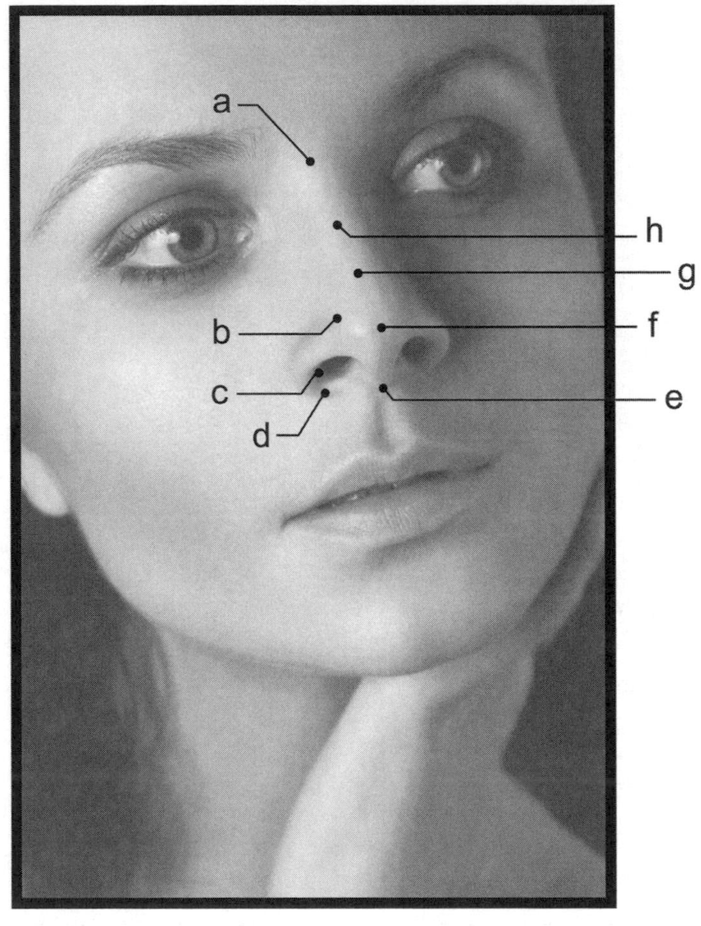

a ______________________ e ______________________

b ______________________ f ______________________

c ______________________ g ______________________

d ______________________ h ______________________

4-9. Label the muscles indicated in the figures.

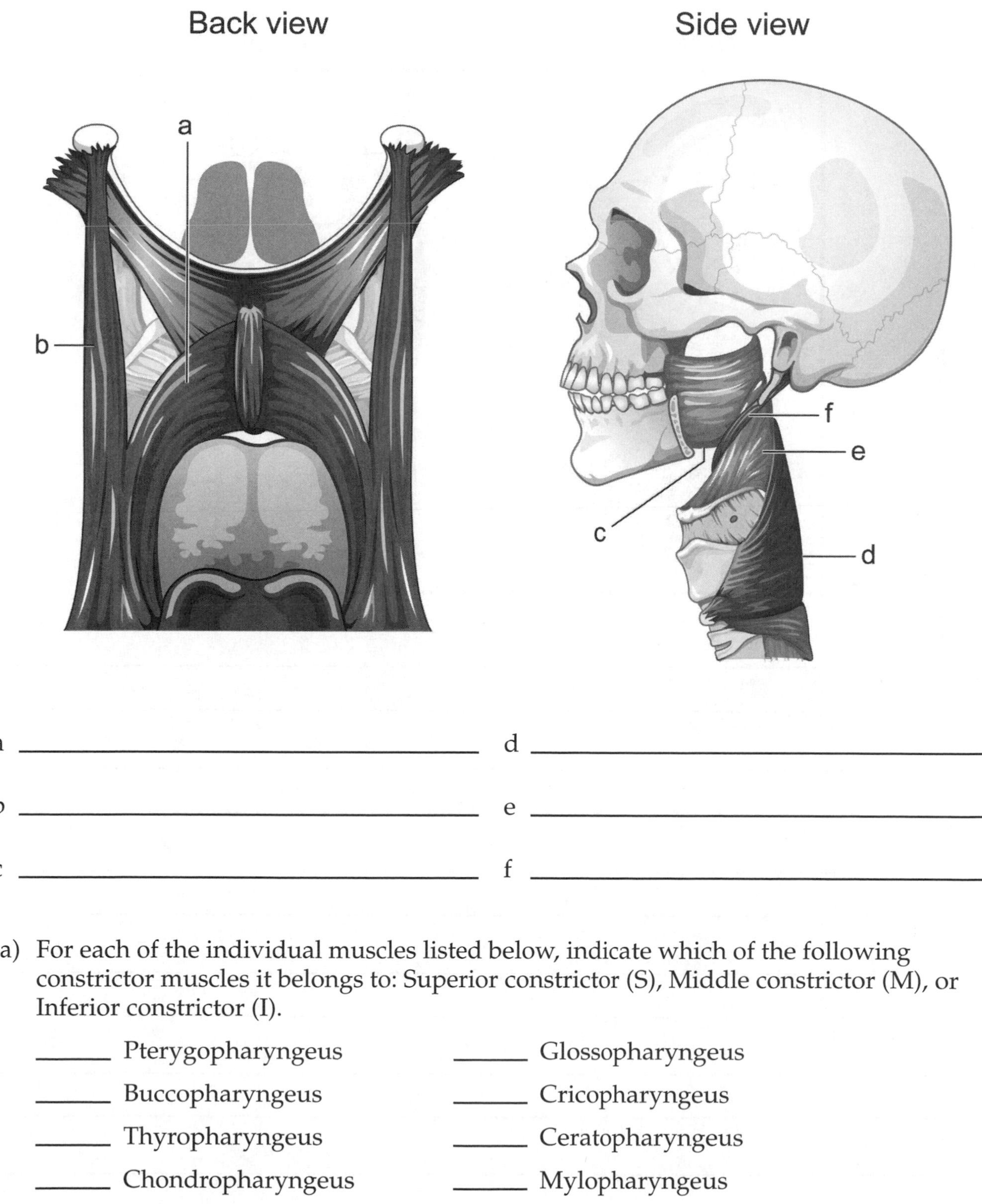

a ______________________ d ______________________

b ______________________ e ______________________

c ______________________ f ______________________

(a) For each of the individual muscles listed below, indicate which of the following constrictor muscles it belongs to: Superior constrictor (S), Middle constrictor (M), or Inferior constrictor (I).

_____ Pterygopharyngeus _____ Glossopharyngeus

_____ Buccopharyngeus _____ Cricopharyngeus

_____ Thyropharyngeus _____ Ceratopharyngeus

_____ Chondropharyngeus _____ Mylopharyngeus

4–10. The figures below illustrate the forces exerted by muscles of the pharynx. Provide the name of each muscle and briefly describe the consequence(s) of the force(s) exerted.

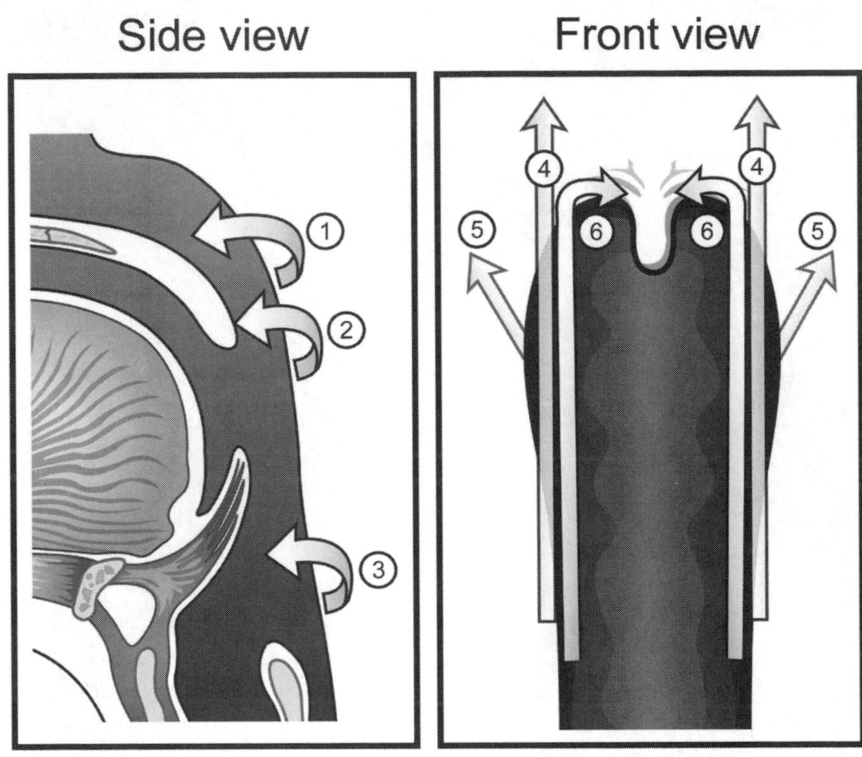

① ____

② ____

③ ____

④ ____

⑤ ____

⑥ ____

4-11. Label the muscles indicated in the figures.

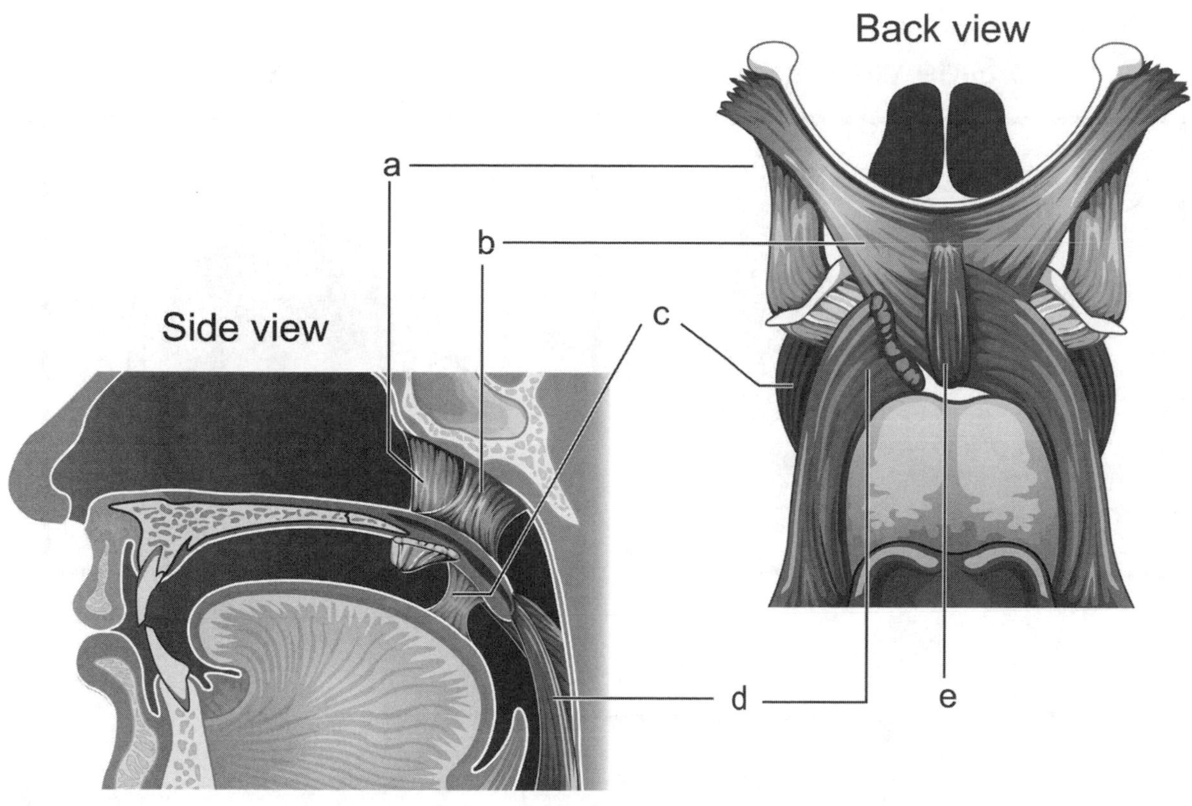

a ______________________ d ______________________

b ______________________ e ______________________

c ______________________

(a) Which of these is the only intrinsic muscle of the velum? ______________

(b) Activation of the palatal tensor plays a significant role in tensing the velum. True or false [Circle one]

(c) The palatal tensor has an important function in opening the ______________.

4–12. The figures below illustrate the forces exerted by muscles of the velum. Provide the name of each muscle and briefly describe the consequence(s) of the force(s) exerted.

Side view

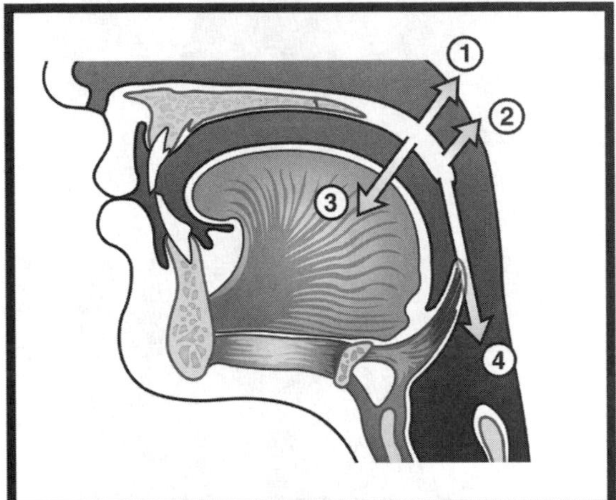

Left oblique view

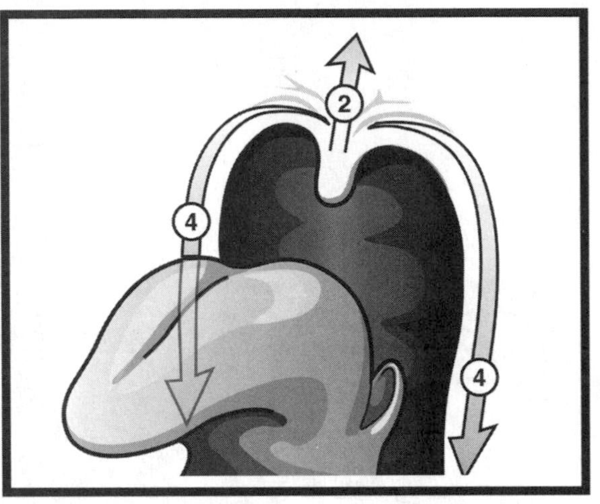

Front view

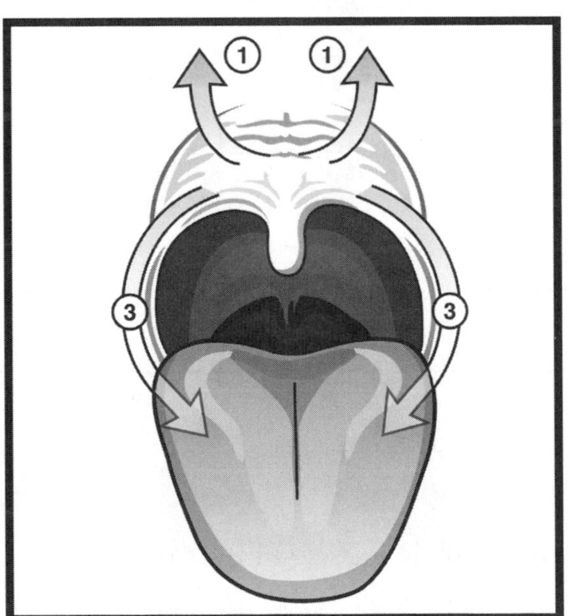

① ______________________________

____

② ______________________________

____

③ ______________________________

____

④ ______________________________

____

4–13. Label the muscles indicated in the figures.

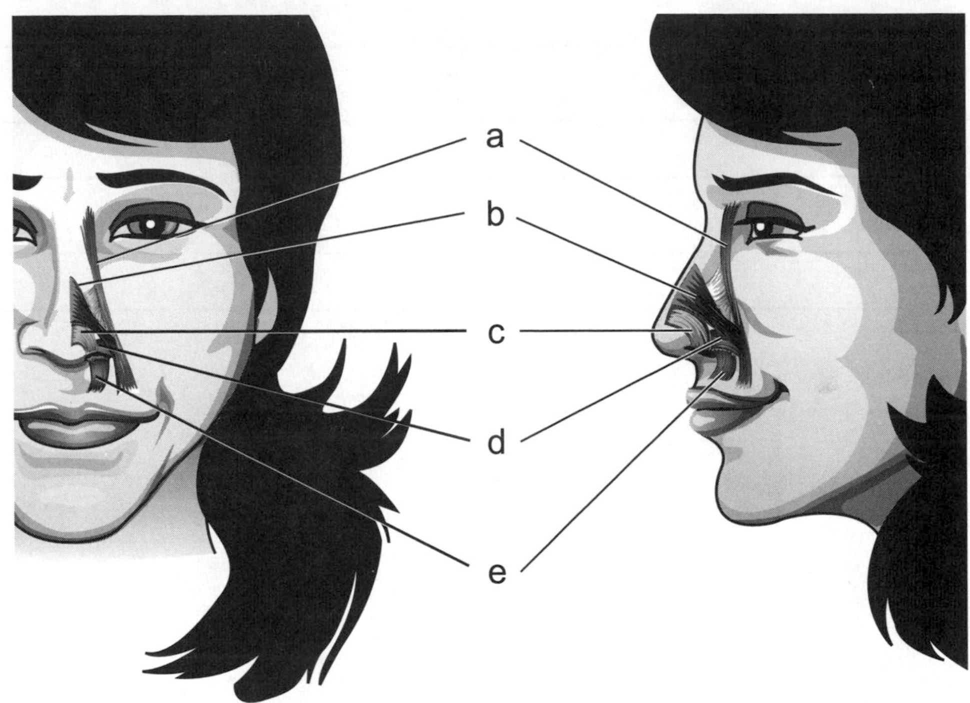

a ________________________________ d ________________________________

b ________________________________ e ________________________________

c ________________________________

(a) Which muscle has the longest name of any muscle in animals? ____________________

____

4-14. Describe the movements that can change the shape and size of the pharyngeal tube. Use the figures below as guides.

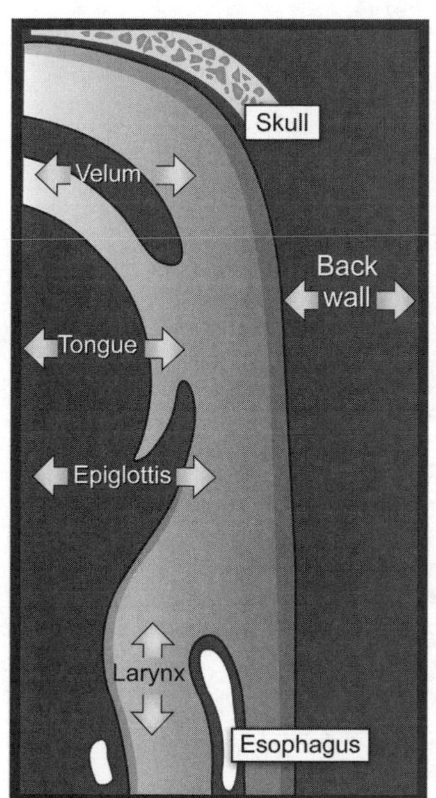

Side view

Front view

(1) ____

____

(2) ____

____

(3) ____

____

(4) ____

____

4–15. The figure below depicts four possible ways to close the velopharynx. Which muscles are most likely responsible for each of these movement patterns?

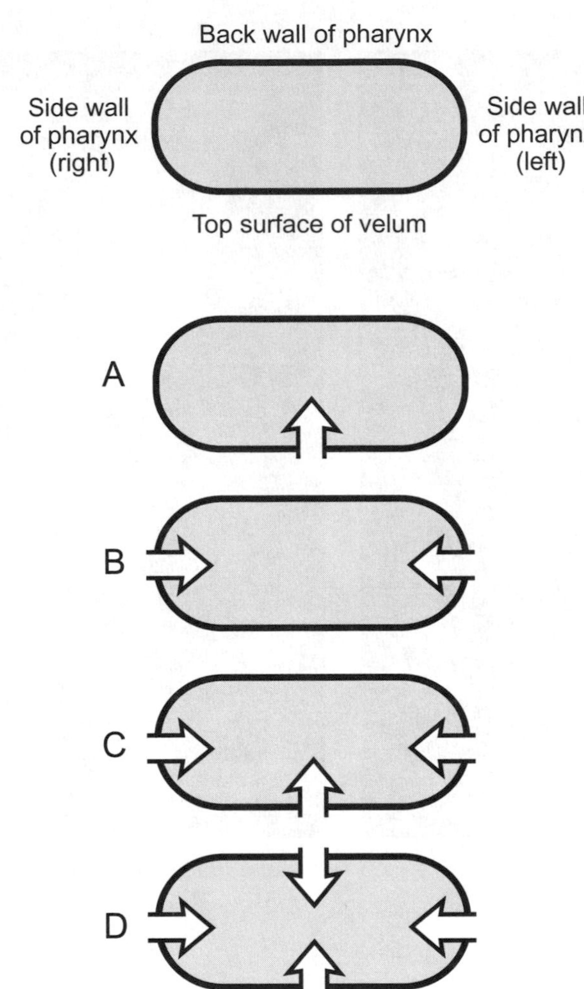

A ____

____

B ____

____

C ____

____

D ____

____

4-16. Complete the following items regarding functions of the velopharyngeal-nasal muscles.

(a) Muscles of the pharynx are listed below. Place a check mark indicating their potential action(s). Note that some muscles may have check marks in more than one column.

	Constricts Pharynx	**Widens Pharynx**	**Raises Pharynx**
Superior constrictor			
Middle constrictor			
Inferior constrictor			
Salpingopharyngeus			
Stylopharyngeus			
Palatopharyngeus			

(b) Muscles of the velum are listed below. Place a check mark indicating their potential action(s). Note that some muscles may have check marks in more than one column.

	Pulls Velum Upward	**Pulls Velum Down-ward**	**Pulls Velum Backward**	**Pulls Velum Forward**	**Shortens and Increases Bulk of Velum**
Palatal levator					
Uvulus					
Glossopalatine					
Pharyngopalatine					

(c) When the velum elevates, it takes on a hooked appearance, creating what are called the velar eminence and velar dimple (see Figure 4–14 in your textbook). Explain why this happens.

____

____

(d) Muscles of the nose are listed below. Place a check mark indicating their potential action(s).

	Constricts Anterior Nares	**Widens Anterior Nares**
Levator labii superioris alaeque nasi		
Anterior nasal dilator		
Posterior nasal dilator		
Nasalis		
Depressor alae nasi		

(e) The muscles of the outer nose are relevant to velopharyngeal-nasal function, but they also play an important role in ______________________.

4-17. Complete the following items regarding control variables of velopharyngeal-nasal function.

(a) Would velopharyngeal-nasal airway resistance most likely increase, decrease, or stay the same in the following situations? [Write increase, decrease, or same]

Velopharynx moves from closed to open: ____________

Velopharynx is open and nasal cavities become congested: ____________

Velopharynx is closed and nasal cavities become congested: ____________

Velopharynx is open and airflow through it increases: ____________

Velopharynx is open and the depressor alae nasi muscles contract: ____________

(b) Which of the following probably would require the greatest velopharyngeal sphincter compression force? [Check one]

_____ Singing a soft note

_____ Glass blowing

_____ Humming loudly

_____ Whistling

(c) Rank order the following according to the acoustic impedance offered by the velopharyngeal-nasal pathway. [1 = least; 3 = most]

_____ Production of "mmmmmm"

_____ Production of "eeeeeeeeee" with the velopharynx closed

_____ Production of "eeeeeeeeee" with the velopharynx open slightly

4-18. Complete the following items regarding the neural substrates of velopharyngeal-nasal function.

(a) The pharyngeal plexus is made up of: [List the cranial nerves, along with their numbers]

Number	**Name**
_____	____________________
_____	____________________
_____	____________________

(b) The pharyngeal plexus innervates which two parts of the velopharyngeal-nasal apparatus? [Check two]

_____ Pharynx

_____ Velum

_____ Outer nose

(c) Motor innervation to the muscles of the velum is provided by the ________________, except for the palatal tensor muscle, which is innervated by cranial nerve _____.

(d) Motor innervation to the muscles of the outer nose is supplied by cranial nerve _____.

(e) Sensory innervation to the pharynx and velum is provided by which of the following cranial nerves? [Check three]

_____ V	_____ X
_____ VII	_____ XI
_____ IX	_____ XII

(f) Our ability to sense the position and movement of the velum is quite good or poor. [Circle one]

4-19. Complete the following items regarding ventilation and velopharyngeal-nasal function.

(a) The part(s) of the normal velopharyngeal-nasal apparatus that offer(s) the greatest resistance to airflow during resting tidal breathing is/are the [Check one]

______ velopharynx.

______ internal nasal valves.

______ superior nasal conchae.

______ posterior part of the nasal cavities.

(b) The resistance to airflow offered by the external nasal valve [Check one]

______ can be decreased by the nasal dilator muscles.

______ can be decreased by the nasalis and depressor alae nasi muscles.

______ is infinite in the normal nose.

______ never changes.

(c) The internal and external nasal valves become smaller or larger [Circle one] during inspiration. This serves to raise or lower [Circle one] the resistance of the nasal airway.

(d) Indicate whether the following statements are True (T) or False (F). If a statement is false, write a revised statement that is true.

______ The two sides of the nose change their relative resistance in an alternating and cyclic pattern.

____

____

______ Total nasal resistance changes substantially hour to hour.

____

____

______ Nasal cycling is thought to be due to changes in air temperature.

______ Most breathing is done through the mouth.

______ The switch from nasal to oral breathing occurs when nasal pathway resistance exceeds 1.0 LPS.

(e) Explain how the application of a nose mask might change the nasal pathway resistance.

4-20. Complete the following items regarding velopharyngeal-nasal function and speech production.

(a) A person has a greater probability of having airtight velopharyngeal closure when sustaining which one of the following vowels and which one of the following consonants? [Circle two]

/u/ /æ/ /m/ /s/

(b) Why does velar height tend to be greater for high vowels than low vowels? Provide two possible explanations.

(c) For which of the following phrases is velopharyngeal closure most critical? [Check one]

_____ "I'm lying low in a hollow."

_____ "Toss the frisbee to Sue."

Explain why. ____

(d) The velopharynx is more likely to be open during the vowel in the word seen or seat. [Circle one]

Explain why. ____

____

____

(e) The observation of single motor unit activity in outer nose muscles during speech production indicates that [Check one]

_____ the speaker needs to clear the nasal airway of mucus.

_____ the nasal muscles may assist in valving the nasal airway during speech production.

_____ there is a neural impairment (there should be no activity in outer nose muscles).

_____ none of the above.

(f) During running speech production, inspirations are usually routed through the mouth only, nose only, or both the mouth and nose. [Circle one]

(g) What are two benefits of using the inspiration strategy noted above in item (f)?

____

____

4-21. Complete the following items regarding gravity, development, age, and sex.

(a) Explain why there might be relatively less activation of the palatal levator muscles and relatively more activation of the pharyngopalatine muscles when speaking in a supine position compared to an upright position.

____

____

____

____

____

____

(b) It should be easier for a person with weak palatal levator muscles to raise the velum when in a(n) upright or supine [Circle one] body position.

(c) Indicate whether the following statements about the velopharynx are True (T) or False (F). If a statement is false, write a revised statement that is true.

_____ The velopharynx is usually closed during vocalization in the first month of life.

____

____

_____ Six-month-old infants sometimes close the velopharynx and sometimes open the velopharynx during vocalization.

____

____

_____ Children close the velopharynx for oral sound production by 3 years of age (and probably much earlier).

____

____

_____ Temporal patterns associated with velopharyngeal opening/closing are the same in adults and children.

____

____

_____ Unlike young adults, who close the velopharynx during oral sound production, older adults (age 60 years and above) tend to open the velopharynx during oral sound production, probably due to age-related weakening of the velopharyngeal muscles.

____

____

_____ Although certain details of velopharyngeal function during speech production may differ between males and females, these differences are generally minor and not clinically significant.

____

____

(d) Explain how the nasopharyngeal tonsils ("adnoids") change during development and their potential significance to velopharyngeal closure.

____

____

____

____

4-22. Complete the following items regarding measurement of velopharyngeal-nasal function.

(a) A common way to visualize the velopharynx from above is to insert a rigid or flexible [Circle one] endoscope through the nasal cavities.

(b) Would it be possible to use an endoscope to view the velopharynx from below? Yes or No [Circle one]

If yes, what type of endoscope could be used (rigid or flexible) and where would it be positioned for best viewing?

____

____

____

____

(c) A lateral x-ray image shows the velum in contact with the posterior pharyngeal wall. Does this mean that the velopharynx is closed? Yes, No, or Maybe [Circle one]

Explain your answer.

____

____

____

____

(d) If you measured nasal airflow in a normal speaker, what would you expect to find for the following speech samples? [Check the appropriate answer]

	Nasal Airflow Throughout	Nasal Airflow During Part	No Nasal Airflow
Sustained "m"	______	______	______
Sustained "s"	______	______	______
"Socks	______	______	______
"Sample"	______	______	______

(e) Nasal airflow tracings recorded during speech production are shown below. They were recorded by placing a mask (attached to a pneumotachograph) over the nose.

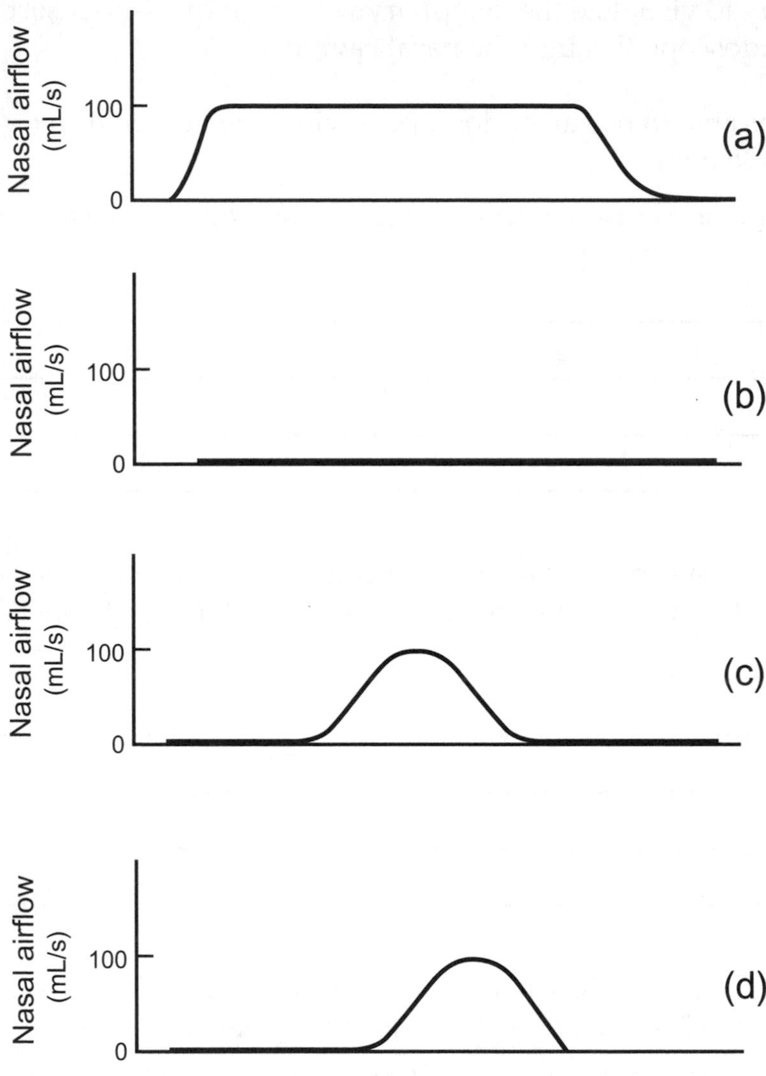

Which tracing represents nasal airflow during the following activities? [Answer a, b, c, or d]

______ Production of the word "team"

______ Humming

______ Production of the word "emu"

______ Production of the word "seat"

(f) The nasal airflow tracing below was recorded during the production of the sentence, "Sally cooked rice."

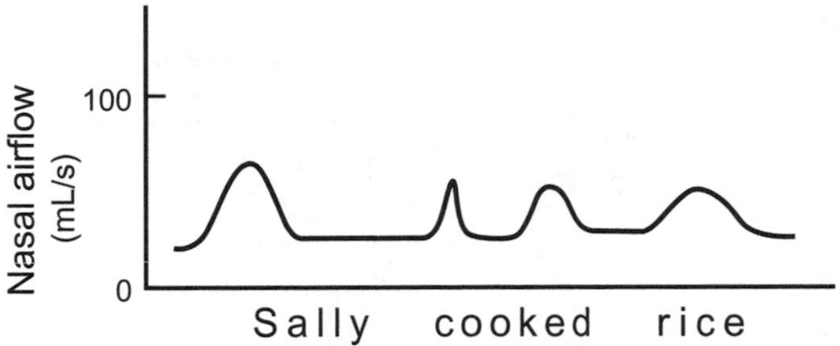

What could you conclude from this airflow tracing?

____

____

____

____

(g) The velopharyngeal orifice area can be estimated by a method developed by Warren and DuBois (1964; see Figure 4–29 in your textbook). Estimate the velopharyngeal orifice area using the formula and the values given below for oral pressure (P_1, in dynes/cm^2), nasal pressure (P_2, in dynes/cm^2), and nasal flow (in cubic centimeters per second, cc/s). The formula is:

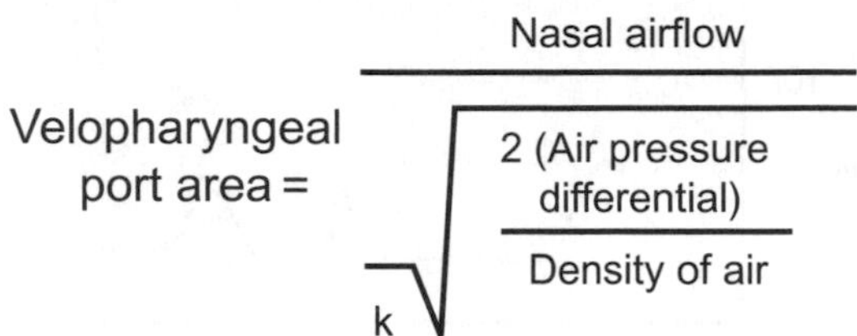

Note that dynes/cm^2 is a unit of measure for pressure that is much smaller than cmH_2O (specifically, 1 cmH_2O ≈ 980 dynes/cm^2, so 1 dyne/cm^2 ≈ 0.001 cmH_2O). Also, note that k is a constant that adjusts for the fact that airflow is often turbulent during speech production, rather than laminar (smooth). The suggested value for k is 0.65, density of air ≈ .001 (gm cm^3), and the air pressure differential = $P_1 - P_2$.

Velopharyngeal orifice area is expressed in square centimeters (cm^2). Calculate the velopharyngeal orifice area from the oral pressure, nasal pressure, and nasal flow values given below.

Oral Pressure (P_1; dynes/cm^2)	Nasal pressure (P_2; dynes/cm^2)	Nasal Flow (cc/s)	Velopharyngeal Orifice Area (cm^2)
100	80	200	________
100	0	0	________
100	20	30	________

Indicate which of the calculated values above best describes the velopharyngeal orifice area for:

Sustained vowel with normal voice quality ________

Sustained vowel with hypernasal voice quality ________

Sustained /m/ ________

(h) The tracings below represent simultaneously recorded oral pressure, nasal pressure, and nasal airflow during the production of "papapa."

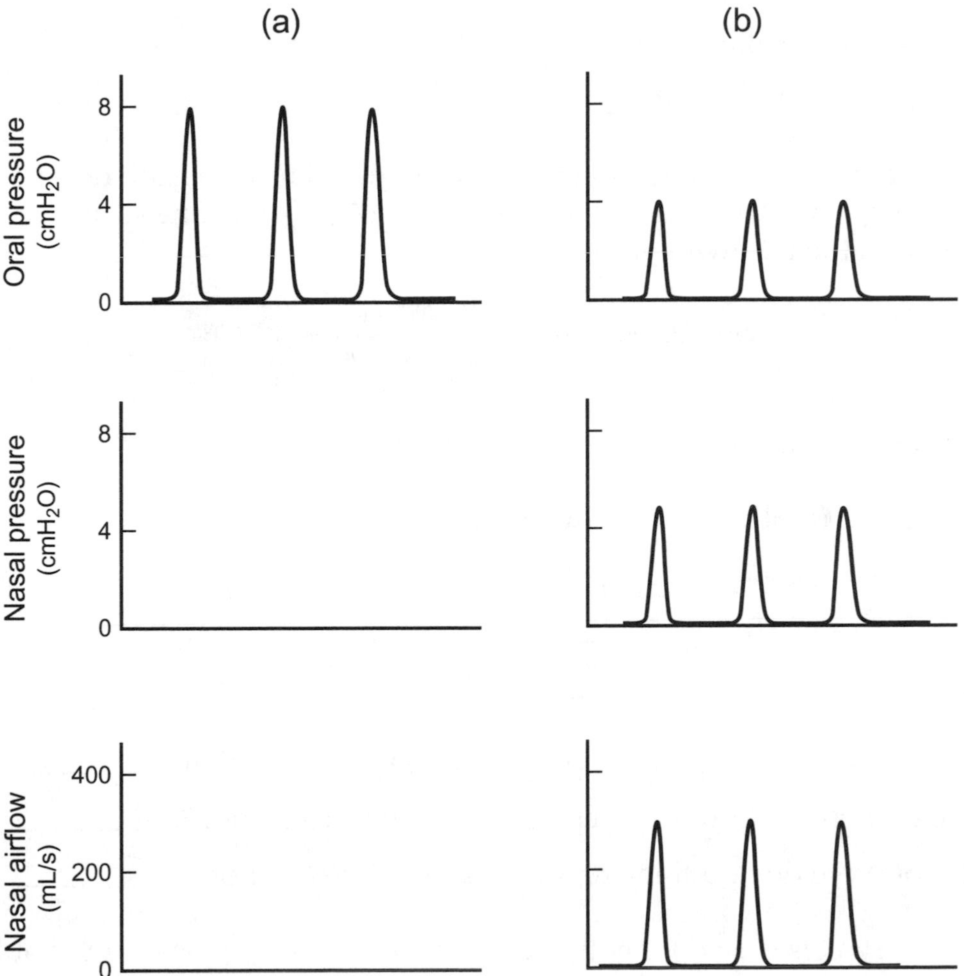

What can be concluded about velopharyngeal function from the tracings in (a)?

____

What can be concluded about velopharyngeal function from the tracings in (b)?

____

Can tracheal pressure be estimated from the tracings in (a)? If so, what is it?

____

Can tracheal pressure be estimated from the tracings in (b)? If so, what is it?

____

(i) Nasalance is a(n) [Check one]

_____ perceptual measure.

_____ acoustic measure.

_____ aeromechanical measure.

_____ physiological measure.

Nasalance is determined by sensing the acoustic signal near the anterior nares and near the mouth. The root mean square amplitude (A_{RMS}) of the nasal and oral signals are entered into the following formula:

$$\text{Nasalance} = \frac{\text{Nasal } A_{RMS}}{\text{Nasal } A_{RMS} + \text{Oral } A_{RMS}} \times 100\%$$

Calculate the nasalance for the following values:

Nasal A_{RMS}	**Oral A_{RMS}**	**Nasalance**
5	80	_______%
120	10	_______%
20	80	_______%

Which one of these do you think represents an /m/ production? _______

Which one of these do you think represents an /ɑ/ production? _______

Which one of these do you think represents an /i/ production? _______

If the velopharynx is closed for both the /ɑ/ and /i/ productions, why would the /ɑ/ have a lower nasalance value than /i/?

____

____

4-23. Complete the following items regarding velopharyngeal-nasal disorders and clinical professionals.

(a) It is possible for someone to have a submucous cleft (an opening in the bony palate that is covered by mucosal tissue) and complete velopharyngeal closure during oral sound production.

Would there be nasal airflow during the production of, "Take out the trash"? Yes or No [Circle one] Why?

____

____

The nasalance values would likely be normal, abnormally high, or abnormally low [Circle one] during the production of, "Take out the trash"? Why?

____

____

(b) Why does surgical removal of the nasopharyngeal tonsil sometimes result in velopharyngeal air leakage during oral sound production?

____

____

____

____

(c) It is reasonable to conclude that someone with an abnormally short velum could have produced the airflow tracing shown in Question 4–22 (f) for the sentence, "Sally cooked rice." True or False [Circle one]

(d) Someone with a neuromotor disease might [Check one]

______ not be able to close the velopharynx.

______ close the velopharynx abnormally slowly.

______ close the velopharynx for only a short period before it opens again.

______ Any of the above might occur in someone with a neuromotor disease.

(e) Match each of the following clinical professionals with a role he or she might serve a client with a velopharyngeal-nasal disorder.

Clinical Professional	Potential Role
_____ Speech-language pathologist	(a) Oversees medical team for clients with cleft palates and other craniofacial disorders
_____ Otorhinolaryngologist	(b) Constructs prostheses to replace missing body parts
_____ Neurologist	(c) Surgically repairs and/or reconstructs parts of the body
_____ Prosthodontist	(d) Manages depression and grief that might accompany a velopharyngeal-nasal disorder
_____ Plastic surgeon	(e) Diagnoses diseases of the nervous system
_____ Psychologist	(f) Evaluates velopharyngeal competence for speaking and swallowing

5

Pharyngeal-Oral Function and Speech Production Questions

5-1. Label the bones and other structures indicated in the figures.

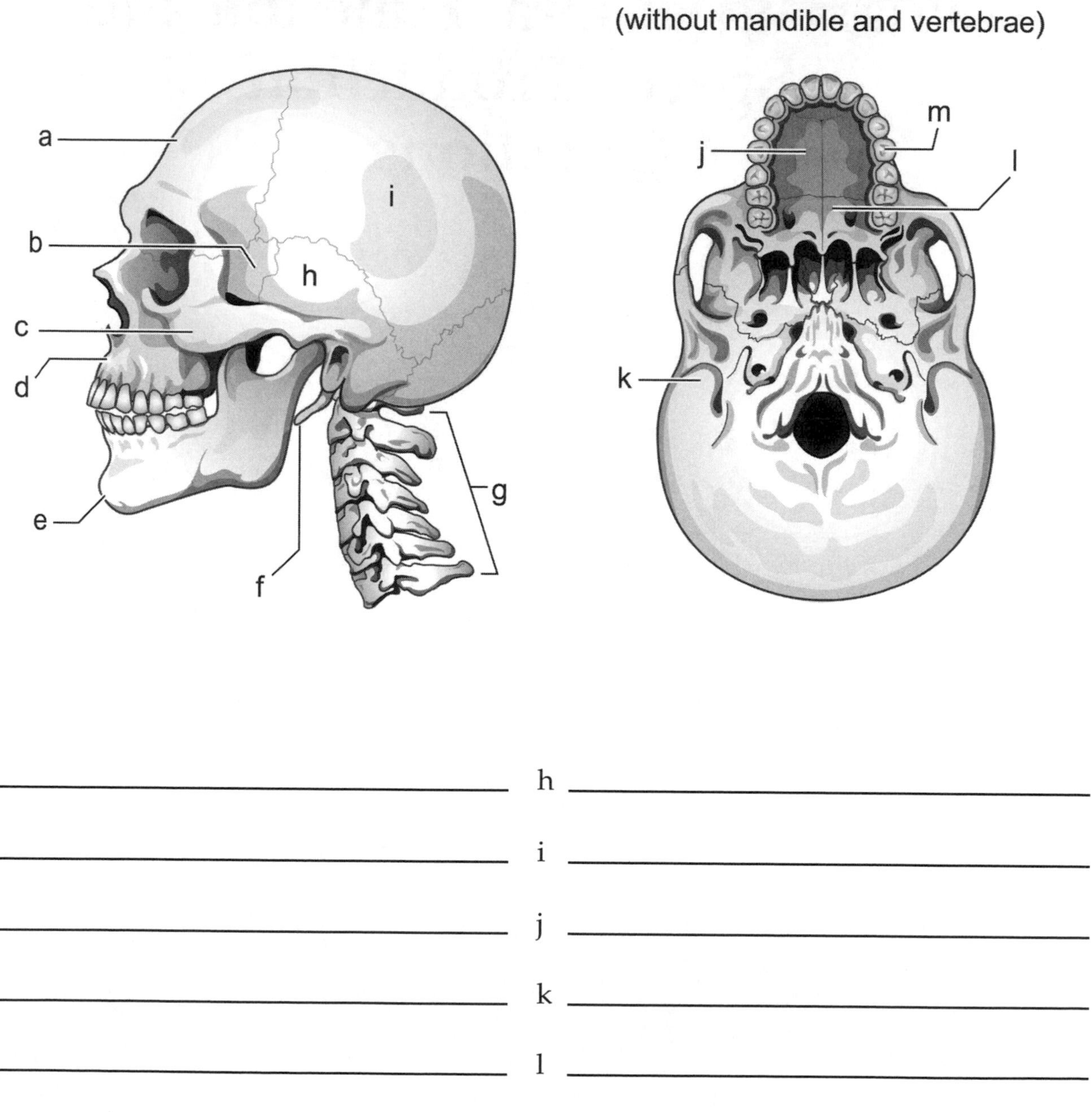

a ______________________________

b ______________________________

c ______________________________

d ______________________________

e ______________________________

f ______________________________

g ______________________________

h ______________________________

i ______________________________

j ______________________________

k ______________________________

l ______________________________

m ______________________________

5–2. Label the processes indicated in the figures.

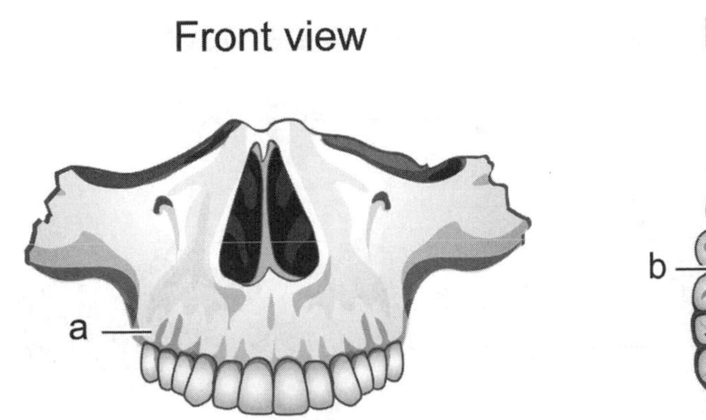

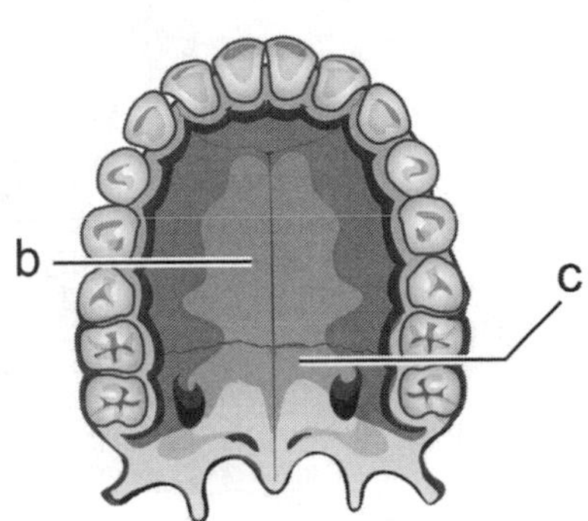

a ______________________ c ______________________

b ______________________

(a) These processes make up a structure called the ______________.

(b) This structure forms the roof of the __________ cavity and the floor of the __________ cavities.

5–3. Label the parts of the mandible indicated in the figures.

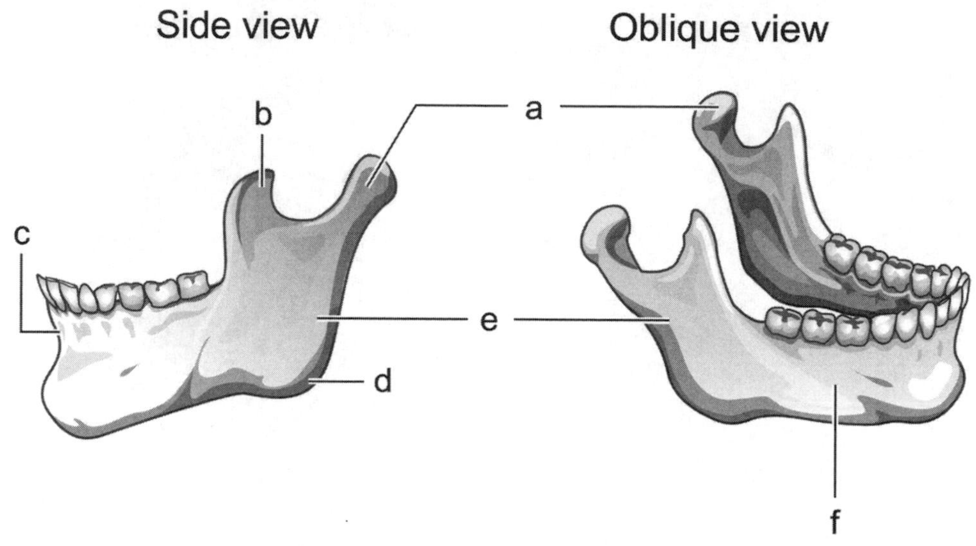

a ______________________ d ______________________

b ______________________ e ______________________

c ______________________ f ______________________

5–4. Label the teeth indicated in the figure.

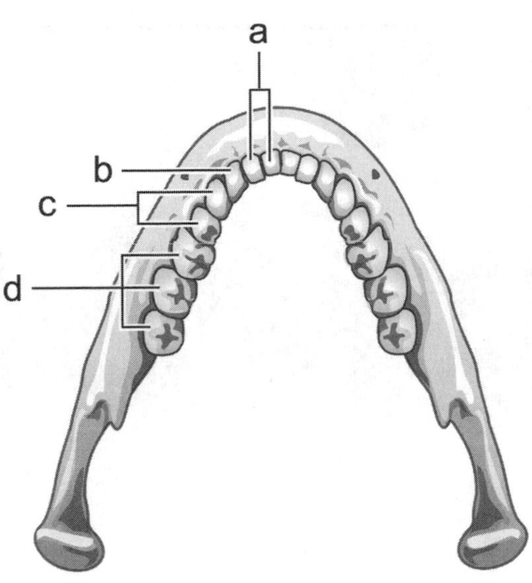

a ______________________ c ______________________

b ______________________ d ______________________

(a) How many permanent teeth are in the mandible (shown above)? ________

(b) How many permanent teeth are in the maxilla? ________

(c) How many baby teeth are typically in the mandible? ________

(d) How many baby teeth are typically in the maxilla? ________

5–5. Label the ligaments indicated in the figure.

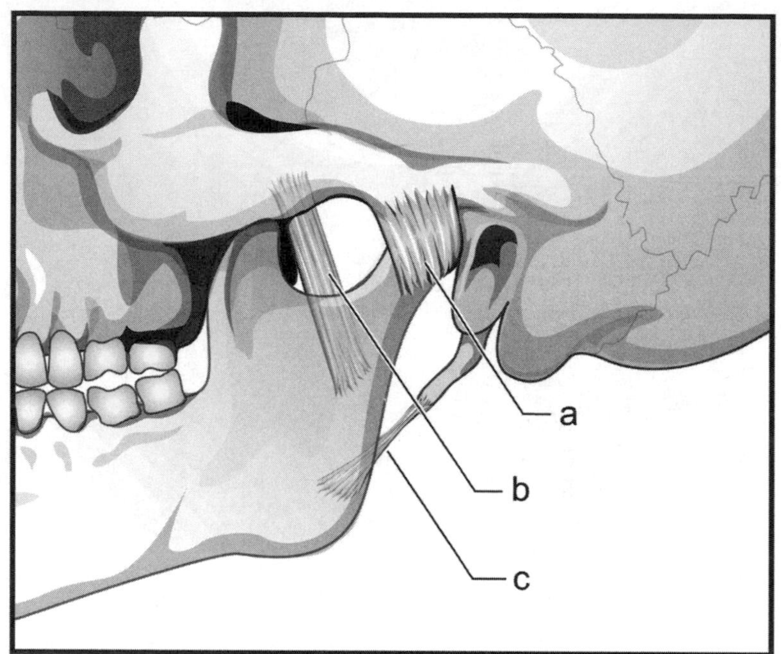

a ______________________ c ______________________

b ______________________

(a) What joint is shown in the figure? ______________________

(b) Describe the three movements of the mandible made possible by this joint (and its pair).

____

____

____

5-6. Label the regions of the pharyngeal-oral apparatus indicated in the figure.

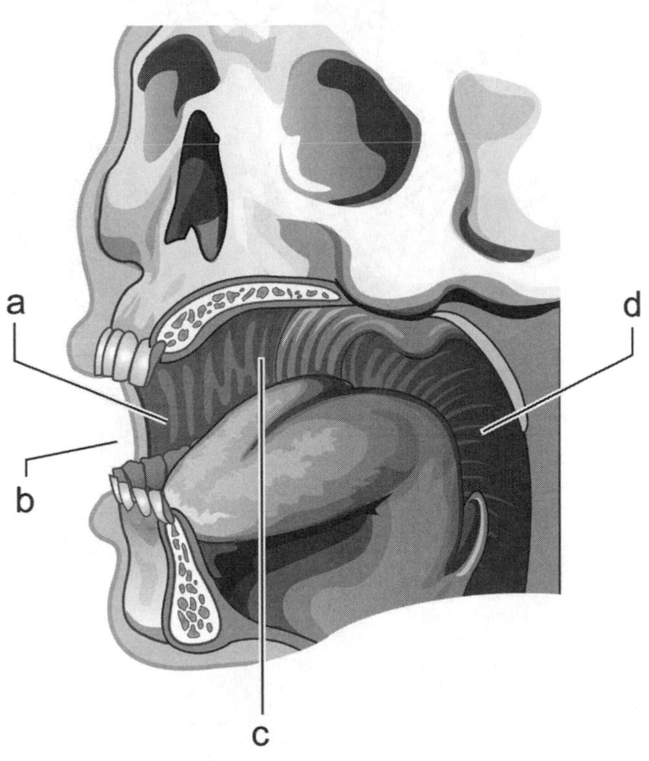

a ______________________ c ______________________

b ______________________ d ______________________

(a) The buccal cavity (not indicated in the figure) is located between the ______________ and ______________ on the inside and the ______________ and ______________ on the outside.

(b) What structure serves as the boundary between the oral cavity and the pharyngeal cavity?

____

5–7. Label the parts of the tongue indicated in the figure.

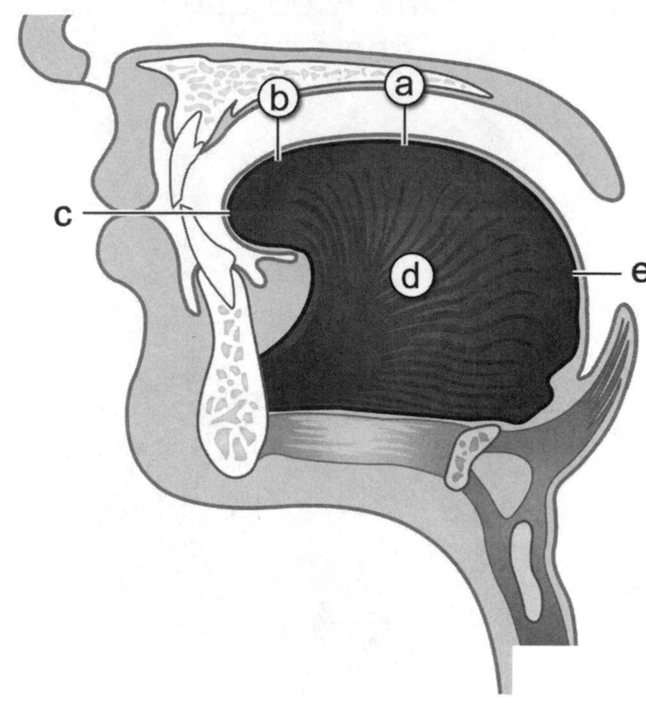

a ______________________________ d ______________________________

b ______________________________ e ______________________________

c ______________________________

(a) This scheme for subdividing the tongue is considered to be a(n) anatomical or functional [Circle one] scheme.

(b) Do the parts of the tongue correspond to specific muscles or muscle groups? ________

(c) The mucosa that covers the tongue houses small structures called ______________.

5–8. Label the muscles of the mandible indicated in the figures.

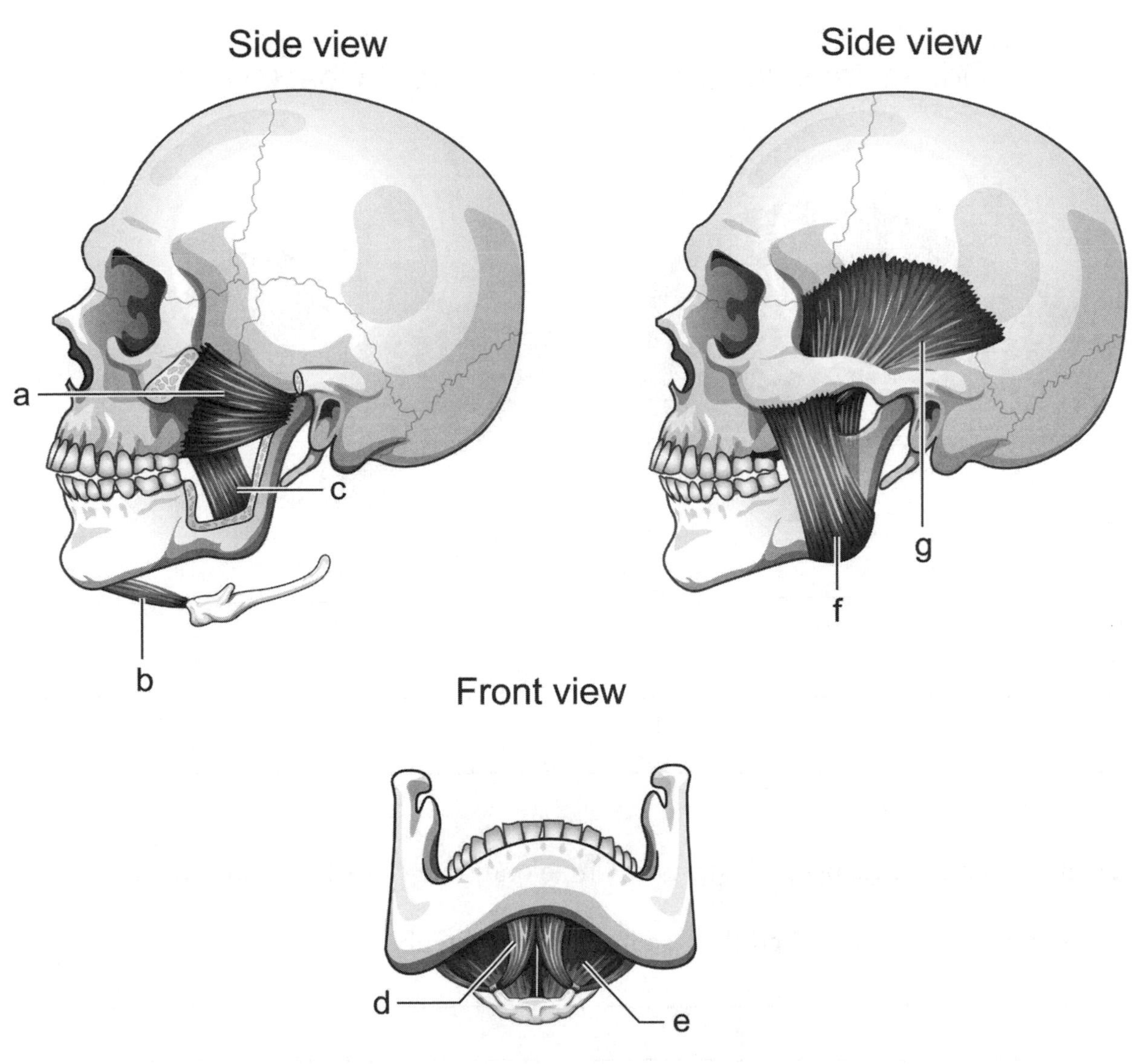

a ______________________ e ______________________

b ______________________ f ______________________

c ______________________ g ______________________

d ______________________

5–9. Label the muscles of the tongue indicated in the figures.

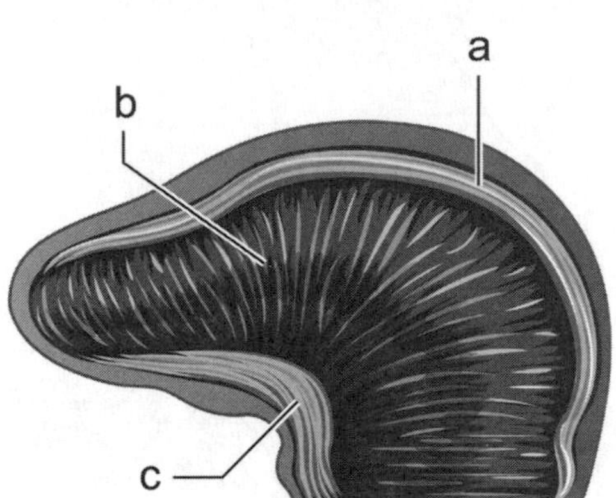

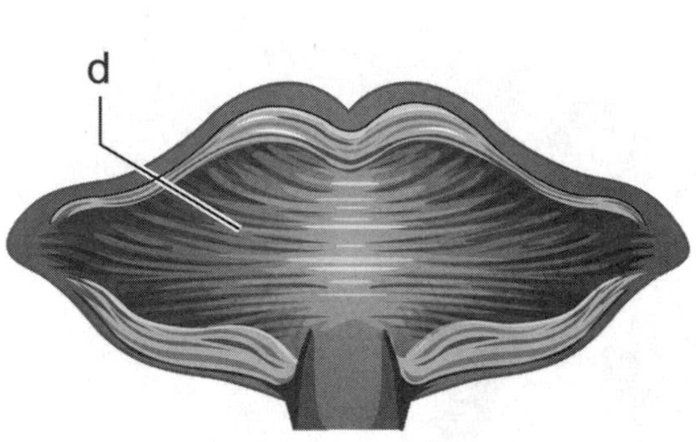

a ______________________ c ______________________

b ______________________ d ______________________

(a) These are called intrinsic or extrinsic [Circle one] muscles of the tongue.

(b) Explain why they are called that (as indicated in [a] above).

____

____

5-10. Label the muscles of the tongue indicated in the figure.

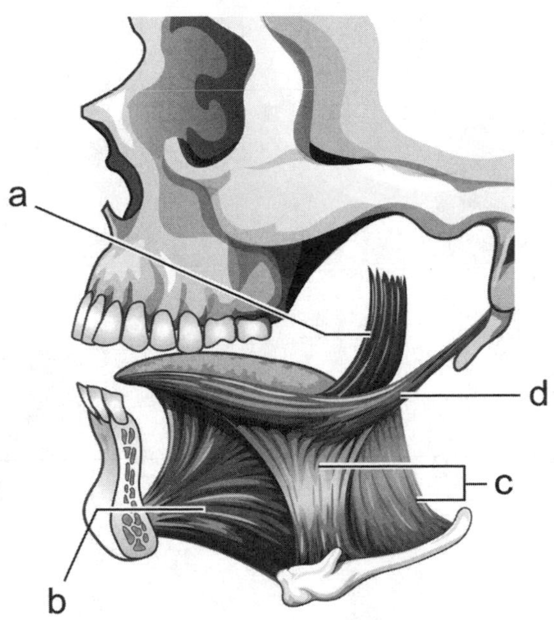

a ______________________ c ______________________

b ______________________ d ______________________

(a) These are called intrinsic or extrinsic [Circle one] muscles of the tongue.

(b) Explain why they are called that (as indicated in [a] above).

____

____

5–11. Label the muscles of the lips indicated in the figures.

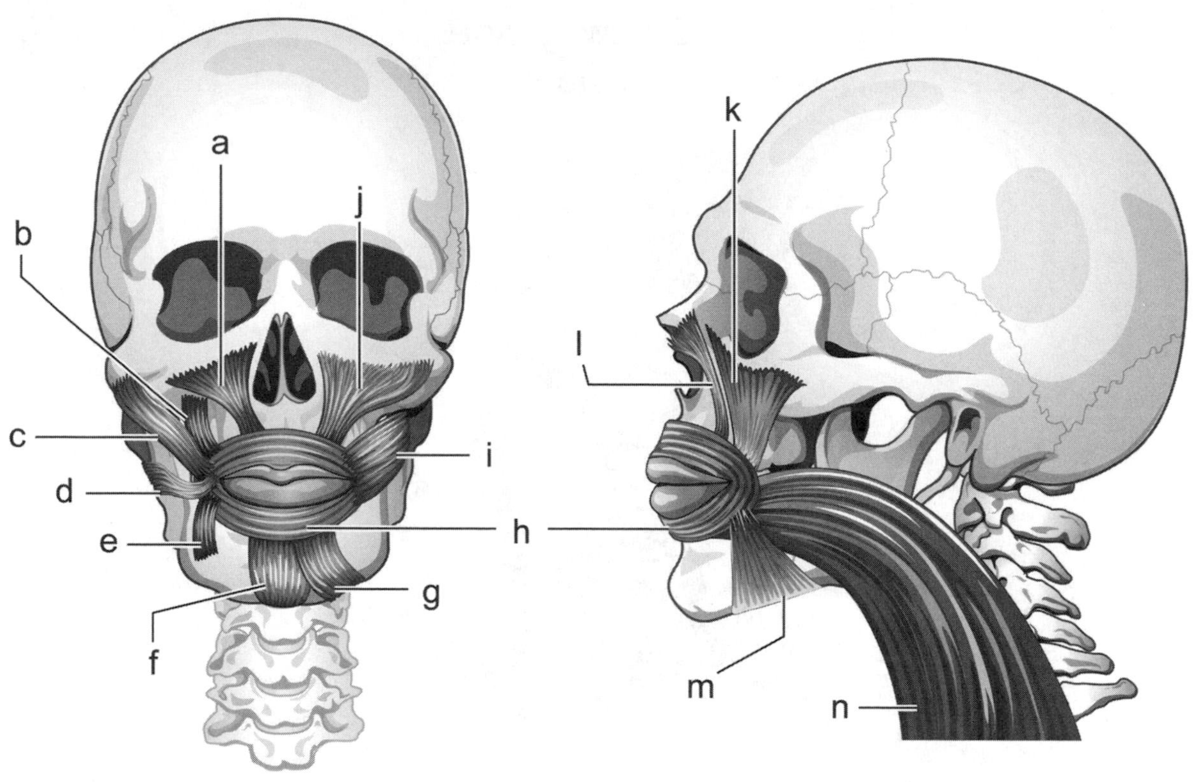

a ______________________ h ______________________

b ______________________ i ______________________

c ______________________ j ______________________

d ______________________ k ______________________

e ______________________ l ______________________

f ______________________ m ______________________

g ______________________ n ______________________

5-12. Complete the following items regarding movements of the pharynx.

(a) The walls of the laryngopharynx and oropharynx can be moved inward by contraction of the ________________ constrictor muscles and the ________________ constrictor muscles.

(b) The walls of the pharynx can be moved outward by contraction of the ________________________ muscles.

(c) Other structures that can change the size/shape of the pharyngeal tube are the tongue and epiglottis, among others. True or False [Circle one]

5-13. Muscles of the mandible are listed below. Place a check mark indicating their potential influence(s) on the mandible. Note that some muscles may have check marks in more than one column.

	Raise	**Lower**	**Move Forward**	**Move Backward**	**Move Side to Side**
Masseter					
Temporalis					
Internal pterygoid					
External pterygoid					
Digastric (anterior belly)					
Mylohyoid					
Geniohyoid					

5-14. Muscles of the tongue are listed below. Match the muscle with its potential influence(s) on the tongue.

Muscle	Potential Influence(s) on the Tongue
______ Superior longitudinal	(a) Moves back of tongue forward; moves front of tongue backward; moves center of tongue downward
______ Inferior longitudinal	(b) Moves tongue upward and backward; pulls sides of tongue upward; shortens tongue; pulls tongue tip toward the side
______ Vertical	(c) Shortens tongue; turns tip and sides upward
______ Transverse	(d) Moves tongue downward and backward
______ Styloglossus	(e) Flattens tongue
______ Palatoglossus	(f) Narrows and elongates tongue
______ Hyoglossus	(g) Moves back of tongue upward, backward, and inward
______ Genioglossus	(h) Shortens tongue; turns tip downward

5-15. A large number of muscles can move the lips in many ways. List the muscles according to their influence(s) on the lips. [Hint: Use Figure 5–15 in the textbook to help construct most of your answers.]

Upper Lip

Move upward

____

____

Evert (turn outward)

____

Move downward

____

____

Lower Lip

Move upward

____

____

Move downward

____

____

Evert (turn outward)

____

Mouth Corners

Upward

____

____

____

____

____

Downward

____

____

____

____

Upward and sideways

____

____

____

Downward and sideways

____

____

Backward and sideways

____

____

____

____

____

____

Upward and inward

____

____

Downward and inward

____

____

Inward and toward midline

____

____

____

Compress Lips, Cheeks, and/or Mouth Corners Against Teeth and/or Alveolar Processes

____

____

____

____

The muscle that moves the lips in the greatest number of directions is the

______________________.

5-16. Complete the following items regarding control variables of pharyngeal-oral function.

(a) Adjustments of the upper and lower lips can change the length and cross-sectional dimensions of the [Check one]

_____ oral vestibule.

_____ oral cavity.

_____ pharyngeal cavity.

_____ laryngeal cavity.

(b) Adjustments of the velum can change the [Check one]

_____ length of the oral vestibule.

_____ length of the oral cavity.

_____ length of the pharyngeal cavity.

_____ cross-sectional dimension of the pharyngeal cavity.

(c) Lowering the mandible can [Check one]

_____ change the length of the oral vestibule and oral cavity.

_____ change the cross-sectional dimensions of the oral vestibule and oral cavity.

_____ change the length and change the cross-sectional dimensions of the oral vestibule and oral cavity.

_____ not change the dimensions of the oral vestibule and oral cavity.

(d) Changes in the length and cross-sectional dimensions of different regions of the pharyngeal-oral lumen cause changes in the acoustic signal that emanates from it. True or False [Circle one]

(e) Contact pressure between two oral-pharyngeal structures is influenced by [Check one]

_____ the muscular pressure exerted.

_____ surface tension between the two surfaces.

_____ gravity.

_____ the muscular pressure exerted, surface tension between the two structures, and gravity.

(f) List the structures that the tongue can generate contact pressure against.

_____________________ _____________________

_____________________ _____________________

_____________________ _____________________

(g) List the structures that the lips can generate contact pressure against.

____

____

(h) A decrease in the cross-sectional area of the pharyngeal-oral lumen generally causes a(n) increase or decrease [Circle one] in airway resistance.

(i) Airway resistance in the region of the lips is lower or higher [Circle one] during panting than during whistling.

(j) When the tongue is sealed airtight against the hard palate, airway resistance is [Check one]

_____ very low.

_____ infinite (that is, the highest possible).

_____ approximately 1 cmH_2O/LPS.

_____ approximately 10 cmH_2O/LPS.

(k) As the mouth increases in size (that is, as the lips move farther apart), pharyngeal-oral acoustic impedance usually increases or decreases. [Circle one]

(l) As the tongue moves upward toward the hard palate, pharyngeal-oral acoustic impedance usually increases or decreases. [Circle one]

5-17. Complete the following items regarding the neural substrates of pharyngeal-oral control.

(a) Motor innervation for the pharyngeal muscles comes from cranial nerves ______ (____________________), ______ (____________________), and possibly ______ (____________________). [Provide number and name]

(b) Motor and sensory innervation for most of the mandibular muscles comes from cranial nerve ______ (____________________). [Provide number and name]

(c) Motor innervation for most of the tongue muscles comes from cranial nerve ______ (____________________). [Provide number and name], the exception being the palatoglossus muscle which receives motor innervation from cranial nerve ______ (____________________). [Provide number and name]

(d) Motor innervation for most of the lip muscles comes from cranial nerve ______ (____________________). [Provide number and name]

(e) Bell's palsy is a condition that affects cranial nerve ______ (____________________). [Provide number and name]

5-18. Fill in the American English vowel chart by inserting the appropriate vowel in each of the boxes.

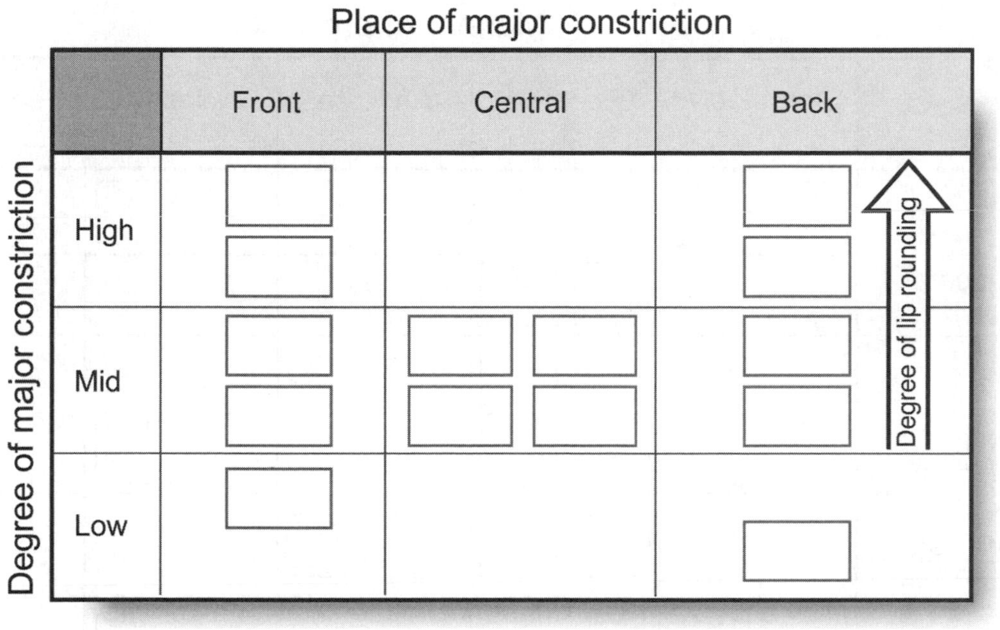

Place of major constriction

Degree of major constriction	Front	Central	Back
High			
Mid			
Low			

Degree of lip rounding

(a) The Front place refers to a constriction between the tongue and the

____________________.

(b) The Central place refers to a constriction between the tongue and the

____________________.

(c) The Back place refers to a constriction between the tongue and the

____________________ or the ____________________.

(d) A High degree of constriction refers to a large or small [Circle one] cross-sectional area of the airway.

5–19. Fill in the American English consonant chart by inserting the appropriate consonant(s) in each of the boxes. Note that "–" means voiceless and "+" means voiced.

Manner of production

Place of production

	Stop-plosive		Fricative		Affricate		Nasal		Semivowel	
	–	+	–	+	–	+	–	+	–	+
Labial (lips)										
Labiodental (lip–teeth)										
Dental (tongue–teeth)										
Alveolar (tongue–gum)										
Palatal (tongue–hard palate)										
Velar (tongue–velum)										
Glottal (vocal folds)										

(a) Stop-plosive consonants that are released through the nasal cavities are said to be ________________.

(b) Consonants that involve a stop (obstruction) component include stop-plosive consonants and ________________ consonants.

(c) The nasal manner means that the velopharynx is <u>open</u> or <u>closed</u>. [Circle one]

(d) Consonants that are produced with the least amount of airway constriction are called ________________.

5-20. Complete the following items regarding the speech production stream.

(a) Although it is convenient to categorize speech sounds according to a phonetic code (that is, place-constriction-lip rounding for vowels and place-manner-voicing for consonants), it gives the impression that sounds are strung together like "beads on a string." Explain why this is not an accurate way to conceptualize speech production.

____

____

____

____

(b) Coarticulation is defined as ______________________________.

(c) Which of the following is an example of forward coarticulation (also called right-to-left coarticulation)? [Check one]

_____ Lip rounding during the production of /s/ in "pots."

_____ Lip rounding during the production of /t/ in "two."

_____ Lip rounding during the production of /m/ in "mice."

_____ Lip rounding during the production of /s/ in "caboose."

(d) Which of the following is an example of backward coarticulation (also called left-to-right coarticulation)? [Check one]

_____ Lip rounding during the production of /s/ in "pots."

_____ Lip rounding during the production of /t/ in "two."

_____ Lip rounding during the production of /m/ in "mice."

_____ Lip rounding during the production of /s/ in "caboose."

(e) What does forward coarticulation (also called anticipatory coarticulation) suggest about how the nervous system controls speech production?

____

____

____

(f) What does backward coarticulation (also called carryover coarticulation) suggest about the nature of the articulators?

____

____

____

(g) Theories that view the speech production process as a series of continuously unfolding and often overlapping movements of the different articulators have been called ________________ Theory or ________________ Theory.

5–21. Indicate whether the following statements about development, age, and sex are True (T) or False (F). If a statement is false, write a revised statement that is true.

_____ The infant's pharyngeal-oral apparatus is smaller than an adult's pharyngeal-oral apparatus, but essentially the same in configuration (shape).

____

____

_____ The infant's pharyngeal-oral apparatus continues to grow at least into adolescence and possibly adulthood.

____

____

_____ Children have slower speech production rates than adults.

____

____

_____ Children have more stable (less variable) speech production movements than adults.

____

____

_____ Adult-like pharyngeal-oral movements for speech production are not acquired until the teenage years.

_____ Overall, the pharyngeal-oral apparatus gets smaller with age in adults and changes the resonance characteristics accordingly.

_____ Articulatory rate and overall speaking rate (inclusive of pauses) slow with age in adults.

_____ The duration of speech segments becomes shorter with age in adults.

_____ Variability in speech production movements increases with age in adults.

_____ The pharynx is longer in men than women.

_____ During speech production the articulators tend to move slower in men than in women.

5-22. Complete the following items regarding measurement of pharyngeal-oral function.

Figure 5–28 in the textbook depicts movements of the tongue, lips, and mandible (as tracked by pellet points) during the production of a vowel sequence using the x-ray microbeam system [read the figure caption for details of what is depicted in the figure]. Use the figure to answer the questions (a) through (d) below.

(a) During the production of which vowel is the tongue at its highest position? ____________

(b) During the production of which vowel is the tongue at its lowest position? ____________

(c) During the production of which vowel is the tongue at its most backward position?

____

(d) Which lip (lower lip or upper lip) moves farther during the production of the vowel sequence? ____________

(e) The x-ray microbeam system was developed, in part, to address the problem of the relatively high radiation risk that was posed by the earlier x-ray imaging systems. True or False [Circle one]

(f) Strain-gauge systems can be used to track and measure [Check one]

______ force production of selected articulators.

______ movements of selected articulators.

______ electrical activity in the muscles of selected articulators.

______ both force production and movements of selected articulators.

(g) Electromagnetic sensing systems can be used to track and measure [Check one]

______ force production of selected articulators.

______ movements of selected articulators.

______ electrical activity in the muscles of selected articulators.

______ both force production and movements of selected articulators.

(h) Electromagnetic sensing systems for measuring movements of the articulators are similar to magnetometer systems for measuring movements of the breathing apparatus. True or False [Circle one]

(i) Electropalatographic monitoring requires the construction of ____________________

____.

(j) Magnetic resonance imaging can only be used to produce static images, not images of articulatory movements. True or False [Circle one]

(k) The pharyngeal-oral structures that are best visualized with ultrasound imaging are the ____________________ and the ____________________.

(l) Consider Figure 5–32 in the textbook. What does this figure indicate about the movement of the lateral pharyngeal walls during successive /ɑ/ and /k/ productions?

____

____

____

What muscle causes the inward movement of the pharyngeal walls at the level where the ultrasound transducer is placed?

____

(m) Describe how oral air pressure is measured.

____

____

____

____

____

____

(n) What is the effect on oral pressure when there is a velopharyngeal leak or when the lips do not seal completely during the production of /p/?

____

____

____

(o) If you wanted to calculate the airway resistance at a constriction where the tongue is close to the alveolar ridge during an /s/ production, what measurements would you need to make? [Check one]

_____ The force of the tongue against the alveolar ridge

_____ The area of the glottis between the tongue and the alveolar ridge

_____ Pressure on both sides of the constriction and airflow through the constriction

_____ Airflow on both sides of the constriction and alveolar pressure

5-23. Complete the following items regarding pharyngeal-oral disorders and clinical professionals.

(a) Name five conditions that could cause pharyngeal-oral impairments.

_____

_____

_____

_____

_____

(b) What is a glossectomy?

_____

_____

_____

(c) If a client has a weak tongue due to a neuromotor disease, which of the following consonants would be most difficult for him to produce? [Check all that apply]

_____ /m/

_____ /t/

_____ /k/

_____ /p/

_____ /s/

_____ /h/

_____ /n/

(d) Which of the following professionals would be most likely to be involved in the evaluation and/or management of a client with a pharyngeal-oral impairment (who did not have impairments of other parts of the body)? [Check all that apply]

______ Dentist

______ Pulmonologist

______ Prosthodontist

______ Neurologist

______ Psychologist

______ Physical therapist

______ Plastic surgeon

______ Otorhinolaryngologist

______ Podiatrist

______ Speech-language pathologist

6

Brain Structures and Mechanisms for Speech, Hearing, and Language Questions

6–1. What is the difference between a nerve and a tract?

____

____

6–2. If the cerebral hemispheres were cut into front and back halves, in which anatomical plane is the cut made?

____

In which anatomical plane is the cut made when it separates the cerebral hemispheres into upper and lower halves?

____

6–3. Clusters of cell bodies deep within the cerebral hemispheres are called ____________, and in a fixed brain have a ____________ color.

6–4. What is the difference between a nucleus and a ganglion?

____

____

6–5. What is the difference between lateralization of function and specialization of function in the cerebral hemispheres?

____

____

6–6. Below is a line drawing of the cerebral hemispheres.

(a) Identify the plane of the view.

(b) Identify the lobes of the cerebral hemispheres that can be seen in this view.

(c) Show the boundaries of the lobes (of the ones that are shown in this view) and name them.

(d) Identify the location of the primary motor cortex and the primary somatosensory cortex.

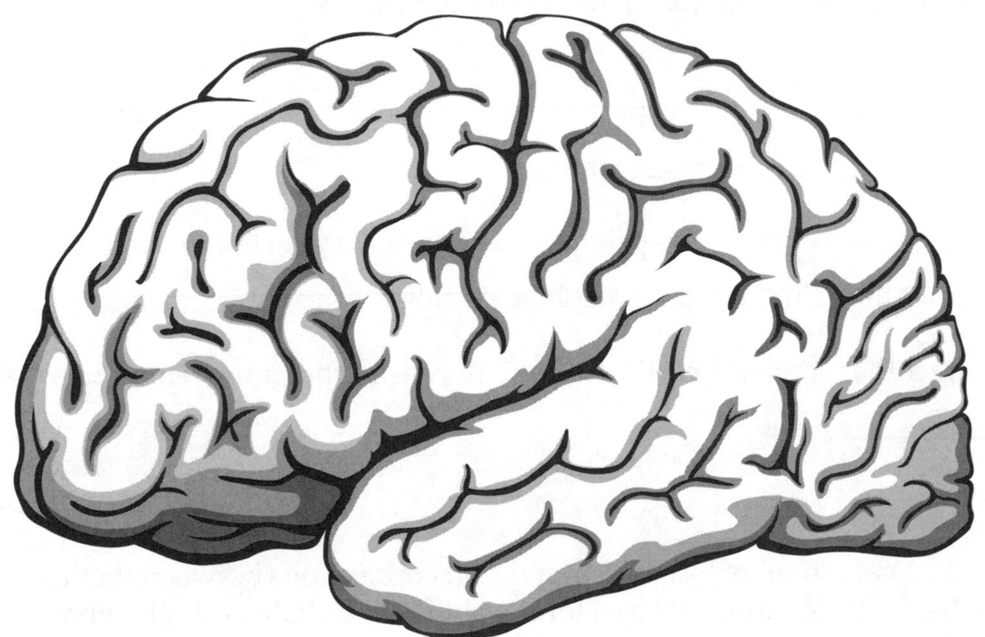

6–7. State two major functions of the frontal lobes.

____

____

6–8. State two major functions of the parietal lobes.

____

____

6–9. Describe the hidden "shelf" of the dorsal surface of the temporal lobe. Then, in two sentences or less, state why it is proper to say that the frequency arrangement along the basilar membrane of the cochlea is "projected" onto the auditory cortex.

____

____

____

____

6–10. Answer the following questions about fiber tracts:

(a) A fiber tract that connects the primary sensory cortex in the left and right hemispheres is called a/an ______________ tract.

(b) A fiber tract that connects the primary somatosensory cortex in the left hemisphere with Broca's area (in the left hemisphere) is called a/an ______________ tract.

(c) A fiber tract that connects cortical cells with cells in the brainstem is called a/an ______________ tract

6–11. In a classical model of brain "centers" and connections between them for speech and language, what is the anatomical basis for the ability to imitate verbally what someone says (as when a clinician asks, repeat the following three syllables: /ba/-/sta/-/da/)?

____

____

6–12. What is the point made in the text about the extent of corpus callosum fibers, as seen in Figure 6–5 (upper right) and Figure 6–10 in the textbook?

____

____

6–13. What is the internal capsule and where is it located? Identify two major tracts that contribute to it.

6–14. Using a box-and-arrows format, draw the major structures of the cortico-striatal-cortical, and cortico-cerebello-cortical loops.

6–15. Below is a line drawing of the ventral surface of the brainstem. Locate on this surface the approximate exit/entry location of cranial nerves V, VII, VIII, IX, X, XI, and XII.

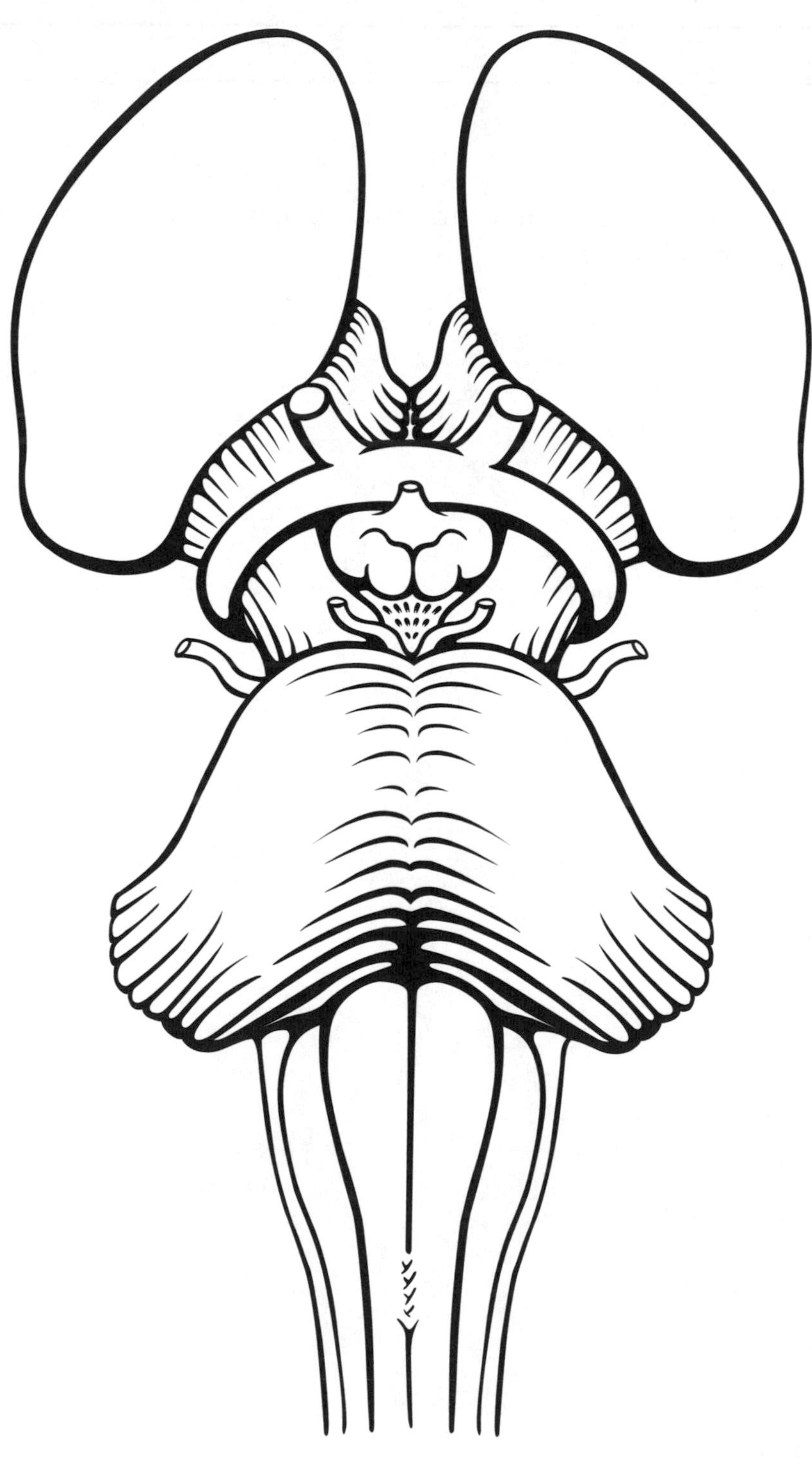

6–16. The table below shows speech/hearing relevant cranial nerves in the first column and two additional columns labeled "Motor" and "Sensory." For each cranial nerve listed in the first column, put an "X" under "Motor" or "Sensory," if the nerve has that function. For each nerve, provide an example of its motor function (if that function is checked) and/or its sensory function. If both "motor" and "sensory" columns are checked for a particular nerve, provide an example for both functions.

Cranial Nerve	Motor	Sensory
V		
VII		
VIII		
IX		
X		
XI		
XII		

6–17. For the following signs, indicate which cranial nerve may be damaged and on which side of the brainstem the damage is located.

Sign	Cranial Nerve	Side
Drooping corner of left lip, flattened left nasolabial fold, lack of furrowed brow on left forehead		
Failure of left side of soft palate to elevate for /a/		
Lack of sensation (e.g., to touch with a Q-tip) on right side of upper lip		
Absence of taste on both sides of posterior part of tongue		
Atrophy of right half of tongue		
Failure of left masseter to bulge when patient bites down		

6–18. The fibers of the corticospinal tract run through the midbrain as the ________________, through the pons as the ________________, and through the medulla as the ________________.

6–19. Describe in four or five sentences how the cerebellum is connected to the rest of the central nervous system.

____

____

____

____

____

____

6-20.

(a) Give an example of a brainstem motor nucleus that is associated with more than one cranial nerve.

___

(b) Give an example of a brainstem sensory nucleus that is associated with multiple cranial nerves.

___

6-21. The brainstem is said to consist of three major levels: the midbrain, the pons, and the medulla. One way to consider brainstem anatomy is to look at surface features of the ventral and dorsal brainstem (such as Figures 6–20 and 6–21 in the textbook), and another way is to study transverse (horizontal) sections through different levels of the brainstem. Based on your study of the transverse sections of the brainstem shown in the textbook, what specific anatomical landmarks do you think could be used to identify the level (midbrain, pons, and medulla) of an unlabeled, transverse section of the brainstem?

___

___

___

___

___

___

6-22. Using boxes and arrows, draw the nervous system components that are involved in the stretch reflex. What is the basic function of a stretch reflex?

6-23. Why is it important to know which cranial nerve nuclei are innervated bilaterally and which are innervated contralaterally? Give a specific example of why this information is important when performing a cranial nerve exam.

6-24. What does the term "upper motor neuron lesion" mean?

6–25. Below is a line drawing of a transverse section of the spinal cord and nerves attached to that section. Label at least five anatomical parts of this section and/or nerves.

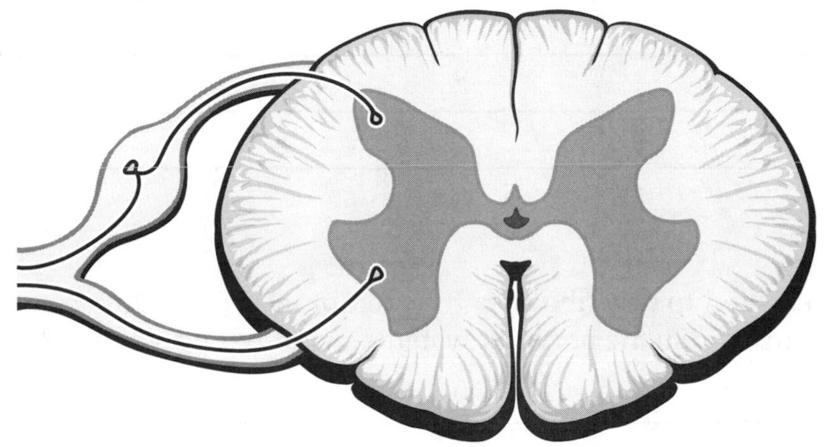

6–26. What is the primary difference between neurons and glial cells?

____

____

____

6–27. Briefly describe how neurotransmitters are manufactured within the brain and how they end up in the terminal segments of neurons.

____

____

____

____

____

____

6–28. Why is it appropriate to refer to the neuromuscular junction as a synapse? What part of the neuromuscular junction is analogous to a postsynaptic membrane in a central nervous system synapse? Which neurotransmitter is associated with neuromuscular junctions?

6–29. Assume you were asked to describe why the membrane of a neuron's soma was so important to signal transmission in the nervous system—what would you say?

6–30. List the layers of the meninges from most superficial (closest to the scalp) to most deep. How are the meninges related to the ventricular system?

6–31. Below is a line drawing of the ventricles. Label the important structures of the ventricles as described in the text and identify an adjacent nucleus or tract for each labeled ventricle structure.

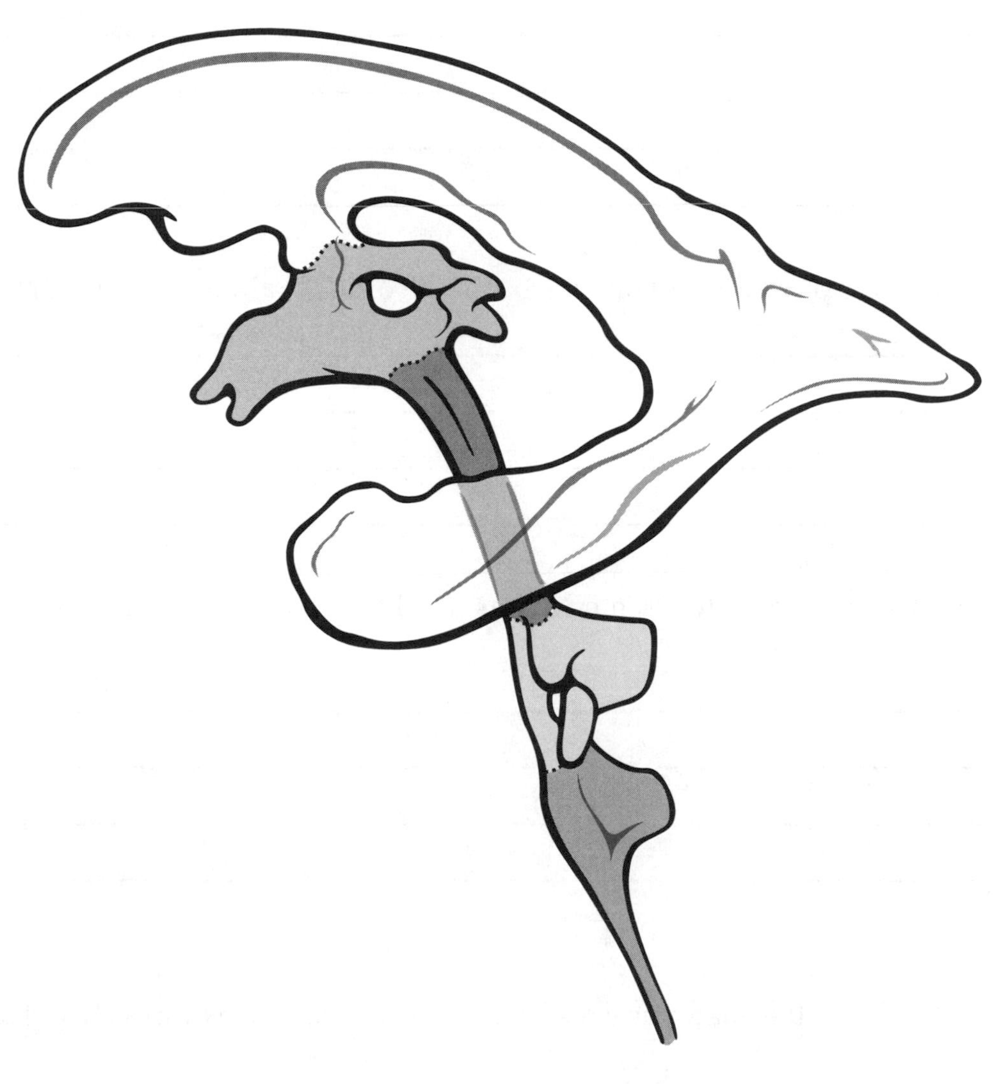

6–32. Answer the following questions about the blood supply to the brain.

(a) What is the distinction between the "anterior" and "posterior" blood supply to the brain?

____

____

____

____

(b) What is the circle of Willis and on which surface of the brain is the structure visible?

____

____

____

____

(c) Write a brief statement (3 to 5 sentences) as to why the MCA is so important to speech and language function.

____

____

____

____

6–33. In DIVA, what is the anatomical distinction between apraxia of speech and dysarthria?

____

____

____

____

____

7

Acoustics Questions

7–1. Pages 380–382 of the textbook present information on storage of energy by air molecules when they are displaced from the rest position and are in motion. The stored energy is expressed in the form of forces exerted by the air molecules as they are displaced from and move around their rest positions. Based on this information, use the top graph below to show how recoil force (y-axis) varies with distance of an object from its rest position (x-axis, 0 position), and the bottom graph to show how inertial force (y-axis) varies with the mass of an object (x-axis). In both graphs, force increases upward on the y-axis, but actual numerical values are not important (hence the labeling of the y-axes in "arbitrary units"). The general "shape" of the functions relating forces to the x-axis variables is of primary interest. In both graphs, use circles to plot a hypothetical force value at each x-axis value, and then connect the circles across all the plotted points to show the shape of the function.

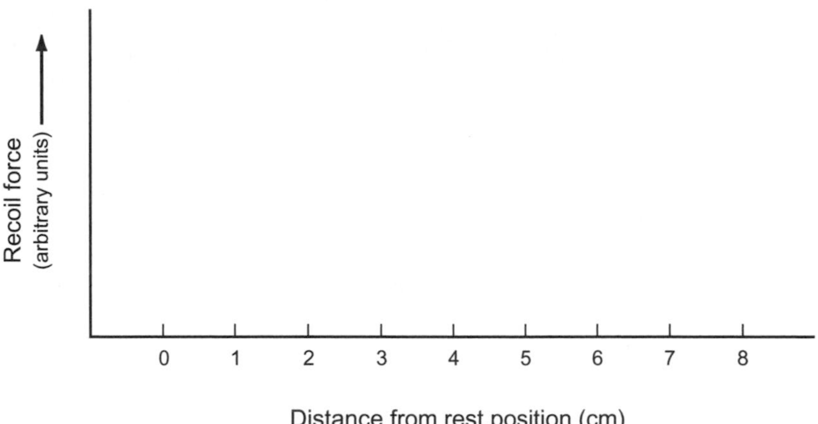

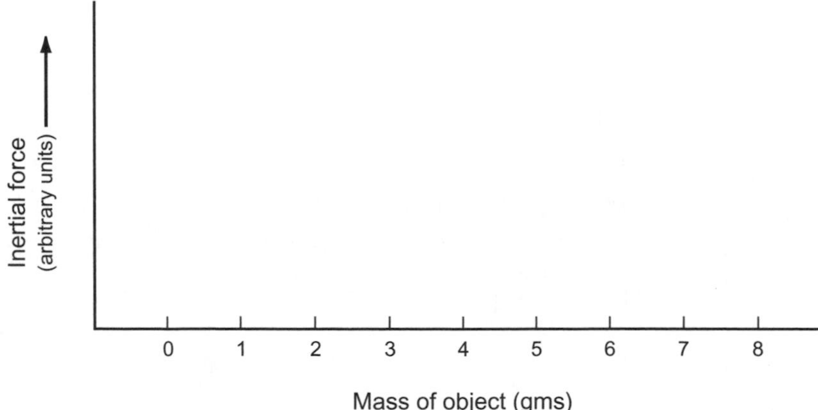

7–2. Periods of vibration can be expressed in seconds (s) and milliseconds (ms), but the latter units are preferred in descriptions of speech events (because so many speech events occur over time intervals of less than 1 s). A series of time values, give in s or ms, are listed in the left column. In the right column write the corresponding time using the other units (e.g., if given the value in s, write it in ms, and vice versa).

Original Time Value	**Stated in Alternative Time Units**
10 ms	__________
4 s	__________
0.1 s	__________
0.0001 s	__________
325 ms	__________
1.8 ms	__________
15 s	__________
1325 ms	__________

7–3. From the information provided in the waveform shown below, determine the period (T) of vibration and then compute the frequency of the vibration.

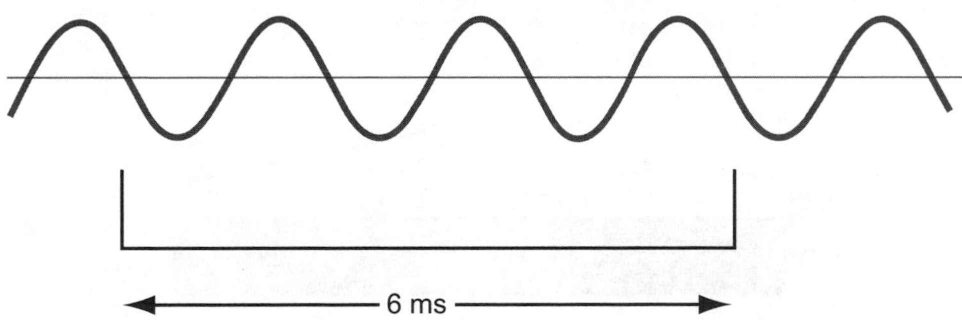

(a) Period (T) = ____________

(b) Frequency of vibration = ____________

7–4. In Figure 7–5 of the textbook, the wavelengths of the 100 Hz and 1000 Hz sounds are said to extend, " . . . from the leading edge of the first high pressure region to the leading edge of the next high pressure region" (p. 387). Immediately below, the pressure wave of the 100 Hz sound is reproduced from the textbook and two of the four arrows marked "P_{atm}" show what is meant by "leading edge of a high pressure region." More specifically, the leading edge is the location in space of P_{atm} *preceding* the location of highest positive pressure as the sound wave extends across space. In the figure below, the two P_{atm} arrows that are the leading edges are the first and third ones. The inset of Figure 7–5 in text, showing a plot of pressure as a function of distance, shows that the leading edge as defined above is at points #1 and #3 along this plot; #3 precedes the next highest, positive pressure location that is not shown in the inset, as only a single wavelength is plotted.

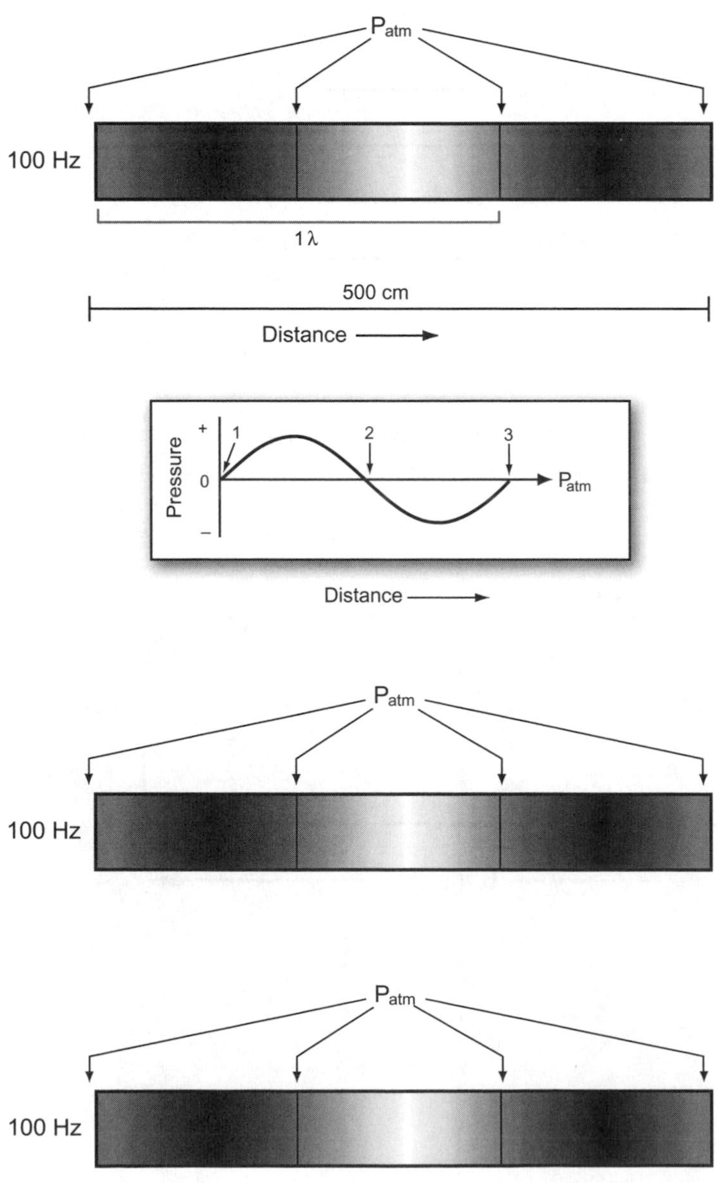

It should be understood that when identifying a wavelength from an image of pressure variation across distance, as in the top part of the image above, the selection of a starting point along the pressure variation, to identify a single wavelength, is arbitrary. We used the leading edge of the first high pressure region as a convenient starting point, but other starting points could have been chosen to illustrate the identification of a single wavelength. Using the two reproductions (above) of the 100 Hz pressure variation from Figure 7–5 in the textbook, show a single wavelength with a starting point of (1) the location of maximum pressure and (2) the location of P_{atm} following the first maximum pressure.

7-5. Compute the wavelengths for each of the frequencies listed on the *x*-axis of the graph below and plot them, connecting the plotted points with a continuous curve. Scale and label the *y*-axis appropriately.

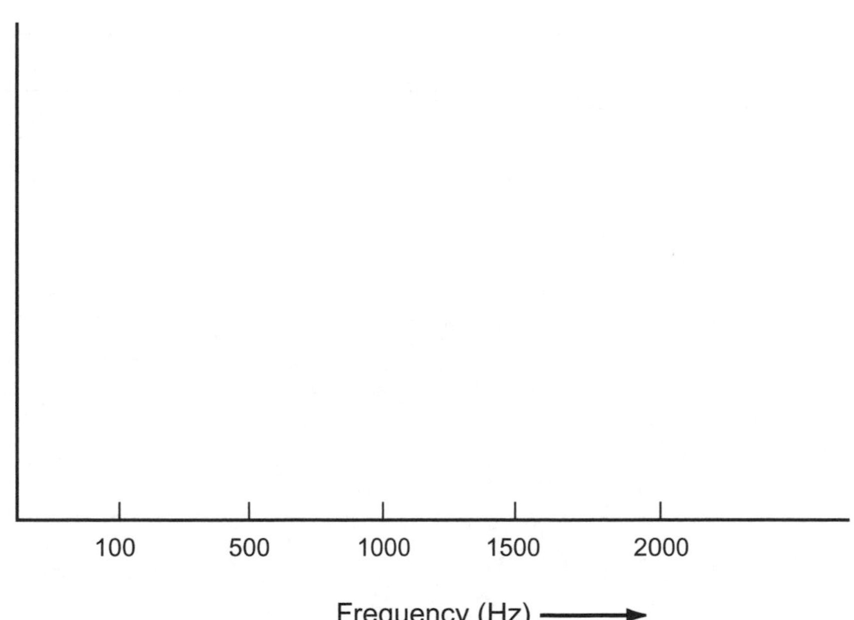

7–6. Given that sinusoidal waveforms are derived from motion around a circle, how would you adjust the motion to:

(a) decrease the period (T) of the sinusoidal waveform.

____

____

____

(b) decrease the frequency (F) of the sinusoidal waveform.

____

____

(c) increase the amplitude of the sinusoidal waveform.

____

____

7-7. Using Formula (4) in the textbook (p. 391) and the table of sines provided below, plot the amplitudes as a function of time (given below as time "steps" ranging from "0" to "9," see left-most column) for the following data, where A = 10. Label your plot completely.

Plot these data

Time	Angle
0	0
1	40
2	80
3	120
4	160
5	200
6	240
7	280
8	320
9	360

Use these sine values

Angle (degrees)	Sine	Angle	Sine
0	0.0000	190	−0.1736
10	0.1736	200	−0.3420
20	0.3420	210	−0.5000
30	0.5000	220	−0.6428
40	0.6428	230	−0.7660
50	0.7660	240	−0.8660
60	0.8660	250	−0.9397
70	0.9397	260	−0.9848
80	0.9848	270	−1.0000
90	1.0000	280	−0.9848
100	0.9848	290	−0.9397
110	0.9397	300	−0.8660
120	0.8660	310	−0.7660
130	0.7660	320	−0.6428
140	0.6428	330	−0.5000
150	0.5000	340	−0.3420
160	0.3420	350	−0.1736
170	0.1736	360	−0.0000
180	0.0000		

7-8. The graph below shows a spectrum of a complex, periodic acoustic event.

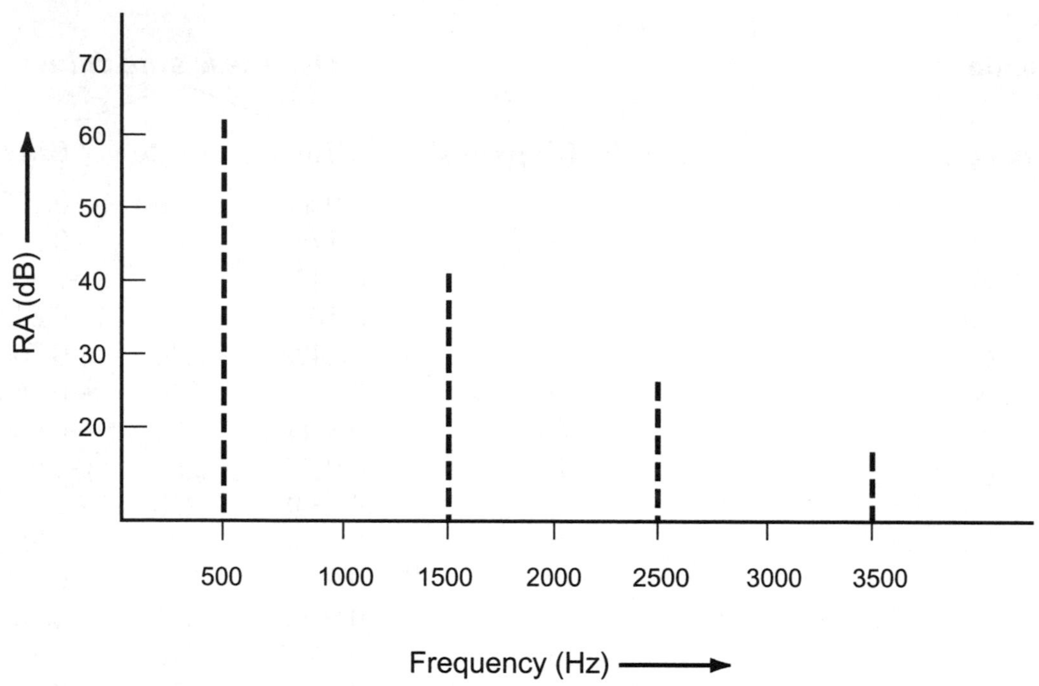

(a) Based on this spectrum, show the individual components of this event in the form of fully labeled waveforms (the waveforms must show the period of the individual components).

(b) What is the period of the complex periodic event? ___________

7-9. Look at the spectra shown below.

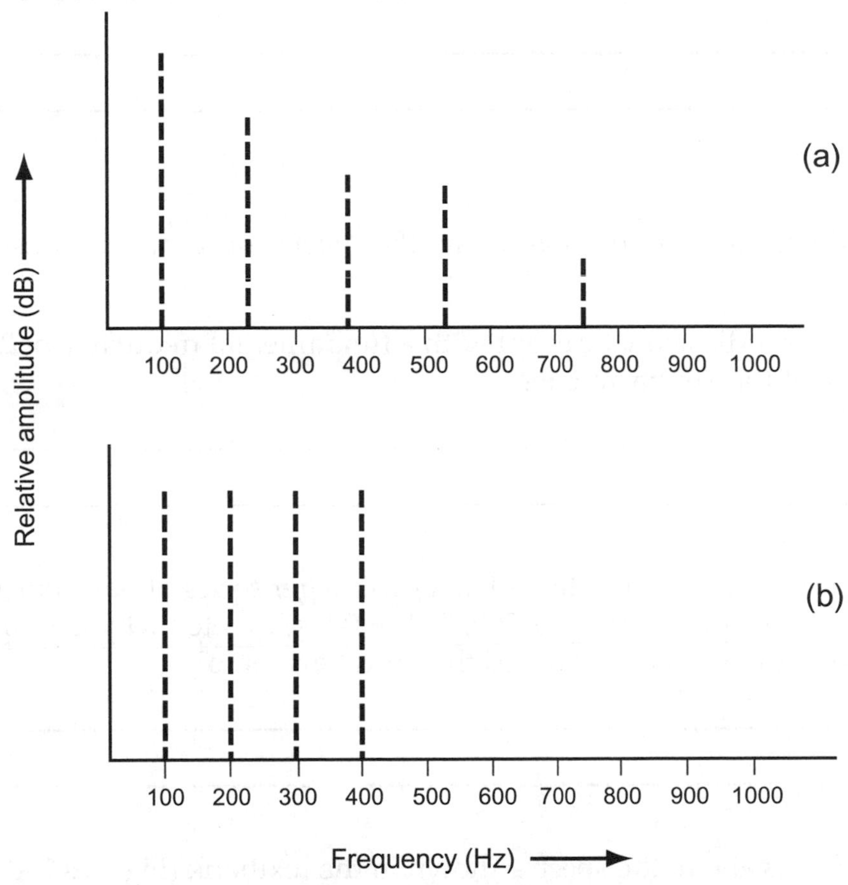

(a) Which one of these spectra shows a complex periodic acoustic event? ____________

(b) Which shows a complex aperiodic acoustic event? ____________

(c) Explain in a simple statement of one or two sentences how you know the correct answers for the two questions above.

____

____

____

7–10. In no more than two sentences, explain the difference between a time-domain and frequency-domain display of an acoustic event.

____

____

____

7–11. Answer the following questions about the spectra of complex acoustic events:

(a) In a complex periodic acoustic event with a fundamental frequency of 250 Hz, what is the frequency of the 7th harmonic?

____

____

(b) In a harmonic spectrum consisting of an odd-integer series of harmonics (e.g., frequency components at 100, 300, 500, 700, 900 Hz, . . . etc.) why isn't the third frequency component (500 Hz) called the third harmonic?

____

____

(c) In the waveforms above the spectra shown in the textbook (Figures 7–8 and 7–9), the amplitude-by-time displays are the result of many different individual frequency components summing their amplitude-by-time characteristics to produce a complex acoustic event. Which aspect of the summation of many different waveforms is *not* shown in these spectra?

____

____

7–12. Based on textbook material (pp. 398–400), answer the following general questions about mechanical resonance:

(a) What are the two properties that can change the resonant frequency of a vibrating object?

____

(b) How would you change the values of those properties to *decrease* the resonant frequency of an object?

___

___

(c) Explain in a sentence or two how simultaneous changes in the values of the two properties from (a) can result in an *unchanged* resonant frequency?

___

___

7-13. How are mechanical resonators and Helmholtz resonators analogous?

___

___

___

___

7-14. The two equations shown below are for the resonant frequency of a spring-mass model (Equation 1) and the resonant frequency of a Helmholtz resonator (Equation 2). The two equations both show, within the square root sign, variables whose values can change the resonant frequency of a resonator.

$Fr = 1/2\pi * \sqrt{K/M}$ (Equation 1)

$Fr = c/2\pi * \sqrt{S/Vl}$ (Equation 2)

(a) Which variable(s) in Equation 2 relate(s) to "K" in Equation 1? Write a sentence that states how the acoustic variable(s) is (are) analogous to the mechanical variables symbolized by "K."

___

___

(b) Which two variables in Equation 2 relate(s) to the "M" in Equation 1? Write a sentence that states how the acoustic variable(s) is(are) analogous to the mechanical variable symbolized by "M."

___

___

7-15. Why does a tube open at both ends or open at only one end (i.e., one end closed, one end open) have *multiple* resonant frequencies?

7-16. Compute the first three resonant frequencies for tubes open at both ends and having lengths of: (a) 8 cm, (b) 12 cm, and (c) 16 cm. Use your computed values for the three tube lengths to plot them on the frequency-by-tube-length chart shown below. At each tube length, use unfilled circles for the lowest resonance (R1), unfilled squares for the second resonance (R2), and unfilled triangles for the third resonance (R3) (as shown to the right of the graph). When all the data are plotted, write a sentence summarizing the results of your calculations. Scale the *y*-axis appropriately.

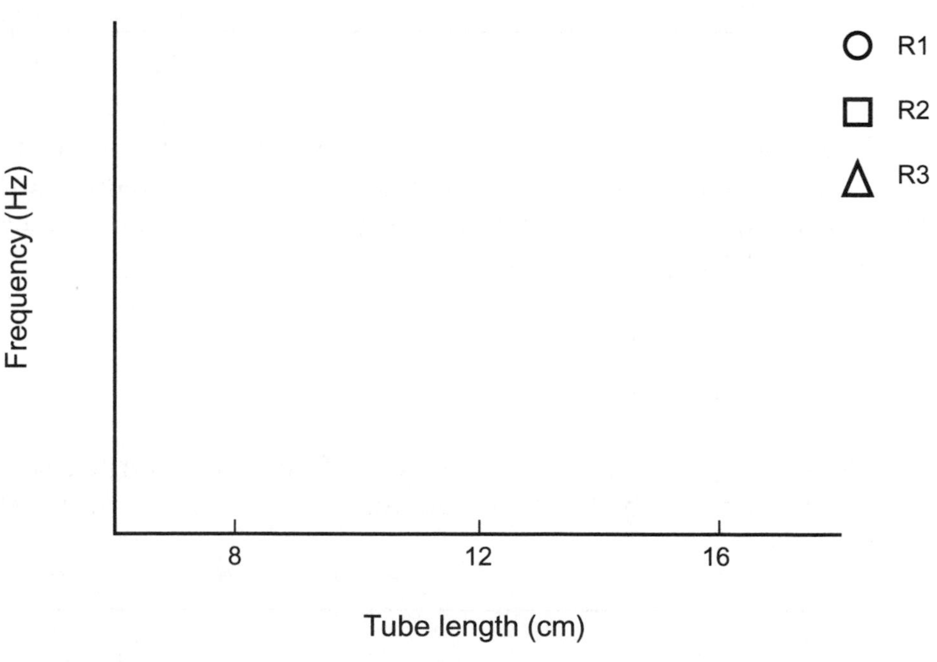

7-17. Using the graph from Question 7–16, compute and plot the first three resonant frequencies (R1, R2, R3) for tubes of the same length but with one end closed. Plot the data with *filled* symbols, using circles for R1, boxes for R2, triangles for R3. Write a summary statement that compares the data for the two tube types (both ends open vs. one end closed).

7-18. Explain, in a single sentence, why the resonant frequencies of a tube open at both ends are determined by a formula called the *half-wavelength rule*. Provide a similar explanation for the *quarter-wavelength rule*, which applies to tubes open at one end and closed at the other.

7–19. The graph below shows two resonance curves, one represented by a dashed line and the other by a solid line.

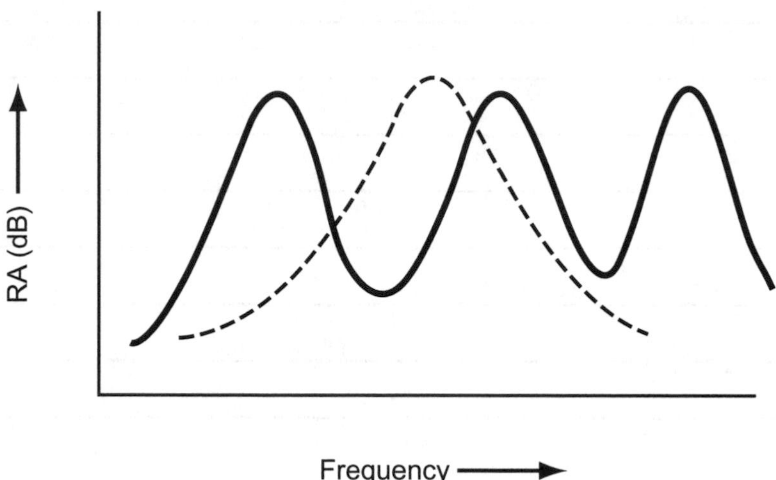

(a) If you were shown this graph and asked which curve is from a Helmholtz resonator and which is from a tube resonator, what would be your answer (based solely on the information provided by this graph)?

____

____

____

____

(b) Briefly explain your answer.

____

____

7-20. When a tube resonates, why are there multiple locations of maximum pressure within the tube?

____

____

____

7-21. Use the information provided in this graph to estimate the resonant frequency and bandwidth of the resonator. Show your work on the graph.

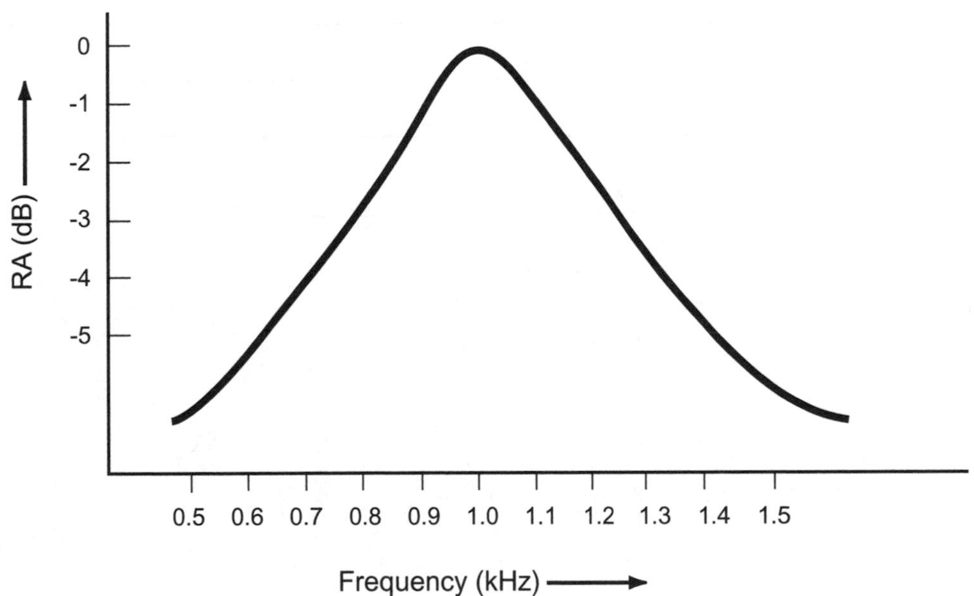

Resonant frequency ______________________________

Bandwidth ______________________________

7-22. How is vibratory energy lost in the vocal tract?

7-23. Why is the concept of a resonator "shaping" an input equivalent to the concept of a resonator as a filter?

7-24. Below are two resonance curves from the same resonator, but with different damping conditions.

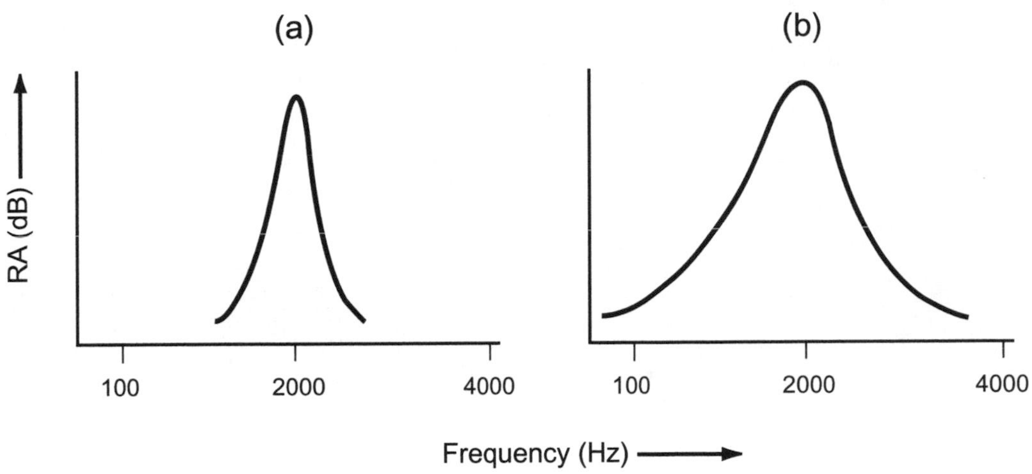

(a) Which resonance curve shows a more lightly damped resonator?

____

(b) Draw two time-domain graphs—fully labeled—that correspond (roughly) to the damping difference between (a) and (b) above.

Acoustic Theory of Vowel Production Questions

8-1. Examine the two glottal area (Ag) functions shown below in (a) and (b).

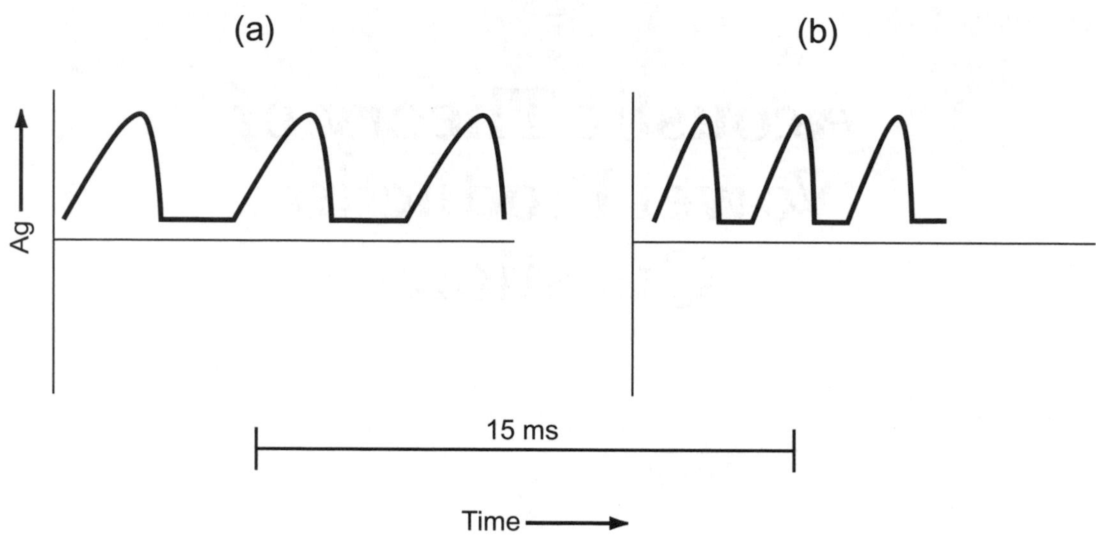

(a) Which Ag function has the longer closed phase? ___________

(b) Which Ag function shows a higher fundamental frequency (F0)? ___________

(c) Roughly estimate the F0s of the two glottal area functions, based on the information given in the two functions.

____

____

____

8-2. Explain in a sentence or two how a speech scientist can "recover" the glottal waveform from a vocalic acoustic signal recorded in front of the lips.

____

____

____

8–3. Shown below is a reproduction of Figure 8–4 (p. 420) from the textbook. On the figure, show how you would make an adjustment to the Vg function that would reduce the relative amplitude of higher frequency harmonics in the glottal spectrum, but leave the F0 unchanged.

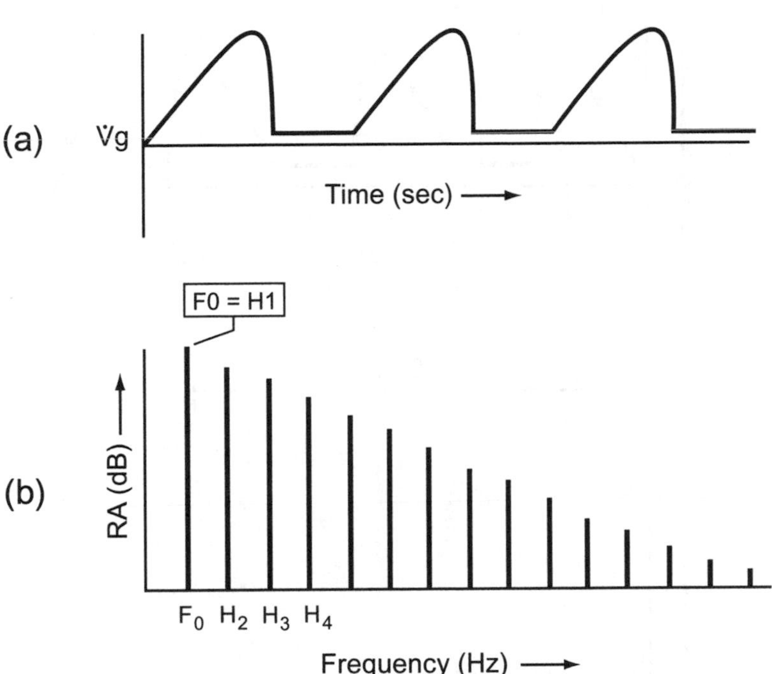

8–4. Using the glottal waveform shown on top as a reference, draw a new glottal waveform on the axes below the time bar, showing a wave that would be associated with a wider spacing between the harmonic components of the spectrum (as compared to the spacing associated with the reference glottal waveform).

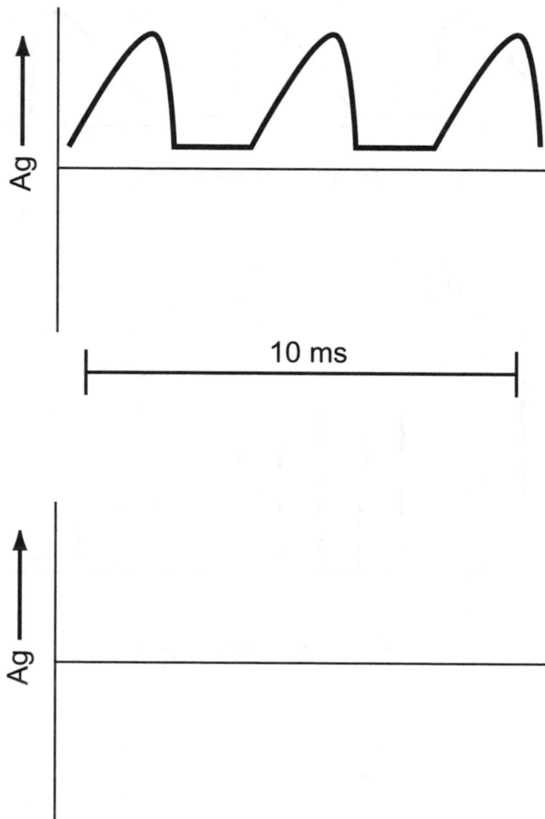

8–5. Answer the following questions about the glottal spectrum.

(a) What is meant by "tilt of the glottal spectrum"?

____

____

____

(b) Describe in one or two sentences what it means to have a glottal spectrum that is *less tilted* than normal.

____

____

____

(c) Which aspect of vocal fold vibration controls the tilt of the glottal spectrum?

____

____

8–6. In a few sentences, write a statement demonstrating that you understand the potential clinical significance of the relationship between the cyclic movements of vocal fold vibration and the glottal spectrum that is produced by that vibration.

____

____

____

____

____

____

8–7. Why is the correct acoustic (resonator) model of the vocal tract a tube closed at one end?

8–8. Answer the following questions about vocal tract area functions.

(a) Write a one-sentence definition of the term "vocal tract area function."

(b) Using your knowledge of vowel phonetics and Figure 8–10 (p. 428 in the textbook) as a model, sketch the general shape of the expected vocal tract area function for the vowel /u/. Label the axes of your graph.

8-9. What is the technical distinction between a theoretical versus output spectrum associated with vowel production?

8-10. Output spectra of vowels typically show peaks that decline in amplitude with increasing frequency; what is the explanation for this decrease?

8-11. Figure 8–11 (p. 429) from the textbook is reproduced below. The output spectrum shows three peaks as indicated by the labels. What kind of *articulatory* adjustment could move the second peak in this spectrum from its current location near the 20th harmonic to a region near the 10th harmonic?

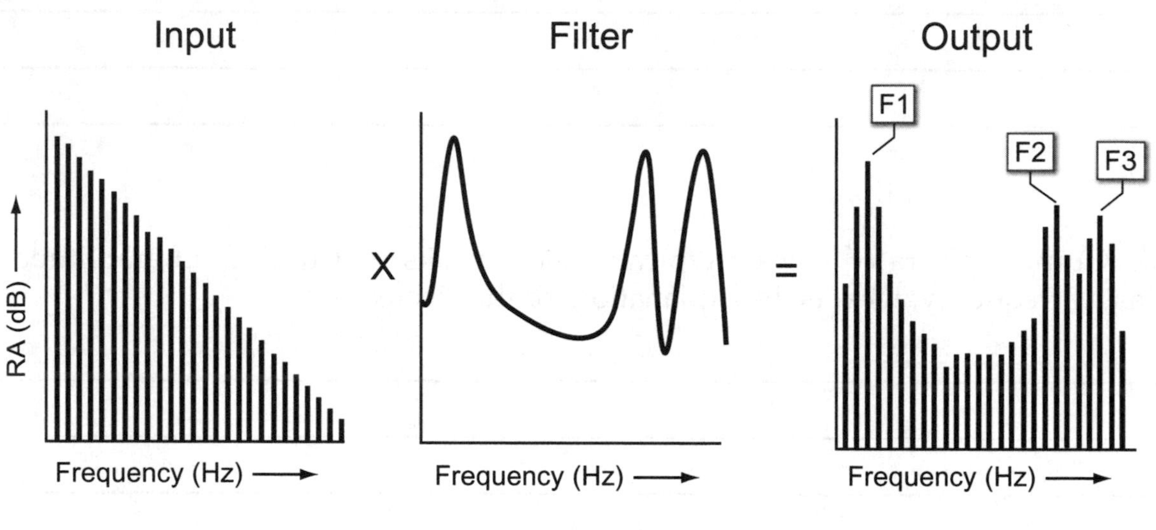

8-12. Give an example of the independence of source and filter in the acoustic theory of vowel acoustics.

8-13. What is a formant and what is the relevance of formants to acoustic descriptions of vowels?

8-14. Examine the vowel spectra of Figure 8–13 in the textbook (p. 433). There are peaks in these spectra, known to you as formants, but there is also energy at other frequencies. Based on information presented on p. 434 in the textbook, how can you explain the tendency of peaks in vowel spectra to "stand out" (i.e., to be "well defined" as peaks) against the other energy in the spectrum? What articulatory conditions might produce a vowel spectrum in which the formants would not "stand out" as clearly, relative to the other energy in the spectrum?

8–15. Shown below in (a) is a velocity distribution for one of the resonances of a tube closed at one end. Which resonance is shown? How do you know the answer? Draw the corresponding pressure distribution for this resonance, in the tube labeled (b).

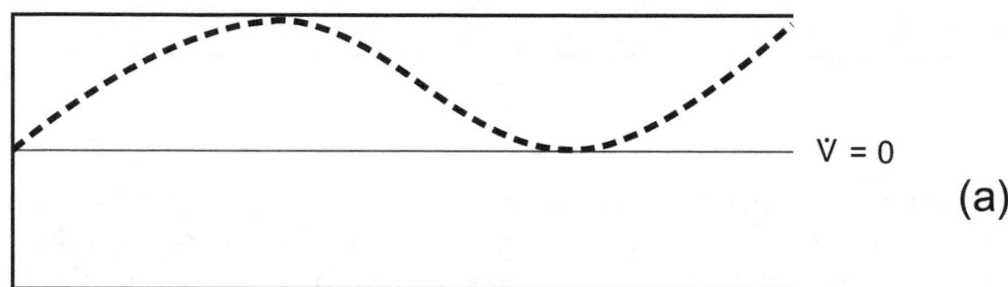

Which resonance is shown? ______________________________

How do you know the answer? ______________________________

8-16. In the tube shown below, the downward-pointing arrow shows the location of a constriction and the height of the shaded box at that location shows the magnitude of the constriction (the top of the shaded box is close to the upper boundary of the tube, indicating a relatively tight constriction).

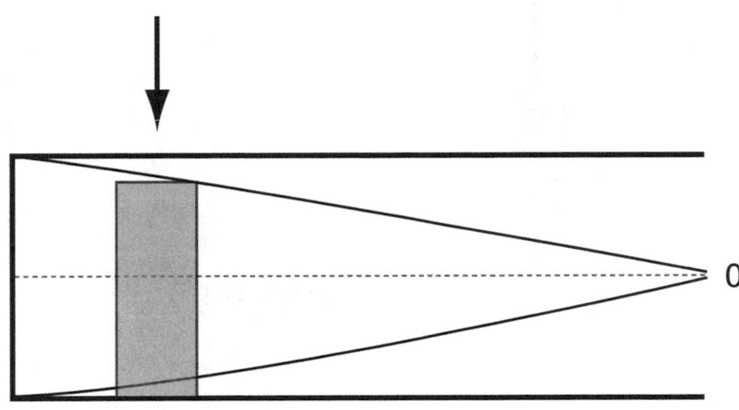

(a) Which distribution of energy is shown and how do you know?

____

____

(b) Using the conditions shown above as a reference, show two separate constriction changes that could lower (i.e., cause a decrease in) the resonant frequency shown in the tube.

8–17. The resonant circuit shown below contains the same components as the one shown in Figure 8–17 (p. 441) of the text.

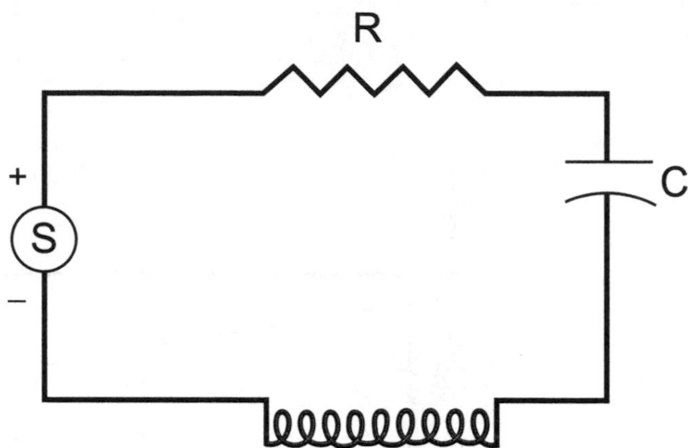

(a) Circle the electrical component(s) whose *increased* magnitude would *decrease* the resonant frequency of the circuit.

(b) Draw a box around the component(s) whose *decreased* magnitude would *increase* the frequency of the circuit.

(c) Put an "X" through the component(s) whose changes in magnitude do not affect the resonant frequency but do affect the tuning of the circuit's resonance curve.

8–18. Which tube resonant mode is affected the most by variations in tongue height?

How can the tongue height rule of Stevens and House (1955) be explained within the framework of perturbation theory?

8-19. In the textbook, this summary statement appears: " . . . increases in tongue advancement result in an increasing F2 and a decreasing F1." Draw tube models to demonstrate why this is the case for a relatively tight constriction.

8-20. When a talker rounds her lips while producing the vowel /i/, what is the explanation, according to perturbation theory, for the decrease in *all* resonant frequencies of the vocal tract?

____

____

____

8–21. What kinds of data are available in support of the acoustic theory of vowel production?

Thought question: Examine the data (from males) below from a study by Lee et al. (1999), and based on these data, state why they provide general support for one important aspect of the acoustic theory of vowel production. Are there any deviations from that support?

		Vowel		
Age of Speaker		/ɑ/	/i/	/u/
5	F1	1166	467	477
	F2	1750	3041	1508
	F3	3412	3653	3136
9	F1	1011	382	471
	F2	1601	2979	1603
	F3	3245	3536	3198
15	F1	731	310	343
	F2	1316	2350	1316
	F3	2507	2964	2433

Data from Lee, S., Potamianos, A., & Narayanan, S. (1999). Acoustics of children's speech: Developmental changes of temporal and spectral parameters. *Journal of the Acoustical Society of America, 105,* 1455-1468. (see data Table on pp. 1461–1462).

9

Theory of Consonant Acoustics Questions

9-1. Why is the theory of vowel acoustics incomplete for the case of consonant acoustics?

9-2. What is an antiresonance and why does it occur?

9-3. Explain the following statement: The spectrum of a nasal murmur consists of a mix of resonances and antiresonances. Include in your answer comments on which cavities contribute to the resonances and antiresonances in this spectral mix.

9-4. Why are nasal murmurs less intense as compared to adjacent vowels?

9–5. Examine the two spectra below, which were computed for speech sounds recorded at the same mouth-to-microphone distance.

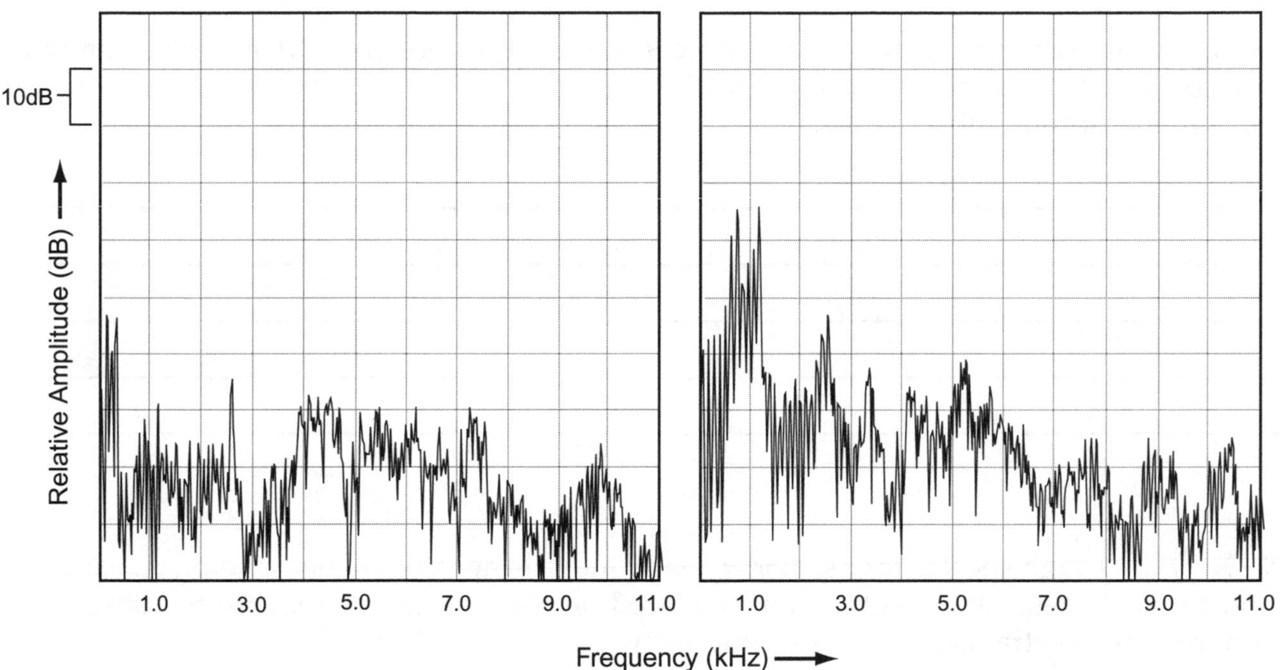

(a) Based on what you see, identify the one (left or right) most likely to be associated with a nasal murmur. ________

(b) Identify the one (left or right) most likely associated with a vowel. ________

(c) How did you make your choice?

____

____

____

____

9-6. The spectrum of a nasalized vowel includes resonances from the ________________ and the ________________ cavities.

9-7. Examine the spectra shown in Figure 9–4 of the textbook (p. 463) and based on what you see, explain why the nasalized vowels /ɑ/, /ɛ/, and /u/ are less intense than the corresponding non-nasalized vowels.

____

____

____

____

____

9-8. Draw rough spectra for /s/ and /ʃ/ and indicate approximately where you expect to find the main resonance with an arrow placed on each spectrum. Explain the differences between the spectra. Label all axes completely.

9-9. Define "frication source" and give two different examples of how such a source is generated within the vocal tract.

9-10. Based on the discussion in the textbook concerning the relative intensity of fricative source spectra across different fricatives, what informal experiment could you perform to show how the intensity of a sustained /f/ can be increased without any change in the *production* of the /f/? (*Hint*: Answer requires imagination!)

9-11. State, in a single sentence, the general difference between the fricative spectra for /s/ and /ʃ/ versus the fricative spectra for /f/ and /θ/.

9-12. For fricatives produced with a constriction between the tongue and palate, what is the primary determinant of the resonant frequency of the aperiodic energy?

9-13. How can the relative "flatness" versus "peakiness" of a spectrum be measured?

Draw a relatively flat versus peaky spectrum and show how the measure(s) would distinguish the spectral difference. Label all axes completely.

9-14. Why are values for P_o (oral air pressure) slightly different for voiceless versus voiced stops? And why is this pressure difference relevant to stop acoustics?

9–15. Shown below are three pairs of VCV (vowel-consonant-vowel) acoustic waveforms (one member of each VCV pair on the left, one on the right).

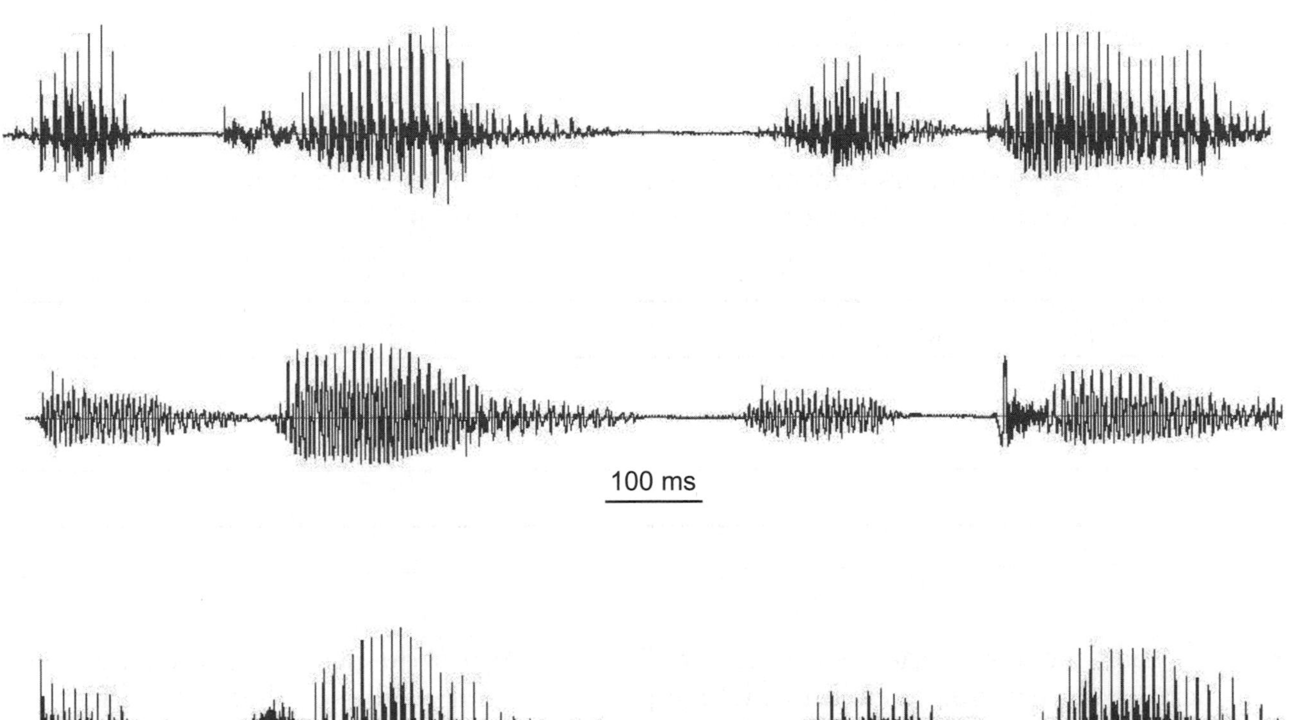

(a) For each pair, indicate the one that shows a voiced stop and the one that shows a voiceless stop.

Top row: Left is __________, right is __________.

Middle row: Left is __________, right is __________.

Bottom row: Left is __________, right is __________.

(b) State at least two separate reasons for each of the choices.

9-16. How does an understanding of speech aeromechanics explain the acoustic events during and following the release of a voiceless stop consonant?

9-17. What aspects of the theory of fricative and stop acoustics are interchangeable? Another way to ask this question is: which principles of the acoustic theory for fricatives also apply to the acoustic theory for stops?

9-18. What is voice-onset time (VOT) and why is it different in voiceless as compared to voiced stops?

10

Speech Acoustic Analysis Questions

10–1. In a few sentences, explain how the German scientist H. von Helmholtz applied the principle of resonance to the study of the resonant frequencies of vowels.

10–2. In the recording of acoustic signals, what does "transduction" mean? What are some potential problems with accurate transduction?

10–3. Shown below are two vowel waveforms (one on the left, one on the right, with a roughly 100-ms pause between them) produced by the same talker, an adult male just shy of 60 years of age.

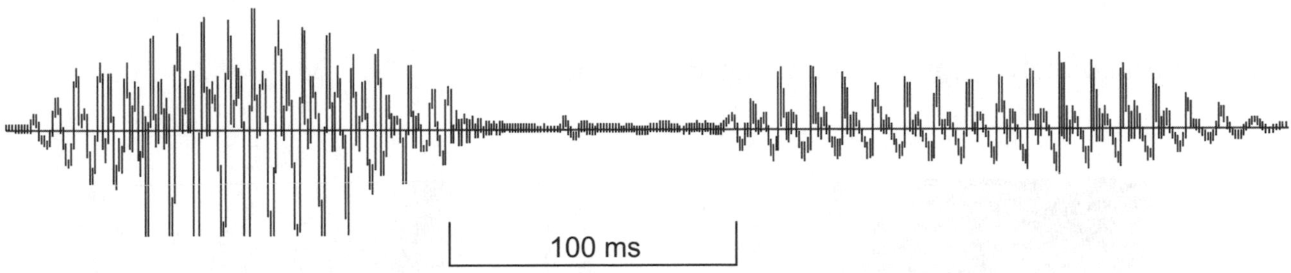

(a) Based on the material on pp. 494–497 in the textbook, what is the quantitative (measurable) information that can be obtained from this display?

____

____

____

(b) What qualitative interpretation of frequency differences between the two waveforms can be made simply by looking at them?

____

____

____

10–4. What is a formant transition?

____

____

10–5. Immediately below is an unlabeled spectrogram.

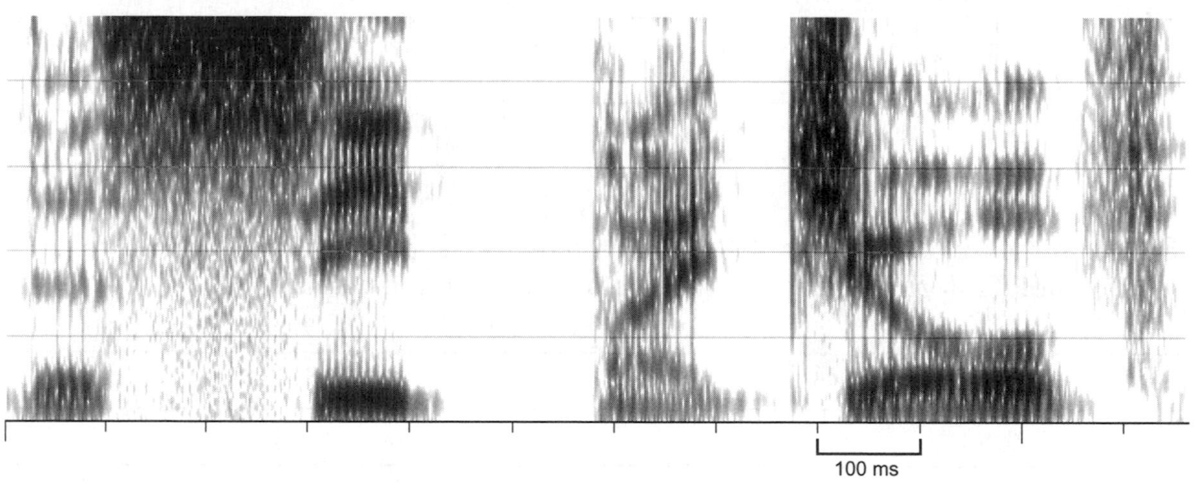

(a) Label the axes.

(b) Identify one (any) region of energy that is clearly greater (more intense) than one other region of energy.

(c) Identify a vowel that has an F2 around 2000Hz.

(d) Identify a vowel with a large formant transition.

(e) Identify a fricative with very intense energy in the higher frequencies.

10–6. When frequency analysis of a speech acoustic signal is performed, what is meant by the term "analysis band"?

____

____

10–7. What was the major scientific advance and what was the advantage of the sound spectrograph?

____

____

10–8. Using Figure 10–8 (p. 502) in the textbook and the associated textbook discussion as a guide, answer the following questions concerning the appearance of phonetic events on the spectrogram below.

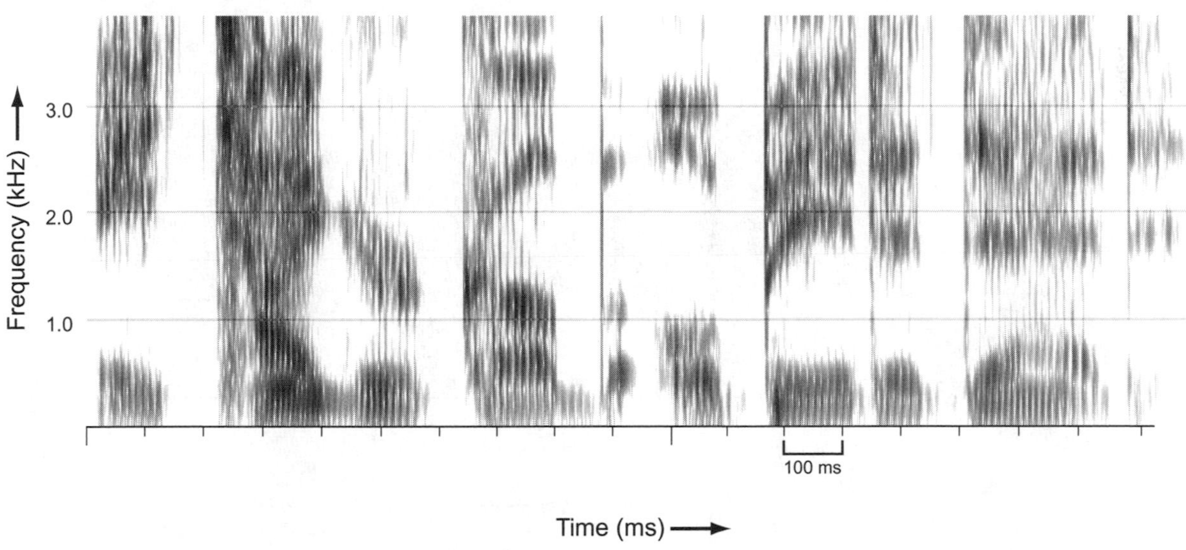

(a) How many stop bursts can you identify on the spectrogram above? Number the identified stop bursts from 1 to *n* (where *n* equals the total bursts identified), starting with the left-most burst. What criteria did you use to identify these events as stop bursts?

____

____

____

(b) For the same spectrogram, which stops (using your numbers) are voiced and which are voiceless? What criteria did you use to make these decisions?

____

____

____

(c) How many fricatives and vowels can be identified in the spectrogram below? What criteria were used to make these identifications?

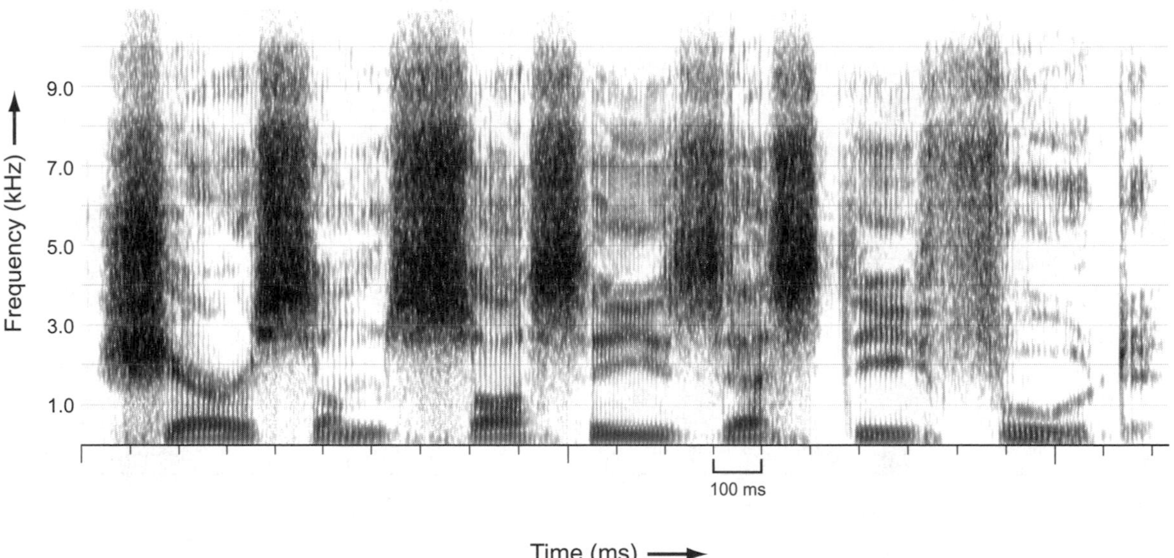

____

____

____

(d) In the spectrogram below two words are shown, each with a well-defined vocalic interval.

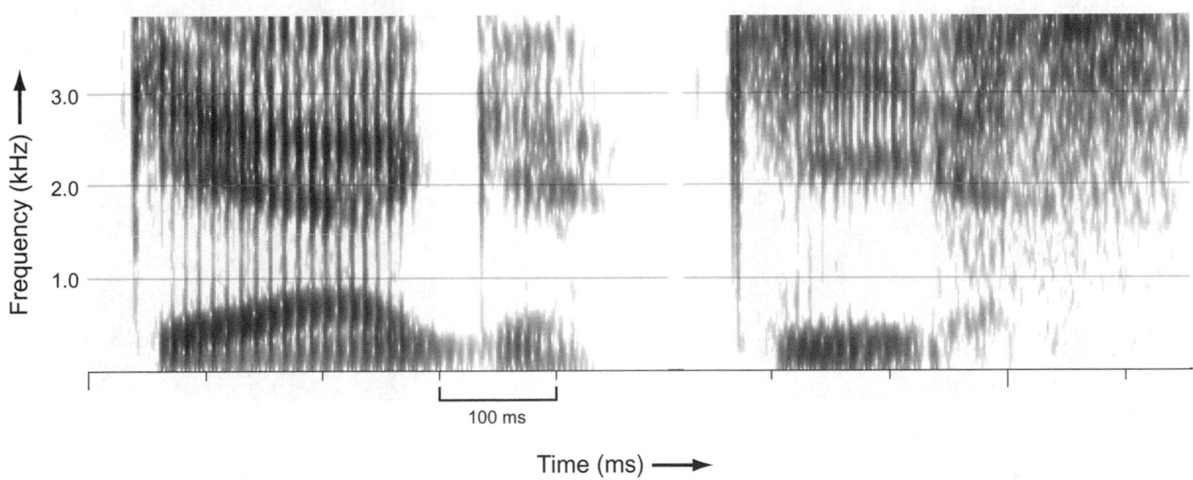

Identify the vocalic interval (left or right word) for which spectral slices from a brief "window" taken at two different points would produce *different* spectral characteristics.

____

____

Identify the vocalic interval for which spectral slices taken at two different times would produce essentially the *same* spectra.

____

____

(e) The spectrogram below shows two productions of the word "gab" ([gæb]).

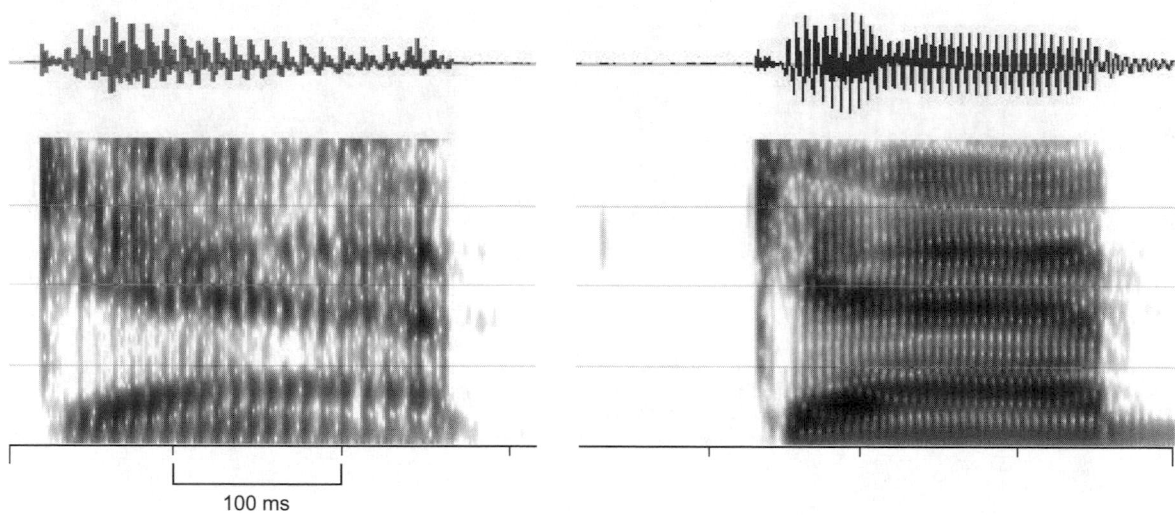

Which production (left or right spectrogram) has the higher F0? ________________

How do you know? ____

____

For either one of the productions, compute the average F0 for the middle 100 ms of the vowel.

____

____

10–9. What are the types of sounds (the phonetic classes of sounds) for which you would expect to see more or less regularly spaced glottal pulses extending from the bottom to top (or nearly to the top) of a spectrogram?

____

____

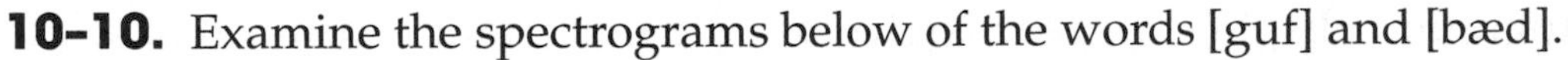

10-10. Examine the spectrograms below of the words [guf] and [bæd].

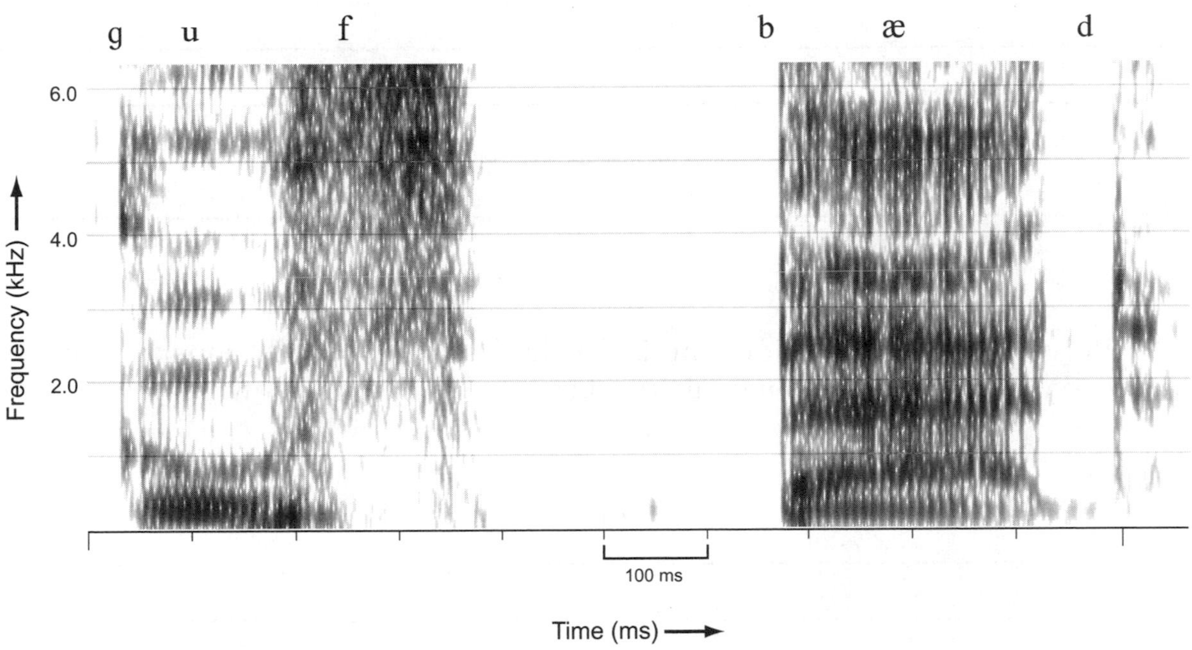

(a) Based on the information available in these displays, estimate the frequencies of the first three formants for the two vowels using conventional measurement concepts for "target" formant frequencies of vowels, as discussed in the textbook (pp. 504–505).

	/u/	/æ/
F1		
F2		
F3		

(b) How do the values you measured for F1and F2 compare to the values shown in Figure 11–2 (p. 523) of the textbook?

____

____

____

____

10–11. In a spectrographic display of speech, what are the important features that allow you to distinguish between a vowel interval (such as /i/) versus a voiceless fricative interval (such as/s/)?

____

____

____

____

10–12. Provide the segmentation criteria for the following sound sequences and place segmentation marks on the phonetically unlabeled spectrograms below.

"a bag" /eɪbæg/

____

____

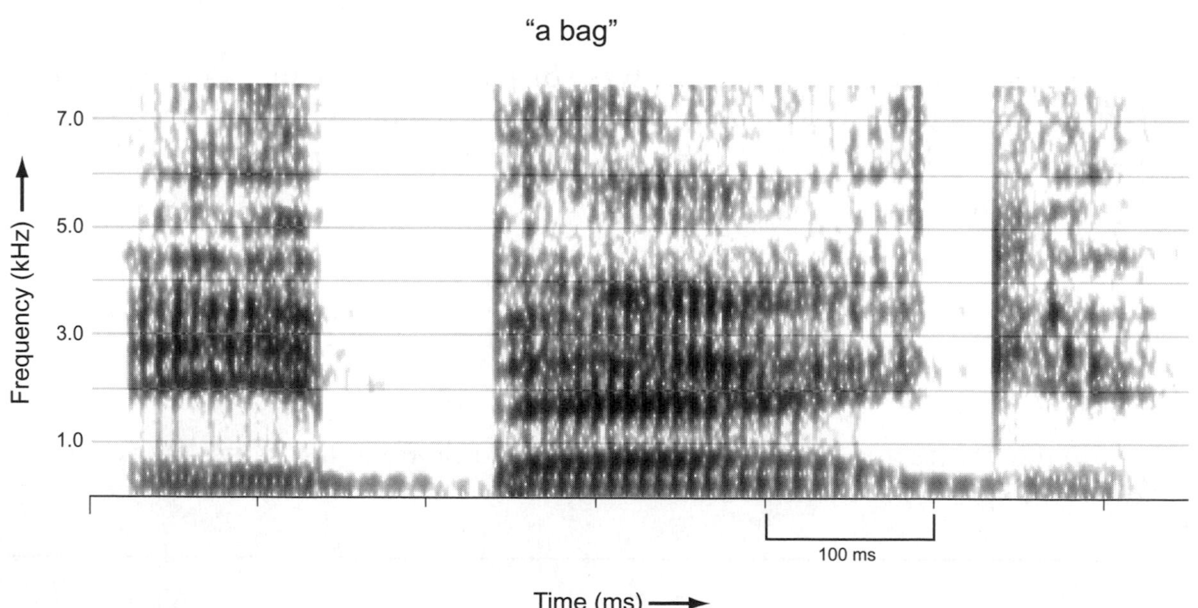

"stop sign" /stɑpsaɪn/

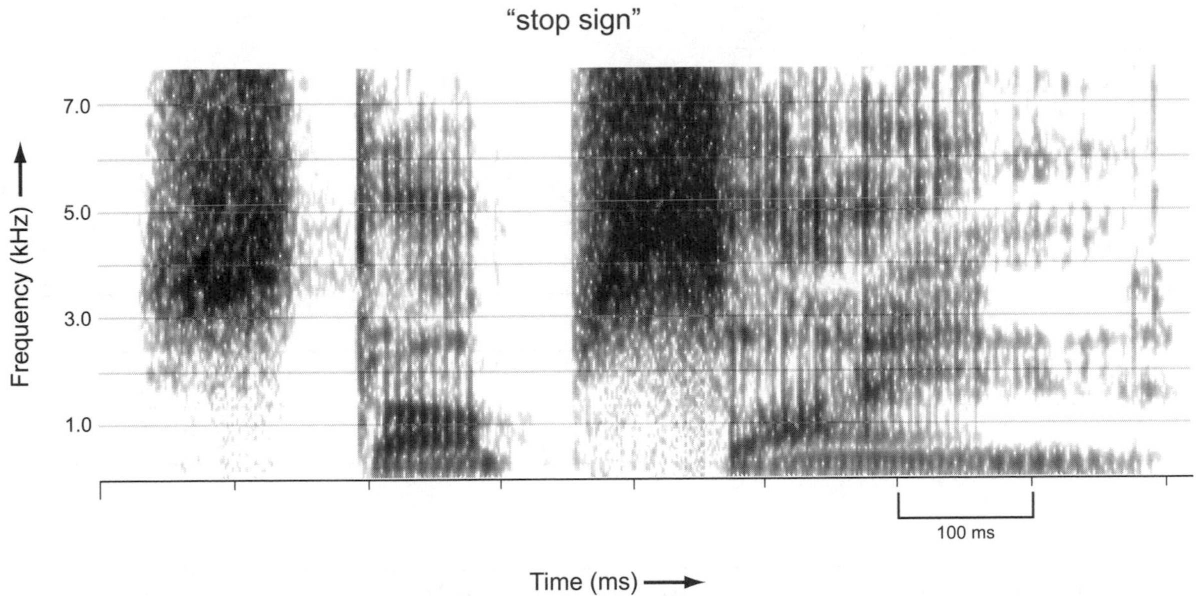

"ellisfink" /ɛlɪsfɪŋk/

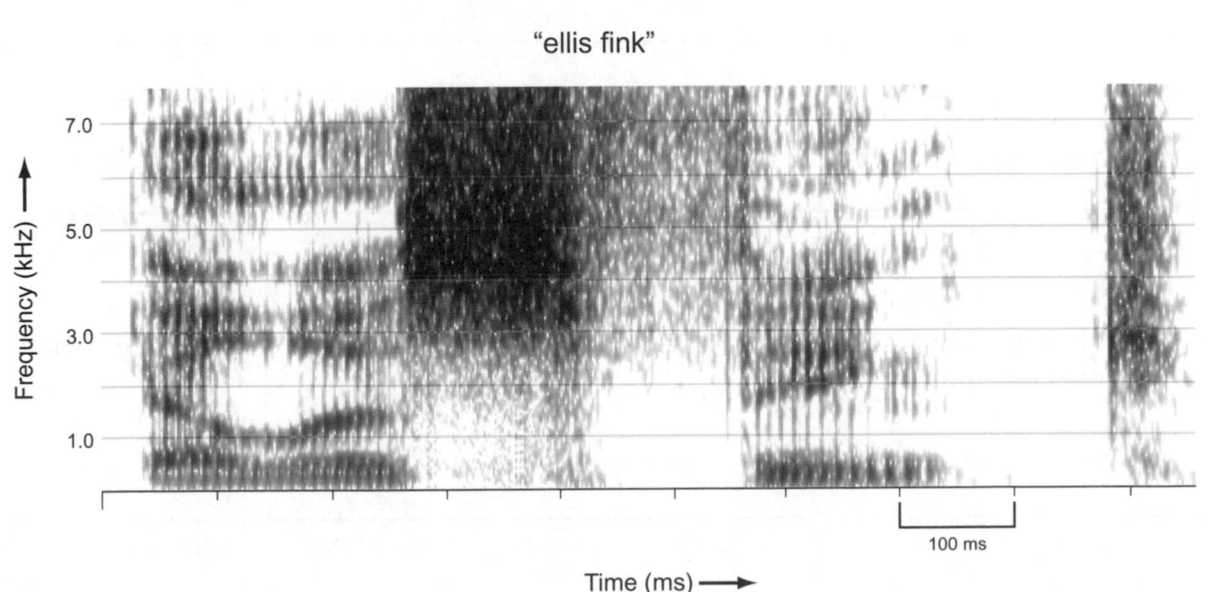

10–13. In Figure 10–10 of the textbook (p. 511), the pitch tracker did a fairly good job of estimating the F0 for the vocalic sequences in "blue spot" and "normal."

(a) What are the ranges (make your best estimate) of the F0 variation in both of these vocalic sequences?

blue spot ________

normal ________

(b) What brief description can you provide for the F0 contours over both the "blue spot" and "normal" sequences?

____

____

____

____

10–14. What is the main difference between analog and digital representation of a speech signal? What adjustments can be made to computer processing of a speech signal (when it is input to the analysis program) to make the digital representation as close as possible to the analog representation?

____

____

____

____

____

____

10–15. What is meant by the term "analysis window" when applied to LPC estimates of vowel formant frequencies?

____

____

10–16. Below is a spectrogram of the word "gag," and above the spectrogram, three horizontal lines are shown as the sizes (durations) of three potential analysis windows for estimating the target formant frequencies of the vowel. Which window is the preferred one and why?

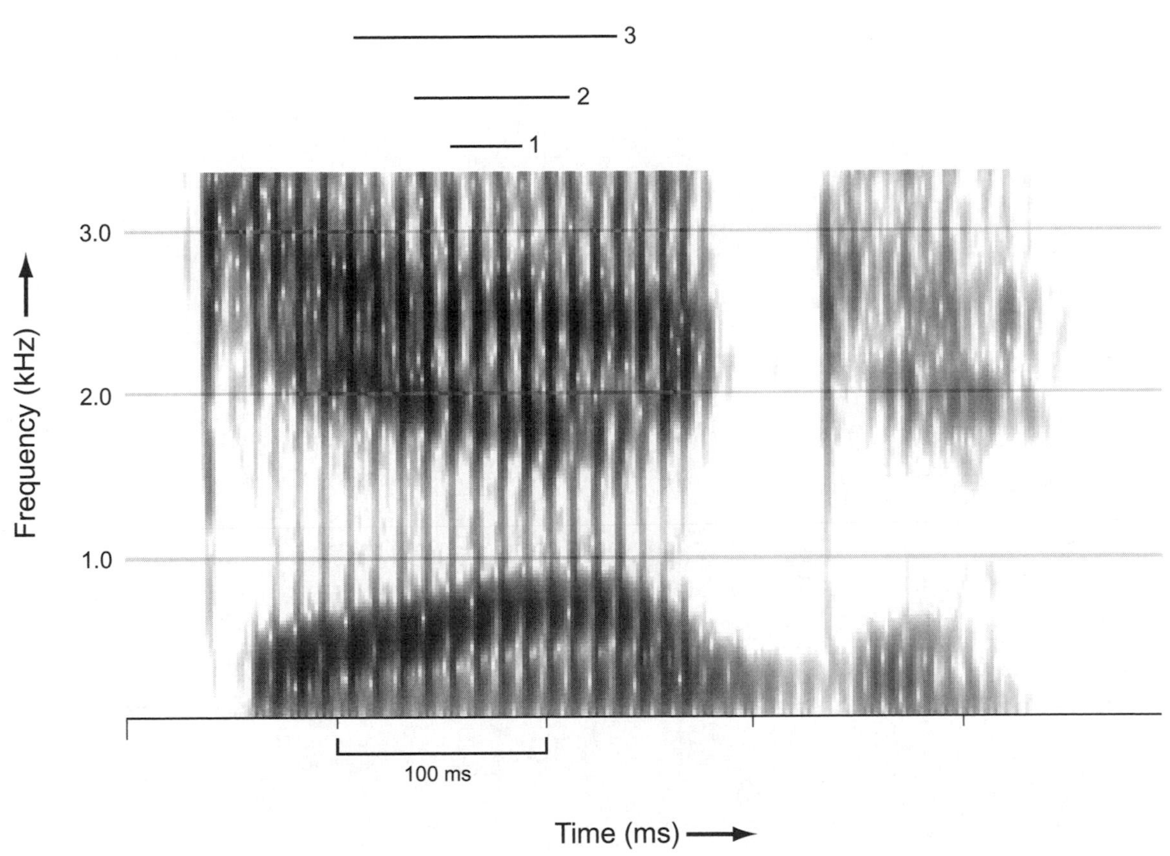

____

____

____

____

11

Acoustic Phonetics Data Questions

11-1. Below are two sets of spectrograms, one (top) of the American English corner vowels /i/, /æ/, /ɑ/, and /u/ produced as relatively brief, isolated vowels, and the other (bottom) of these same vowels produced in a /ˈhɛdVd/ frame where the first syllable (/hɛ/) is stressed and the second syllable has a /dVd/ syllable form containing the same vowels that were spoken in isolation. The utterances were all produced by a 59-year-old healthy male.

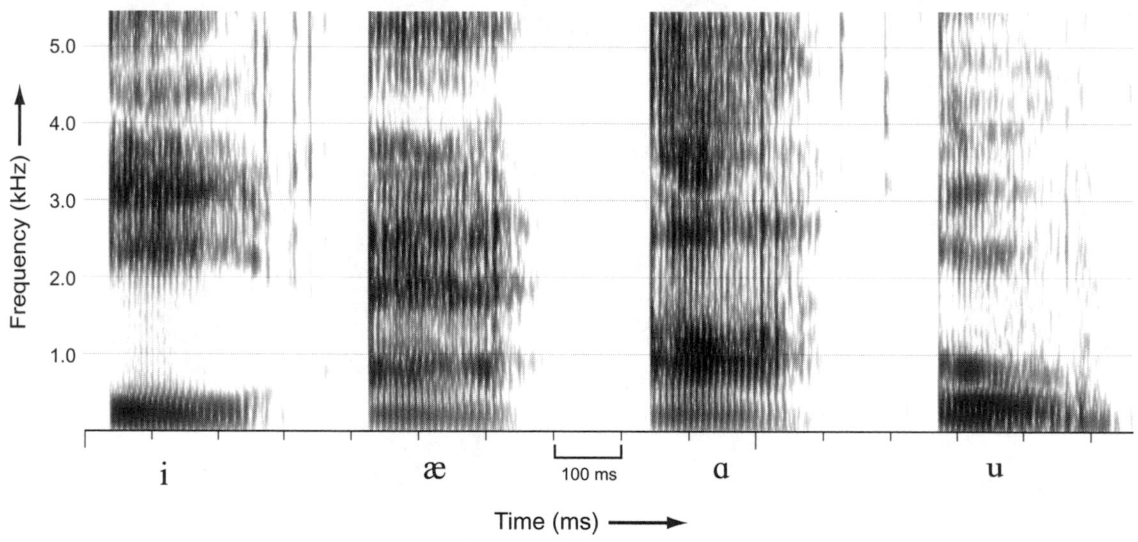

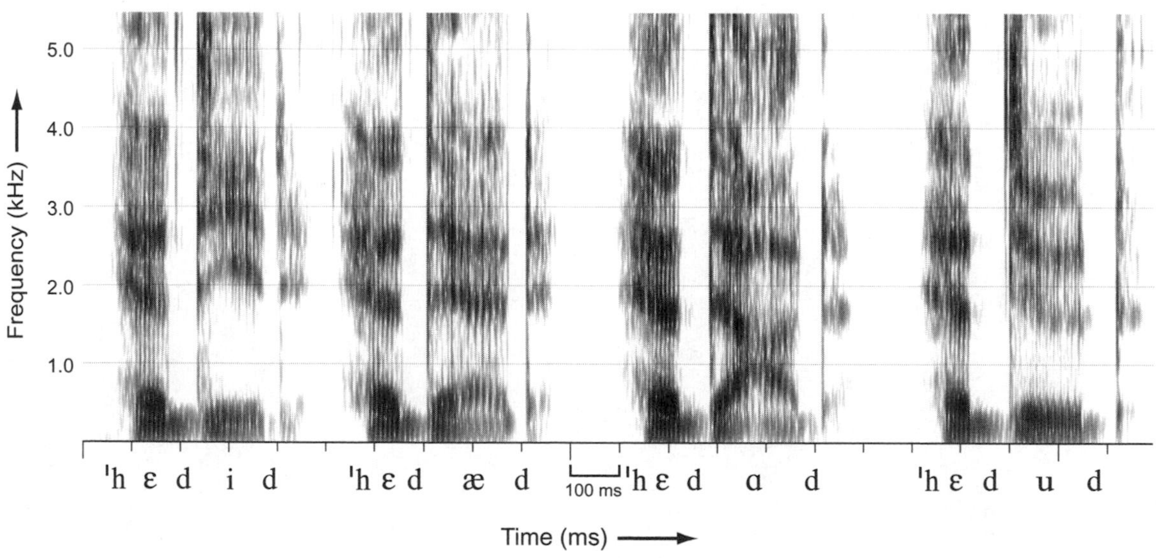

(a) Using the frequency calibration lines and distance-to-frequency conversion (in which a mm-to-Hz conversion is established using a ruler), measure the first three formant frequencies of the isolated vowels and of the vowels in the /dVd/ forms. Plot the values on the F1–F2 and F2–F3 graphs shown below. Use filled squares for the isolated vowel data points, and unfilled squares for the vowels in /dVd/ context.

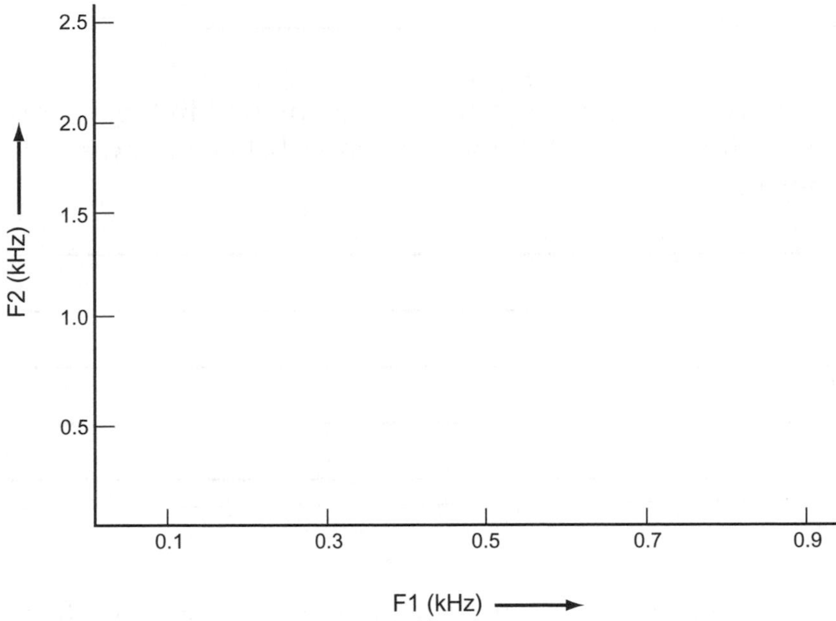

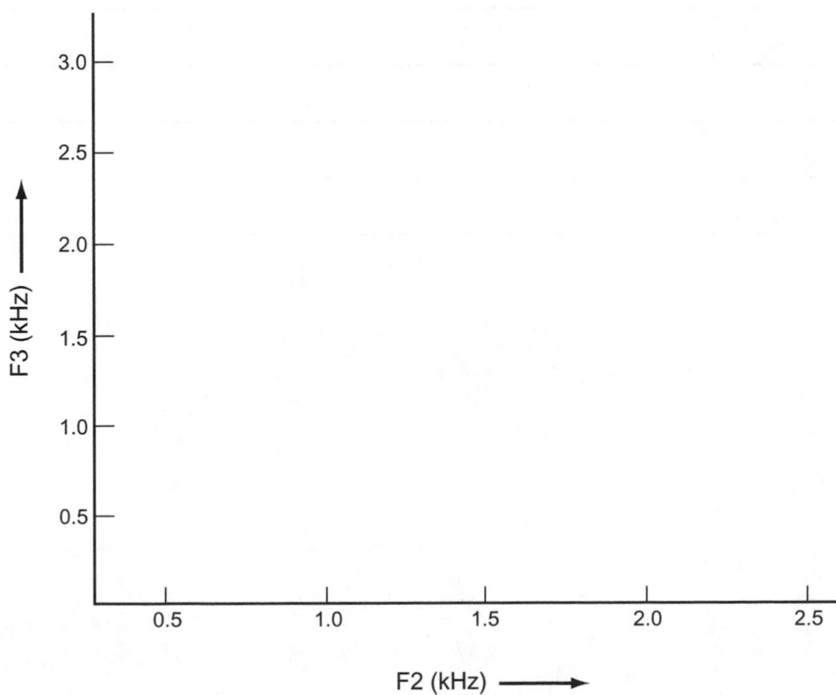

(b) How do the isolated vowel data compare with the corner vowel data from Hillenbrand et al. (1995) shown in Figure 11–2 of the textbook?

(c) In a sentence or two, describe the pattern of data plotted in the figures and provide a likely articulatory interpretation of the differences between vowels in isolated versus /dVd/ utterances.

11-2. What is the potential clinical significance of measures of vowel formant frequencies?

11–3. Answer the following questions concerning the Mandarin versus American English vowel formant frequency data plotted in Figure 11–6 (p. 529) of the textbook:

(a) Both groups of female speakers (the Mandarin and American English speakers) attempted to produce the same vowels, but the Mandarin speakers clearly produced different formant frequencies than the American speakers for both shared and new vowels. Based on the plotted vowels, which group produced an overall larger vowel space?

____

(b) For this set of vowels, in which articulatory dimension do the Mandarin speakers seem *less flexible* as compared to the American speakers? (*Hint*: Review Stevens & House rules, Chapter 8 of textbook).

____

11–4. What is a "null context" vowel?

____

____

11–5. What is articulatory undershoot? In an F1–F2 plot, what are the reference points required to describe the degree of undershoot resulting from a particular speaking condition?

____

____

____

____

____

11–6. Give two examples of intrinsic differences in vowel duration.

____

____

11-7. Give three examples of extrinsic factors that affect vowel duration.

11-8. Design a connected speech sample in which the vowel /æ/, in a CVC form, has a duration that is just about as long as it can be in any imaginable "natural" (real-life) utterance.

11-9. Below is a spectrogram of a VNV sequence, where V = vowel and N = nasal murmur. Below the spectrogram is a spectral "slice" taken from a 25-msec window centered around the temporal middle of the nasal, as shown on the spectrogram. Show the resonances and antiresonances on both the spectrogram and the spectral slice displays, and show the correspondences between the two display types.

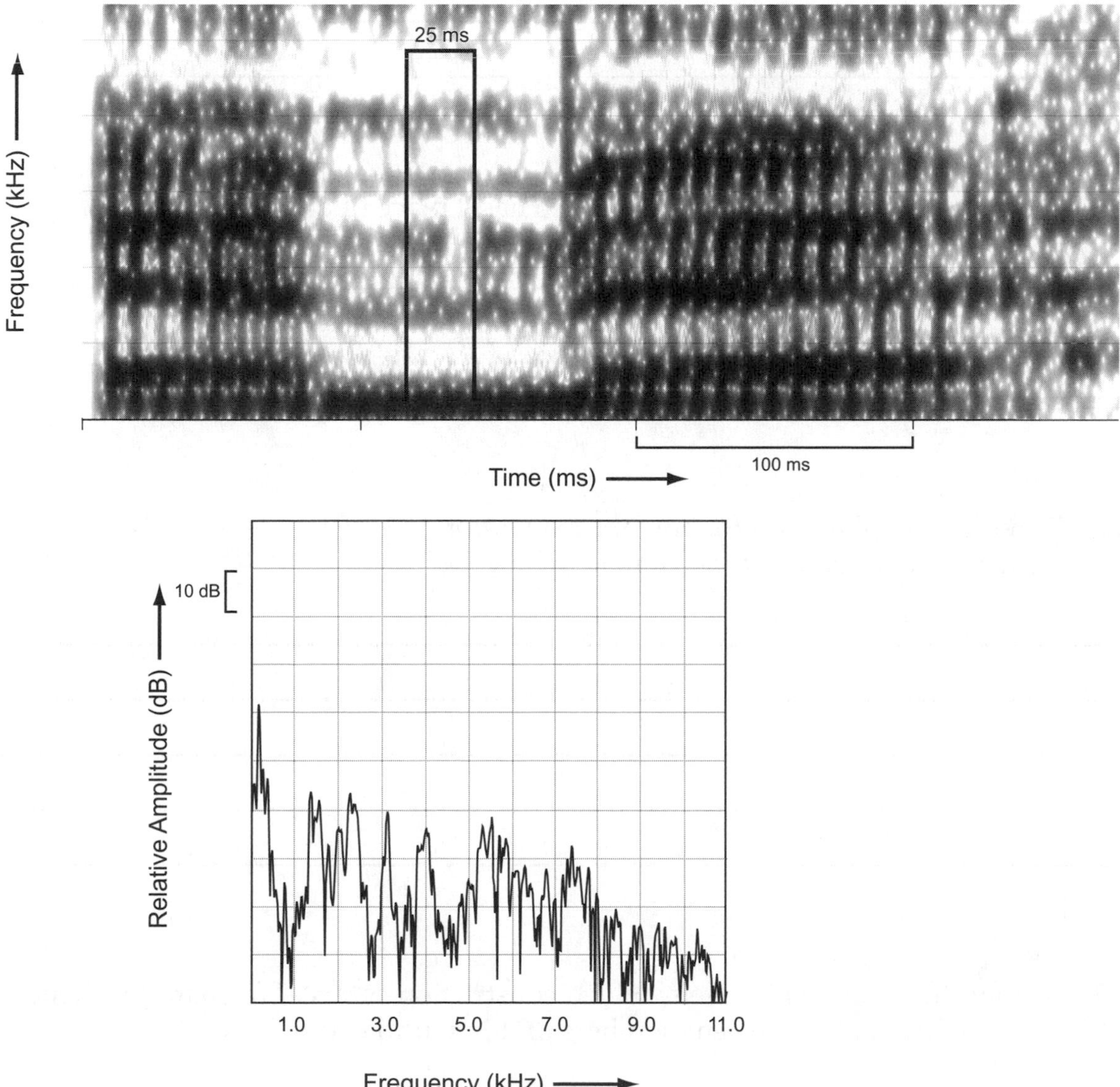

11-10. What are the potential acoustic cues, within a nasal murmur, to nasal place of articulation?

Why are these cues to nasal place of articulation less than perfectly reliable?

11-11. What are potential *non*murmur cues to nasal place of articulation?

11-12. Provide an explanation for how the expression $(A1 - P1)_{oral} - (A1 - P1)_{nasal}$ can serve as an acoustic index of velopharyngeal inadequacy.

11-13. Among the four semivowels, which constriction-interval formant frequencies are most likely to differentiate between members of this sound class?

11-14. Explain in a single sentence how it is known from speech acoustic data that a rapidly changing vocal tract configuration is an essential component of semivowel articulation.

11-15. Examine the spectrogram below and identify the fricatives you believe are: (a) sibilants and (b) nonsibilants. What is the basis of your choices? For each fricative you identify, make a general "by-eye" estimate of the location of the primary frequency peak (or peaks) in the middle 50 ms of the fricative segment.

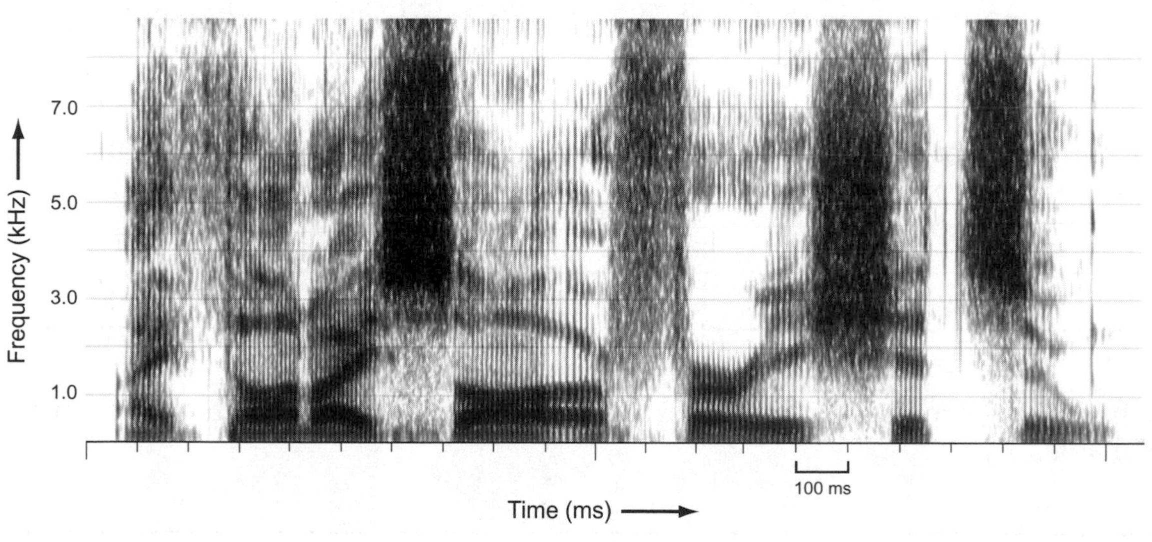

11–16. Using the shape of a normal distribution as a reference (see Figure 11–22, p. 558, of the textbook), circle the expected value of skewness and kurtosis as "positive," "negative," or "close to zero" (i.e., like a normal distribution) for the following hypothetical cases of speech spectra:

Spectrum Description				
Fricative with sharp peak	Kurtosis =	positive	negative	close to zero
Vowel	Skewness =	positive	negative	close to zero
Nasal murmur	Skewness =	positive	negative	close to zero
/p/ burst	Skewness =	positive	negative	close to zero
/f/	Kurtosis =	positive	negative	close to zero
/r/	Skewness =	positive	negative	close to zero

11–17. (a) What articulatory characteristic typically determines the value of the first spectral moment (M1) for a lingual fricative?

(b) Why is the second spectral moment (M2) of nonsibilants typically greater than M2 of sibilants?

11–18. Why are the durations of voiceless fricatives determined in large part by laryngeal components of articulation?

11-19. Based on information presented in the textbook, what are the spectrographic clues that suggest an /h/ segment?

____

____

11-20. The figure below is a reproduction of Figure 11–28 of the textbook (p. 572), minus the labels "Stop onset" and "Stop release." The stop onset is indicated by the left-hand edge of the rectangle below the laryngeal devoicing gesture (LDG), and the stop release by the right-hand edge of the rectangle. Using this figure as a guide, what are several *articulatory changes* that can cause the VOT of a voiceless stop to vary, assuming phonetic context and the speaker are held constant? (That is, the only changes you can make to modify VOT are to the physiologic events depicted in the figure below).

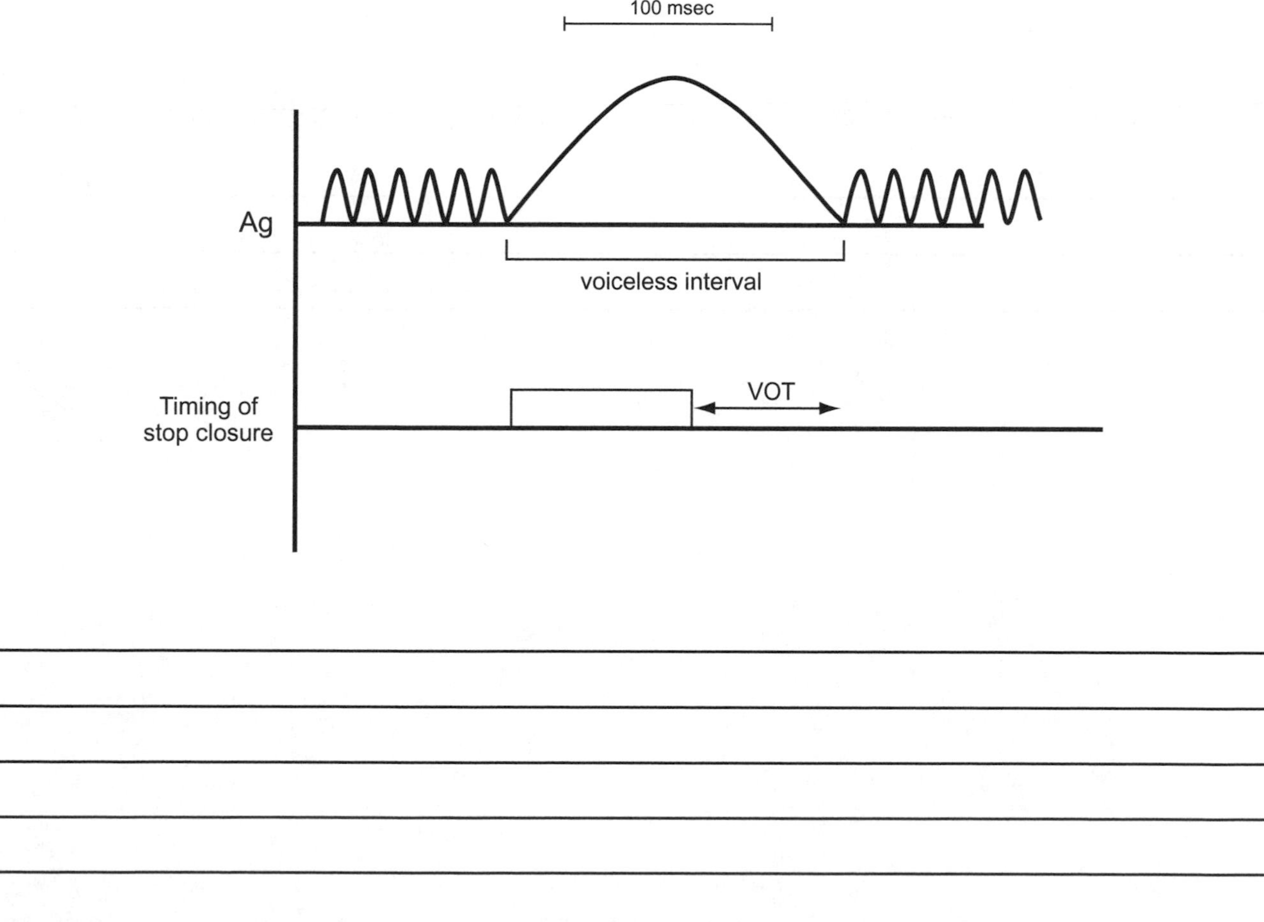

____

____

____

____

____

____

11-21. Answer the following two questions about voice onset time (VOT).

(a) In one or two sentences, explain the difference between positive and negative values of VOT.

____

____

____

(b) What is special about the VOT of voiceless stops when the stop occurs in a same-syllable, s + stop cluster (as in the word "stop" or "skate")?

____

____

____

11-22. What is a "spectral template," as applied to the case of stop-burst acoustics?

____

____

____

11-23. The spectrograms shown below contain two pairs of VCV utterances; one pair on the top row, the other on the bottom row. Based on information provided in the textbook, identify each utterance pair by indicating "stop" or "affricate" above the display of the VCV in which C = singleton stop or C = affricate. Explain the rationale for your choices.

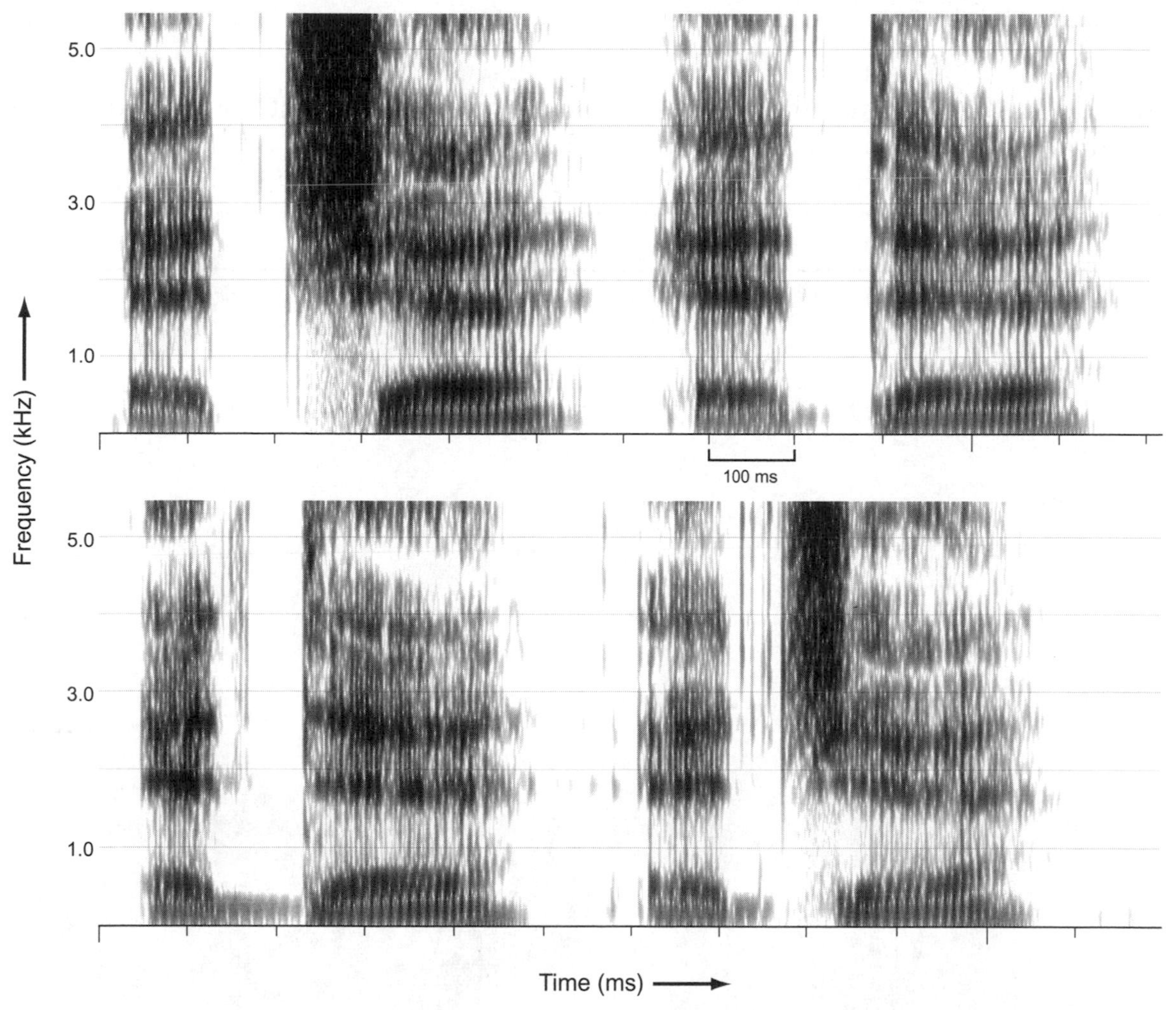

11-24. Answer the two following questions about F0 contours.

(a) How do F0 contours vary across a typical declarative utterance?

(b) How do speakers manipulate F0 to signal their intention to continue speaking versus to indicate that they are finished speaking?

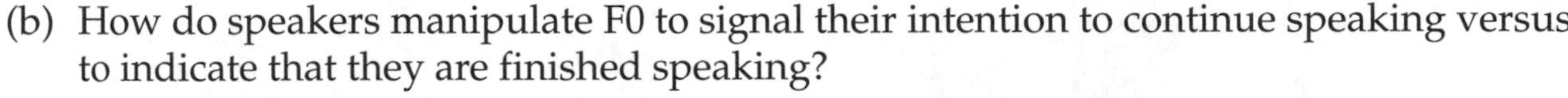

11-25. Shown below are two spectrograms and their associated F0 contours for the phrase, "I love you."

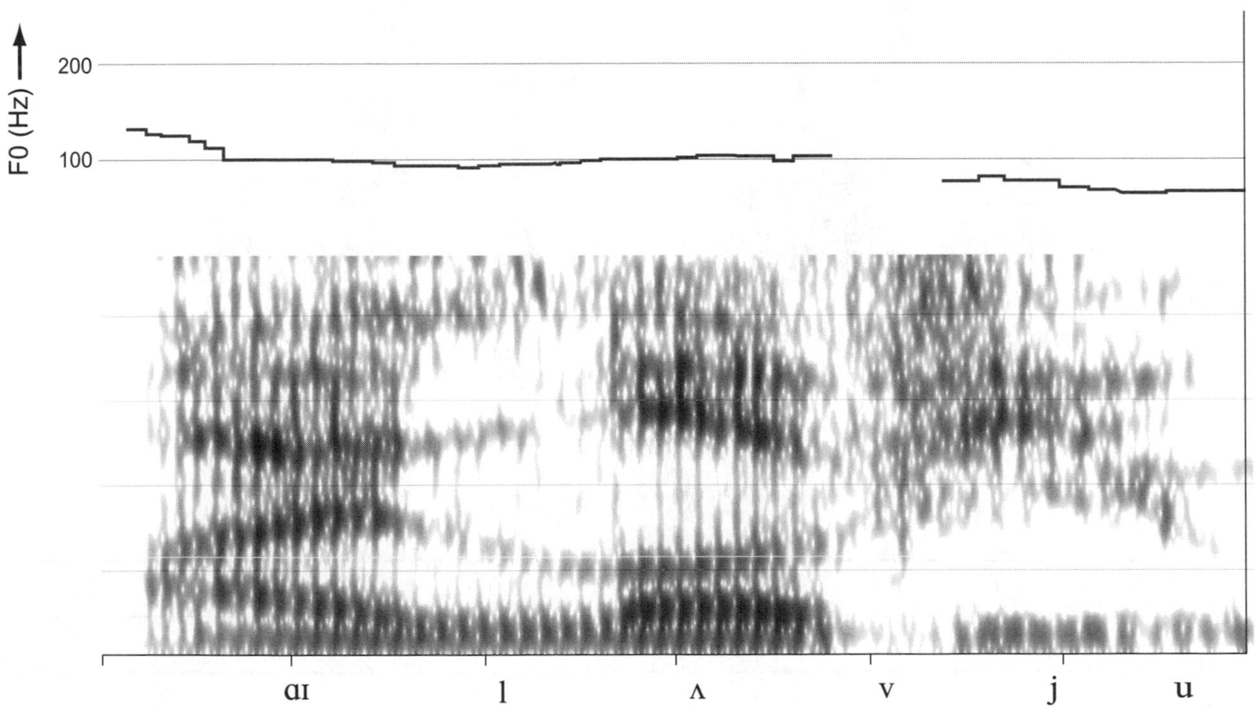

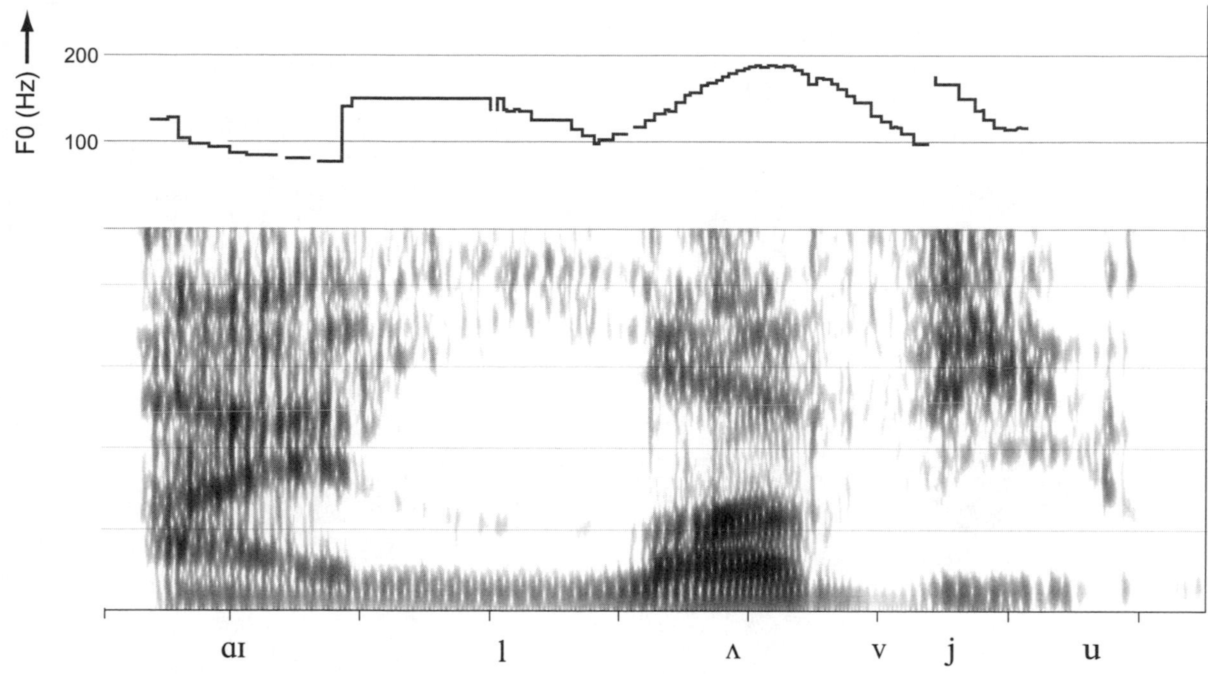

Based on the information provided in the displays and discussed in the textbook, what is the difference in the way these two utterances were spoken?

____

____

12

Speech Perception Questions

12–1. How was an early version of a speech synthesizer used in the discovery of speech acoustic characteristics that were important to the perception of specific characteristics of speech sounds?

12–2. In a few sentences, explain the following statement: "In the classic ba-da-ga experiment conducted at Haskins Laboratories in the early 1950s, the experimenters created a continuum of signals relevant to the perception of place of articulation for stops."

12–3. Explain the difference between an *identification* and *discrimination* experiment in speech perception research. Why was it important for scientists to perform both experiments to "prove" categorical perception in the classic experiments on acoustic cues to place of articulation?

12-4. Based on information discussed in Chapters 11 and 12 of the textbook, why did the scientists at Haskins Labs believe that a "motor theory" of speech perception was necessary?

12-5. Explain how animal perception of speech sounds is related to different theoretical accounts of human speech perception.

12-6. What is the meaning of "duplex" in the phenomenon called "duplex perception"?

How does the "duplex" phenomenon for speech signals relate to the concept of a species-specific human module for speech perception?

How solid is this "duplex" evidence?

12-7. Below are three smoothed spectra of /k/ bursts taken from three different productions. More specifically, the /k/ was produced in three different vowel contexts. Each spectrum was computed from a 25-ms "piece" of the signal extending from the burst into the frication interval. The spectra have been smoothed to eliminate much of the detail typically seen in Fast Fourier Spectra (FFTs).

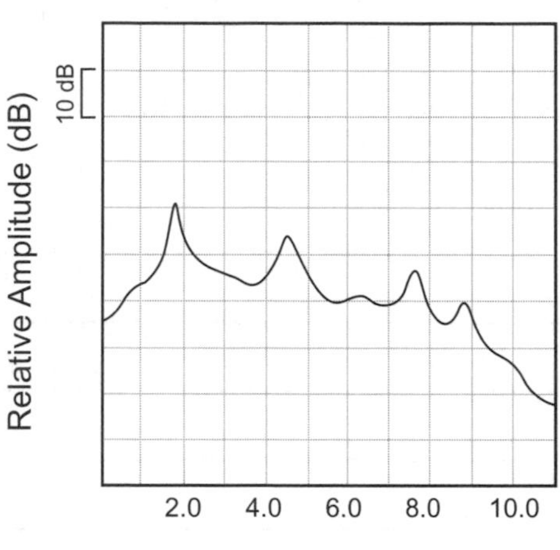

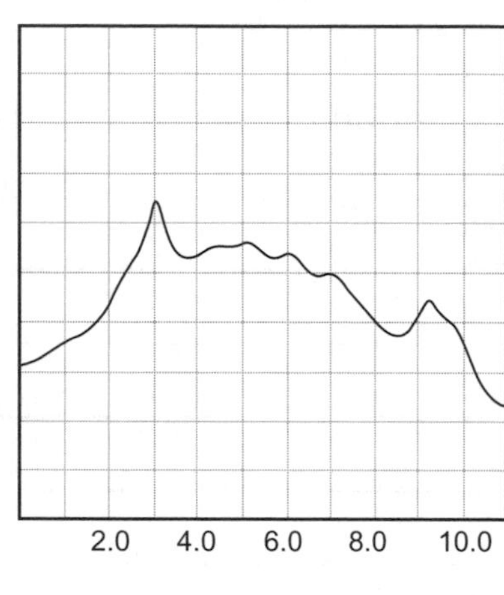

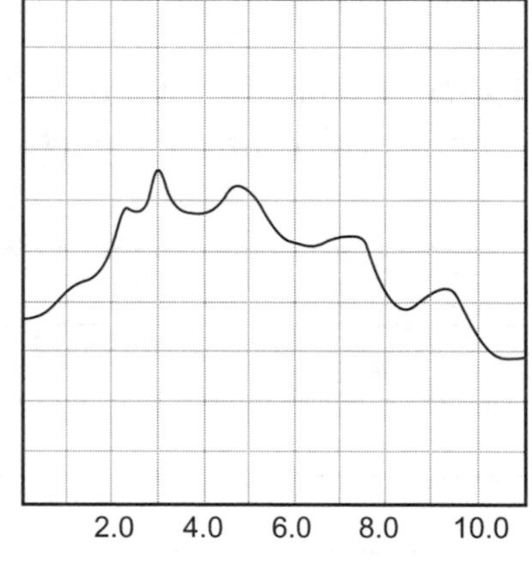

Frequency (kHz) ⟶

(a) In what ways are these three spectra similar?

____

____

(b) In what ways are they different?

____

____

(c) How have these similarities and differences been discussed for relevance to theories of speech perception?

____

____

12–8. Does the phenomenon of "trading relations" support a motor or auditory theory of speech perception? Look at the spectrograms below of /si/ versus /su/ and suggest an experiment in which these signals could be manipulated to demonstrate a trading relations effect. (*Hint*: Look for a difference in the major concentration of frication noise energy between /si/ amd /su/.)

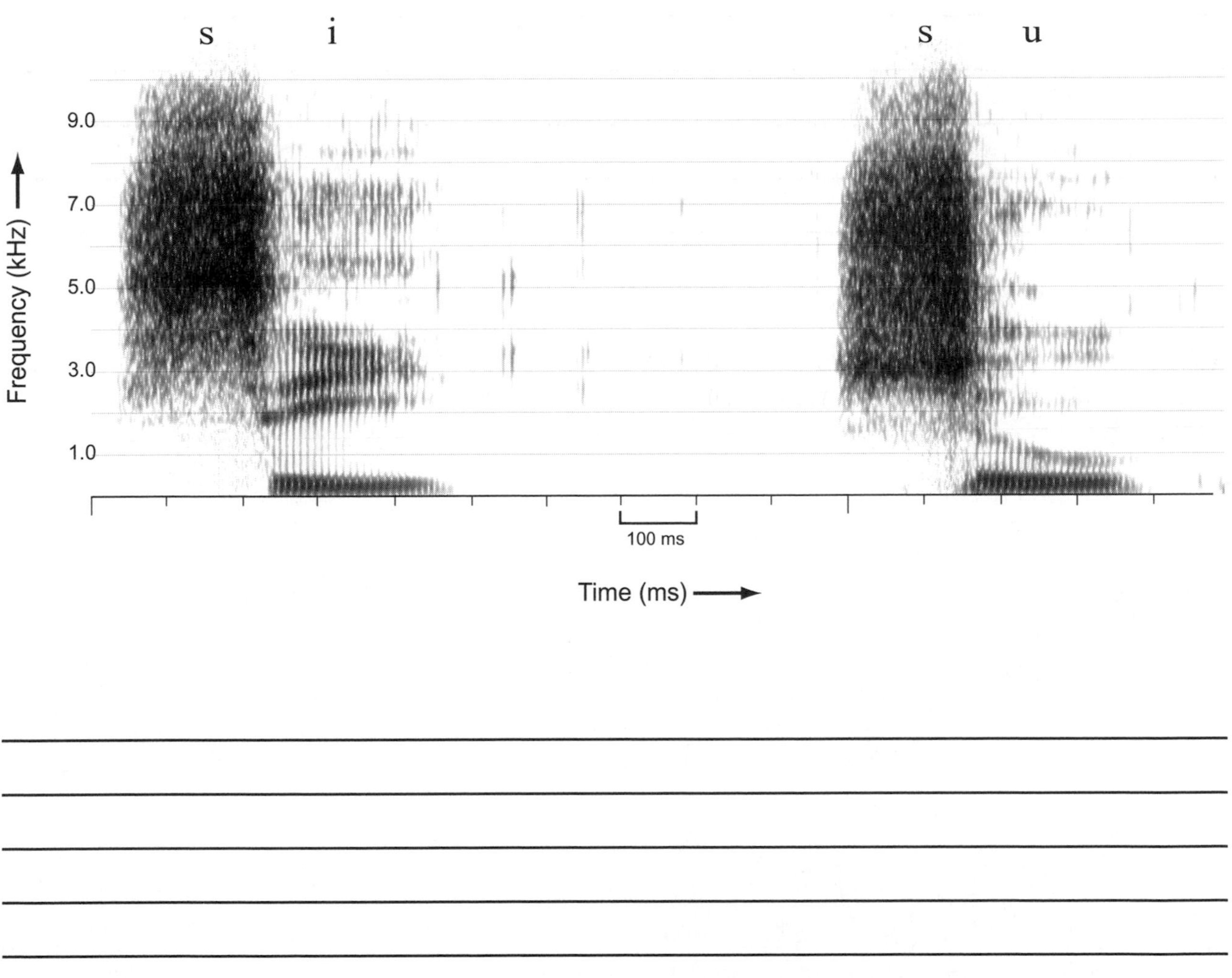

12-9. Why can an explanation of speech perception that relies on general auditory mechanisms (as compared to the specialized mechanisms of the motor theory) survive the reality of substantial acoustic variability for a given sound segment, this variability resulting from changes in phonetic context, speaker identity, style of speech, and so forth?

12-10. Draw an identification-discrimination plot in which the identification data support an interpretation of categorical perception, but the discrimination data do not. Explain your drawing.

12-11. Provide a two or three-sentence explanation of how speech perception in animals has been used to address the controversy between motor versus auditory theories of speech perception.

12-12. In a sentence or two, explain how the "direct realism" view of speech perception is regarded by its proponents as "simpler" than auditory theories of speech perception.

12-13. Why is the idea that words are perceived by matching analysis of acoustic input to a sequence of abstract phonemes not necessarily supported by experimental data?

12–14. Explain the use of speech intelligibility tests as a means to evaluate listener-communication system and speaker proficiency.

13

Swallowing Questions

13–1. Label the structures in the figure.

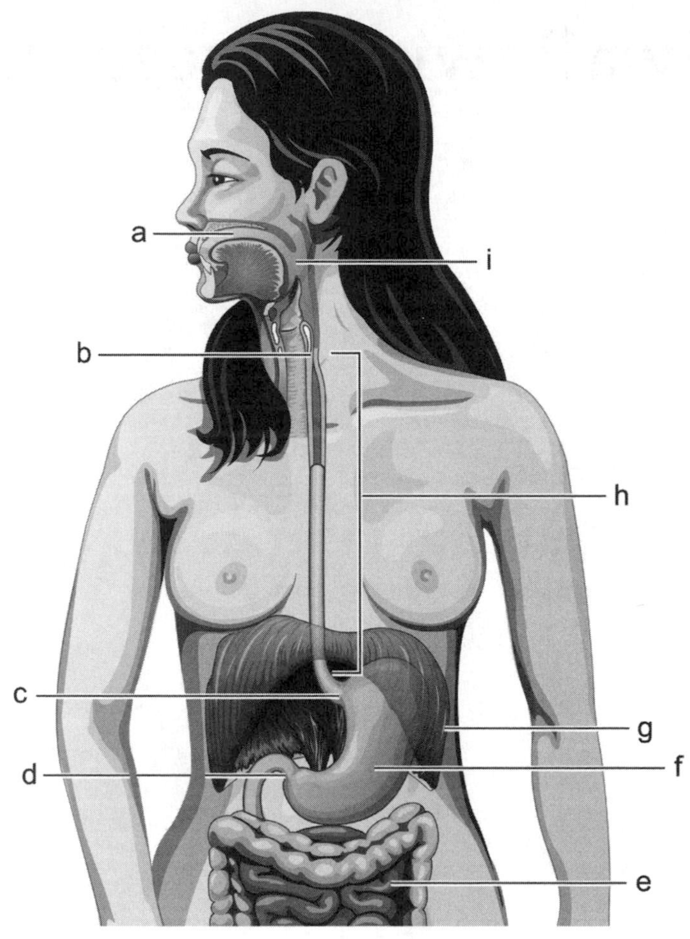

a ____________________

b ____________________

c ____________________

d ____________________

e ____________________

f ____________________

g ____________________

h ____________________

i ____________________

13-2. Complete the following items regarding the anatomy and physiology of selected swallowing structures.

(a) The muscles in the cervical (upper) part of the esophagus are striated or smooth [Circle one] and the muscles in the abdominal (lower) part of the esophagus are striated or smooth. [Circle one] Striated or smooth [Circle one] muscle is considered to be involuntary.

(b) Activation of the ______________________ muscle may cause pressure change within the upper esophageal sphincter. This muscle is considered by some to be part of the ______________________ muscle.

(c) The stomach is made up of striated or smooth [Circle one] muscle.

(d) In general, the forces associated with swallowing are higher or lower [Circle one] and the movements are faster or slower [Circle one] than those associated with speaking.

(e) The resting pressures in the upper and lower esophageal sphincters are higher or lower [Circle one] than the resting pressures in the esophagus and stomach.

(f) What might happen if the pressure in the stomach were greater than the pressure in the lower esophageal sphincter?

____

____

13-3. Complete the following items regarding the phases of swallowing.

(a) Match each of the following events with the appropriate phase of swallowing:

______ The velopharynx closes.	(a) Oral preparatory phase
______ A solid bolus is masticated.	(b) Oral transport phase
______ The bolus moves by peristalsis.	(c) Pharyngeal transport phase
______ The constrictor muscles contract sequentially.	(d) Esophageal transport phase
______ The upper esophageal sphincter begins to open.	
______ A liquid bolus is contained in the anterior oral cavity.	
______ The velum begins to elevate.	
______ The bolus moves toward the pharynx.	
______ The larynx elevates and closes.	
______ The bolus enters the upper esophageal sphincter.	
______ The epiglottis moves backward and downward.	
______ The back of the tongue elevates to separate the oral cavity from the pharyngeal cavity.	

(b) Define *deglutition.* Is deglutition exactly the same as *swallowing*?

____

____

____

____

(c) Define *bolus.*

____

____

(d) Define *apnea*.

____

(e) Which phase of swallowing includes an obligatory apneic period? ______________

(f) How long (in seconds) is the oral preparatory phase of swallowing? ___________

(g) How long (in seconds) is the oral transport phase of swallowing? ___________

(h) How long (in seconds) is the pharyngeal transport phase of swallowing? ___________

(i) How long (in seconds) is the esophageal transport phase of swallowing? ___________

(j) Do the phases of swallowing overlap? _______ Explain your answer.

____

____

13–4. Complete the following items regarding breathing and swallowing.

(a) The apneic interval usually lasts approximately ___________.

(b) Following a single swallow, it is most common to inspire or expire. [Circle one]

(c) Why is it considered beneficial to expire following a swallow?

____

____

____

(d) During sequential swallowing of liquid, it is not uncommon to experience mild feelings of dyspnea. True or false [Circle one]

(e) Swallowing usually occurs at lung volumes that are [Check one]

______ smaller than the resting expiratory level.

______ near total lung capacity.

______ slightly larger than the resting expiratory level.

______ unpredictable.

13-5. Complete the following items regarding the neural control of swallowing.

(a) Which six cranial nerves are important for swallowing (provide number and name)?

____

____

____

____

____

____

(b) Which 22 spinal nerves are important for swallowing?

____

____

____

(c) The cranial nerve that innervates the cervical (upper) esophagus is ______________.

(d) The lower regions of the esophagus are under the control of the ________________ nervous system.

(e) Cortical regions of the brain play a strong role in the control of the

________________ and ________________ phases of swallowing.

The brainstem has primary control over the ________________ and

________________ phases of swallowing.

13-6. Complete the following items regarding the influences of selected variables on swallowing.

(a) In general, swallowing pudding takes more time or less time [Circle one] and higher forces or lower forces [Circle one] than swallowing water.

(b) In general, movements are larger when swallowing a larger bolus compared to a smaller bolus. True or False [Circle one]

(c) Laryngeal penetration is more common when swallowing thinner or thicker [Circle one] liquids and when swallowing smaller or larger [Circle one] boluses.

(d) Does taste influence the pressures exerted during swallowing? Yes or No [Circle one]

(e) It takes longer to initiate a swallow of a warm bolus compared to a cold bolus. True or False [Circle one]

(f) Describe at least one way that sequential swallows differ from single swallows.

____

____

____

(g) Give an example of how it is possible to change the way you swallow.

____

____

____

(h) Certain features of the swallow differ with body position. True or False [Circle one]

13-7. Complete the following items regarding development, age, and sex.

(a) The first swallow usually occurs a few hours after birth. True or False [Circle one]

(b) Suckling is characterized by [Check one]

______ forward and backward (horizontal) movements of the tongue.

______ large vertical movements of the mandible.

______ up and down (vertical) movements of the tongue.

______ both forward and backward (horizontal) movements of the tongue and large vertical movements of the mandible.

(c) Suckling creates greater forces than sucking. True or False [Circle one]

(d) Infants can swallow and breathe at the same time. True or False [Circle one]

(e) Infants usually begin eating solid foods around [Check one]

_____ 1 month of age.

_____ 6 months of age.

_____ 1 year of age.

_____ 2 years of age.

(f) After age 60 years, swallowing generally becomes faster or slower. [Circle one]

(g) Women tend to swallow faster and with greater force than men. True or False [Circle one]

13–8. Complete the following items regarding measurement of swallowing.

(a) A videofluoroscopic swallow study is also called a(n) [Check one]

_____ FEES.

_____ barium swallow study.

_____ modified barium swallow study.

_____ endoscopic swallow study.

(b) Manometry is considered the "gold standard" for evaluation of the swallow. True or False [Circle one]

(c) Which phases of swallowing can be visualized using videofluoroscopy? [Check all that apply]

_____ Oral preparatory phase

_____ Oral transport phase

_____ Pharyngeal transport phase

_____ Esophageal transport phase

(d) A videofluoroscopic swallow examination is performed by a

_____________________________________, who runs the x-ray equipment, and a

_____________________________________, who presents the liquid and food and

instructs the client on the swallowing tasks.

(e) Define *laryngeal penetration.*

____

____

(f) Define *aspiration.*

____

____

(g) Laryngeal penetration and aspiration can be detected with [Check all that apply]

______ videofluorscopy.

______ flexible endoscopy.

______ magnetometry.

______ manometry.

(h) The swallowing evaluation procedure that allows direct viewing of the vocal folds from above is the [Check one]

______ modified barium swallow study.

______ flexible endoscopic evaluation of swallowing (FEES).

______ ultrasound assessment.

______ manometric evaluation.

(i) Manometry provides a way to measure <u>movement</u> or <u>pressure</u>. [Circle one]

13–9. Complete the following items regarding swallowing disorders and clinical professionals.

(a) Define *dysphagia*.

___

___

___

(b) Give an example of a psychogenic swallowing disorder.

___

(c) Could a glossectomy cause a swallowing disorder? Yes or No [Circle one] Why or why not?

___

___

___

(d) Briefly state why following conditions might cause a swallowing disorder.

Bilateral paralysis of the facial muscles

___

___

___

Removal of a vocal fold

___

___

___

A stroke in the brainstem

___

___

___

Chronic obstructive pulmonary disease

____

____

____

(e) A speech-language pathologist is responsible for the evaluation and management of oropharyngeal or esophageal [Circle one] dysphagia.

(f) If a client has a disorder of esophageal motility, his management is directed by a

______________________.

(g) A/an ______________ therapist provides devices and behavioral strategies for improving a client's ability to feed himself or herself.

Answers

CHAPTER 1

1-1 Neural level
Muscular level
Structural level
Aeromechanical level
Acoustic level
Perceptual level

1-2 Breathing subsystem
Laryngeal subsystem
Velopharyngeal-nasal subsystem
Pharyngeal-oral subsystem

1-3

Forensics is the use of data for legal applications. Examples include use of data for the purpose of speaker identification from audio recordings and to support a legal claim of someone who has sustained an injury that has impaired quality of life.

CHAPTER 2

2-1

a. Clavicle
b. Ribs
c. Pelvic girdle
d. Costal cartilage
e. Sternum

2-2

a. Scapula
b. Coccygeal
c. Sacral
d. Lumbar
e. Thoracic
f. Cervical

2-3

a. Trachea
b. Lung
c. Main-stem bronchi
d. Alveoli

2–4

a. Subclavius
b. Pectoralis minor
c. Subcostals
d. Pectoralis major
e. Sternocleidomastoid
f. Transversus thoracis
g. Serratus anterior
h. Scalenus anterior, medius, posterior

2–5

a. External intercostals
b. Internal intercostals

2–6

a. Latissimus dorsi
b. Serratus posterior inferior
c. Serratus posterior superior
d. Levatores costarum
e. Quadratus lumborum
f. Lateral iliocostalis lumborum
g. Lateral iliocostalis thoracis
h. Lateral iliocostalis cervicis

2–7

a. Diaphragm
b. Opening for vena cava
c. Central tendon of diaphragm
d. Opening for aorta
e. Opening for esophagus

2–8

a. Rectus abdominis
b. Transversus abdominis
c. External oblique
d. Internal oblique

2-9

	Inspiratory	Expiratory
Muscles of the Rib Cage Wall		
Sternocleidomastoid	X	
Scalenus anterior, medius, and posterior	X	
Pectoralis major	X	
Pectoralis minor	X	
Subclavius	X	
Serratus anterior	X	
External intercostal	X	
Internal intercostal (between ribs)		X
Internal intercostal (between costal cartilages)	X	
Transversus thoracis		X
Latissimus dorsi	X	X
Serratus posterior superior	X	
Serratus posterior inferior		X
Lateral iliocostalis cervicis	X	
Lateral iliocostalis thoracis	X[1]	X[1]
Lateral iliocostalis lumborum		X
Levatores costarum	X	
Quadratus lumborum		X
Subcostal		X
Muscle of the Diaphragm		
Diaphragm	X	
Muscles of the Abdominal Wall		
Rectus abdominis		X
External oblique		X
Internal oblique		X
Transversus abdominis		X

[1]"Contraction of the lateral iliocostalis thoracis muscle stabilizes large segments of the back of the rib cage wall and makes them move in concert with either the rib elevation or depression caused by the cervical and lumbar elements of the muscle group, respectively" (p. 17, Hixon et al., 2014).

2-10

Component	Passive Force		Active Force	
	Inspiratory	Expiratory	Inspiratory	Expiratory
Pulmonary apparatus		X		
Chest wall	X	X	X	X
Rib cage wall	X	X	X	X
Diaphragm	X		X	
Abdominal wall	X	X		X

2-11

Muscle(s)	Move RC outward	Move RC inward	Move DI footward	Move DI headward	Move AB outward	Move AB inward
RC inspiratory	X			X		X
RC expiratory		X	X		X	
DI (with RC fixed)			X		X	
DI (with AB fixed)	X			X		
AB	X			X		X

2-12

a. Inspiratory reserve volume
b. Tidal volume
c. Expiratory reserve volume
d. Residual volume
e. Vital capacity
f. Functional residual capacity
g. Inspiratory capacity
h. Total lung capacity

2–13

(a) TLC for a man who is 5 feet, 6 inches tall: **6.34 L**
Ht = 5.5 feet × 0.3048 = 1.68 meters
(7.99 × 1.68) – 7.08 = 6.34 liters

TLC for a woman who is 5 feet, 6 inches tall: **5.30 L**
Ht = 5.5 feet × 0.3048 = 1.68 meters
(6.60 × 1.68) – 5.79 = 5.30 liters

Women have smaller TLCs than men.

(b) RV for a man who is 5 feet, 6 inches tall and 25 years old: **1.52 L**
Ht = 5.5 feet × 0.3048 = 1.68 meters
(1.31 × 1.68) + (0.022 × 25) – 1.23 = 1.52 L

RV for a man who is 5 feet, 6 inches tall and 75 years old: **2.24 L**
Ht = 5.5 feet × 0.3048 = 1.68 meters
(1.81 × 1.68) + (0.016 × 75) – 2.00 = 2.24 L

RV increases with age.

(c) Your TLC: (Answers will vary.)

Your RV: (Answers will vary.)

Your vital capacity (VC): (Answers will vary.) Calculate as follows: TLC – RV = VC

Decrease; TLC does not change significantly with age, whereas RV increases. Therefore, VC decreases with age.

2–14

__d__ End of an inspiration for resting tidal breathing

__e__ End of an expiration for resting tidal breathing

__c__ End of an inspiration for conversational speaking

__b__ End of an inspiration for classical singing

__f__ End of an expiration for vigorous laughing

__a__ End of an inspiration for a vital capacity maneuver

__g__ End of an expiration for a vital capacity maneuver

2-15

(a) 230 cmH_2O

(b) −125 cmH_2O

(c) 0 cmH_2O

(d) 25 cmH_2O

(e) Right. This is because in the supine body position, gravity pulls in the expiratory direction on all parts of the breathing apparatus, whereas in the upright body position, gravity pulls in the inspiratory direction on the diaphragm-abdomen part of the breathing apparatus.

(f) The relaxation characteristic does not extend to 100% VC because the recoil force of the breathing apparatus compresses the pulmonary apparatus (and the air molecules within it) to a smaller volume (size). You can demonstrate this to yourself if you inspire as much air as you can, close your larynx (or upper airway), and completely relax your breathing muscles. You should feel yourself compress to a smaller size. The relaxation characteristic does not extend to 0% VC because the recoil force of the breathing apparatus expands the pulmonary apparatus (and the air molecules within it) to a larger volume. You can demonstrate this to yourself if you expire as much air as you can, close your larynx (or upper airway), and completely relax your breathing muscles. You should feel yourself expand to a larger size.

2-16

__f__ Abrupt sniffing

__c__ Conversing loudly in a noisy restaurant

__e__ Relaxation at the end of a quiet breath

__b__ Loud yelling

__a__ Maximum expiratory effort near total lung capacity

__g__ Maximum inspiratory effort near residual volume

__d__ Conversing at usual loudness

2–17

(a) __d__ Largest abdominal wall diameter

__b__ Smallest abdominal wall diameter

__a__ Largest rib cage wall diameter

__c__ Smallest rib cage wall diameter

(b) Red shading: The area outlined by the relaxation characteristic (dashed line) and the curved solid line (running from Total lung capacity to Residual volume) to the left of the relaxation characteristic.

(c) Green shading: The area outlined by the relaxation characteristic (dashed line) and the curved solid line (running from Total lung capacity to Residual volume) to the right of the relaxation characteristic.

2–18

__c__ Classical singing

__b__ Running as fast as possible

__d__ Conversational speaking

__f__ After eating a large meal

__a__ Pulling in the abdominal wall inward to look as thin as possible

__g__ Pushing out the abdominal wall to look as fat as possible

__e__ Resting tidal breathing

2–19

(a) phrenic nerve; C3–C5

(b) True

(c) Nearly all of the rib cage wall muscles

All the abdominal wall muscles

(d) Abnormally small vital capacity (VC)

Abnormally small inspiratory reserve volume (IRV)

No expiratory reserve volume (ERV)

Abnormally small total lung capacity (TLC)

(e) Yes

The diaphragm would still be intact, and the diaphragm is the most powerful and important of all the breathing muscles.

(f) brainstem

(g) voluntarily; automatically

(h) both oxygen and carbon dioxide

(i) increase

(j) mechanoreceptors

(k) True

(l) A person who has lost function of all spinal motor neurons would lose neural innervation to the diaphragm and muscles of the rib cage wall and abdominal wall. Thus, the only way the person might be able to breathe would be to activate neck muscles (such as the sternocleidomastoid muscles) to lift the rib cage wall to generate a small inspiration. Alternatively, the person might be able to learn glossopharyngeal breathing, a form of positive-pressure breathing that resembles that of a frog (see sidetrack titled Ribbit, Ribbit in your textbook). Most likely, however, the person will be given a ventilator, such as that shown in Figure 2–45 in your textbook.

2–20

(a) 0.45 L

(b) 450 mL

(c) 4.5 L

(d) Answers will vary. Estimate your tidal volume by multiplying your vital capacity by 10% (e.g., 5 L × 10% = 0.5 L)

(e) –0.5 LPS

(f) 0.5 LPS

(g) –1 cmH_2O

(h) 1 cmH_2O

(i) smaller

(j) oxygen; carbon dioxide

(k) False

Active force from the diaphragm drives inspiration. In upright body positions, the abdominal wall muscles are also activated throughout the resting tidal breathing cycle. (See Figure 2–25 in your textbook.)

2–21

(a) –30 cmH_2O

(b) 60% VC

(c) 37 cmH_2O

(d) 8 cmH_2O

(e) rib cage wall inspiratory muscles

(f) all

(g) small

2–22

(a) larger

(b) 5 to 10 cmH_2O

(c) more

(d) more

(e) Stretches the diaphragm

Stretches the expiratory muscles of the rib cage wall

(f) less

(g) expiratory rib cage wall muscular pressure and abdominal wall muscular pressure, with the latter predominating.

(h) Yes

(i) Larger

People often speak at larger lung volumes when they produce louder speech so that they can take advantage of the higher expiratory recoil pressure that prevails at larger lung volumes.

(j) Yes

Although people sometimes speak at larger lung volumes to produce louder speech (see previous question), it is not necessary to do so. Volume and pressure for speech production can be thought of as independent variables.

2-23

(a) inspiratory rib cage wall muscles; diaphragm

(b)

	Upright Running Speech Production	Supine Running Speech Production
Abdominal wall muscles	On	Off
Expiratory rib cage wall muscles	On	On

(c) Some air should be expired when you open your airway in supine.

This happened because gravity has expired the breathing apparatus, primarily by the abdominal content pushing the diaphragm headward.

(d) larger

No

(e) generally the same

2–24

(a)

Tidal Volume (L)	Breathing Rate (BPM)	Minute Ventilation (LPM)
0.50	12.0	6.0
0.60	10.0	6.0
0.75	10.0	7.5
1.10	7.5	8.25

(b) 3 Heavy exercise

2 Reading aloud continuously (without breaks)

1 Resting tidal breathing

(c) They take deeper inspirations.

They expend more air during speaking.

They often blow off air.

They speak at larger than usual lung volumes (well above the resting level).

They increase ventilation.

(d) hyperventilate; decrease

2–25

(a) Answers will vary. Expected values are 16 to 20 syllables/breath group for young adults.

(b) decrease

(c) The 75-year-old man

(d) Yes

(e) False

(f) False. Speech breathing becomes adult like by age 10 years.

(g) True

(h) more

2–26

(a) The person is not wearing a noseclip.

(b) Some of the expired volume could escape through the nose, so the vital capacity measure obtained may be artificially small.

2–27

(a) 0.4 L

(b) 2.6 L

(c) 2.2 L

(d) 1.4 L

(e) 4.0 L

(f) residual volume

2–28

(a) 2.0 L

(b) 10 s

(c) 0.2 LPS

(d) 2.0 LPS

2–29

(a) Peak 1 = 7.0 cmH_2O

Peak 2 = 6.0 cmH_2O

Peak 3 = 5.5 cmH_2O

Peak 4 = 4.5 cmH_2O

Peak 5 = 3.0 cmH_2O

Peak 6 = 2.0 cmH_2O

(b) Alveolar pressure was decreasing over the course of the breath group.

(c) The oral pressure drops to zero between the peaks because the vocal folds have come together to produce the vowel. During these periods of voicing, the oral pressure does not provide an accurate estimate of alveolar pressure.

2-30

(a) You generated at least 10 cmH_2O alveolar pressure.

(b) You would place the tip of the straw at the 5 cmH_2O mark.

2-31

(a) _CW_ Spinal cord injury

_PA_ Asthma

_CW_ Cerebral palsy

_F_ Malingering

_PA_ Emphysema

_F_ Misuse

(b) functional disorders of breathing.

disorders of the chest wall.

disorders of the pulmonary apparatus.

(c) pulmonologist

(d) Speech-language pathologist

Pulmonologist

Respiratory therapist

Neurologist

Physical therapist

Psychologist

CHAPTER 3

3–1

a. Epiglottis
b. Cricoid cartilage
c. Arytenoid cartilages
d. Thyroid cartilage
e. Hyoid bone

3–2

a. Notch
b. Superior cornu
c. Lamina
d. Prominence
e. Angle
f. Inferior cornu
g. Facet

3–3

a. Anterior arch
b. Facet for thyroid cartilage
c. Facet for arytenoid cartilage
d. Lamina

3–4

a. Corniculate cartilage
b. Vocal process
c. Muscular process
d. Apex
e. Facets

3–5

a. Body
b. Lingual surface
c. Petiolus
d. Laryngeal surface

3–6

a. Lesser cornu

b. Body

c. Greater cornu

3–7

a. Anterior ceratocricoid ligament

b. Lateral ceratocricoid ligament

c. Posterior ceratocricoid ligament

(a) cricothyroid joints

(b) rotate and slide; rotate and slide

3–8

a. Anterior cricoarytenoid ligament

b. Posterior cricoarytenoid ligament

(a) cricoarytenoid joints

(b) rock and slide

3–9

a. Supraglottal region (vestibule)

b. Quadrangular membrane

c. Ventricular ligament

d. Vocal ligament

e. Conus elasticus

f. Cricoid cartilage

g. Subglottal region

h. Vocal fold

i. Laryngeal ventricle

j. Ventricular fold

3–10

(a) __b__ Epithelium

__d__ Superficial layer of the lamina propria

__a__ Intermediate layer of the lamina propria

__e__ Deep layer of the lamina propria

__c__ Muscle

(b) muscle

deep layer of the lamina propria

(c) intermediate layer of the lamina propria

superficial layer of the lamina propria

epithelium

(d) The glottis is the opening between the vocal folds.

(e) membranous; 60%; cartilaginous; 40%

3–11

a. Thyroepiglottic ligament
b. Vocal ligament
c. Middle cricothyroid ligament
d. Lateral cricothyroid membrane
e. Conus elasticus
f. Ventricular ligament
g. Quadrangular membrane
h. Hyothyroid membrane
i. Middle hyothyroid ligament
j. Cricotracheal membrane
k. Lateral hyothyroid ligament

3–12

a. Thyroarytenoid
b. Lateral cricoarytenoid
c. Transverse arytenoid
d. Posterior cricoarytenoid
e. Oblique arytenoid
f. Cricothyroid

(a) intrinsic

(b) Both ends of each muscle have attachments within the larynx.

3–13

(a) external thyroarytenoid muscle; thyromuscularis; internal thyroarytenoid muscle; thyrovocalis; vocal

(b) decrease

(c) A *vocal fold* consists of a vocal ligament, internal thyroarytenoid muscle, and external thyroarytenoid muscle. In contrast, a *vocal cord* consists of only a vocal ligament and internal thyroarytenoid muscle.

(d) posterior cricoarytenoid; lateral cricoarytenoid; arytenoid

(e) oblique; epiglottis

(f) lengthening; fixed-length

3–14

a. Thyrohyoid
b. Sternothyroid
c. Inferior constrictor

(a) extrinsic

(b) One end of each muscle attaches within the larynx and one end of each muscle attaches outside the larynx.

3–15

a. Digastric
b. Sternohyoid
c. Omohyoid
d. Mylohyoid
e. Genioglossus
f. Geniohyoid
g. Hyoglossus
h. Stylohyoid

(a) supplementary

(b) They do not insert directly into the larynx, but influence its position and stability.

3-16

(a)

	Shortens Vocal Folds	Tenses Vocal Folds	Lengthens Vocal Folds	Abducts Vocal Folds	Adducts/ Compresses Vocal Folds
Thyroarytenoid	X	X			X
Posterior cricoarytenoid			(X)[1]	X	
Lateral cricoarytenoid	(X)[2]				X
Arytenoid					X
Cricothyroid		X	X		

[1]The posterior cricoarytenoid muscles lengthen the vocal folds as they abduct them. They also secure the posterior parts of the vocal folds and act as antagonists to the cricothyroid muscles as the cricothyroid muscles lengthen and tense the vocal folds. However, the posterior cricoarytenoid muscles are not viewed as primary vocal fold lengtheners.

[2]The lateral cricoarytenoid muscles counteract the lengthening action of the posterior cricoarytenoid muscles during vocal fold abduction. They are also able to shorten the effective vibrating length of the vocal folds through the mechanism of medial compression. However, the lateral cricoarytenoid muscles are not viewed as primary vocal fold shorteners.

(b)

	Moves Housing Upward	Moves Housing Downward	Moves Housing Forward	Moves Housing Backward
Sternothyroid		X	X	
Thyrohyoid	X			
Sternohyoid		X		
Omohyoid		X		X
Digastric: anterior belly	X		X	
Digastric: posterior belly	X			X
Stylohyoid	X			X
Mylohyoid	X		X	
Geniohyoid	X		X	
Hyoglossus	X			
Genioglossus	X		X	

(c) Tracheal tug tends to pull the vocal folds downward and toward the sides, thus abducting the vocal folds.

(d) medial compression

3–17

(a) __1__ Whispering

__4__ Coughing vigorously

__2__ Singing softly

__3__ Speaking loudly

(b) decrease

increase

increase

decrease

(c) __c__ Bearing down while lifting something heavy

__a__ Inspiring

__b__ Whispering

__b__ Producing a voiceless consonant (like /s/)

__b__ Producing breathy voice

(d) low

(e) increases

(f) lateral; medial

(g) decrease

3-18

(a)

Number	Name
X	Vagus
XI	Accessory

(b) recurrent; vagus

(c)

Cranial Nerves	Spinal Nerves
V	C1
VII	C2
X	C3
XI	
XII	

(d) X

3-19

(a) The vocal folds adduct momentarily while tracheal pressure builds. This is followed by an abrupt release of vocal fold adductory force and release of turbulent airflow that may be audible.

(b) The vocal folds are brought close to each other (but not approximated) forming a narrow glottis. Air is forced through the narrow glottis, creating turbulent airflow that is usually audible.

(c) (b) and (c)

(d) __F__ *Revised:* The acoustic disturbance that constitutes the voice source corresponds to the part of the vibratory cycle during which the vocal folds move together and the laryngeal airway closes.

__T__ Vocal fold vibration is usually characterized by a vertical phase difference in which the vocal folds come together at the bottom before they come together at the top.

__F__ *Revised:* The vertical phase difference is caused by air pressure pushing apart the lower portion of the vocal folds before pushing apart the middle and upper portions of the folds.

__T__ The average air pressure within the glottis is greater in a converging glottis than in a diverging glottis.

__F__ *Revised:* Vocal fold vibration is sometimes initiated by simultaneous expiratory airflow and vocal fold approximation. It can also be initiated with expiratory airflow either preceding or following vocal fold approximation (soft or hard vocal attack, respectively).

__F__ *Revised:* The minimum tracheal pressure needed to vibrate the vocal folds is approximately 2 to 3 cmH_2O.

(e) translational—moving laterally away from and toward the midline;

rotational—rotation around a pivot point located between the top and bottom of the medial surface of the vocal fold cover

(f) recoil force of the vocal fold tissue exceeds the intraglottal air pressure.

intraglottal air pressure begins to decrease.

(g) high; abrupt

3–20

(a) the rate at which the vocal folds vibrate.

(b) pitch

(c) increases; decreases; increases

(d) The cricothyroid muscles can increase the stiffness of the vocal folds by stretching them and the thyroartenoid muscles can increase their internal stiffness by contracting muscle fibers that make up the vocal folds. The cricothyroid and thyroartenoid muscles usually work together to increase vocal fold stiffness, which, in turn, increases fundamental frequency. This is the primary frequency adjusting mechanism used in voice production.

(e) No. There is a wide range of relative activation of the cricothyroid and thyroarytenoid muscles that can be used to produce a given fundamental frequency. This is illustrated in Figure 3–41 in your textbook.

(f) Activation of the lateral cricoarytenoid muscles can generate force between the vocal folds in the region of the vocal processes and create medial compression. Greater medial compression may decrease the effective vibrating length of the vocal folds and thereby increase fundamental frequency. This is considered to be a secondary frequency adjusting mechanism.

(g) Elevation of the larynx, probably through actions of thyrohyoid muscles, is believed to increase the stiffness of the vocal folds and their covers and cause an increase in fundamental frequency. This is considered to be a secondary frequency adjusting mechanism.

(h) Vocal fold stiffness

(i) increase; 2 to 4 Hz

(j) To produce the highest possible fundamental frequency, you would likely activate the cricothyroid and thyroarytenoid muscles maximally and raise your larynx using your thyrohyoid muscles, and you might increase your tracheal pressure using your abdominal wall and expiratory rib cage wall muscles.

3-21

(a) loudness

(b) breathing; laryngeal; pharyngeal-oral

(c) increase; increase; increase

(d) (b)

(e) The waveforms in (b) are higher in amplitude and show a faster decrease in glottal area than the waveforms in (a).

(f) midrange of sound pressure levels.

(g) midrange of fundamental frequency levels.

(h) To produce the highest sound pressure level possible, you would likely inspire deeply (to take advantage of high expiratory recoil pressure at large lung volumes) and activate your abdominal wall and expiratory rib cage wall muscles to generate a high tracheal pressure, activate your lateral cricoarytenoid and arytenoid muscles to generate a high laryngeal opposing pressure, and lower the mandible and tongue and raise the velum to minimize the impedance to the sound emanating from the mouth.

3-22

(a) pulse; modal; loft

(b) loft; modal; pulse

(c) loft

(d) pulse

(e) different

The fundamental frequency is the rate of vocal fold vibration or the number of vibration cycles per unit time. The fundamental frequency is the highest in the upper (loft) set of waveforms because there are more cycles in the same time period than in the other two sets of waveforms.

(f) True. This is illustrated in Figure 3–44 in your textbook.

3-23

(a) For example, the vocal folds abduct and adduct quickly during production of voiceless consonants. For another example, the vocal folds directly contribute to creating the sound source for glottal stops and glottal fricatives.

(b) cricothyroid; thyroarytenoid

(c) intonation contour

(d) Vowels

(e) increase; increase

(f) voice quality

3-24

(a)

Age (years)	Male F0 (Hz)	Female F0 (Hz)
1	475	475
3	300	300
6	250	250
10	250	250
20	125	215
50	110	195
80	130	190
100	155	180

(b) length and thickness (mass) of the vocal folds.

(c) The male larynx increases in size and changes shape quickly during the pubescent years, whereas the female larynx goes through less extensive change.

(d) In young women, the gap is typically located in the posterior part of the larynx.

In elderly women, the gap typically is located along the membranous portion of the vocal folds.

(e) Chronological age is the number of years since birth. Physiological age is more difficult to quantify and is related to health status. A person can be old chronologically and much younger physiologically, and vice versa.

3-25

(a) Sustained vowel, such as "eeeeeeeee." Running speech activities cannot be used because the tongue is being held in place by the examiner.

(b) Because the endoscope is routed through the nose, it is possible to produce anything, including sustained productions and running speech activities (e.g., "Get me to the church on time").

(c) The stroboscopic light flashes at a rate that is just slightly different than the fundamental frequency, thereby resulting in the light flashing at slightly different points in each successive vocal fold vibratory cycle. This creates the optical illusion that vocal fold vibration is occurring in slow motion. The advantage of viewing vocal fold vibration with a stroboscopic light source is that the eye is able to resolve the slower images (the rate actual vocal fold vibration is too high to be "seen" with the naked eye).

(d) higher; lower

(e) Yes

(f) pneumotachometer.

(g) electroglottograph.

(h) 0 mL/s

This corresponds to the times when the vocal folds are approximated.

200 mL/s

This corresponds to the times when the vocal folds are apart maximally.

(i) 100 mL/s

The vocal folds have not yet fully approximated. This is an example of a soft vocal attack.

(j) The decrease in airflow may be due to a decrease in tracheal pressure, an increase in laryngeal airway resistance, or both.

(k) Tracheal air pressure = 7 cmH_2O

Pharyngeal air pressure = 0 cmH_2O

Translaryngeal airflow = 0.2 LPS

Laryngeal airway resistance = 35 cmH_2O/LPS

3-26

(a) __N__ Parkinson disease

__F__ Habit of using an abnormally high pitch

__ST__ Cancerous tumor on the vocal folds

__ST__ Gunshot wound to the larynx

__F__ Pretending to be aphonic (without voice)

__N__ Traumatic brain injury

(b) functional

(c) Speech-language pathologist

Laryngologist

Phonosurgeon

Neurologist

Psychologist

CHAPTER 4

4-1

a. Temporal bone
b. Alveolar process
c. Frontal bone
d. Nasal bone
e. Zygomatic bone
f. Maxillary bone
g. Mandible
h. Styloid process
i. Cervical vertebrae
j. Mastoid process

4-2

a. Maxillary bone
b. Vomer bone
c. Nasal choana
d. Palatal bone

4-3

a. Foramen magnum
b. Ramus of mandible
c. Velum
d. Root of tongue (and lingual tonsil)
e. Laryngeal aditus
f. Esophagus
g. Pyriform sinus
h. Epiglottis
i. Faucial isthmus
j. Nasal choana

(a) lower

(b) esophagus

4-4

a. Nasal cavities
b. Velum
c. Tongue
d. Epiglottis
e. Hyoid bone
f. Cricoid cartilage
g. Esophagus
h. Laryngopharynx
i. Oropharynx
j. Nasopharynx

(a) nasopharynx

(b) nasal choanae

(c) The boundary between the nasopharynx and oropharynx is somewhat arbitrary because the structures in this area are moveable. In the figure it is shown to be at the approximate level of the hard palate.

(d) hyoid bone.

4-5

a. Hard palate
b. Anterior faucial pillar
c. Posterior faucial pillar
d. Palatine tonsil
e. Velum

(a) oropharynx

(b) soft palate; uvula

(c) middle

4–6

a. Frontal bone
b. Nasal bone
c. Ethmoid bone
d. Vomer bone
e. Maxillary bone
f. Palatine bone

(a) septum; cartilage and bone

4–7

a. Superior nasal concha
b. Middle nasal concha
c. Inferior nasal concha
d. Nasal vestibule

(a) large

(b) True

(c) cilia

4–8

a. Root
b. Ala
c. Anterior naris
d. Base
e. Septum
f. Apex
g. Dorsum
h. Bridge

4–9

a. Palatopharyngeus
b. Salpingopharyngeus
c. Superior constrictor
d. Inferior constrictor
e. Middle constrictor
f. Stylopharyngeus

(a)

S	Pterygopharyngeus	S	Glossopharyngeus
S	Buccopharyngeus	I	Cricopharyngeus
I	Thyropharyngeus	M	Ceratopharyngeus
M	Chondropharyngeus	S	Mylopharyngeus

4-10

① The superior constrictor muscle constricts the lumen of the upper pharynx.

② The middle constrictor muscle constricts the lumen of the middle pharynx.

③ The inferior constrictor muscle constricts the lumen of the lower pharynx.

④ The salpingopharyngeus muscle pulls the lateral walls of the pharynx upward and inward and decreases the width of the pharyngeal lumen.

⑤ The stylopharyngeus muscle pulls upward on the pharynx and pulls the lateral wall toward the side and increases the width of the pharyngeal lumen.

⑥ The palatopharyngeus muscle pulls the lateral pharyngeal walls inward and decreases the width of the pharyngeal lumen. It also pulls upward on the pharynx.

4-11

a. Palatal tensor

b. Palatal levator

c. Glossopalatine

d. Pharyngopalatine

e. Uvulus

(a) Uvulus

(b) False.

It used to be thought that the palatal tensor muscle tensed the velum, but more recent research shows that it does not have the mechanical means to do so.

(c) eustachian tube

4-12

① The palatal levator muscle lifts the velum upward and backward.

② The uvulus muscle shortens and lifts the velum and increases the thickness of its posterior segment.

③ The glossopalatine muscle pulls downward and forward on the velum.

④ The pharyngopalatine muscle pulls downward and backward on the velum.

4-13

a. Levator labii superioris alaeque nasi

b. Nasalis

c. Anterior nasal dilator

d. Posterior nasal dilator

e. Depressor alae nasi

(a) Levator labii superioris alaeque nasi

4-14

(1) The pharyngeal tube can be lengthened and shortened through downward and upward movements of the larynx.

(2) The pharyngeal tube can be constricted and dilated through inward and outward movements of the lateral pharyngeal walls.

(3) The pharyngeal tube can be constricted and dilated through forward and backward movements of the posterior pharyngeal wall.

(4) The pharyngeal tube can be constricted and dilated through backward and forward movements of the velum, tongue, and epiglottis.

4-15

A. The palatal levator muscle can move the velum upward and backward (and the uvulus muscle might also help extend the velum backward).

B. The superior constrictor muscle can move the lateral pharyngeal walls inward.

C. The palatal levator muscle can move the velum upward and backward (and the uvulus muscle might also help extend the velum backward). The superior constrictor muscle can move the lateral pharyngeal walls inward.

D. The palatal levator muscle can move the velum upward and backward (and the uvulus muscle might also help extend the velum backward). The superior constrictor muscle can move the lateral pharyngeal walls inward and the posterior pharyngeal wall inward.

4-16

(a)

	Constricts Pharynx	Widens Pharynx	Raises Pharynx
Superior constrictor	X		
Middle constrictor	X		
Inferior constrictor	X		
Salpingopharyngeus	X		X
Stylopharyngeus		X	X
Palatopharyngeus	X		X

(b)

	Pulls Velum Upward	Pulls Velum Down-ward	Pulls Velum Backward	Pulls Velum Forward	Shortens and Increases Bulk of Velum
Palatal levator	X		X		
Uvulus	X				X
Glossopalatine		X		X	
Pharyngopalatine		X	X		

(c) The velum takes on a hooked appearance when it elevates because the major lifting muscle, the palatal levator muscle, inserts near the middle of the length of the velum.

(d)

	Constricts Anterior Nares	**Widens Anterior Nares**
Levator labii superioris alaeque nasi		X
Anterior nasal dilator		X
Posterior nasal dilator		X
Nasalis	X	
Depressor alae nasi	X	

(e) facial expression

4–17

(a) decrease

increase

same

increase

increase

(b) Glass blowing

(c) __1__ Production of "mmmmmm"

__3__ Production of "eeeeeeeee" with the velopharynx closed

__2__ Production of "eeeeeeeee" with the velopharynx open slightly

4–18

(a)

Number	Name
IX	Glossopharyngeal
X	Vagus
XI	Accessory

(b) Pharynx

Velum

(c) pharyngeal plexus; V (trigeminal)

(d) VII

(e) V, VII, X

(f) poor

4–19

(a) internal nasal valves

(b) can be decreased by the nasal dilator muscles.

(c) larger; lower

(d) __T__ The two sides of the nose change their relative resistance in an alternating and cyclic pattern.

__F__ *Revised:* Total nasal resistance remains relatively constant (even though the resistance of each side changes).

__F__ *Revised:* Nasal cycling is thought to be regulated by the suprachiasmatic nucleus of the hypothalamus.

__F__ *Revised:* Most breathing is done through the nose.

__F__ *Revised:* The switch from nasal to oral breathing occurs when nasal pathway resistance reaches 4.0 to 4.5 cmH_2O/LPS.

(e) The pressure of the mask on the tissue surrounding the nose can compress and deform the nasal pathway and increase its resistance. See sidetrack in your textbook titled The Masked Man's Nose.

4-20

(a) /u/ /s/

(b) One explanation is that the velum is mechanically connected to the tongue through the glossopalatine muscles. Therefore, when the tongue is low (as during low vowel production), elevation of the velum is restricted compared to when the tongue is high (as during high vowel production).

A second explanation is that high vowels are more apt to be perceived as nasal than low vowels due to differences in their acoustic characteristics. Greater velar elevation protects against the perception of nasality in high vowels, which have a higher oral acoustic impedance. Velar elevation is not as critical to protecting against the perception of nasality in low vowels, which have a lower oral acoustic impedance.

(c) "Toss the frisbee to Sue."

"Toss the frisbee to Sue" has several high-pressure consonants (/t/, /s/, /f/, /z/, /b/) and velopharyngeal closure is important for producing high oral pressure.

(d) seen

The velopharynx is more likely to be open during the vowel in the word "seen" because the velopharynx begins to open in anticipation of the upcoming nasal consonant. In contrast, a closed velopharynx is required for production of the /t/ in "seat."

(e) the nasal muscles may assist in valving the nasal airway during speech production.

(f) both mouth and nose

(g) First, allowing air to flow through both the mouth and nose minimizes the airway resistance and thereby maximizes the speed of the inspiration. Second, this strategy takes advantage of the humidification and filtration functions provided by nasal inspiration.

4–21

(a) In the supine body position, gravity pulls the velum toward the posterior pharyngeal wall. This means that the velum does not have to move as far as it does in an upright body position to achieve velopharyngeal closure; thus, relatively less activation of the palatal levator muscles is required to close the velopharynx. In contrast, relatively greater activation of the pharyngopalatine muscles is needed to open the velopharynx in supine because gravity is not working with these muscles as it is in upright.

(b) supine

(c) __F__ *Revised:* The velopharynx is usually open during vocalization in the first month of life.

__T__ Six-month-old infants sometimes close the velopharynx and sometimes open the velopharynx during vocalization.

__T__ Children close the velopharynx for oral sound production by 3 years of age (and probably much earlier).

__F__ *Revised:* Temporal patterns associated with velopharyngeal opening/closing are more variable in children than adults.

__F__ *Revised:* Both young adults and older adults close the velopharynx during oral sound production.

__T__ Although certain details of velopharyngeal function during speech production may differ between males and females, these differences are generally minor and not clinically significant.

(d) The nasopharyngeal tonsils, commonly referred to as the "adnoids," enlarge during childhood and then begin to atrophy after about age 10 years. As the adnoids shrink, the child adapts to this structural change and continues to achieve velopharyngeal closure when needed. However, if the child has insufficient velar tissue, the shrinking of the adnoids may result in the inability to close the velopharynx. Also, if the adnoids are removed surgically, it may take time for the child to learn to close the velopharynx under these new structural circumstances.

4–22

(a) flexible

(b) Yes

Either a flexible or rigid endoscope could be used. It would be positioned in the pharynx with the camera lens facing upward toward the velopharynx.

(c) Maybe

The velum may be in contact with the posterior and lateral pharyngeal walls and the velopharynx may be closed airtight. However, it also may be that the velopharynx is open along the sides of the velum. It is not possible to determine this from a lateral x-ray image.

(d)

	Nasal Airflow Throughout	**Nasal Airflow During Part**	**No Nasal Airflow**
Sustained "m"	X		
Sustained "s"			X
"Socks			X
"Sample"		X	

(e) d Production of the word "team"

a Humming

c Production of the word "emu"

b Production of the word "seat"

(f) The person who generated this tracing had a continuous velopharyngeal leak (i.e., the velopharynx never closed), as indicated by the fact that airflow never went to zero. Airflow increased during production of high-pressure consonants (the /s/ in "Sally" and "rice" and the /k/ and /kt/ in "cooked").

(g) 1.5 cm^2

0 cm^2

0.1 cm^2

0 cm^2

0.1 cm^2

1.5 cm^2

(h) The velopharynx is closed.

The velopharynx is open.

Yes, tracheal pressure can be estimated to be 8 cmH_2O.

No, an accurate estimate cannot be made due to the presence of a velopharyngeal leak; however, one can conclude that tracheal pressure is at least 4 cmH_2O.

(i) acoustic measure.

5.9%

92.3%

20.0%

92.3%

5.9%

20.0%

There is a lower oral (acoustic) impedance for /ɑ/ than /i/.

4-23

(a) No

There would be no airflow because the velopharynx is closed and there is mucosal tissue covering the cleft, so there is no air leak.

abnormally high

Nasalance values would be abnormally high because the transfer of acoustic energy across the region with the submucous cleft would be greater than in a normal speaker.

(b) The nasopharyngeal tonsil provides additional tissue that may contribute to velopharyngeal closure. When this is suddenly removed (rather than slowly receding over a period of years), it may be difficult for the speaker to compensate immediately for its loss.

(c) True

An abnormally short velum would explain the fact that there is nasal airflow throughout the utterance. Other conditions could explain this nasal airflow pattern as well.

(d) Any of the above might occur in someone with a neuromotor disease.

(e) __f__ Speech-language pathologist

__a__ Otorhinolaryngologist

__e__ Neurologist

__b__ Prosthodontist

__c__ Plastic surgeon

__d__ Psychologist

CHAPTER 5

5-1

a. Frontal bone
b. Sphenoid bone
c. Zygomatic bone
d. Maxilla
e. Mandible
f. Styloid process
g. Cervical vertebrae
h. Temporal bone
i. Parietal bone
j. Maxilla
k. Mastoid process
l. Palatine bone
m. Permanent teeth

5-2

a. Alveolar process
b. Palatine process of maxilla
c. Horizontal process of palatine bone

(a) maxilla

(b) oral; nasal

5-3

a. Condylar process
b. Coronoid process
c. Alveolar process
d. Angle
e. Ramus
f. Body

5-4

a. Incisors
b. Canine
c. Premolars
d. Molars

(a) 16

(b) 16

(c) 10

(d) 10

5-5

a. Temporomandibular ligament

b. Sphenomandibular ligament

c. Stylomandibular ligament

(a) Temporomandibular joint

(b) Upward and downward (hinge-like)
Forward and backward (gliding)
Side to side (gliding)

5-6

a. Oral vestibule

b. Oral airway opening

c. Oral cavity

d. Pharyngeal cavity

(a) gums and teeth; lips and cheeks

(b) anterior faucial pillars (palatoglossal arch)

5-7

a. Dorsum

b. Blade

c. Tip

d. Body

e. Root

(a) functional

(b) No

(c) taste buds

5-8

a. External pterygoid
b. Geniohyoid
c. Internal pterygoid
d. Digastric (anterior)
e. Mylohyoid
f. Masseter
g. Temporalis

5-9

a. Superior longitudinal
b. Vertical
c. Inferior longitudinal
d. Transverse

(a) intrinsic

(b) They are called intrinsic muscles of the tongue because both their origins and insertions are within the tongue.

5-10

a. Palatoglossus
b. Genioglossus
c. Hyoglossus
d. Styloglossus

(a) extrinsic

(b) They are called extrinsic muscles of the tongue because they have their origins in structures outside the tongue and their insertions in the tongue.

5-11

a. Zygomatic minor
b. Incisivus labii superioris
c. Zygomatic major
d. Risorius
e. Incisivus labii inferioris
f. Mentalis
g. Depressor labii inferioris
h. Orbicularis oris
i. Buccinator
j. Levator labii superioris
k. Levator anguli oris
l. Levator labii superioris aleque nasi
m. Depressor anguli oris
n. Platysma

5–12

(a) inferior; middle

(b) stylopharyngeus

(c) True

5–13

	Raise	Lower	Move Forward	Move Backward	Move Side to Side
Masseter	X			X	X
Temporalis	X			X	X
Internal pterygoid	X				X
External pterygoid		X	X		X
Digastric (anterior belly)		X			
Mylohyoid		X			
Geniohyoid		X			

5–14

__c__ Superior longitudinal
__h__ Inferior longitudinal
__e__ Vertical
__f__ Transverse
__b__ Styloglossus
__g__ Palatoglossus
__d__ Hyoglossus
__a__ Genioglossus

5-15

Upper Lip

Move upward
- Levator labii superioris
- Levator labii superioris aleque nasi (lip segment)
- Zygomatic minor

Move downward
- Orbicularis oris
- Depressor anguli oris

Evert (turn outward)
- Levator labii superioris

Lower Lip

Move upward
- Orbicularis oris
- Mentalis
- Levator anguli oris

Move downward
- Depressor labii inferioris
- Platysma

Evert (turn outward)
- Depressor labii inferioris
- Mentalis

Mouth Corners

Upward
- Orbicularis oris
- Zygomatic major
- Zygomatic minor
- Levator anguli oris
- Incisivus labii superioris

Downward
- Orbicularis oris
- Depressor anguli oris
- Incisivus labii inferioris
- Platysma

Backward and sideways
- Orbicularis oris
- Buccinator
- Risorius
- Zygomatic major
- Levator anguli oris
- Platysma

Upward and inward
- Orbicularis oris
- Incisivus labii superioris

Upward and sideways

Orbicularis oris

Zygomatic major

Levator anguli oris

Downward and sideways

Orbicularis oris

Platysma

Downward and inward

Orbicularis oris

Incisivus labii inferioris

Inward and toward midline

Orbicularis oris

Incisivus labii superioris

Incisivus labii inferioris

Compress Lips, Cheeks, and/or Mouth Corners Against Teeth and/or Alveolar Processes

Orbicularis oris

Buccinator

Risorius

Platysma

orbicularis oris

5–16

(a) oral vestibule

(b) length of the pharyngeal cavity

(c) change the length and change the cross-sectional dimensions of the oral vestibule and oral cavity

(d) True

(e) the muscular pressure exerted, surface tension between the two structures, and gravity.

(f) Pharynx
Velum
Hard palate
Alveolar process of the maxilla
Teeth
Lips

(g) Teeth
Other lip

(h) increase

(i) lower

(j) infinite (i.e., the highest possible)

(k) decreases

(l) increases

5–17

(a) IX (glossopharyngeal); X (vagus); XI (accessory)

(b) V (trigeminal)

(c) XII (hypoglossal); X (vagus)

(d) VII (facial)

(e) VII (facial)

5–18

Place of major constriction

Degree of major constriction

	Front	Central	Back
High	i beat ɪ bit		u tooth ʊ hook
Mid	e capon ɛ bet	ɝ word ɚ onward ʌ above ə above	o boast ɔ taught
Low	æ bat		ɑ calm

Degree of lip rounding

(a) alveolar process of the maxilla

(b) hard palate

(c) velum; posterior pharyngeal wall

(d) small

5-19

Manner of production

Place of production	Stop-plosive –	Stop-plosive +	Fricative –	Fricative +	Affricate –	Affricate +	Nasal –	Nasal +	Semivowel –	Semivowel +
Labial (lips)	p pole	b bowl						m sum		w watt
Labiodental (lip–teeth)			f fat	v vat						
Dental (tongue–teeth)			θ thigh	ð thy						
Alveolar (tongue–gum)	t toll	d dole	s seal	z zeal				n sun		l lot
Palatal (tongue–hard palate)			ʃ ash	ʒ azure	tʃ choke	dʒ joke				j,r yacht, rot
Velar (tongue–velum)	k coal	g goal						ŋ sung		
Glottal (vocal folds)			h hot							

(a) imploded

(b) affricate

(c) open

(d) semivowels

5-20

(a) If you were to watch the articulators produce a sequence of speech sounds (such as a word or a sentence), you would not be able to segment one sound from another. Rather, you would see the articulators moving continuously through one point to another with little to no hesitation. Interestingly, there is a relatively poor correspondence between the phonetic descriptors for vowels and consonants and the articulatory events associated with the creation of the speech sounds.

(b) the influence of one sound on another.

(c) Lip rounding during the production of /t/ in "two."

(d) Lip rounding during the production of /s/ in "caboose."

(e) Forward coarticulation provides evidence that the nervous system plans ahead for the production of upcoming sounds. For example, the plan for the production of the final /u/ in "construe" is manifested as the beginning of lip rounding that occurs during the production of sounds that come before the /u/. According to the theory of feature spreading, a look ahead operator within the nervous system scans ahead to determine the upcoming features in the sequence and, in those cases where a particular feature is not specified, anticipatory coarticulation of an upcoming feature can begin.

(f) Backward coarticulation appears to reflect the fact that the articulators have inertial properties, which means that they are not able to move instantaneously from one position to another. For example, the fact that the velopharynx remains open for a short period at the beginning of the vowel in the word "nap" indicates that it takes time for the velopharynx to move from an open configuration to a closed configuration.

(g) Articulatory Phonology; Gesture

5–21

__F__ *Revised:* The infant's pharyngeal-oral apparatus is smaller than an adult's pharyngeal-oral apparatus and different in configuration.

__T__ The infant's pharyngeal-oral apparatus continues to grow at least into adolescence and possibly adulthood.

__T__ Children have slower speech production rates than adults.

__F__ *Revised:* Children have more variable speech production movements than adults.

__T__ Adult-like pharyngeal-oral movements for speech production are not acquired until the teenage years.

__F__ *Revised:* Overall, the pharyngeal-oral apparatus gets larger with age in adults and changes the resonance characteristics accordingly. Specifically, the resonant frequencies become lower because the air spaces are larger.

__T__ Articulatory rate and overall speaking rate (inclusive of pauses) slow with age in adults.

__F__ *Revised:* The duration of speech segments becomes longer with age in adults. This is one reason that speech production is slower in older adults than younger adults.

__T__ Variability in speech production movements increases with age in adults.

__T__ The pharynx is longer in men than women.

__F__ *Revised:* During speech production the articulators tend to move faster in men than in women.

5-22

(a) /i/

(b) /ɑ/

(c) /u/

(d) lower lip

(e) True

(f) both force production and movements of selected articulators.

(g) movements of selected articulators.

(h) True

(i) an acrylic plate to fit the hard palate of the individual

(j) False

(k) dorsum of the tongue; lateral pharyngeal walls

(l) The lateral pharyngeal walls move inward during /ɑ/ productions and outward during /k/ productions.

Middle constrictor muscle

(m) One end of a small catheter is placed behind the lips (in the oral vestibule or farther back in the oral cavity) and the other end is connected to an air pressure transducer.

(n) Peak oral pressure is lower than if the velopharynx and lips were sealed airtight.

(o) Pressure on both sides of the constriction and airflow through the constriction

5–23

(a) Developmental speech sound articulation problems

Congenital craniofacial anomalies

Pierre Robin syndrome

Treacher Collins syndrome

Traumatic injuries

Cancer

Neuromotor diseases (cerebral palsy, muscular dystrophy, multiple sclerosis, etc.)

Hearing loss

(and many others)

(b) A glossectomy involves surgical removal (amputation) of the tongue, usually to remove cancerous tissue.

(c) /t/

/k/

/s/

/n/

(d) Dentist

Prosthodontist

Neurologist

Psychologist

Plastic surgeon

Otorhinolaryngologist

Speech-language pathologist

CHAPTER 6

6-1

A nerve is a bundle of axons in the PNS; a tract is a bundle of axons in the CNS.

6-2

Coronal plane

Horizontal plane

6-3

nuclei; grayish

6-4

A nucleus is a group of cell bodies (somata) clustered together *within* the CNS; a ganglion is a cluster of cell bodies just *outside* the CNS, either in the skull just outside the brainstem or along the vertebrae just outside the spinal cord. Ganglia typically contain the first sensory synapses for neuronal information being transmitted into the central nervous system.

6-5

Lateralization of function means that a certain function is represented by neuronal tissue in either the left or right hemisphere; many, if not most, speech and language functions are often said to be lateralized to the left hemisphere in a majority of humans. Specialization of function means that neuronal tissue is specialized for a function, such as the neural tissue in the occipital lobes (both left and right sides) being specialized for vision, or the ventral surface of the frontal lobes (both left and right sides) being specialized for executive function.

6–6

See Figure below.

(a) The view is in the sagittal plane.

(b) The lobes are identified on the figure below.

(c) The boundaries of the lobes (the ones that can be seen in this view) are labeled on the figure and include the central fissure (fissure of Rolando) that is the boundary between the frontal and parietal lobes, and the sylvian fissure (lateral fissure) that is the boundary between the temporal and frontal lobes (anterior part of fissure) and the temporal and parietal lobes (posterior part of fissure). Clear boundaries between the temporal and occipital lobes, and parietal and occipital lobes are not visible in this sagittal view of the left hemisphere

(d) The location of the primary motor cortex (PMC) and primary somatosensory cortex (PSC) is shown on the labeled figure; the PMC is the gyrus immediately anterior to the central fissure, and the PSC is the gyrus immediately posterior to the central fissure.

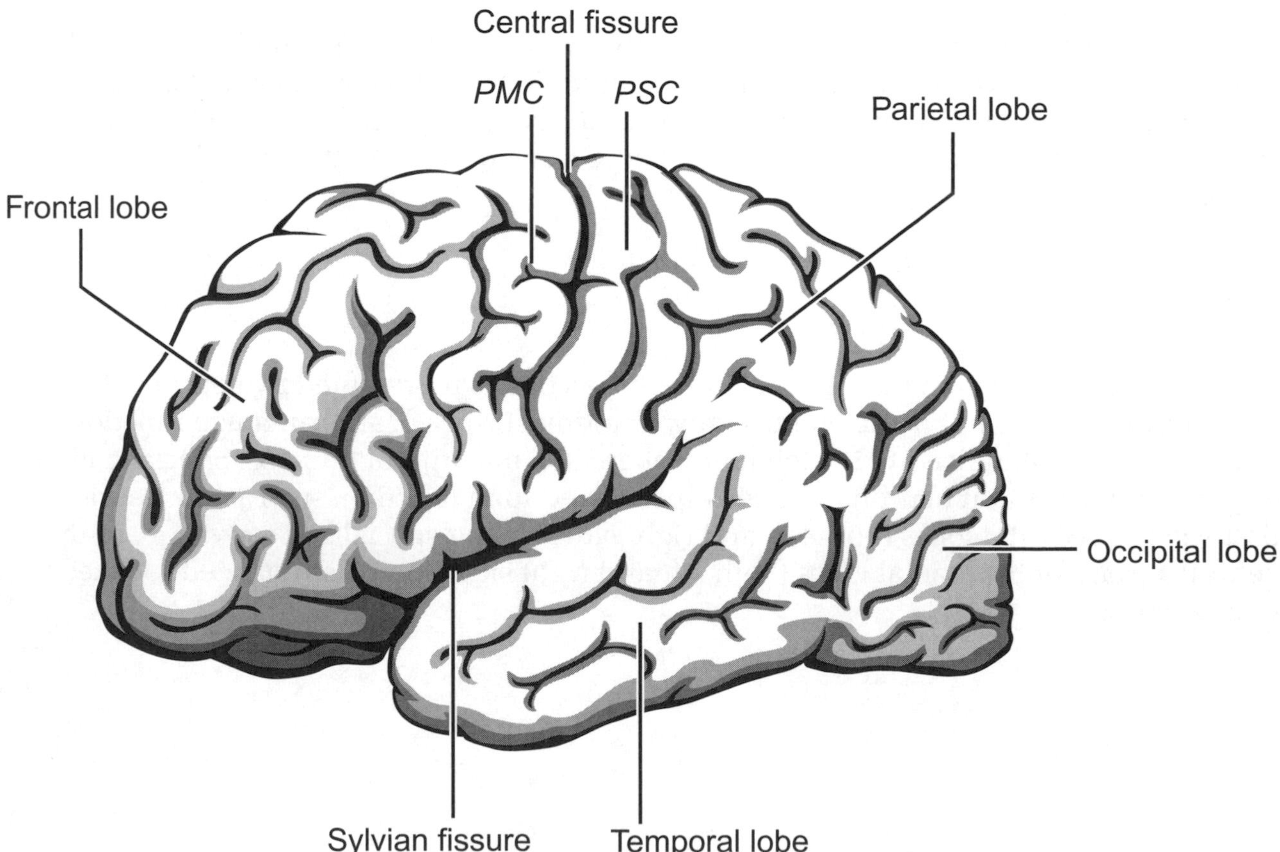

6-7

The frontal lobes are important for executive function, planning of action, and "programming" speech sequences (another form of planning of action).

6-8

The parietal lobes are important for integration of sensory information, body space awareness, and object recognition (as part of integration of sensory information and the attachment of that integration to meaning).

6-9

The superior temporal gyrus of the temporal lobe—the "top" gyrus of the temporal lobe—extends as a shelf of tissue toward the center of the cerebral hemispheres. The anterior part of this shelf of tissue (see Figure 6–7 in the textbook) contains the primary auditory cortex, or the cells that receive input most directly from the end-organ of hearing—the cochlea. Posterior to the primary auditory cortex is the planum temporale, a group of cells that serve as auditory association cortex, performing higher level analyses than those done in the anterior, primary auditory cortex. The planum temporale is thought to be very important to the higher level auditory analyses associated with speech and language perception. The reason why it is proper to say that the frequency arrangement of the basilar membrane is "projected" onto the cells in the primary auditory cortex is because, like the basilar membrane, there is strong evidence of tonotopic arrangement of cells in the primary auditory cortex (but *not* in the planum temporale).

6-10

(a) commissural

(b) association

(c) projection

6-11

The anatomical basis for imitating strings of syllables that are presented aurally (via the auditory system) is the "brain network" consisting of Wernicke's area, the arcuate fasciculus, Broca's area, and the orofacial part of the primary motor cortex. Presumably, the syllables enter the auditory system and are first analyzed in Wernicke's area. They are then sent via the arcuate fasciculus to Broca's area where they are prepared for production by means of an articulatory plan. Broca's area then sends this plan to the orofacial cells in the primary motor cortex, which send commands to the brainstem for execution of the plan.

6-12

The point is that even though in a mid-sagittal section, the fibers of the corpus callosum seem to be limited in their anterior, posterior, and dorsal extent (see Figure 6–5 in the textbook), when DTI images are made of the corpus callosum (see Figure 6–10 in the textbook) the fibers can clearly be seen to reach more anteriorly, more posteriorly, and more dorsally than shown by the midsagittal section.

6-13

The internal capsule is a thick bundle of fibers (white matter) that includes projection fibers, association fibers, and fibers connecting nuclei in the several loops discussed in the textbook. The location of the internal capsule can be described in the sagittal view (in either hemisphere) as immediately inferior to the corona radiata and above the superior margin of the midbrain; in fact, it is the gathering of the corona radiata into a tight bundle that forms the internal capsule. In a horizontal section through the thalamus and several subcortical nuclei of the basal ganglia, the internal capsule forms a boomerang pattern in the anteroposterior dimension with the "knee" of the boomerang forming the most medial part of the structure. The anterior projection of the boomerang—the anterior limb of the internal capsule—is just lateral to the caudate nucleus and medial to the putamen. The posterior projection—the posterior limb—is medial to the putamen and lateral to the thalamus.

6-14

See Figures 6–17 (p. 313) and 6–18 (p. 318) in the textbook for complete box-and-arrows drawing of these loops.

6–15

See labeled figure below.

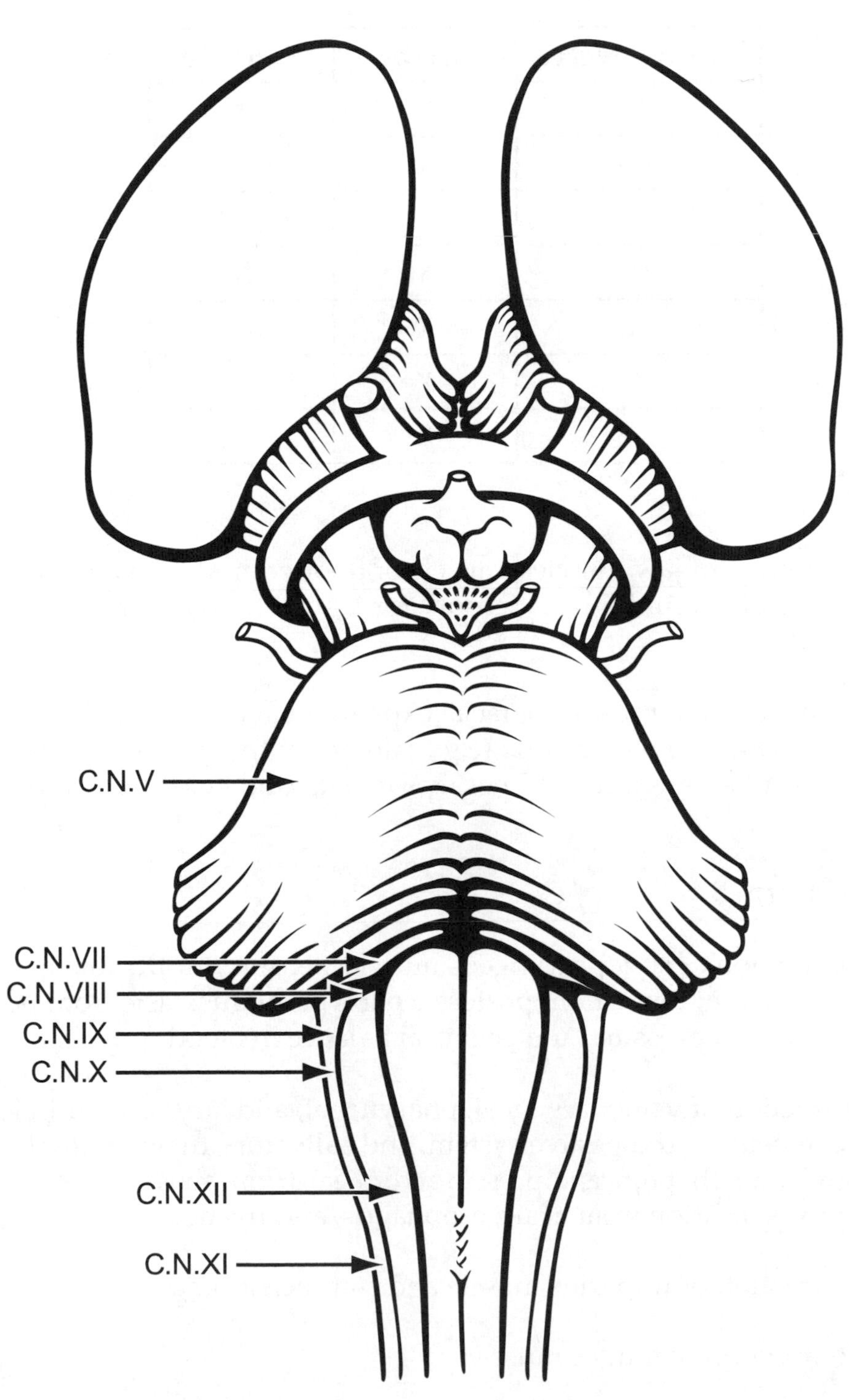

6–16

Example functions given below the table.

Cranial Nerve	Motor	Sensory
V	X	X
VII	X	X
VIII		X
IX	X	X
X	X	X
XI	X	
XII	X	

Motor for V: Contraction of jaw muscles, muscle of floor of mouth, one muscle of velopharynx, and one muscle of middle ear. Sensory for V: Touch, pain, temperature for face, and much of the oral cavity.

Motor for VII: Contraction of muscles of facial expression and one muscle of middle ear, plus control of certain autonomic function (e.g., salivary output to mouth). Sensory for VII: Touch from parts of external ear and perhaps tonsils, and taste from anterior two-thirds of tongue.

Sensory for VIII: Hearing.

Motor for IX: Contraction of stylopharyngeus muscle. Sensory for IX: Touch, pain, and pressure from the eardrum; touch from posterior parts of tongue; taste from posterior tongue; detection of blood pressure; and chemical balance in blood.

Motor for X: Contraction of velopharyngeal, pharyngeal, and laryngeal muscles; control of smooth muscle in heart and digestive system; and salivatory function in pharynx and larynx. Sensory for X: touch, pain, and pressure from eardrum; sensation from meninges, pharynx, and larynx; sensation from heart, esophagus, and trachea.

Motor for XI: Contraction of trapezius muscle and sternocleidomastoid muscle

Motor for XII: Contraction of tongue muscles.

6–17

Sign	Cranial Nerve	Side
Drooping corner of left lip, flattened left nasolabial fold, lack of furrowed brow on left forehead	VII	L
Failure of left side of soft palate to elevate for /a/	X	L
Lack of sensation (e.g., to touch with a Q-tip) on right side of upper lip	V	R
Absence of taste on both sides of posterior part of tongue	IX	L, R
Atrophy of right half of tongue	XII	R
Failure of left masseter to bulge when patient bites down	V	L

6–18

crus cerebri; pontine fascicles; pyramids

6–19

The cerebellum is connected to the rest of the CNS by three major tracts, the cerebellar peduncles. Broadly, the inferior cerebellar peduncle connects the cerebellum to parts of the brainstem and the spinal cord; the middle cerebellar peduncle connects the cerebellum to brainstem structures; and the superior cerebellar peduncle connects the cerebellum to the thalamus.

6–20

(a) A brainstem motor nucleus that is associated with more than one cranial nerve is the nucleus ambiguus. This columnar nucleus that runs the superior–inferior extent of the lateral medulla gives off fibers that contribute to cranial nerves IX (glossopharyngeal), X (vagus), and possibly XI (accessory).

(b) A brainstem sensory nucleus that is associated with multiple cranial nerves is the sensory nucleus of V, which receives fibers from cranial nerves V, VII, IX, and X.

6–21

In horizontal slices of the *midbrain*, the small hole in the posterior half of the section is the cut cerebral aqueduct (see, for example, Figure 6–23 in the textbook). This small hole is an excellent landmark for midbrain slices because the aqueduct widens into the fourth ventricle as it enters the pons. A horizontal slice through the midbrain may also be identified by the strip of tissue on the anterior edge of the section, the crus cerebri, and by the substantia nigra, which is immediately posterior and stains opposite to the crus cerebri. (The crus cerebri is a tract; the substantia nigra is a nucleus. See the contrast in Figure 6–23 of the textbook.) Horizontal slices of the *pons* can be identified by the fibers running across (left to right and right to left) the ventral half of the section, these being fibers of the cerebellar peduncles; by the wide cavity, the fourth ventricle, just posterior to the posterior edge of the section; and by the two bumps of tissue in the floor of the fourth ventricle, these being the abducens nuclei. Figures 6–24 and 6–26 in the textbook show these pontine landmarks. Horizontal slices of the *medulla* can be identified by the unusually shaped olivary nuclei in the ventrolateral part of the slice and by the ventral pyramids separated by the well-defined anterior fissure (see Figure 6–27 in the textbook).

6–22

See the box-and-arrows figure below. The basic function of the stretch reflex is to detect stretch of main (striated) muscle fibers and to "correct" the stretch back to the pre-stretch length by means of the fast loop between the muscle spindle and the alpha motor neurons in the spinal cord or brainstem that innervate these same muscle fibers, and cause them to contract to counter the stretch.

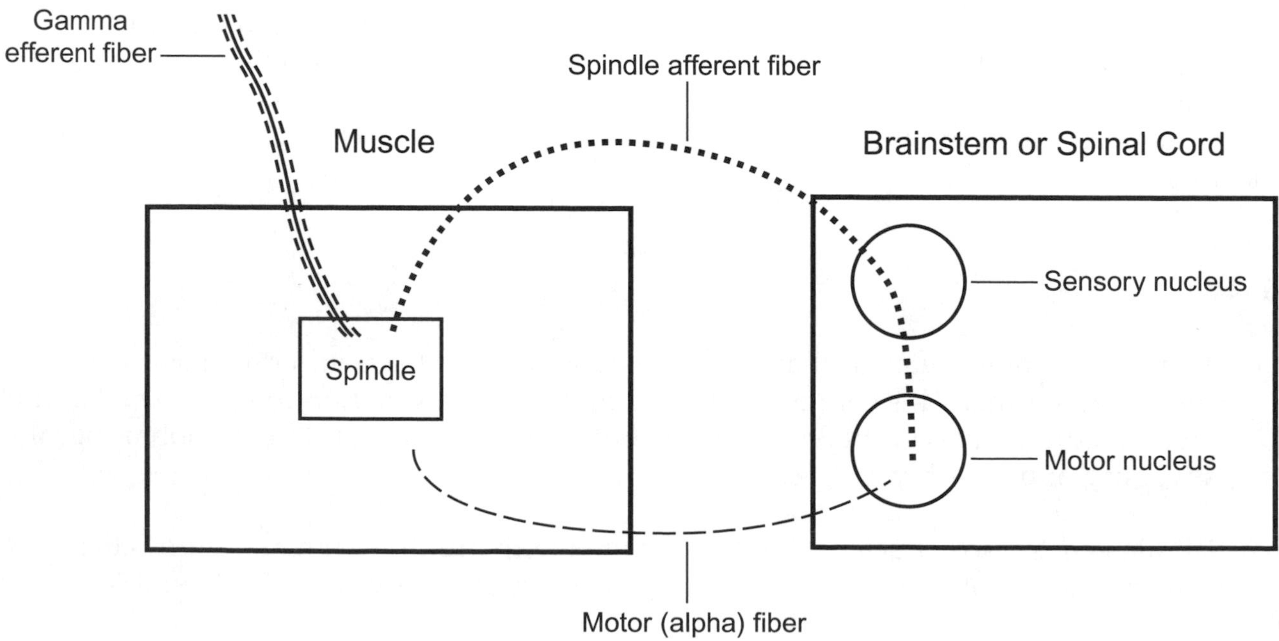

6-23

It is important to know the innervation pattern of the cranial nerve nuclei because this knowledge allows you to make good estimates of site-of-lesion from clinical signs. For example, it is important to know that facial nucleus neurons that innervate muscles of the upper face are innervated bilaterally, whereas facial nucleus neurons that innervate muscles of the lower face are innervated contralaterally. Knowledge of this innervation pattern allows a clinician to interpret lower lip drooping on the left side, with no observable weakness in the upper left half of the face, as an upper motor neuron lesion on the right side. Another example is how the bilateral innervation of the nucleus ambiguus permits an inference of lower motor neuron damage when a person's velum elevates on only one side when he or she is asked to say "ah." Because the nucleus ambiguus contains the cells that control elevation of the soft palate, their bilateral innervation means that if the lesion was in the upper motor neuron of one side, the healthy, opposite side would provide innervation to these cells, allowing both sides of the velum to lift when saying "ah." If the velum elevates only on one side when the person says "ah," the logical inference is that the lesion is in the lower motor neuron on the side showing weakness—in the final common pathway to the muscles of the velopharynx.

6-24

"Upper motor neuron lesion" means that a lesion is somewhere between the cortical motor neurons, and the brainstem and cranial nerve (or spinal cord) motor cells. An upper motor neuron lesion cannot be *in* the brainstem or spinal cord motor cells—that would be a lower motor neuron lesion.

6-25

See labeled drawing below.

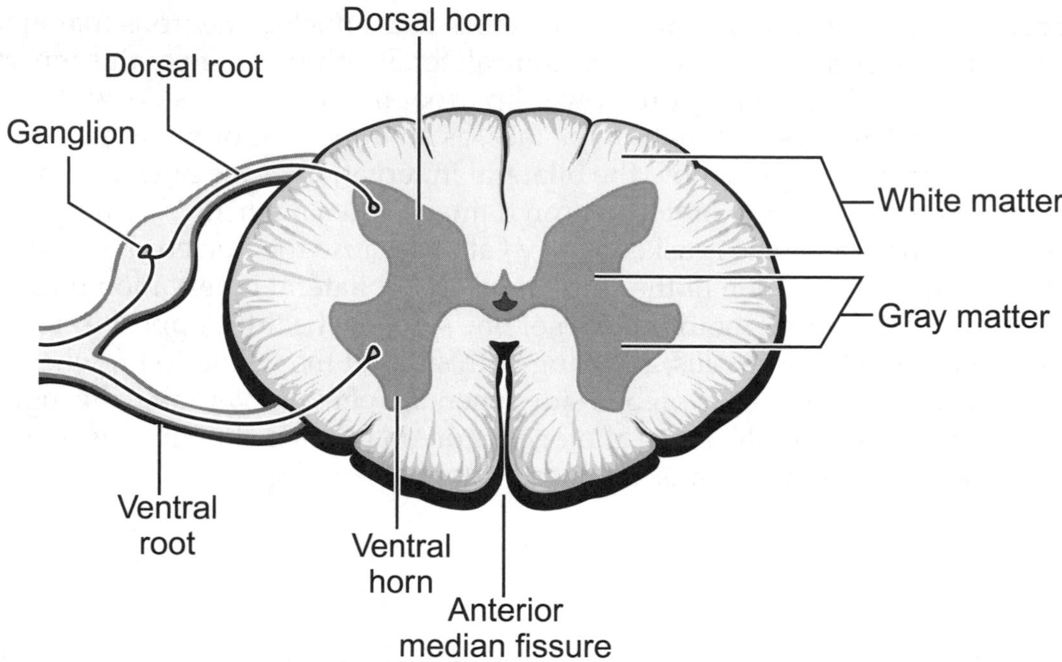

6-26

The primary difference between neurons and glial cells is that neurons are the *signaling cells* of the nervous system—they transmit information from one cell to the next—whereas glial cells serve more "housekeeping" roles in the nervous system. These housekeeping roles include clean up of waste material, nutritive support of neurons, and the creation and deposit of myelin onto neuron axons.

6-27

Neurotransmitters are manufactured in the cell soma by the action of the organelles described in the textbook. The neurotransmitters manufactured within the soma, or a chemical precursor of the neurotransmitter eventually stored in the terminal segment, are transported from the soma to the terminal segments of the neuron along microtubules, which are like tracks connecting the soma to the terminal segments. The manufactured molecules "ride" down these microtubules, from soma to terminal segment, and sometimes undergo further chemical change as they make the trip to the terminal segment. When the neurotransmitter molecules reach the terminal segment, they are packaged for storage and future release into the synaptic cleft.

6–28

The neuromuscular junction qualifies as a synapse because it has a presynaptic membrane (the membrane of the terminal segment of the motor axon), neurotransmitter packaged within the terminal segment of this axon, and a postsynaptic membrane called a motor endplate in which specialized receptors are embedded (this is analogous to the postsynaptic membranes of the dendrites in the CNS, which contain receptors specialized for particular neurotransmitters). The neurotransmitter at neuromuscular junctions is acetylcholine and the receptors in the postsynaptic membrane are specialized to receive acetylcholine (that is, acetylcholine binds to these receptors).

6–29

The soma membrane is so important to signal transmission within the CNS because its permeability can be changed selectively and at different times to the passage of different molecules. More specifically, the membrane can have its properties changed so that positively charged ions are allowed to pass through it or are blocked from passing through it. Depending on whether the membrane is permeable to positive ions or impermeable to them, the neuron may or may not fire a signal that is transmitted to another neuron. The membrane changes its properties according to the effect of enzymes acting upon it. A disease process that affects the ability of the membrane to change its permeability selectively (to different ions) and at proper times may affect the ability of neurons to conduct signaling in a proper way.

6–30

The meninges have three layers: the most superficial being the dura mater, the next deep being the arachnoid mater, and the deepest being the pia mater. The dura adhere to the inner surface of the skull and the pia follow the contours of the gyri and sulci of the cerebral hemispheres. The meninges are related to the ventricular system because cerebrospinal fluid (CSF) flows in the subarachnoid space, which is a small volume between the arachnoid mater and pia mater, and CSF is returned to the venous blood flow via the arachnoid villa, which protrude from the arachnoid space into the sinuses between layers of the dura mater (see Figure 6–36 in the textbook).

6–31

See the labeled drawing below. Adjacent to the frontal horn of the lateral ventricle: caudate nucleus and corpus callosum; adjacent to the occipital horn of lateral ventricle: corpus callosum; adjacent to temporal horn of lateral ventricle: tail of caudate nucleus and hippocampus; adjacent to third ventricle: thalamus; adjacent to cerebral aqueduct: midbrain tissue (central gray of midbrain); adjacent to fourth ventricle: cerebellum, pons, and medulla; adjacent to central canal: gray matter of spinal cord.

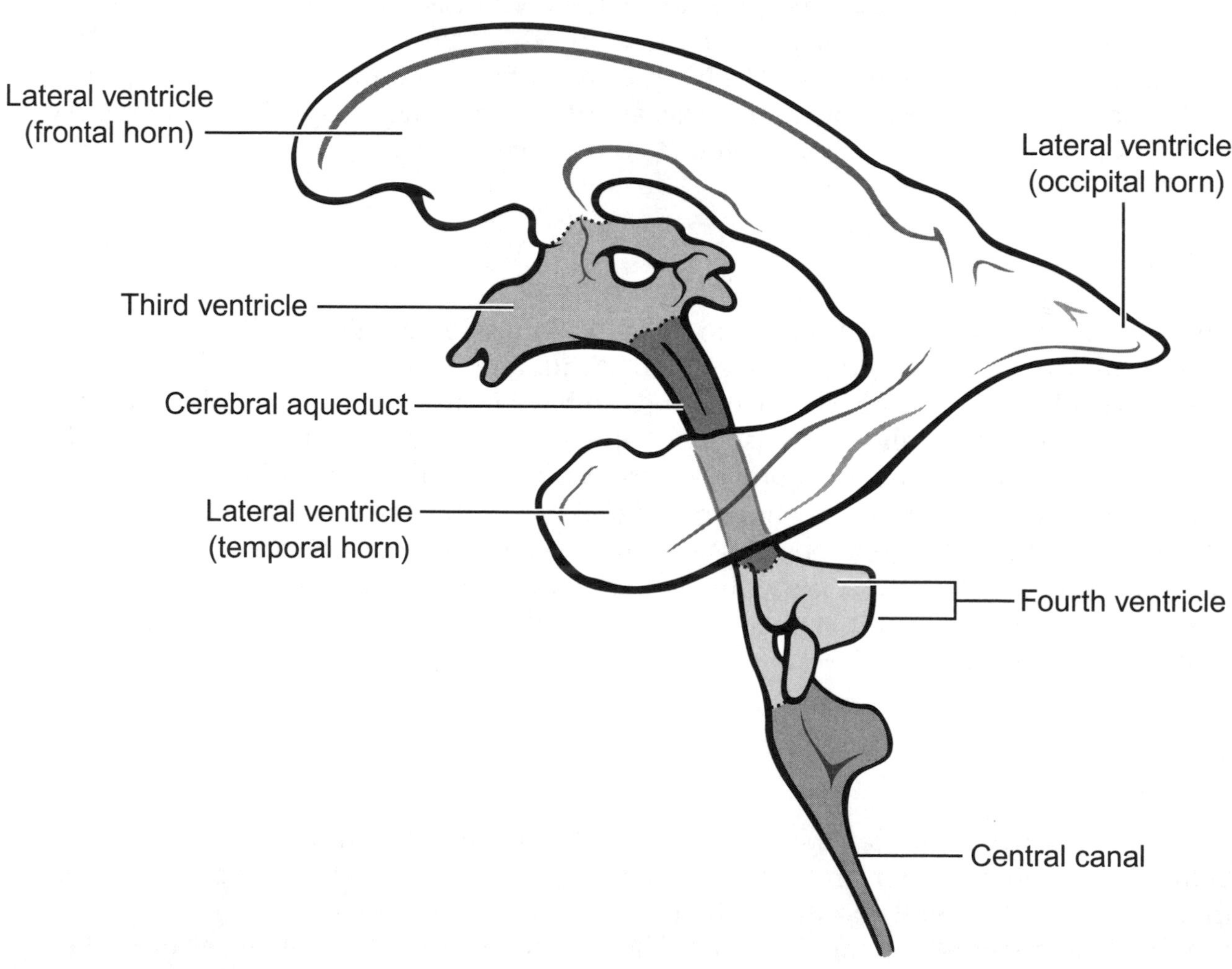

6-32

(a) The distinction between the anterior and posterior blood supply of the brain is based on the primary origin of the blood. The anterior supply in a hemisphere derives from the internal carotid artery on the same side of that hemisphere, whereas the posterior supply derives from the basilar artery, an axial artery formed by the converging vertebral arteries.

(b) The Circle of Willis is a connection of arteries at the base of the brain, formed by arteries that are branches of the internal carotid and basilar arteries. The circle of arteries includes the posterior cerebral arteries, the posterior communicating arteries, the anterior cerebral arteries, and the anterior communicating arteries.

(c) The MCA is so important to speech and language function because it is the main supply to the cortical and subcortical structures of the frontal, temporal, and parietal lobes (typically left hemisphere) that have been implicated in speech and language functions of the brain. Strokes involving the left MCA typically result in some loss of speech and language function, the severity of which depends on whether the loss of blood flow is general (meaning, at the origin of the MCA) or more local (as in one of the smaller arteries given off by the MCA to, for example, regions of the frontal lobe in the vicinity of Broca's area).

6-33

In DIVA, the anatomical distinction between apraxia of speech and dysarthria is that "planning" tissue is located in the lateral-ventral pre-motor cortex (lvPMC), an area just anterior to the primary motor cortex where cells for control of orofacial structures are located. "Execution" tissue is located in the orofacial region of the primary motor cortex, close to where the primary motor cortex meets the sylvian fissure. In DIVA, damage to lvPMC results in apraxia of speech, while damage to orofacial regions of primary motor cortex results in dysarthria.

CHAPTER 7

7-1

Both force functions increase as the *x*-axis value increases. Recoil force increases with increased distance from the rest position (stated in alternate terms, with increased stretch or compression from the rest position of an elastic object) and inertial force increases with the mass of an object, measured here in grams.

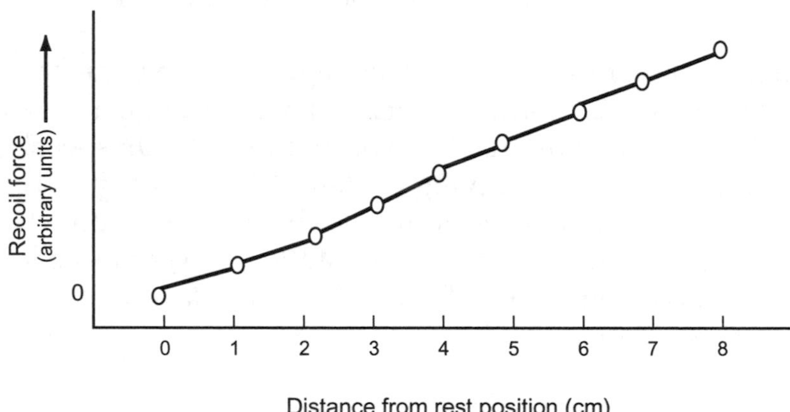

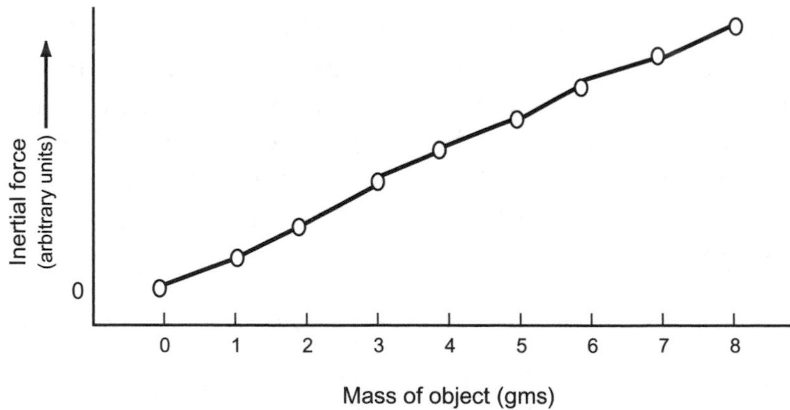

7-2

Original Time Value	Stated in Alternative Time Units
10 ms	0.010 s
4 s	4000 ms
0.1 s	100 ms
0.0001 s	0.1 ms
325 ms	0.325 s
1.8 ms	0.0018 s
15 s	15000.00 ms
1325 ms	1.325 s

7-3

(a) The period of vibration is 2 ms; this is known because the time interval of 6 ms shown below the sinusoid spans 3 complete cycles of vibration.

(b) For a period of 2 ms, the frequency is $F = 1/T = F = 1/0.002 = 500$ Hz.

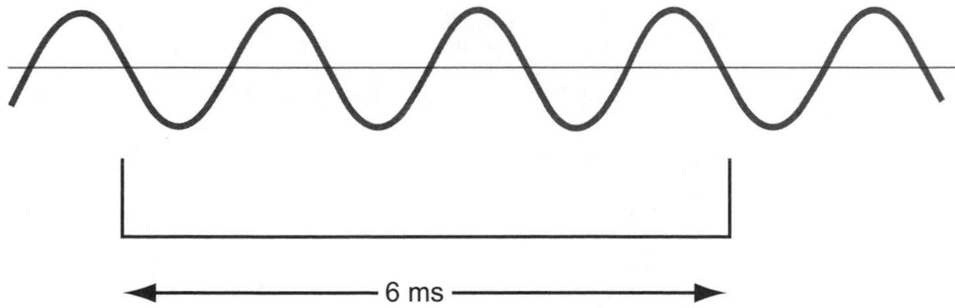

7-4

Top: Starting point; location of maximum pressure.

Bottom: Starting point; location of P_{atm} following the first maximum pressure.

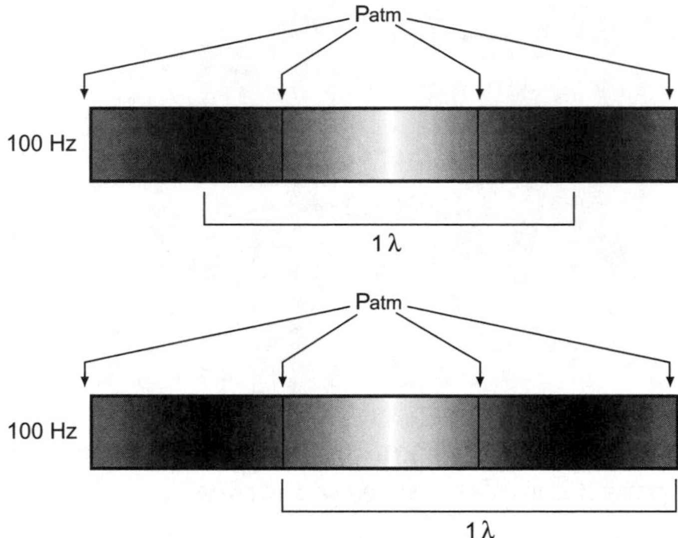

7-5

Using the formula $\lambda = c/f$, where c (speed of sound in air) = 33,600 cm/s, the wavelengths for the frequencies on the x-axis are as follows: 100 Hz: 336 cm (~132 inches); 500 Hz: 67.2 cm (~26.5 in); 1000 Hz: 33.6 cm (~13.2 in); 1500 Hz: 22.4 cm (~8.83 in); 2000 Hz: 16.8 cm (~6.62 in).

The plot below shows the data in centimeters; the y-axis is scaled from 0 to 350 cm to capture the full range of the data.

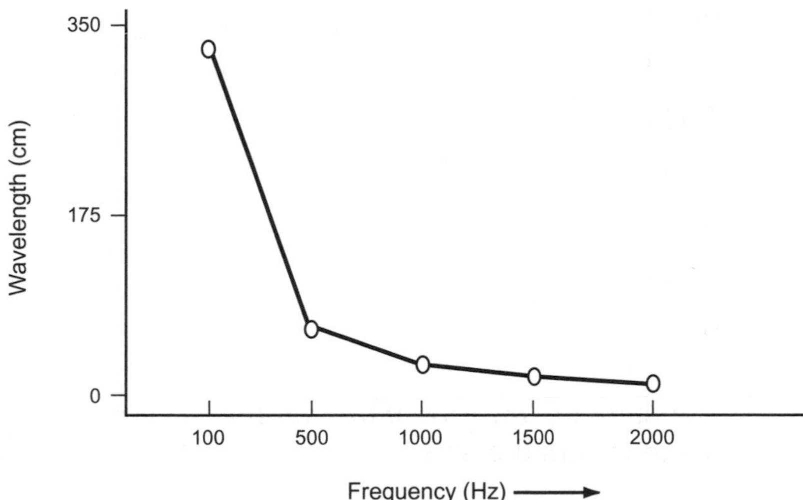

7-6

(a) Make the circular motion *faster* (faster motion will produce shorter periods).

(b) Make the circular motion *slower* (slower motion will increase the period, which is associated with a decreased frequency).

(c) Make the circle *bigger*; motion around a bigger circle will be associated with a waveform having greater maximum amplitude.

7-7

Using the formula D = A sin (ϕ), the amplitudes for the angles to be plotted are:

Time	Angle	Amplitude
0	0	0
1	40	6.428
2	80	9.848
3	120	8.660
4	160	3.420
5	200	−3.420
6	240	−8.660
7	280	−9.848
8	320	−6.428
9	360	0

Note that the graph below, showing the plot of the computed amplitudes, is a sine wave; the numbers on the *x*-axis represent the time-steps shown in the left-most column immediately above.

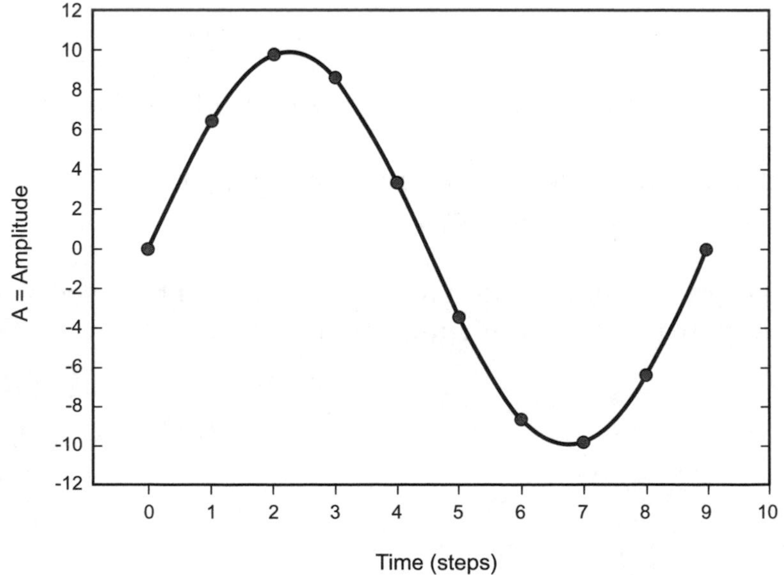

7-8

(a) The periods are 2 ms (500 Hz); 0.66 ms (1500 Hz); 0.4 ms (2500 Hz); and 0.28 ms (3500 Hz). These were computed by applying the formula T = 1/F.

(b) The period of the complex periodic waveform is T = 2 ms, because the period of a complex periodic waveform is always the period of the lowest frequency component.

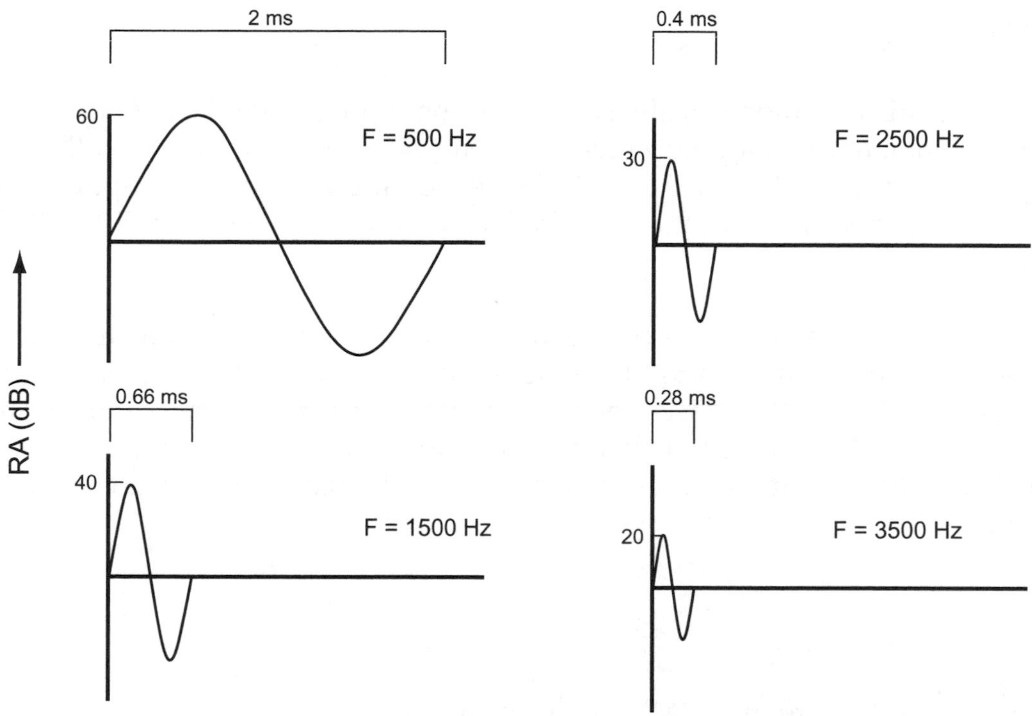

7-9

(a) Spectrum (*b*) shows a complex periodic acoustic event.

(b) Spectrum (*a*) a complex aperiodic acoustic event.

(c) This is known by examination of the frequency components shown in the two spectra. In (*b*), the higher frequency components are related to the fundamental frequency (the lowest frequency) by whole number multiples; in (*a*), they are not.

7-10

A time-domain display of an acoustic event shows amplitude of the signal as a function of time; a frequency-domain display shows the relative amplitudes of the frequency components of the signal (amplitude by frequency) averaged over some user-selected time interval (which is often short, at least for applications in speech acoustics).

7-11

(a) 1750 Hz (7 × 250).

(b) Because the third harmonic is always 3 times the fundamental frequency (F0; F0 = first harmonic). In the frequency series 100, 300, 500, 700, 900, and so forth, the third harmonic is 3 × 100 = 300 Hz. 500 Hz is the third frequency component of this harmonic spectrum, but it is the fifth harmonic of the spectrum (5 X 100 Hz = 500 Hz).

(c) Phase; different phase relations between the component sinusoids would produce a waveform that maintained the same period but showed different details in the amplitude-by-time pattern. The frequency components remain the same but the way in which all the individual components sum to produce the amplitude-by-time fluctuations is different when phase relations are changed among the component sinusoids.

7-12

(a) The two properties are mass (M) and stiffness (K).

(b) To decrease the resonant frequency of a vibratory object, increase M or decrease K (changing one while the other is held constant).

(c) If the M and K of a vibrating object are changed so that the simultaneous changes offset each other, the properties change but the resonant frequency stays the same. For example, the frequency-lowering effect of increased M could be offset by the frequency-raising effect of increased K; the overall result being the same resonant frequency as before the properties were changed.

7-13

The conceptual properties that make mechanical and Helmholtz resonators analogous are that the masses and stiffnesses of mechanical resonators—using objects having different weights (masses) and springs that vary in the degree to which they can be stretched or compressed (stiffness)—are analogous to the "plug" of air that occupies the neck of a Helmholtz resonator (the mass) and the volume of air that occupies the bowl of the resonator (the compliance, which is the inverse of stiffness).

7-14

(a) The "K" in Equation (1) represents stiffness, and the variable "V" in Equation (2) is the acoustic analog to "K." In the equation for the resonant frequency of a Helmholtz resonator, "V" stands for the volume of the resonator bowl (Figure 7–12 in the textbook, and discussion on pp. 402–403), and increases in "V" decrease the stiffness (increase the compliance) of the resonator. "V" and "K" are essentially the same variable, with the qualification that increases in "V" make the acoustic resonant system less stiff (more compliant); whereas, increases in "K" make the mechanical resonant system more stiff. A larger "V" means the air molecules are easier to displace with an applied force (i.e., they have more room to be displaced by an applied force), which is similar to a lesser value of "K," which indicates that the spring is more easily displaced by an applied force.

(b) The "M" in Equation (1) represents mass, and the variables "S" and "l" in Equation (2) are both acoustic analogs to "M." The acoustic variable "l" is directly analogous to the "M" in a mechanical resonant system because increasing the length of the resonator neck is like adding weight to a mass (in the acoustic resonator, there are more air molecules in a longer plug of air with all other factors being equal). The acoustic variable "S" is *functionally* analogous to the mechanical "M"; as "S" decreases, the speed of air molecules moving through the neck increases and this creates increased inertia because the molecules have to be accelerated to greater speeds and decelerated from those greater speeds. Greater acceleration/deceleration requirements are functionally equivalent to the effect of greater mass—more time is required to achieve the top speeds when the opening of the neck is narrower.

7-15

The resonant frequencies of tubes occur at frequencies having wavelengths whose pressure characteristics "match" the ends of the tubes. At a closed end, there must be a pressure maximum along the wavelength; at an open end, the pressure must equal atmospheric pressure. A wavelength that satisfies these requirements will set up a "standing wave" within the tube, generating maximum pressures and therefore maximum amplitudes of vibration (consistent with the definition of resonance: a frequency at which there is maximal vibratory energy). This pressure-matching criterion is met by the wavelengths of *many* frequencies, as illustrated in Figures 7–14 and 7–15 of the textbook. Multiple standing waves will be established in a vibrating tube: the tube, therefore, has multiple resonant frequencies.

7–16

The resonant frequencies for a tube open at both ends and with the three lengths (8, 12, 16 cm) are given in this table:

Tube Length (cm)	R1	R2	R3
8	2100	4200	6300
12	1400	2800	4200
16	1050	2100	3150

These resonances were computed with the formula $f_r = n * c/2l$, where $n = 1, 2, 3 \ldots$ n, c = speed of sound in air (33,600 cm/s), and l = tube length. See the graph under Answer 7–17 for the plotted data and a brief summary of the results.

7–17

The resonant frequencies for a tube closed at one end with the three lengths are given in this table:

Tube Length (cm)	R1	R2	R3
8	1050	3150	5250
12	700	2100	3500
16	525	1575	2625

These resonances were computed with the formula $f_r = (2n - 1) * c/4l$, where $n = 1, 2, 3 \ldots$ n, c = speed of sound in air, and l = tube length. The graph below shows the plotted data for both tubes (open at both ends, unfilled symbols; closed at one end, filled symbols; R1 = circles, R2 = boxes, R3 = triangles).

The summary of these data is that the resonant frequencies of all tubes decrease as the length of the tube increases; when tube length is the same for tubes open at both ends versus closed at one end (e.g., 12 cm), the resonances of a tube closed at one end are lower than the resonances of tube open at both ends.

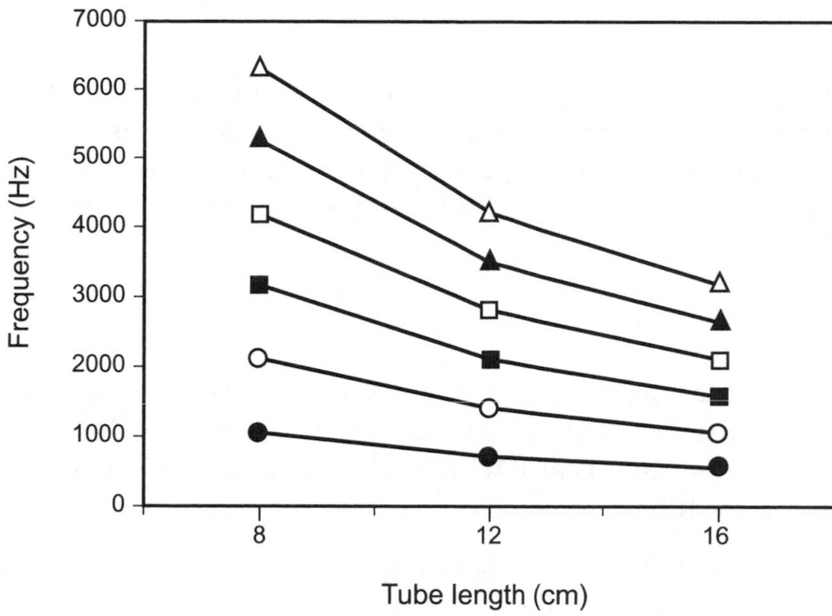

7-18

The formula for the resonances of a tube open at both ends is called the half-wavelength rule because the lowest resonance of the tube is a frequency whose wavelength is twice the length of the tube (i.e., half the wavelength "fits" into the tube to match the pressures along the wavelength to the pressures at the ends of the tube). The formula for the resonances of a tube closed at one end and open at the other end is called the quarter-wavelength rule because the lowest resonance of the tube is a frequency whose wavelength is four times the length of the tube (i.e., a quarter of the wavelength "fits" into the tube to match the pressures along the wavelength to the pressures at the ends of the tube).

7-19

(a) The resonance curve shown by the dashed line must be from a Helmholtz resonator, and the resonance curve shown by the solid line must be from the tube resonator.

(b) This is because the dashed resonance curve has only a single peak (i.e., a single resonance), which is characteristic of Helmholtz resonators; the solid line shows multiple peaks (multiple resonances), which is characteristic of tube resonators.

7-20

There are multiple locations of maximum pressure within a resonating tube because the multiple superimposed resonance modes have multiple locations of maximum pressure throughout the length of the tube, especially for the higher frequency resonances where the pressure distributions involve multiple wavelengths that "fit" inside the tube.

7-21

The resonant frequency was estimated from the curve by dropping a vertical line from the peak of the curve to the frequency (x) axis and noting where the line intersects the axis. As shown below, the intersection is at 1000 Hz, so the resonant frequency indicated by this curve is, by definition, 1000 Hz.

The bandwidth was estimated by designating the amplitude of the curve at its peak as 0 dB and scaling the y-axis in "dB down" steps (in 1 dB increments) from this 0 dB point. A horizontal line was extended from –3 dB across the graph to intersect the resonance curve along its left and right "tails," and from these intersection points vertical lines were dropped to the frequency (x) axis (see left and right dashed lines in figure below). The left line intersects the frequency axis at roughly 790 Hz, the right vertical line at roughly 1240 Hz. The bandwidth is therefore 1240 minus 790 Hz, or 450 Hz, which is the frequency range between the 3-dB down points on the resonance curve.

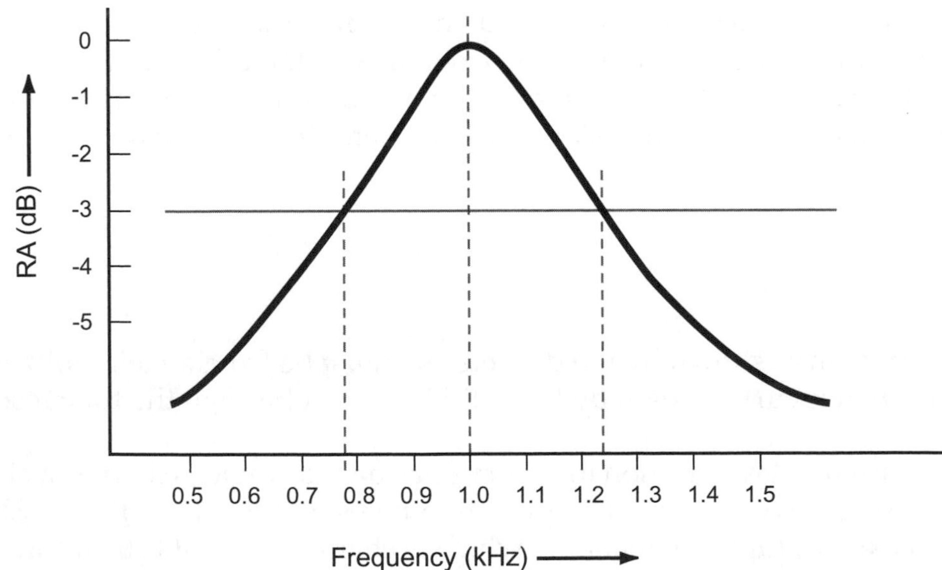

7–22

Vibratory energy is lost in the vocal tract by friction (molecules rubbing against each other and against the walls of the vocal tract), absorption of vibratory energy in air by structures of the vocal tract, and radiation of sound from the outlet of the vocal tract (the lip section of the vocal tract) to the atmosphere.

7–23

To say that a resonator "shapes" an input is to say that the amplitudes in an input signal are emphasized or de-emphasized by the resonance curve of a resonator. At frequency locations where a resonance curve has high amplitude, the energy in the input signal is "passed" and output at high levels; at frequency locations where the resonance curve has low amplitude, energy in the input signal barely "makes it through" as output. This description is basically the same as a description of a filter. A filter allows certain frequencies to pass through and "rejects" other frequencies. Therefore, a resonance curve can be thought of as a filter that is imposed on an input signal (see Figure 7–18 in the textbook).

7–24

Resonance curve (a) shows the more lightly-damped resonator, because its bandwidth is much narrower than the bandwidth shown in (b). The two waveforms shown below labeled (a) and (b) correspond to the spectra (a) and (b) in this question. Waveform (a) takes a longer time to "die out," for its amplitude to diminish over time to zero, as compared to waveform (b). The longer decay time is consistent with less energy loss.

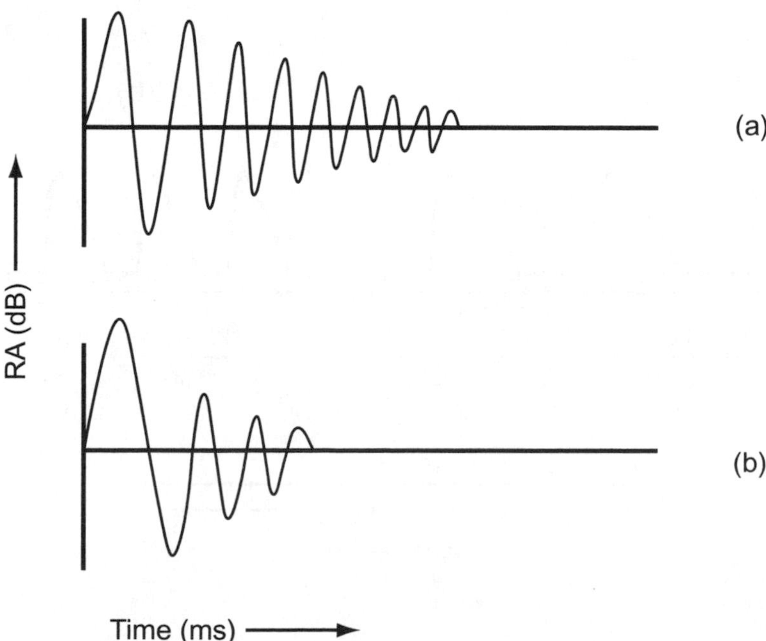

CHAPTER 8

8-1

(a) The Ag function in (a) has the longer closed phase, as indicated by the longer horizontal line, just above the baseline, between the "open" parts of the cycle.

(b) The Ag function in (b) has a higher fundamental frequency because the period of the cycles in (b) is shorter than the period of the cycles in (a) (see the marked periods below).

(c) A rough estimate of the F0 in both glottal waveforms was determined as follows. First, the common time axis for both waveforms is shown by a line length labeled as equivalent to 15 ms. The length of the line was measured with a millimeter rule as 66 mm (line length may be different in the printed version), so to determine the conversion of distance to time, divide the time (15 ms) by the length of the time line (66 mm) to find that 1 mm = 0.23 ms. Using this distance-to-time conversion, the period of a single glottal cycle was measured for both waveforms by choosing the instant of glottal closure as the starting point and the succeeding instant of glottal closure as the ending point of a cycle (see the boundaries of the marked periods in the figure below). The cycle in glottal waveform (a) was 22 mm long, which when converted to time equals T = 22 × .23 = 5.1 ms; F = 1/T gives F =1/.0051 = 196 Hz; the cycle in glottal waveform (b) was 12 mm long, which converted to time equals T = 12 × .23 = 2.76 ms; F = 1/T gives F =1/.00276 = 362 Hz. Your measurement of the time line may differ slightly from the one here, but the results should not be too different from the F0s given here.

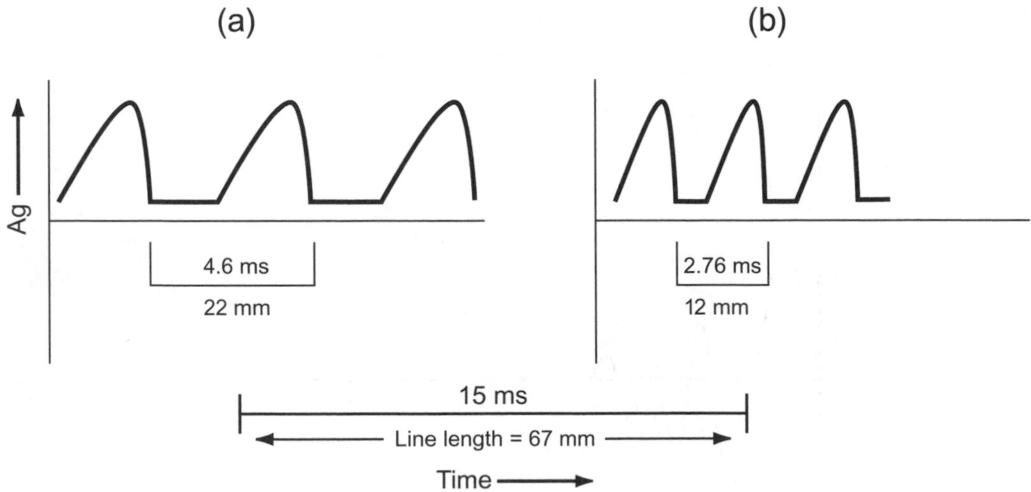

8-2

When a speech signal is recorded in front of the lips, it contains the influences of the acoustic result of both the vibrating vocal folds and the resonating vocal tract. To recover the part due only to the vibrating vocal folds (the glottal waveform), the resonances of the vocal tract must be removed from the recorded signal. This can be done by applying an inverse filter to the recorded signal. This filter is a mirror image of the resonances of the vocal tract, as if the resonance curve determined for a particular vocal tract configuration is "flipped" on the *y*-axis (i.e., the relative amplitude axis). When the signal recorded in front of the lips is processed by this "flipped" resonance curve, the resonant frequencies of the vocal tract are filtered out of the signal, leaving only the glottal waveform at the output of the filter.

8-3

The adjustment to the glottal waveform is shown below. The adjustment involves decreasing the slope (speed) of the closing phase, shown by the light gray line for each of the three cycles superimposed on the original glottal waveform. This adjustment in vocal fold vibration will decrease the energy in the higher harmonics of the glottal spectrum. The F0 is not changed because the periods of the glottal waveform remain the same as they were before the speed of the closing phase was adjusted. This occurs because the slower closing phase is also associated with a *shorter* closed phase. The sum of the open phase plus closed phase—that is, the period of vocal fold vibration—remains the same in the original versus the closing-phase adjusted waveforms.

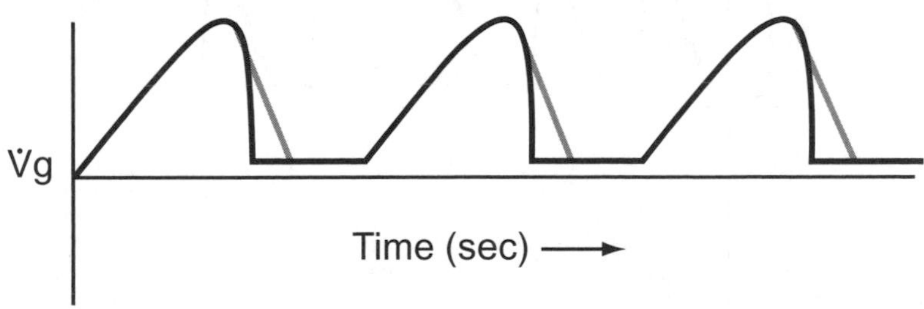

8-4

The new waveform shows a shorter period than the original waveform. (This can be deduced by simple visual analysis of the greater number of cycles in the lower, as compared to upper graph: both waveforms have the same time scale shown by the 10-ms calibration bar). The shorter period of the new waveform means that the fundamental frequency (F0) is higher, and therefore the harmonics of the glottal spectrum are more widely spaced than those of the original glottal spectrum. Because the glottal spectrum is composed of a consecutive-integer series of harmonics, the higher the F0, the greater the frequency range between consecutive harmonics.

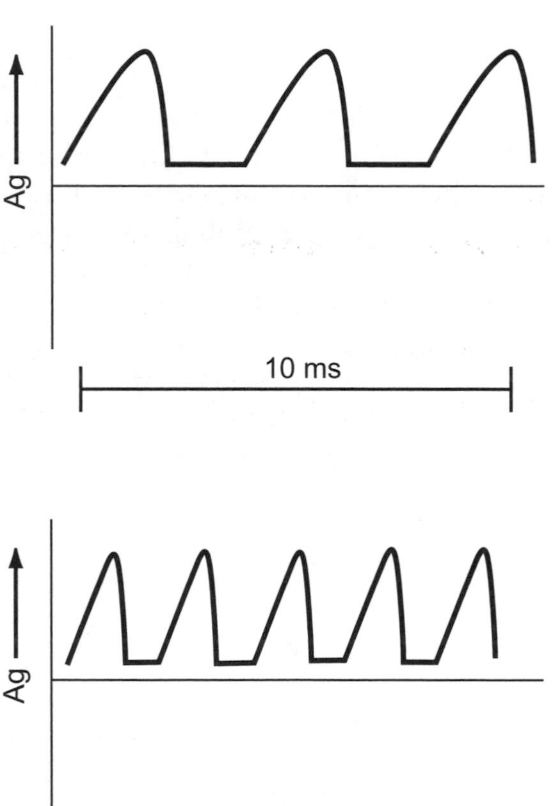

8-5

(a) "Tilt of the glottal spectrum" refers to the decrease in harmonic amplitude with increasing frequency of the harmonics. A glottal spectrum with rapidly decreasing harmonic amplitudes, as frequency increases, is said to be very tilted; a spectrum with harmonic amplitudes that do not decrease very dramatically with increasing frequency is said to be less tilted. As explained in the textbook, a glottal spectrum with no tilt (a theoretical example, not possible for natural glottal spectra) would be one in which all harmonics had the same amplitude (i.e., a flat spectrum). A glottal spectrum with infinite tilt (again, theoretical) would be one in which there was only a single harmonic, the F0.

(b) The "normal" glottal spectrum has harmonics whose amplitudes decrease by about 12 dB for each octave increase in harmonic frequency (e.g., for an F0 of 100 Hz the harmonic amplitude at 600 Hz is about 12 dB less than at 300 Hz, and the harmonic amplitude at 1200 Hz is about 12 dB less than at 600 Hz). A glottal spectrum less tilted than the normal 12 dB per octave would have an overall tilt of about 8 dB per octave (anything less than 12 dB per octave).

(c) Tilt of the glottal spectrum is primarily controlled by the speed of the closing phase of vocal fold vibration; faster than normal closing speeds result in less tilted spectra, slower than normal closing speeds result in more tilted spectra.

8–6

The clinical significance of the relationship between the cyclic motions of vocal fold vibration and the glottal spectrum produced by the vibration is as follows: Voice quality is dependent on the "tilt" of the glottal spectrum, with hyperfunctional voices (those sounding relatively "pressed") having a spectrum tilted less than normal (too much energy in the higher harmonics) and hypofunctional voices (those sounding relatively "breathy" or weak) having a spectrum tilted more than normal (too little energy in the higher harmonics). Clinically, voices with a pressed quality can often be inferred to have a closing phase of vocal fold vibration that is too fast, and voices with breathy or weak quality can be inferred to have a closing phase that is too slow. Other factors may also account for variations in voice quality, but the speed of the closing phase as well as the duration of the closed phase (which is often correlated with the speed of the closing phase, as described in the textbook) make a strong contribution to voice quality variation along the hypo-hyperfunctional continuum.

8–7

The correct acoustic resonator model for the vocal tract is a tube closed at one end because the resonances of the vocal tract are "excited" each time the vocal folds snap shut during vocal fold vibration. The glottal end of the tube is therefore closed at the instant of vocal tract excitation.

8–8

(a) A vocal tract area function is a plot of the cross-sectional area of the vocal tract tube as a function of the distance from the vocal folds to the lips. Another way to say this is that a vocal tract area function shows the variation in constriction of the vocal tract from glottis to lips.

(b) The graph below shows a rough sketch of the expected vocal tract area function for the vowel /u/. Cross-sectional area of the vocal tract is shown on the *y*-axis, with upward movement on the axis indicating greater areas; the vocal tract from glottis (left end of axis) to lips (right end of axis) is shown on the *x*-axis as small "sections" of the tube as explained in the textbook. /u/ is classified as a high-back rounded vowel, so there is a constriction in the velar region (shown as a very small cross-sectional area toward the back of the vocal tract), a relatively large area in the front of the oral cavity, and another constriction at the lip section of the tract. Remember: this is a sketch of the expected configuration based on the classical phonetic description of /u/ as a high back, rounded vowel. Not every speaker or dialect group produces the vowel in this way.

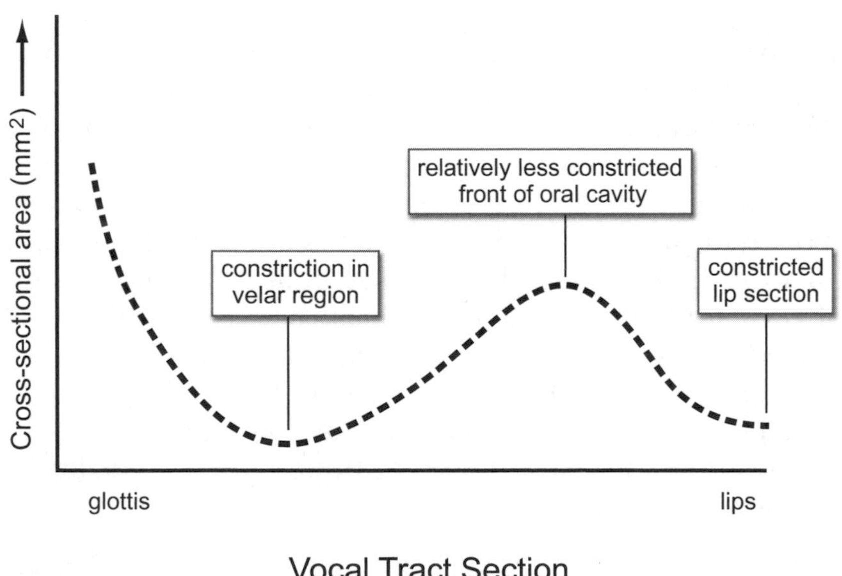

8–9

A theoretical vowel spectrum is *computed* based on the vocal tract area function; an *output* spectrum is measured from a talker's actual production of a vowel.

8-10

The primary explanation for the amplitude decline of vowel-spectra peaks as frequency increases is the decreasing amplitude of the input energy with increasing frequency. The input is the consecutive-integer series of harmonics generated by the vibrating vocal folds. Because the output spectrum reflects the combination of the input and filter energies, peaks in the output spectrum will generally decline with increasing frequency because the input energy is stronger at lower, as compared to higher, frequencies.

8-11

The frequency range of the 2nd peak (F2) is controlled primarily by tongue advancement, with increasing advancement resulting in higher frequencies for the second peak. To move the peak from its location in the figure to a lower frequency, from roughly the 20th to the 10th harmonic, would require retraction of the tongue (somewhat like moving from a high-front to a high-back vowel configuration). In theory, a similar (although perhaps not as dramatic) lowering of the 2nd peak can be produced by rounding the lips without any change in tongue position.

8-12

One example of the independence of the source and filter is a talker's ability to maintain a constant area function (i.e., a vocal tract configuration for a specific vowel) while changing source characteristics such as fundamental frequency (F0) and/or quality. In this case, the filter is constant but the source is changing. The opposite of this is the ability to keep the source fixed (same F0, same quality) while changing the vocal tract configuration (filter), as in changing from an /ɑ/ to /i/ vocal tract tube configuration.

8-13

A formant is a peak in an output spectrum of a vowel. It reflects a resonant frequency of the vocal tract. Formants are relevant to the acoustic description of vowels because the F-pattern, the frequencies of the first three formants, is usually sufficient to distinguish among the vowels of any language. Other information—the relative intensity of the formants, their phases, their bandwidths—are generally not necessary for the *phonetic* categorization of vowels.

8–14

The formant peaks for vowels are "sharply tuned," reflecting resonances with minimal energy loss (see the formant bandwidth data on p. 434 of the textbook). The peaks therefore "stand out" from the rest of the energy in the spectrum. The peaks would not stand out as much for nasalized vowels, where the additional energy loss in the nasal cavities causes the formant peaks to have broader bandwidths and less energy, reducing their distinctiveness relative to the rest of the energy in the spectrum.

8–15

The velocity distribution for the 2nd resonance of the tube is shown.

This is known because ¾ of the full wavelength is shown, and the 2nd resonance of a tube closed at one end always shows ¾ of a full wavelength (first resonance shows ¼, third resonance shows 5⁄4). Tube (b) shows the pressure distribution corresponding to the velocity distribution shown in (a). Again, ¾ of the wavelength is shown, and the maximum pressures (where the dashed lines meet the borders of the tube; where a standing wave would produce maximum pressure inside the tube) occur at locations along the tube where velocity is zero, and vice versa.

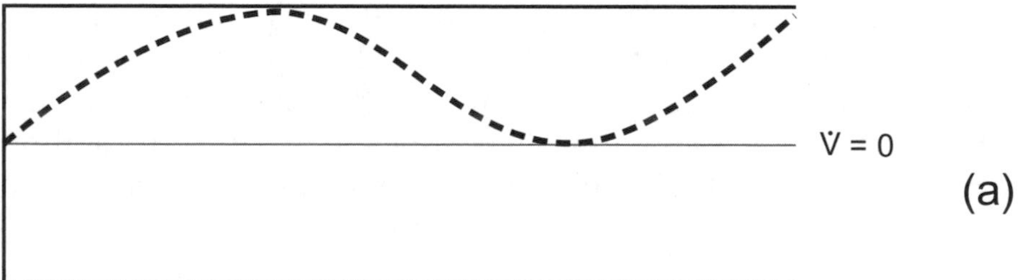

(a)

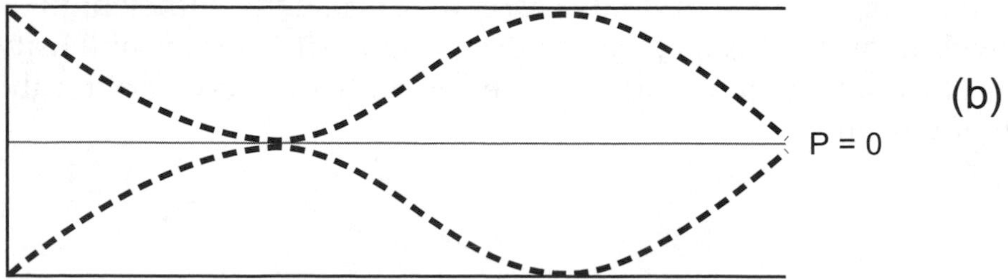

(b)

8–16

(a) In the tube shown below, the pressure distribution for the first resonance is shown. This mode can be instantly identified as a pressure distribution because the energy shows a maximum value at the closed end and a value of zero (P_{atm}) at the open end, which is characteristic of all pressure distributions in tubes closed at one end. Second, it is identifiable as the *first* resonance because ¼ wavelength is shown.

(b) Two separate changes that can be made relative to the reference condition to decrease the frequency of this resonance are shown below. *First*, the tightness of the constriction could be reduced with no change in the location of the constriction. This is illustrated by the original constriction (the lightly shaded gray) and a new constriction (the darkly shaded gray superimposed on the original constriction). By constricting the tube to a lesser degree where the pressure is high (as it is toward the back of this tube's first resonance), the first resonant frequency will decrease (recall that variations in the degree to which a tube is constricted at a given location modify the effect of the constriction on the resonant frequency—less of a constriction in a region of high pressure will make the resonant mode less stiff, therefore decreasing the resonant frequency). *Second*, the constriction can be moved forward, with no change in the degree of the constriction. For this first resonant mode of the tube, the forward movement of the constriction places it in a location where the pressure is less than at the original constriction location (and less pressure means greater velocity). This means that the constriction will move to a location where it decreases the stiffness of this resonant mode (or, alternatively, increases the inertance). The result of this change in constriction location decreases the first resonant frequency of the tube relative to the reference condition.

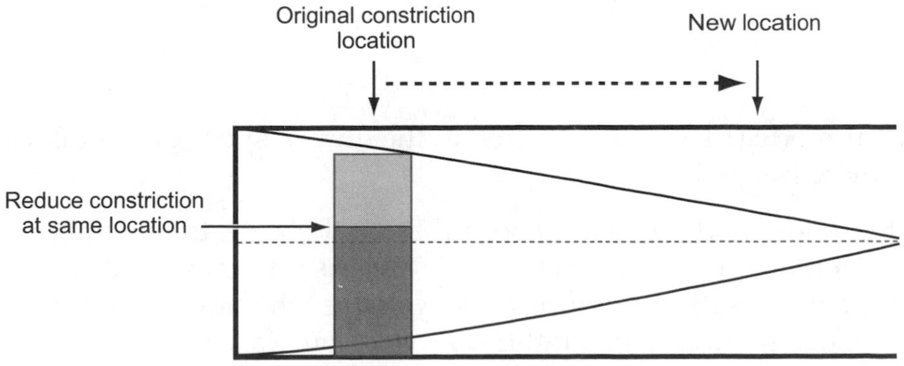

8–17

Both the capacitor and the inductor have a box and circle around them. Increasing the magnitude of the capacitor (circle) is like decreasing its stiffness, therefore, decreasing the resonant frequency of the circuit; increasing the magnitude of the inductor (circle) is like increasing the inertance, thus, decreasing the resonant frequency of the circuit. Decreasing the magnitude of the capacitor (box) is like increasing the stiffness, which increases the resonant frequency of the circuit; decreasing the magnitude of the inductor (box) is like decreasing inertance, which increases the resonant frequency of the circuit. The resistor has an "X" through it (changing its value does not affect the resonant frequency of the circuit, but does change the energy loss within the circuit and therefore the bandwidth of the resonance curve).

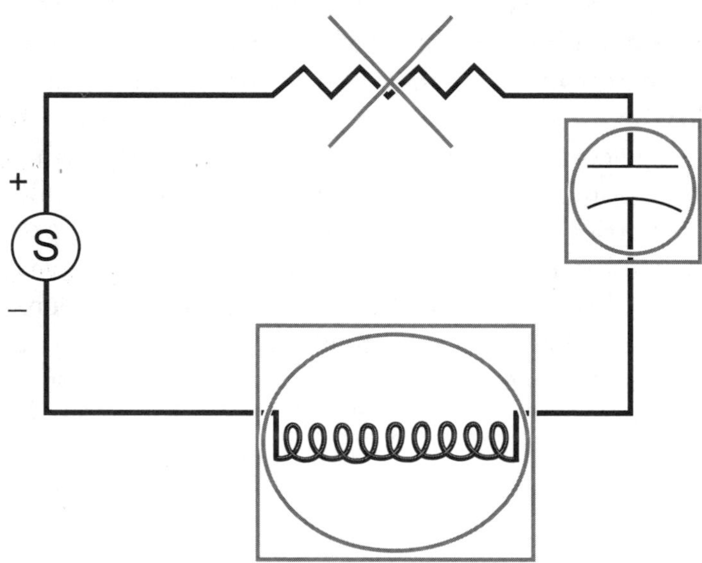

8–18

The first resonant mode (F1 when measured in the output spectrum) is affected most by variations in tongue height.

The best way to understand this within perturbation theory is to remember that the velocity distribution for the first resonant mode increases in magnitude from the closed to open end of the tube, with maximum velocity at the tube outlet. For front vowels, therefore, constrictions of increasing tightness (e.g., from /æ/ to /ɪ/ to /i/; i.e., variations in tongue height) are made in a region of the tube where the velocity is fairly high for the first resonant mode. The tighter the constriction at these high-velocity locations, the greater the increase in inertance and the lower the frequency of the first resonance.

As tongue height increases (as the constriction between the tongue and the palate becomes tighter), the F1 decreases. The same effect holds for back vowels, but the effects of tongue height changes on F1 are not as great as on front vowels because the velocity magnitude in the velar location of the vocal tract is much less than toward the front of the vocal tract.

8–19

Tube models are shown below for the pressure distribution of the 2nd resonant mode (top) and the velocity distribution of the 1st resonant mode (bottom). Advancing the tongue from a back position similar to the constriction location for /u/ (labeled "back" above the tubes) to a front position similar to the constriction location for /i/ (labeled "front" above the tubes) changes the tight constriction from a region of low to high pressure for the 2nd mode (upper tube), therefore increasing the resonant frequency of this mode. The same advancement moves the constriction from a region of relatively lower to higher velocity for the 1st mode (bottom tube), which decreases the resonant frequency of this mode. The relationship of the constriction locations to the energy distributions is indicated by the light vertical lines extending down from the labels above the tubes; note where these lines intersect the respective energy distributions. Tongue advancement therefore changes the second and first resonant modes by raising the frequency of the second mode and lowering the frequency of the first mode.

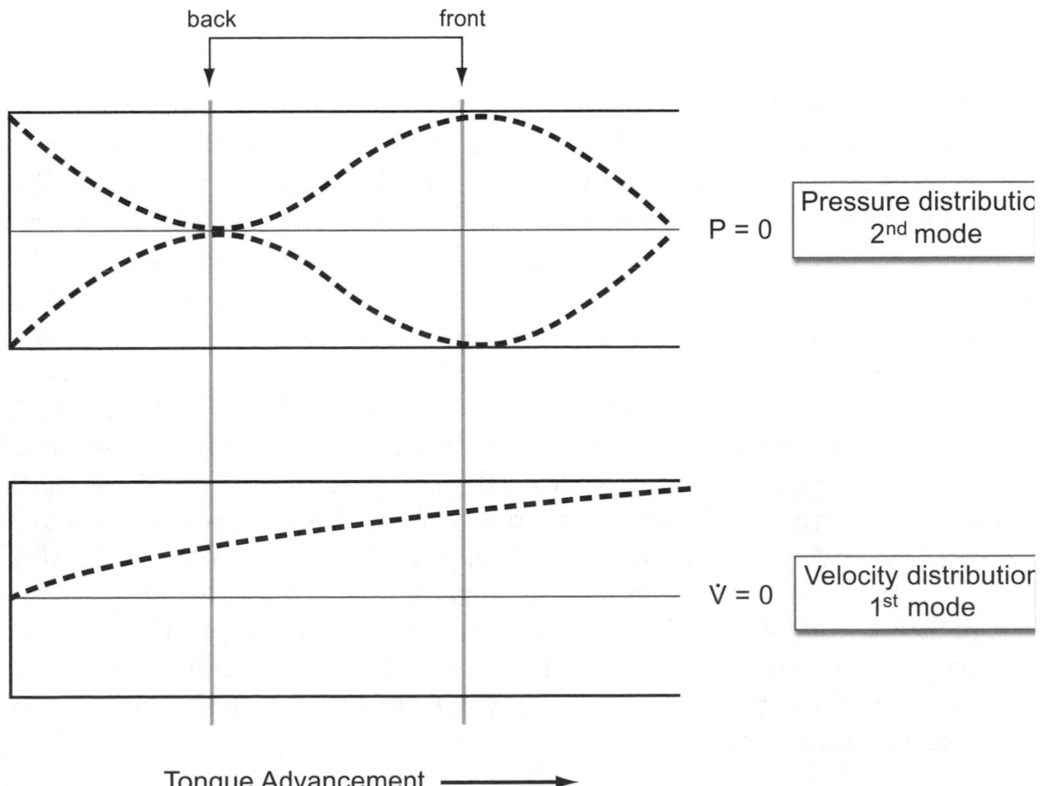

8–20

Rounding the lips is like constricting a tube at the open end. Because velocity of vibrating air molecules is at maximum value at the open end of the tube for *all* resonant frequencies (i.e., for the energy distributions of all wavelengths that "fit" the tube to produce standing waves and therefore resonances), rounding the lips will create a narrower channel at the location of the high-velocity energy and therefore increase inertance, which has the effect of lowering each one of the resonant frequencies of the tube.

8–21

Data from human speech and synthesized speech both support the acoustic theory of vowel production. For example, the formant frequencies of vowels can, for the most part, be explained by the locations and degrees of their constrictions, following the theory developed for how resonances of a tube with uniform cross-sectional area change when a constriction is placed at a specific location within the tube (i.e., when the tube is "deformed" or "perturbed" from its uniform cross-sectional configuration). In other words, the effects of articulatory constrictions on vocal tract formant frequencies are consistent with the effect of constriction location and degree within a simple tube model of resonance. This is a strong form of proof that the vocal tract resonates like a tube open at one end. Similarly, when electrical synthesizers were constructed that mimicked the area functions of the vocal tract, the synthesizer "sounded" like the vowel consistent with an area function modeled after that vowel.

The data from Lee et al. (1999) provide support for the tube model of the acoustic theory of vowel production. If the vocal tract resonates like a tube closed at one end, shorter tubes should have higher resonant frequencies than longer tubes with all other things being equal. The data show averaged vowel formant frequencies for three vowels (/ɑ/, /i/, /u/) for male children at three ages: 5, 9, and 15 years. The vocal tract grows as a child matures, and it is safe to say that a group of 5-year-old children have, on average, shorter vocal tracts than a group of 9-year-old children, who in turn have shorter vocal tracts than a group of 15-year-old children. For a given vowel, if the tube model of vocal tract resonance is correct, the formant frequencies should be highest for the 5-year-old children, and lowest for the 15-year-old children. Taking each formant at a time, compare the F1, F2, and F3 for each vowel across the age groups. You will find an older age group to have lower formant frequencies than a younger age group in all cases except two (the 9-year-old F2 and F3 for /u/ are slightly higher than the 5-year-old F2 and F3 for /u/, which is opposite to expectations if the average 9-year-old vocal tract is longer than the average 5-year-old vocal tract). The theory makes the right predictions about these real data most of the time; the two exceptions probably do not reflect flaws in the theory but rather certain unusual articulatory behaviors (and therefore acoustic outcomes) often associated with the vowel /u/.

CHAPTER 9

9-1

Vowels do not have coupled (shunt) resonators like those in nasal and obstruent acoustics; vowels do not have aperiodic sound sources, which are often located within the vocal tract (and between resonators), as in the case of stops, fricatives, and affricates; and the important frequencies for vowels , those below about 4000 Hz, result in propagation of plane waves in the vocal tract (sound waves propagating only along the long axis of the vocal tract, from glottis to lips). Consonants often have higher frequencies that result in more complex wave propagation (e.g., side-to-side [transverse] sound waves, in addition to plane waves). The addition of wave motions other than planar makes the mathematical basis of the theory much more complicated.

9-2

An antiresonance is a frequency whose energy is "trapped" by a closed resonator; it is like a reverse peak in the spectrum—an inverted peak along the resonance curve, where energy transmission is blocked (just as a regular peak represents a frequency location where energy transmission is maximized). The closed resonator associated with an antiresonance has a resonant frequency based on its dimensions, but does not allow energy at this frequency (and energy at nearby frequencies) to be radiated from the vocal tract.

9-3

The articulation of a nasal murmur involves a closed oral tract and transmission of acoustic energy through the pharyngonasal tract. The spectrum of a nasal murmur includes resonances of the nasal tract (more specifically, the continuous pharyngeal and nasal tracts) and antiresonances of the closed oral tract and the paranasal sinus cavities (which are closed resonators). The spectrum of a nasal murmur therefore is a mix of resonances and antiresonances.

9-4

Nasal murmurs have less intensity than surrounding vowels for two reasons. First, the antiresonances "pull down" energy at the exact frequencies of the antiresonances and at nearby frequencies (much as a resonance emphasizes frequencies at the exact resonant frequency as well as at nearby frequencies). Second, the coupling of the oral and nasal cavities creates greater surface area to absorb sound. A nasal murmur has the surfaces of both the oral and nasal cavities as sound absorbers, and the nasal cavities have extensive surface area and therefore potentially great damping effects on vibratory energy. Peak energies are reduced with greater damping. Because the overall intensity of a speech sound is the sum of energies at each of the frequencies in the sound spectrum, the effect of antiresonances and greater damping during nasal murmurs is to reduce their intensity compared to that of surrounding vowels, which do not have antiresonances and absorption of vibratory energy by the nasal cavities.

9-5

(a) The spectrum on the left is likely from a nasal murmur.

(b) The one on the right is likely from a vowel.

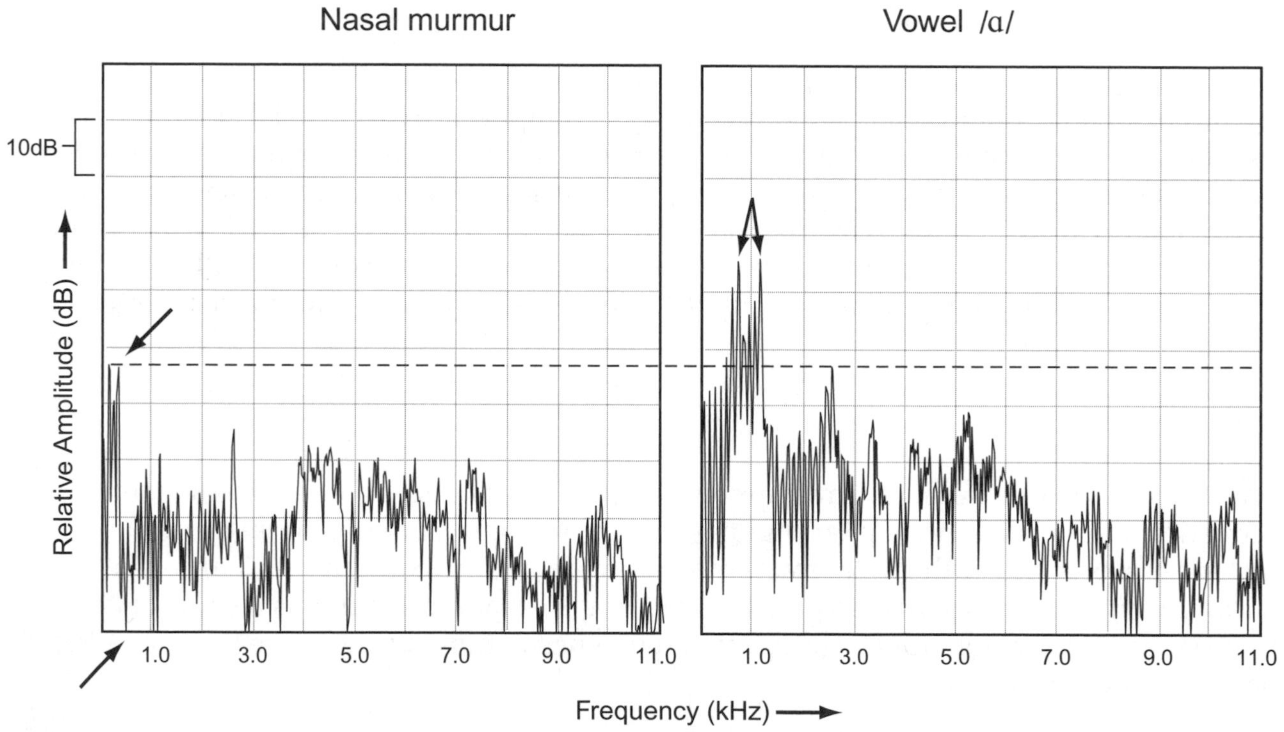

(c) Three pieces of information from the spectra contribute to this choice. *First*, the spectrum on the left has generally lower energy than the spectrum on the right; the dotted line drawn across both spectra shows that the highest peak in the left-hand spectrum is close to 15 dB less intense than the two peaks around 1000 Hz in the right-hand spectrum. The remainder of the energy in the left-hand spectrum is also generally weaker than that in the right hand spectrum. Because the sounds were recorded with the same mouth-to-microphone distance, the intensities of these spectra are directly comparable. Nasal murmurs are typically less intense than vowels (see 9–4 above), so this would suggest the left-hand spectrum is from a murmur. *Second,* the major low frequency peak in the left-hand spectrum is located approximately at 250 to 300 Hz (see downward-pointing arrow, left spectrum), the typical location for the first formant of nasal murmurs. Some vowels (such as /i/) also have a low-frequency first formant around 250 to 300 Hz, but typically they also have a relatively intense second formant around 2300 Hz, which is not seen in this left-hand spectrum. The low-frequency first formant therefore suggests a nasal murmur. *Third,* a pronounced dip in the spectrum (upper-pointing, slanting arrow at the bottom of the left-hand spectrum) is seen around 600 Hz, and other sharp spectral dips are also seen (e.g., close to 1000 Hz, 3000 Hz, and 5000 Hz). The sharp dips suggest antiresonances typical of nasal murmurs; such dips are not seen in the right-hand spectrum. These three pieces of information, taken together, suggest the left-hand spectrum is derived from a nasal murmur. Also, the right hand spectrum contains two relatively intense peaks straddling 1000 Hz (one ~800 Hz, one ~1100 Hz), which suggests the vowel /ɑ/.

9–6

The spectrum of a nasalized vowel includes resonances from the oral cavities and the nasal cavities.

9–7

The nasalized /ɑ/, /ɛ/, and /u/ are less intense than their non-nasalized counterparts because, as easily seen in Figure 9–4 of the textbook, the peaks in the spectra of these three nasalized vowels have lesser amplitude than the corresponding peaks in the non-nasalized spectra (compare the red spectra to the blue spectra in each graph). Overall vowel intensity can be thought of as the sum of all the intensities along the resonance curve for the vowel, so the non-nasalized vowels, with their individual peaks of greater intensity, will have greater overall intensity than their nasalized versions.

9-8

The spectrum to the left is consistent with /s/, the one to the right with /ʃ/. The primary resonance (R) for the /s/ is shown around 5.0 kHz, whereas the primary resonance for /ʃ/ is shown a little above 2.0 kHz. The lower resonance for /ʃ/, as compared to /s/, is a result of the larger front cavity (cavity in front of the fricative constriction) for the former; larger cavities are associated with lower resonant frequencies.

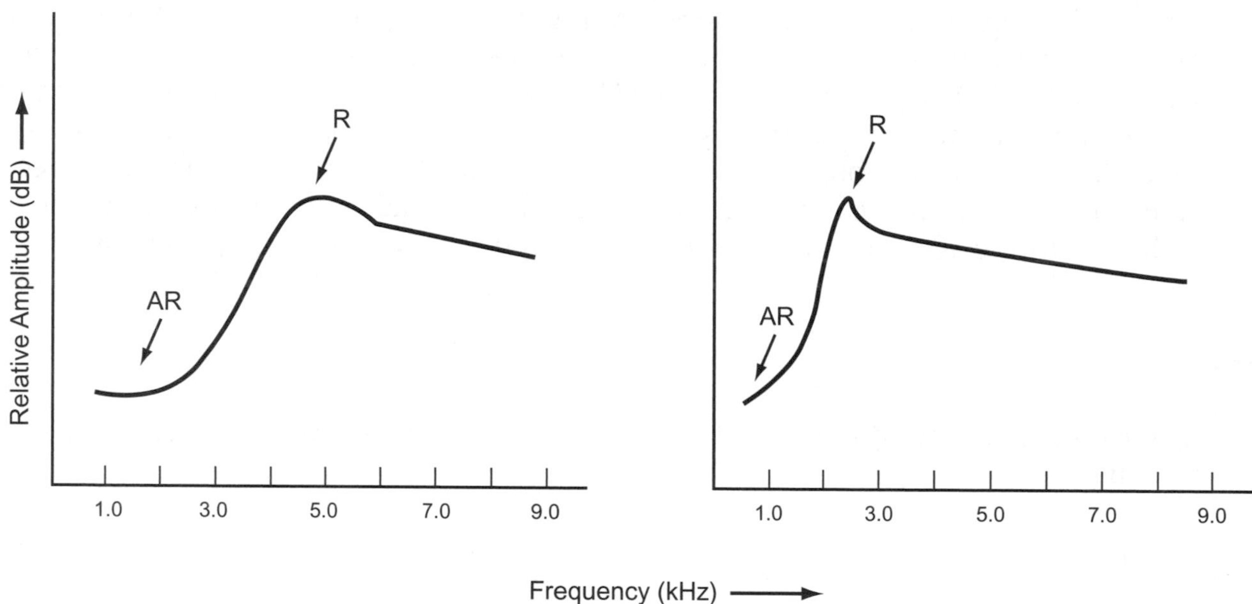

9-9

A frication source is one in which airflow within the vocal tract becomes turbulent in the vicinity of a narrow constriction or when striking an obstacle. "Turbulence" is the term for the type of airflow in which molecules spin in a haphazard fashion, rather than flowing in straight lines (the latter is called "laminar" flow). The acoustic result of turbulent flow is aperiodic energy, and it is this type of energy that is a sound source in fricatives, stops, and affricates. One example of a frication source is when air emerges from a fricative constriction (such as between the tongue and palate for /s/) in a narrow "jet" of flow that has spinning molecules around the borders of the jet. The spinning molecules generate aperiodic acoustic energy and serve as a source for fricatives. A second example is when the air jet strikes the teeth and molecules spin as a result of this collision; this is also a frication source.

9-10

Based on the discussion in the textbook, the intensity of a sustained /f/ can be increased simply by placing an obstacle in the pathway of the airflow exiting the vocal tract. No change in the production effort is required. The turbulence generated at the obstacle will serve as a secondary frication source, resulting in an increase of the overall intensity of the /f/. The waveform below demonstrates the obstacle effect. The signal was recorded with a microphone placed a few centimeters in front of one of the author's lips. After a brief interval of a sustained /f/ without an obstacle (labeled "control frication"), he moved his index finger side to side, in front of his lips, as he continued to sustain the /f/ with constant effort. When his finger met the airstream it served as an obstacle to the flow and generated turbulence and therefore additional aperiodic energy. Note the sudden "jumps" in the height of the waveform, which are brief increases in waveform amplitude produced by a secondary aperiodic source at the finger.

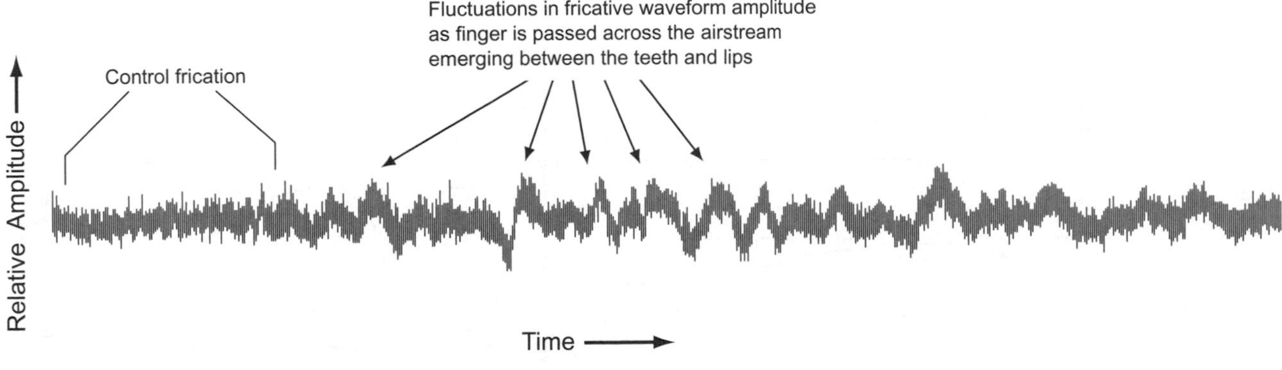

9-11

The fricative spectra for /s/ and /ʃ/ are more intense and more peaky than the fricative spectra for /f/ and /θ/, which tend to be weak and flat.

9-12

The primary determinant of the resonant frequency of the spectrum of fricatives produced with a constriction between the tongue and palate is the size of the cavity in front of the constriction: the larger the cavity, the lower the primary resonant frequency.

9-13

The relative "flatness" versus "peakiness" of spectra is illustrated below. The left spectrum was drawn to be relatively flat, the right spectrum to be relatively peaky. One way to measure this difference is to perform a dynamic range measurement, as illustrated on the two spectra. The dynamic range measures the difference, in dB (see *y*-axis of the graphs), between the lowest and highest energy points on the spectrum. The flatter the spectrum, the smaller the dynamic range in dB. On each spectrum, the lowest energy is indicated by the lower, dashed, horizontal line; the highest energy by the upper, dashed line. The distance between these two lines in dB is shown to the right of each spectrum. The flatter spectrum has a dynamic range of roughly 8 dB, the peakier spectrum a dynamic range of about 18 dB. The relative flatness versus peakiness of two spectra can also be measured using the fourth spectral moment called kurtosis. This is an automatic measurement made by computer-based speech analysis programs.

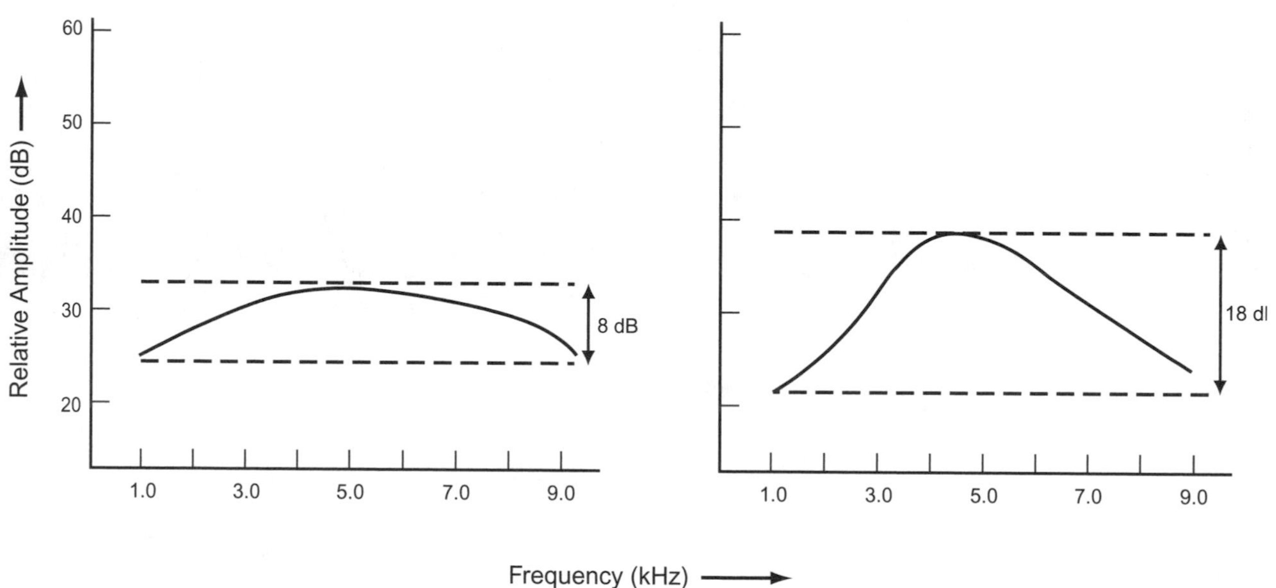

9–14

Values of P_o are higher for voiceless, as compared to voiced stops. The pressure developed inside the vocal tract, above the level of the vocal folds, is higher for voiceless stops (by approximately 1.5 cm/H_2O) because the vocal folds are open for these stops, and the volume of air inside the vocal tract is continuous with the volume of air in the trachea and lungs. When this air is compressed by forces in the respiratory system, the pressure is equivalent throughout the volume (i.e., the alveolar pressure P_{alv} and the tracheal pressure P_t are equal to the oral pressure P_o). On the other hand, voiced stops are produced with the vocal folds vibrating during the stop closure interval. The vibrating vocal folds dissipate some of the aeromechanical energy as air flows through this valve, which results in a reduction of pressure above the folds (P_o) during the closure interval relative to the pressure below the vocal folds (tracheal pressure, or P_t). In the case of voiced stops, $P_{alv} = P_t$ (as in the case of voiceless stops) but P_{alv} and P_t do not equal P_o. The latter pressure is slightly lower than the two former pressures because of the energy loss as air flows through the vocal folds. The P_o difference between voiceless and voiced stops is relevant to stop acoustics, because the higher P_o for voiceless stops explains why bursts are more intense for voiceless as compared to voiced stops (greater P_o in the voiceless case results in higher burst intensity),and why frication intervals are likely to be longer and more intense for voiceless stops (greater P_o for voiceless stops maintains the high flow required for frication over a longer period of time, and greater P_o will create more intense frication noise).

9–15

(a) Top row: Left is <u>voiceless</u>, right is <u>voiced</u>.
Middle row: Left is <u>voiced</u>, right is <u>voiceless</u>.
Bottom row: Left is <u>voiceless</u>, right is <u>voiced</u>.

(b) The first pair of waveforms shows [ɑkɑ] (left) and [ɑgɑ] (right), so the voiceless stop is in the first member of the waveform pair. The evidence in this first pair that the left-hand waveform shows a voiceless stop and the right hand waveform a voiced stop includes: (a) the lack of periodic energy in the left-hand closure interval (see flat line directly beneath [k]) versus evidence of periodic energy during the closure interval on the right (see below [g]); (b) a burst amplitude slightly greater for the left-hand member, as compared to the right-hand member; and (c) a longer VOT for the left-hand, as compared to right-hand waveform (as marked: the VOT interval extends from the burst to the first glottal pulse of the following vowel). The transcription for the other two pairs is provided to show which one is voiceless, and which is voiced; look for similar clues to stop voicing status in these examples.

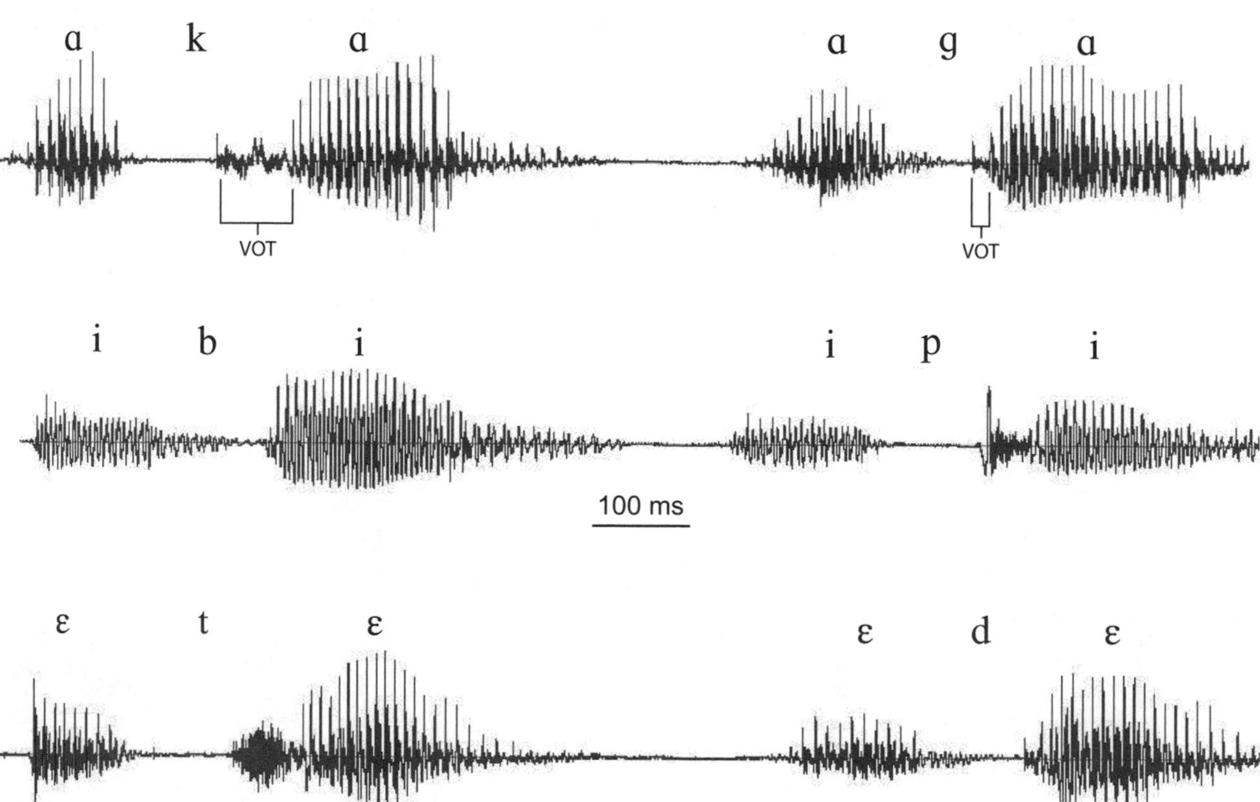

9-16

An understanding of speech apparatus aeromechanics explains the acoustic results during and following release of a stop consonant as follows. First, the acoustic burst is the result of a sudden release of oral pressure developed during the closure interval of a stop. Second, the acoustic frication interval is the result of turbulent flow at the exit of the rapidly expanding constriction (and at obstacles in the path of the flow, if present) as the stop is released into the following vowel. Third, in the case of voiceless stops, the acoustic aspiration interval is the result of turbulent flow in the vicinity of the closing vocal folds as they are brought together for phonation of the following vowel. The table below shows correspondences between these acoustic/aeromechanical events.

Acoustic Event	Aeromechanical Basis
Burst	Sudden release of P_o
Frication	Turbulence at rapidly expanding supralaryngeal constriction(and at obstacles, if present)
Aspiration (for voiceless)	Turbulence at narrowing glottis as vocal folds are brought together for phonation of following vowel

9-17

The theory of stop and fricative acoustics share the concept of aperiodic sources within the vocal tract (such as frication sources), antiresonances (the cavities in back of constrictions), the primary resonance of the spectrum being determined by the size of the cavity in front of the constriction, and the possibility of mixed sources (i.e., simultaneous voicing and aperiodic sources).

9-18

Voice-onset time (VOT) is defined as the interval between the stop burst and the first glottal pulse of the following vowel. Typically, VOT is longer for voiceless, as compared to voiced stops (see Chapter 11 in the textbook). VOT is longer for voiceless stops because the vocal folds are separated during the closure interval to prevent them from vibrating, and the stop burst occurs well before (in milliseconds) the folds are moved back to the midline for the phonation requirements of the following vowel. Thus, for voiceless stops, there is a delay between the burst and the first glottal pulse of the following vowel. In voiced stops, the vocal folds vibrate during the closure interval or are held in the midline position, so when the burst occurs, the folds are ready to vibrate almost immediately (if not simultaneously with the burst).

CHAPTER 10

10-1

Helmholtz used his ear to detect the peak amplitudes, the loudest sounds, produced by the vocal tract in response to tuning fork vibrations, or in the transmission of acoustic energy via a series of resonators he developed (what we now call "Helmholtz resonators"). By selecting tuning forks varying in frequency, striking each one into vibration as it was held close to the lips, and listening to the response of the vocal tract held in various vowel configurations, Helmholtz was able to choose the fork whose frequency appeared to produce the loudest "response." This frequency was thought to correspond to the resonant frequency of the vocal tract for that configuration. Using the same principle but a different method, Helmholtz used the series of resonators he built as a way to transmit acoustic energy between a speaker 's mouth and his (Helmholtz's) ear. The resonators varied from ones with very high resonant frequencies (small ones) to ones with midrange frequencies and ones with very low resonant frequencies (big ones). An assistant phonated a particular vowel into the neck of each of the resonators as Helmholtz listened at a small opening at the bottom of the resonator bowl. He selected the resonator that produced the loudest vowel at his ear as having the frequency that matched the resonance of the vocal tract. Helmholtz reasoned that this match would provide the greatest vibratory energy in the resonator when the vowel was phonated, and hence the loudest sound at his ear.

10-2

"Transduction" is the conversion of one type of energy (e.g., aeromechanical, such as pressure variations) into another type of energy (e.g., electrical, as in voltage variations). One potential problem with transduction is that in the process of converting from one form of energy into another, the details of the original energy variations are not transduced accurately. The resulting transduced signal may not be a faithful representation of the original signal.

10-3

(a) The quantitative information that can be obtained from waveforms is the fundamental frequency (F0). Shown below are estimates of a single period for each waveform, using the 100-ms time calibration given below the waveforms. The repeating glottal pulses of the left waveform are closer together than those of the right waveform, and the measurements for single periods of the respective waveforms demonstrate this. The quantitative measurements show that the left waveform has a higher F0 as compared to the right waveform.

(b) The qualitative information that can be gained by comparing the two waveforms is that their spectra are likely to be different (hence, the difference in detail between the waveforms; in fact, the left waveform is from a brief /u/ and the right waveform is from a brief /ɑ/), and that the left waveform has greater amplitude than the right waveform (in the absence of a calibration for the *y*-axis, or relative amplitude axis, the amplitude difference between the waveforms cannot be measured quantitatively).

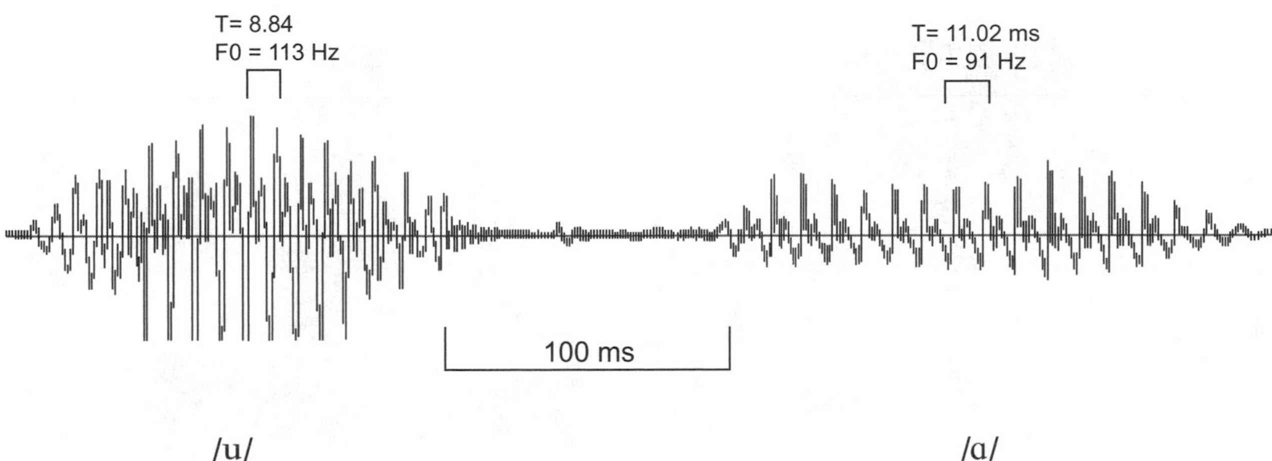

10-4

A formant transition is a change in formant frequency as a function of time.

10-5

See spectrogram below. The *x*- and *y*-axes are labeled; the third axis, relative intensity, is not labeled but is shown as variations of darkness (variations in darkness of the trace, at different time-frequency coordinates, correspond to variations in signal intensity between those time-frequency coordinates). Two examples of relative differences in signal intensity are given: compare the energy difference between the first formants labeled "A" and "B" ("A" is more intense, because the formant band is darker), or between "C" and "D" where the aperiodic energy at "C" is greater than the aperiodic energy at "D." The vowel with F2 roughly at 2.0 kHz is shown (as determined from the frequency calibration lines located at 1.0 kHz intervals as shown along the frequency [*y*] axis). A vowel with a large F2 transition is shown, the transition beginning a little above 1.0 kHz and ending a little below 2.0 kHz; and a fricative with very intense energy in the upper frequencies is shown near the beginning of the utterance.

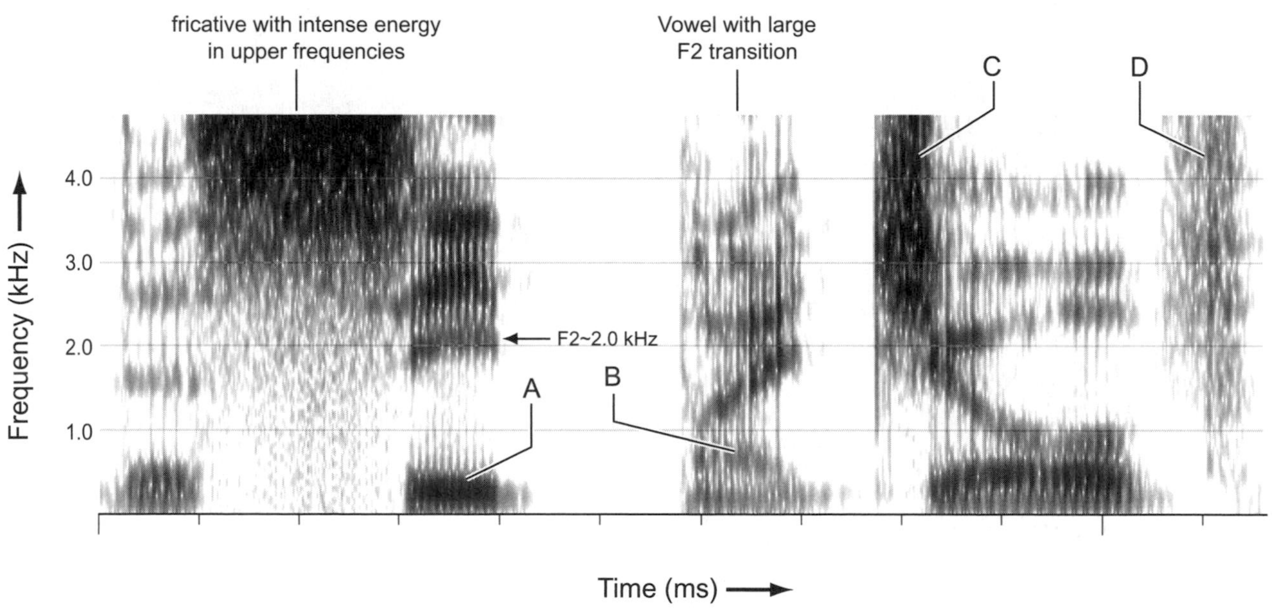

10-6

An "analysis band" is a fixed band of frequencies, for example a 300-Hz band, over which the amount of energy in an acoustic signal is detected and output to some other device (such as the hard disk of a computer) in the form of a magnitude (a voltage, or digital units). When the analysis band is moved continuously across the frequency range of a signal, the output of the band can reconstruct the energy pattern (the spectrum) for a short "piece" of an acoustic signal. An analysis band can be thought of as a filter.

10-7

Spectrograms show the speech acoustic signal and, more precisely, the resonances of the vocal tract as a function of time. This allowed clinicians and researchers to infer the configuration of the vocal tract over time, because the time-varying resonances of the vocal tract reflect, in a lawful way, the changing vocal tract configuration.

10-8

(a, b) In the spectrogram below, 8 bursts are indicated by numbers with downward-pointing lines; the specific stops are shown by the transcription along the bottom of the spectrogram. The criteria used to identify these acoustic events as bursts include a sudden, spike-like acoustic event, a closure interval preceding this event, and possibly the presence of a brief interval of aperiodic energy following the spike-like event (see #1, 3, and 6 for bursts followed by fairly clear intervals of aperiodicity). Most of the bursts are fairly obvious (e.g., #1, 3, 4, 5, 6, 7, 8). Bursts #2, 4, 6, and 8 deserve special comment. Burst #2 is weak, probably because the stop is voiced (see below) and initiates a poststressed syllable (typically weaker than prestressed syllables). Burst #4 probably is not associated with the release of the /b/, but rather reflects the release of a glottal stop (often occurring in words with vowel onsets—in this case, "obeyed"—and especially when initiating a major syntactic unit). Burst #6 is a burst associated with a flap at the end of the words "obeyed" and immediately before the "a," where the "a" was produced as schwa. Finally, burst #8 is an utterance-final stop release; the brief voiced interval following the release, where F2 and F3 extend over a nearly 100-ms interval, is like a voiced relaxation gesture in which the vocal tract returns to a rest position.

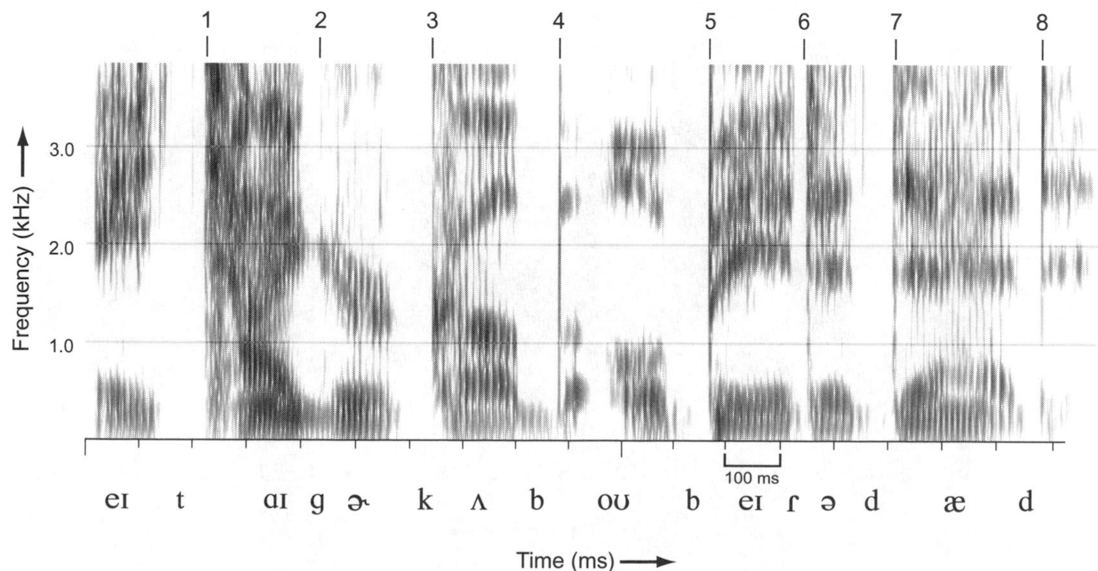

The stops associated with bursts #1 and 3 are voiceless, whereas the other six can all be classified as voiced. Bursts #1 and 3 have preceding closure intervals that clearly lack glottal pulses and both have VOTs in excess of 20 ms (stops with VOTs greater than 20 ms typically are voiceless). The combined criteria of a closure interval lacking glottal pulses and a relatively long VOT are usually sufficient to label a stop as voiceless. Stops #2 and 4 clearly have glottal pulses during the closure intervals and also have short VOTs (but recall that #4 may be a glottal stop). Stops #5 to 8 may show some evidence of glottal pulses during the closure interval, but the voicing energy is often very weak and therefore does not make a compelling case for a voiced stop. However, the short VOT's (less than 20 ms) of each of these stops argue in favor of a voiced stop.

(c) The spectrogram from Question 10–8(c) is reproduced below with phonetic transcription and the labels "F" and "V" to show the locations of fricatives and vowels. The criterion used to identify fricatives is simple: an extended interval of aperiodic energy. "Extended" can be broadly defined as any interval of aperiodic energy exceeding 100 ms. Many of the "F" intervals in the spectrogram are a good deal longer than 100 ms, but a couple (the /z/ and /s/ in "zesty") are close to 100 ms. In general, voiced fricatives are shorter than voiceless fricatives, and fricatives in s + stop clusters are shorter than singleton fricatives (as reviewed in Chapter 11 of the textbook). The vowels in the spectrogram are identified by the appearance of voiced intervals (intervals with vertical, repeating striations reflecting successive cycles of vocal fold vibration), plus dark bands reflecting the resonant frequencies of the vocal tract , that is, the formant frequencies. One of the intervals labeled "V" in the spectrogram may be more properly classified as a "vocalic" rather than a "vowel" (the sequence /eɪr/ in "share"); there is also a voiced interval that is a nasal (the /m/ in "some").

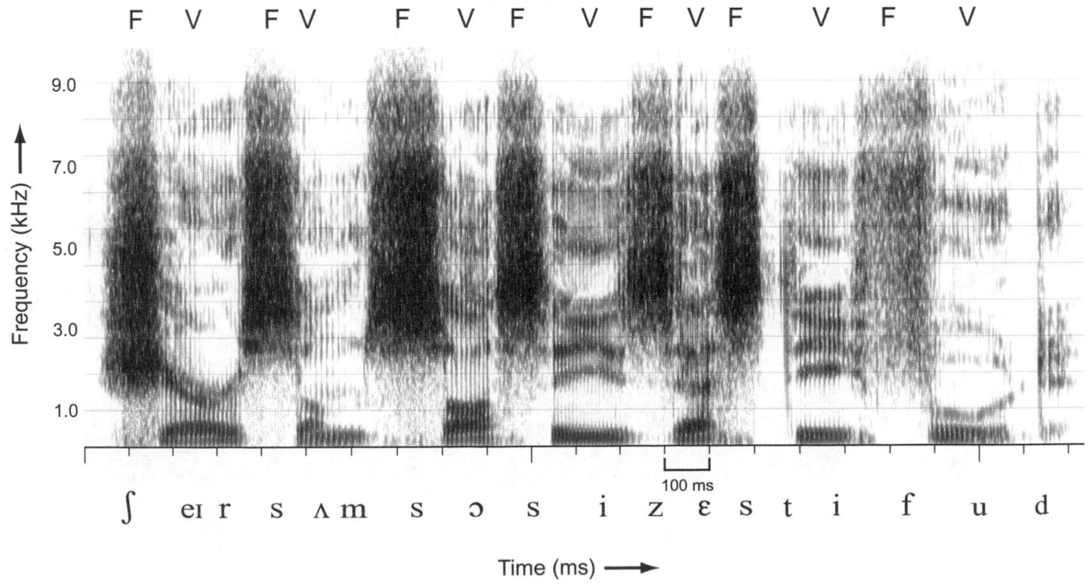

(d) The vocalic event on the left has formant frequencies that are changing quite a bit over time, so the precise spectral characteristics depend on where a spectral slice is taken. For example, in the left-hand spectrogram two time points for spectral slices are shown by the vertical lines extending through the spectrogram; at the first one, near the beginning of the vowel, F1 = 400, F2 = 2150, F3 = 2750 Hz (see short horizontal lines showing approximate location of the formant frequencies). At the second slice toward the end of the vowel, F1 = 700, F2 = 1800, F3 = 2500 Hz. For this vowel, the formant frequencies depend on where the spectral slice is chosen. For the vowel shown in the right-hand spectrogram, F1, F2, and F3 remain fairly "flat" during the entire vocalic interval. At both time slices—one close to the beginning of the vowel, one close to its end—the formants are F1 = 280, F2 = 2250, F3 = 3200 Hz. For this vowel, the spectral characteristics, the formant frequencies, are the same at any time point during the vocalic interval. (The left word is "gag" with the /æ/ produced with a Chicago-type dialect, the right word is "geese.")

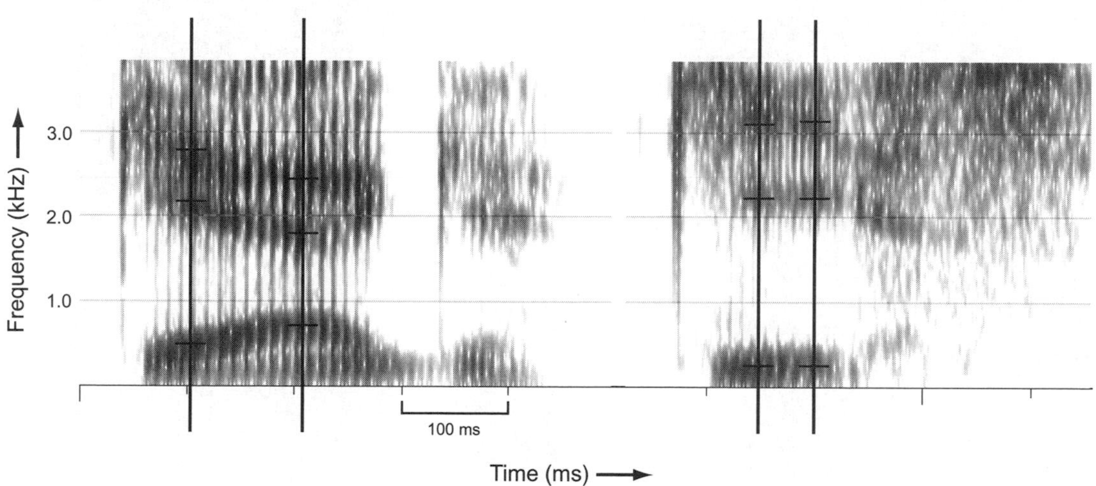

(e) The two productions of "gab" share the same time scale (see the 100-ms calibration), so the relative F0 of the two can be compared by looking at the spacing between successive glottal pulses. The wider this separation, the lower the F0. On this basis, the production of "gab" to the right is the one with the higher F0. By counting the number of pulses within the 100 ms interval, an average F0 can be estimated for each vowel. In the left production there are ~9.5 pulses in the middle 100 ms, which means the average period is 100 ms/9.5 = 10.5 ms, therefore F0 = 1/T = 1/.0105 ~ 95 Hz. The right production has roughly 17 pulses in the 100 ms interval, so the average period is 100 ms/17 = .0059 ms, therefore F0 = 1/.0059 ~ 170 Hz.

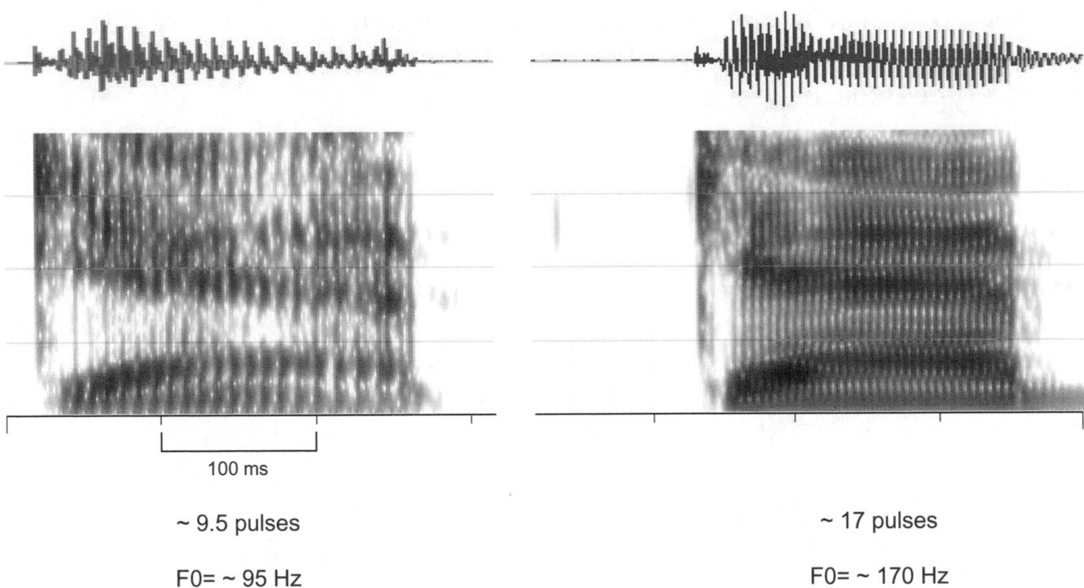

10-9

Regularly spaced glottal pulses would be expected for vowels, diphthongs, semivowels, and nasals, all of which are voiced and produced with an open outlet to the atmosphere (oral in the first three, nasal in the last case). The spacing may change slightly depending on changes in F0 contour over a segment.

10-10

(a) Estimated values of the first three formants of the two vowels are shown below. The measurements were taken at the temporal middle of the vowels (a "conventional" measurement location for "target" formant frequencies) and are estimated based on the frequency calibration lines as shown.

(b) The F1–F2 values for /u/ are in the most extreme, lower left region of the /u/ ellipse shown in Figure 11–2 of the textbook, and the /æ/ values are in the lower, right-hand part of the /æ/ ellipse.

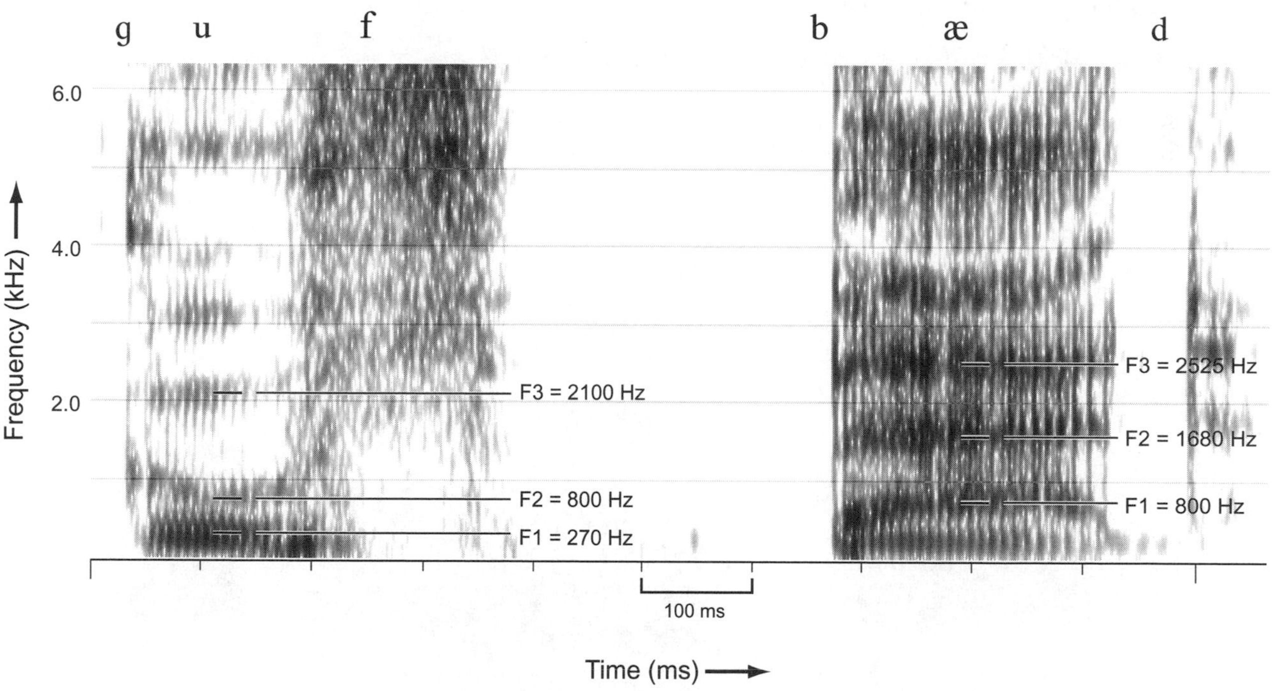

10-11

Vowels are voiced and therefore have repeating glottal pulses shown spectrographically as a series of regularly spaced vertical lines; vowel intervals also show dark bands indicating the resonant frequencies of the vocal tract (the formant frequencies). Voiceless fricatives have relatively long (100 ms and greater) intervals of relatively intense energy. These voiceless fricative intervals do not show repeating patterns because the energy is not periodic.

10–12

Segmentation criteria (upward-pointing arrows indicate the left (initial) and right (final) hand boundaries of the segment between the arrows:

"a bag"

/eɪ/: first glottal pulse to last glottal pulse of vowel/diphthong (this vocalic may be a monophthong or diphthong, depending on dialect of the speaker)

/b/: last glottal pulse of preceding vocalic to burst

/æ/: burst of /b/ (appears to be simultaneous with a glottal pulse) to final glottal pulse preceding the /g/ closure interval

/g/: final glottal pulse of preceding /æ/ to /g/ burst

The segment following the /g/ burst is an end-of-utterance "relaxation" articulatory gesture, lasting about 100 ms; it is not transcribed here as a phonetic segment

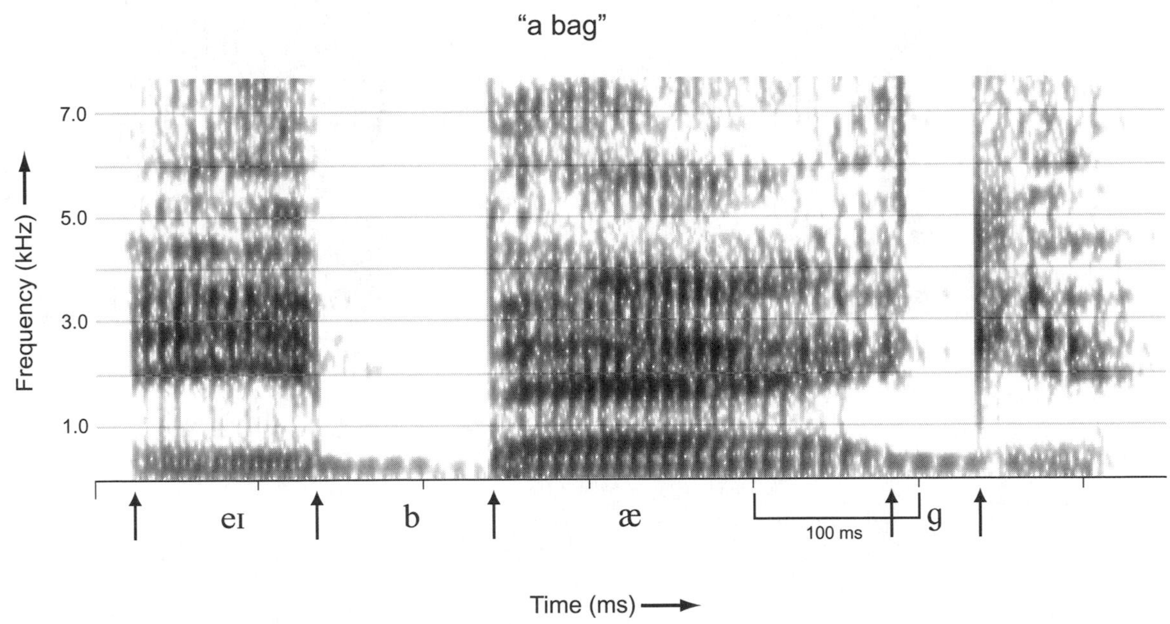

"stop sign"

/s/: onset of frication noise to offset of frication noise (the small amount of aperiodic energy in the /t/ closure interval is common for /s/ + stop cluster production)

/t/: end of preceding, high-energy frication noise to /t/ burst (the arrow just after the burst arrow indicates the first glottal pulse of the following vowel, hence the interval between the burst and the immediately following arrow is the VOT)

/ɑ/: first glottal pulse to last glottal pulse preceding the /p/ closure

/p/: last glottal pulse of preceding /ɑ/ to onset of high-energy frication noise for /s/ (the onset of the frication may be preceded by a weak-intensity burst, but if it is present, it is nearly coincident with the onset of the frication noise)

/s/: onset of frication noise to first glottal pulse of following vowel (in CV syllables where C = voiceless fricative, the first glottal pulse of the following vowel is often a more reliable boundary than the offset of the frication noise)

/ɑɪ/: first glottal pulse of diphthong to last glottal pulse prior to the voiced segment that has clearly reduced energy compared to the diphthong (note at the right-hand arrow, the sudden change in intensity when comparing left of the arrow to right of the arrow; this is a typical segmentation clue when the primary path of sound transmission changes from oral cavity to nasal cavities)

/n/: last glottal pulse of preceding /ɑɪ/ to (roughly) the last glottal pulse of the nasal (utterance-final nasals often present a problem for reliable location of the right-hand boundary of the segment, due to the gradual decline of energy over these segments)

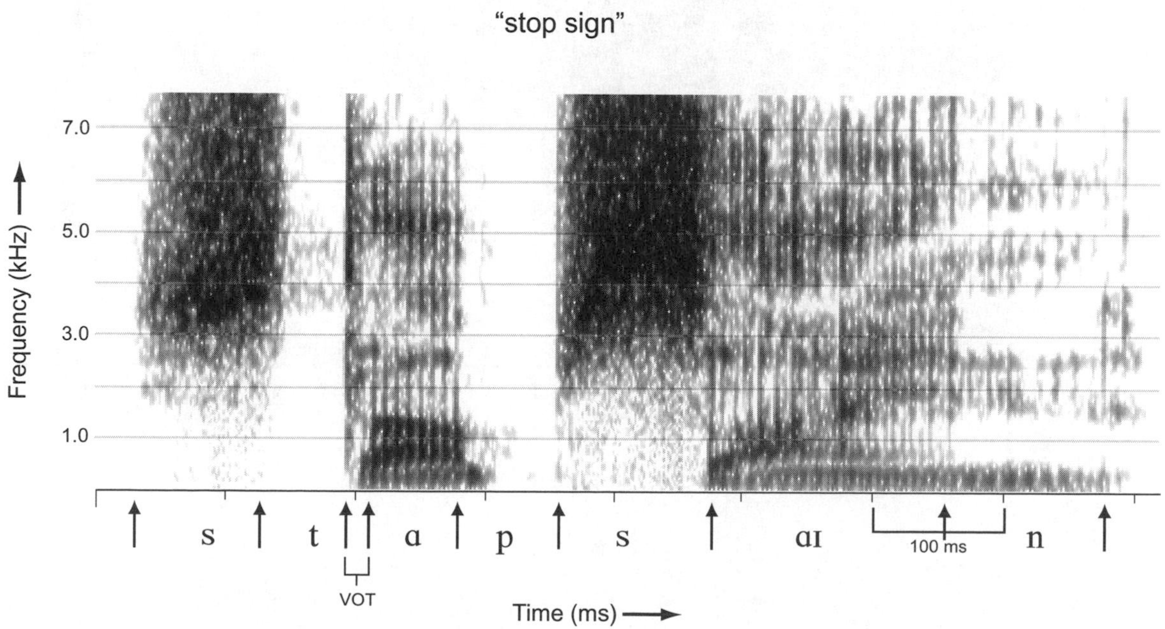

"ellis fink"

/ɛlɪ/: first glottal pulse of the extended vocalic sequence to the last glottal pulse (at the end of /ɪ/). The textbook notes that for sequences of vocalic segments such as this one, the safest segmentation is not to separate the semivowel from the surrounding vowels. In the spectrogram below, the arrows with dashed lines show the /l/ constriction interval segmented from the surrounding vowels, but these decisions can sometimes be difficult to make in a reliable (repeatable) way.

/s/: last glottal pulse of /ɪ/ (alternately, the onset of the high-energy frication noise can be used as the onset of the /s/) to offset of frication noise for /s/ (where the energy changes from relatively high to relative low, see right-hand arrow for /s/)

/f/: offset of high-energy /s/ energy to first glottal pulse of /ɪ/ following the /f/

/ɪ/: first glottal pulse to last glottal pulse prior to dramatic change in energy (energy to the right of the right-hand boundary of /ɪ/ is much weaker as compared to left of this boundary, as in the /ɑɪ/-/n/ boundary for "stop sign," above)

/ŋ/: last glottal pulse of preceding vowel to last glottal pulse of weak-energy voiced segment

/k/: last glottal pulse preceding closure for /k/ to /k/ burst (the energy following this right-hand boundary is the frication interval of the /k/, but as an utterance-final phonetic segment it is not given its own phonetic label)

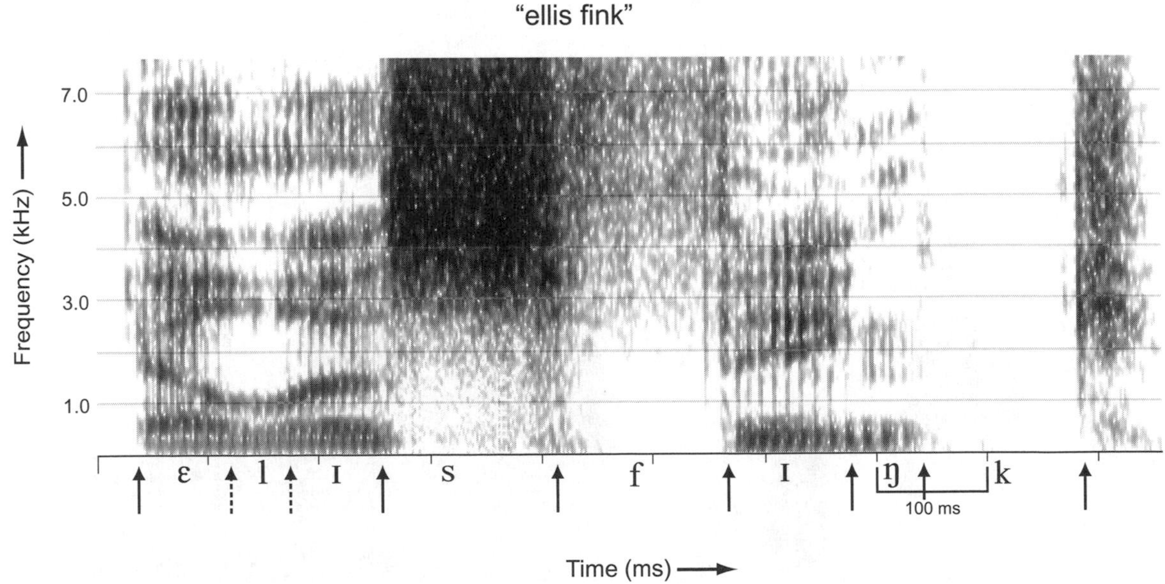

10-13

(a) The F0 over the "blue spot" sequence ranges from about 80 to 150 Hz (range ~70 Hz), with the lowest values at the end of "spot" and the highest at the end of "blue" and beginning of "spot"; and for "normal," the F0 ranges from about 90 to 170 Hz, with the highest values close to the [rm] part of the word.

(b) Both the "blue spot" and "normal" contours can be described as having a rising-falling shape.

10-14

The main difference between an analog and digital representation of a speech signal is that the analog representation shows the energy variations in the signal as a continuous function of time, whereas the digital representation shows the energy fluctuations as a series of discrete samples over time, each of which encodes information on the energy level at all analyzed frequencies of the signal at a single instant in time. By increasing the sampling rate and quantization (number of bits) when the signal is converted from analog to digital representation, the digital representation becomes more like the analog signal.

10-15

An analysis window is an interval of time over which formant frequencies are estimated. The estimates are averaged over the window.

10-16

Window #1 is preferred because it is the shortest, but it is still long enough to produce a reasonable estimate of the formant frequencies. The other two windows are too long, especially because the formant frequencies of this vowel are changing a good deal over time. The longer the analysis window, the more these spectral changes will be "smeared" in the estimate of formant frequencies (see Figure 10–4 in the textbook, p. 496).

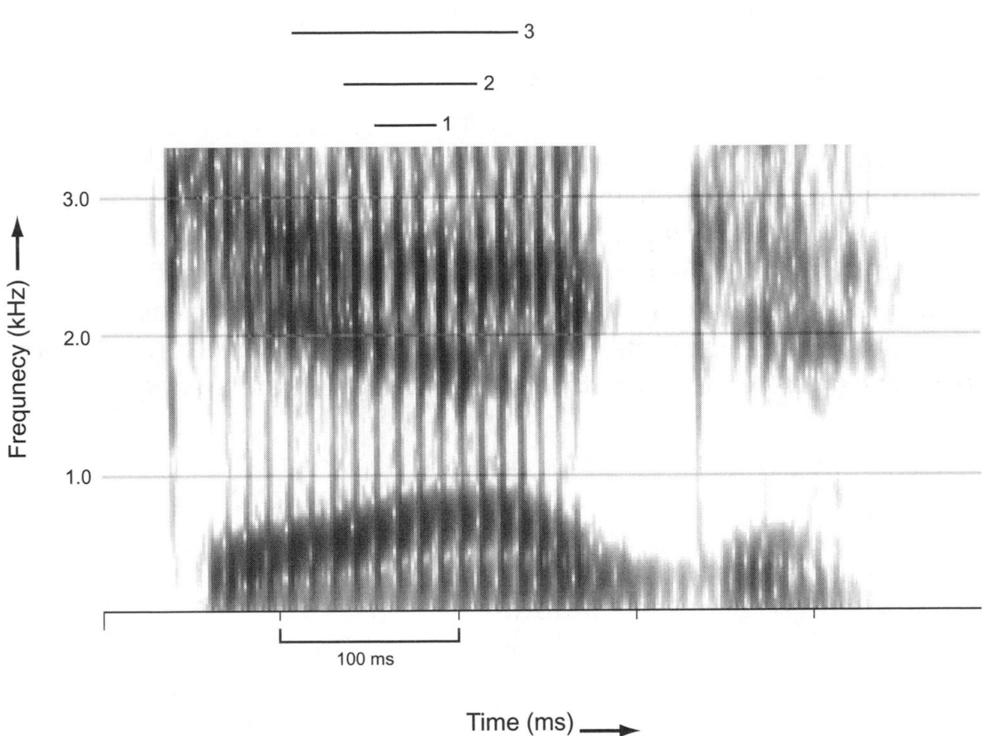

CHAPTER 11

11-1

The formant frequency values are tabled below; under each vowel, the first number is the formant frequency in the isolated production, the second number (*in italics*) the formant frequency in the /dVd/ form. These data were estimated by establishing a distance-to-frequency conversion from the frequency calibration lines, locating the center of each of the first three formants at (roughly) the temporal middle of the vowel, and obtaining the formant frequency as the number of millimeters (then converted to frequency) greater or less than the nearest calibration line.

	/i/	**/æ/**	**/ɑ/**	**/u/**
F1	213, *273*	788, *607*	818, *879*	242, *333*
F2	2333, *2242*	1818, *1788*	1121, *1333*	788, *1637*
F3	3061, *2939*	2516, *2516*	2637, *2514*	2272, *2454*

The plotted data are shown below:

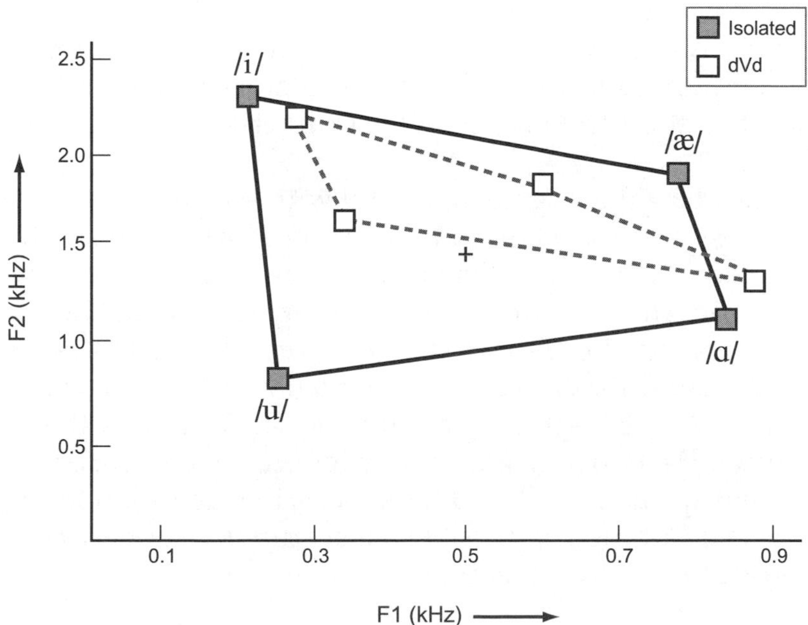

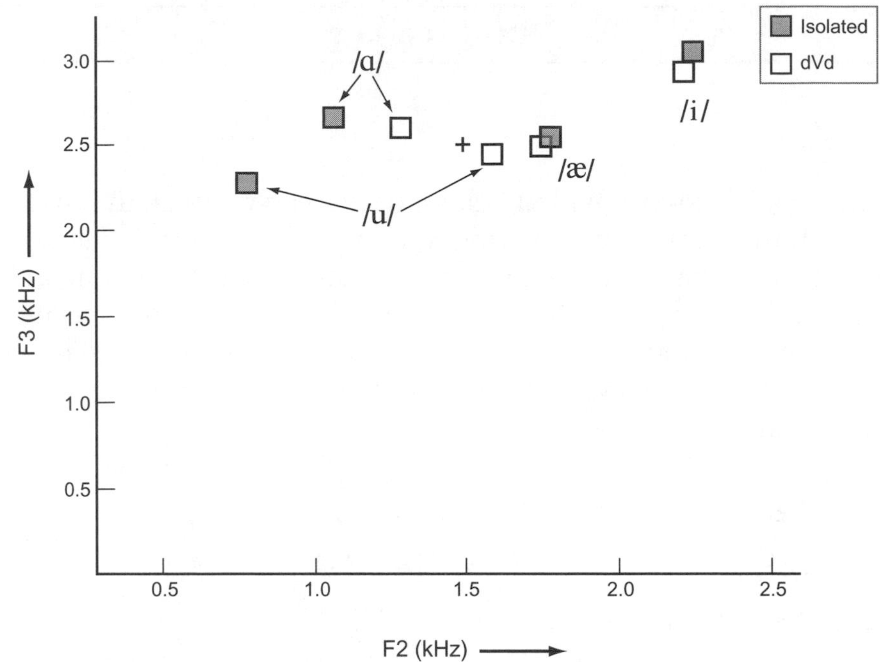

(a) The filled squares in these plots represent data from isolated vowels, the open squares data from vowels in /dVd/ forms. Both plots show a small plus sign marking the F1-F2 or F2-F3 coordinates expected for a male speaker whose vocal tract is in a "schwa" configuration, like that of a tube with a constant cross-sectional area from larynx to lips (a "straight" tube, lacking constrictions). Deviations of plotted points from the plus-sign coordinates can be thought of in articulatory terms as deformations of this "model" straight tube, produced by articulatory behavior. The greater the distance of a plotted point from the schwa coordinates, the greater the deformation.

(b) The isolated F1 and F2 values agree in general with the values for adult males reported by Hillenbrand et al. (1995) and reproduced in the textbook (Figure 11–3). Some of the isolated F1s are lower than those reported by Hillenbrand et al. (compare F1 values for /i/ and /u/) and there is some disagreement for the F1 of /æ/ between the current measures and those shown by Hillenbrand et al. (1995). However, most of the values in the table above fit in the lower left region of the corner vowel ellipses shown in Figure 11–2, as expected for adult-male production of the vowels. The differences between the two sets of data may reflect speaker variability, a difference in context (the current speaker produced the vowels in true isolation, Hillenbrand et al.'s speakers in an /hVd/ frame), or possible dialect differences between the current speaker and those studied by Hillenbrand et al.

(c) The F1–F2 plot shows two quadrilaterals for corner vowels in isolation (solid line) and in /dVd/ form (dashed line). Vowels in isolation clearly produce a "bigger" vowel space, with the coordinates of each vowel relatively far from the schwa coordinates. In articulatory terms, this indicates that the vocal tract configurations for the isolated vowels were substantially deformed from the straight-tube, schwa configuration.

In comparison, the quadrilateral for vowels in /dVd/ forms is much smaller, with coordinates for individual vowels closer to the schwa coordinates, except for /ɑ/. See Figure 11–7 (p. 531) in the textbook for a similar example. The articulatory inference from a comparison of the two quadrilaterals is that vowels produced in /dVd/, poststressed syllables have, using the straight-tube schwa shape as a reference, less "deformed" vocal tract configurations as compared to vowels produced in isolation. The F2–F3 plot shows a similar phenomenon. In every vowel case, the poststressed /dVd/ form results in F2–F3 coordinates closer to the F2–F3 schwa coordinate, as compared to the corresponding case for the isolated vowels.

11-2

Vowel formant frequencies may be interpreted with respect to their underlying articulatory causes. F1 largely reflects variations in the degree to which the vocal tract is open—otherwise known in phonetics as tongue height. Restrictions in F1 variation for a particular talker could reflect restrictions on the talker 's ability to move the jaw and/or tongue for tongue height variations. F2 largely reflects variations in tongue advancement, as well as variations in lip rounding. Restrictions in F2 variation could reflect limitations on the talker 's ability to advance and retract the tongue, and/or to round and spread the lips. These interpretations of F1 and F2 values must be made carefully. In addition, the "size" of the acoustic vowel quadrilateral formed by the F1–F2 coordinates of the four corner vowels in English (and sometimes by just three corner vowels, /ɑ, i, u/), seems to be a measure of overall articulatory flexibility and is often correlated with speech intelligibility (larger the vowel space, higher the intelligibility). Interpretation of size of the acoustic vowel space also requires care and consideration of speaker age, sex, dialect, and perhaps speaking rate.

11-3

(a) The American speakers appear to produce an overall larger vowel space. Connect the plotted points for the vowels and compare the two sets of speakers.

(b) The Mandarin speakers appear less flexible than the American speakers in the articulatory dimension of tongue advancement. Note how Mandarin speakers produce /u, ʊ, ʌ/ with roughly the same F2 (same tongue advancement) while varying tongue height (as inferred from variation along the F1 axis for these vowels). The American speakers also vary tongue height for these vowels but produce much more variation in F2, and by inference, in tongue advancement; some of this latter variation may also be attributed to differences across vowels in lip rounding. Similarly, the Mandarin speakers produce much less F2 variation across /i, ɪ, e/ as compared to the American speakers, suggesting the same articulatory interpretation that the Mandarin speakers use much less variation in tongue advancement to produce these mid to high vowels. Lip rounding should not be a significant issue for these latter vowels, so the data may be more directly interpretable in terms of variation (or the lack thereof) in the tongue advancement/backing dimension.

11-4

A "null context" vowel is a vowel produced either in isolation or an /hVd/ (where V = vowel) context. The idea is to obtain a vowel production that is minimally affected by surrounding phonetic context. The syllable-initial /h/ is assumed to have minimal influence on the vowel articulation. Formant frequencies measured in the null context have been regarded as the ideal "targets" for vowels and as reference points for comparison with formant frequencies from other, non-null contexts. Isolated vowels may appear to be a better representation of the idealized target, and therefore a better null context, but talkers tend to produce isolated vowels in an odd way (e.g., they sing them). The /hVd/ context is considered a more natural utterance and accomplishes the goal of vowel articulation under minimal influence from surrounding context, as shown by Stevens and House in 1963.

11-5

Articulatory undershoot describes the difference between the "target" F1–F2 coordinates for a particular vowel (the "target" formant frequencies being derived from the "null" context) and the production of the same vowel in a non-null context (e.g., where the vowel is surrounded by stops or fricatives, when the vowel is in an unstressed syllable, or part of casual-style speech, etc.). More specifically, the term "undershoot" is used when the formant frequencies move away from the "null" context values in the direction of the values for the schwa. This is illustrated in the hypothetical F1-F2 plot below, where the null context F1-F2 coordinates for the vowel /i/ are plotted as an unfilled circle and the coordinates for /ə/ are plotted as a filled circle.

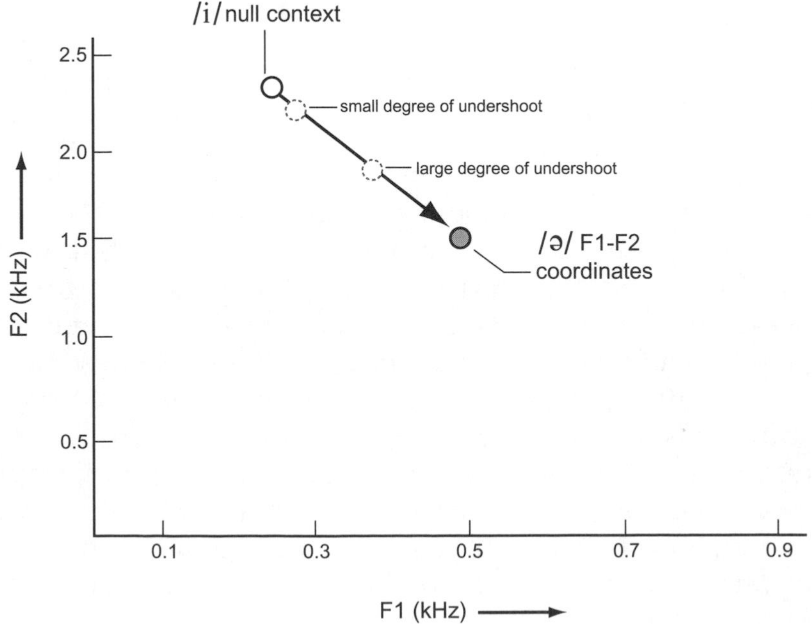

These are the two reference points required to describe the degree of undershoot for a particular vowel. The degree of undershoot can be regarded as the distance of the F1–F2 coordinate values *away from the null-context coordinates and in the direction of the schwa coordinates*. Two different hypothetical degrees of undershoot for the vowel /i/ are illustrated in the figure. The degree of undershoot is greater as the coordinates measured in a particular context move closer to the schwa coordinates (and simultaneously away from the null-context coordinates). The arrow extending from the null context to schwa coordinates can be thought of as one hypothetical "axis" along which undershoot can occur, but undershoot may occur in more complex ways as well (see, for example, the F1–F2 plot for Answer 11–1 above). In some unusual cases, a vowel in context may be at a greater distance from the schwa coordinates as compared to its null context coordinates (see, for example, the case of /ɑ/ in the F1–F2 plot for Answer 11–1 above); this may be a case of hyperarticulation.

11-6

The tense-lax difference for vowels is one example of intrinsic vowel duration differences. Given exactly the same phonetic context and with all other factors held constant, a tense vowel (e.g., /i/) has greater duration than the corresponding lax vowel (such as /ɪ/) (e.g., the vowel in the word "beat" is longer than the vowel in the word "bit"). The same difference is expected for the /e-ɛ/ and /u-ʊ/ pairs. A second example is that of low versus high vowels. With everything else equal, low vowels have greater duration than high vowels ("the vowel in "back" /bæk/ is longer than the vowel in "beak" /bik/; the vowel in "cot" /kɑt/ is longer than the vowel in "coot" /kut/).

11-7

Extrinsic factors that affect vowel durations include: (a) stress of syllable, (b) voicing characteristics of surrounding consonants—especially of the postvocalic consonant, (c) speaking rate, (d) position in utterance, and (e) style of speech (causal versus formal). Other factors such as emotional state may also affect vowel duration indirectly through their influence on speaking rate.

11-8

Start with the vowel /æ/ in the word "dad," where both the initial and final consonants are voiced. If "dad" is spoken in the utterance-final position, with sentence stress (as in an utterance where "dad" was emphasized to make sure the listener understood that it was "Dad" and not, say, "Dan"), and spoken at a very slow speaking rate, the vowel /æ/ would likely be about as long as possible. Surrounding consonants that are voiced, utterance-final position, pre-stressed, and produced at a slow speaking rate, are all factors that lengthen the duration of a vowel. When all these factors are operating simultaneously on the same vowel, it has a very long duration (as in the very slowly spoken sentence, "The guy on the corner was not Dan but DAD").

11-9

Arrows extending from the "piece" of the nasal murmur, defined by the 25-msec window, to the spectral "slice" display, show the correspondences between the spectrogram and spectrum displays for the first four major features (i.e., resonances and antiresonances) of the spectrum. Arrow #1: The nasal murmur F1 seen in the spectrogram corresponds to the low-frequency peak in the spectrum that has the greatest amplitude of any peak within the spectrum; this is consistent with the textbook description of the nasal murmur F1 being a relatively intense resonance located around 250 to 300 Hz. Arrow #2: The arrow extends from the middle of the white space on the spectrogram, centered around 800 Hz, to the prominent and sharp "dip" in the spectrum; this is the primary antiresonance of the nasal murmur, resulting from energy being trapped in the oral cavity. Arrow #3: The arrow extends from the second formant bar of the nasal murmur to the spectrum peak just below 1500 Hz; this is the second nasal resonance. Arrow #4: The arrow extends from the third formant bar of the nasal murmur to the third spectral peak, around 2250 Hz; this is the third nasal resonance. Other correspondences between the spectrographic and "slice-in-time" spectrum display can also be identified.

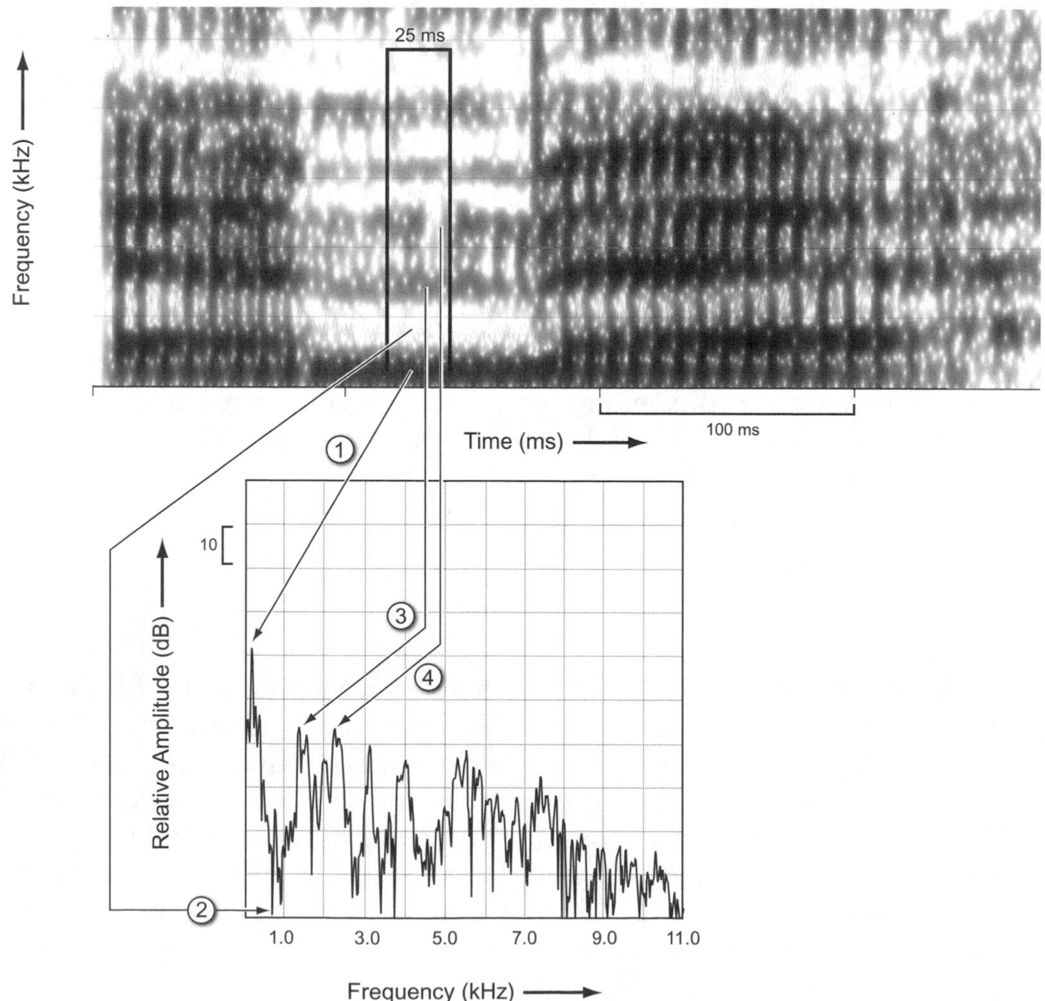

11-10

The potential cues to nasal murmur place of articulation include: (a) the frequency location of the primary antiresonance, which is approximately 700 to 1100 Hz for /m/, 1400 to 2200 Hz for /n/, and above 3000 Hz for /ŋ/; and (b) possibly the frequency locations of the nasal formants F2 through F4.

These cues are less than perfectly reliable because they are highly variable across speakers and are very sensitive to the surrounding phonetic context.

11-11

Potential nonmurmur cues to nasal place of articulation are the formant transition patterns from vowel-to-nasal (VC) or nasal-to-vowel (CV). These patterns, as described in the textbook, are most prominent in F2 and F3.

11-12

The formula $(A1 - P1)_{oral} - (A1 - P1)_{nasal}$ can be used as an index of velopharyngeal inadequacy (VPI). A1 refers to the amplitude of the first formant of a vowel, and P1 to the amplitude of the harmonic peak located at or very close to the frequency where a second nasal resonance is expected when a vowel is nasalized. These two peaks are shown below in an FFT spectrum of a vowel spoken in the non-nasalized CVC syllable (/bib/). A1 on the spectrum points to the first formant of the vowel /i/ (note the second and third formants of this vowel, roughly at 1950 Hz and 2600 Hz, respectively), and P1 points to a harmonic peak almost exactly at 1000 Hz. The region right around 1000 Hz is the expected location for the second nasal resonance (a resonance of the combined pharyngeal and nasal cavities, when they are coupled by velopharyngeal [VP] port opening). If the VP port is closed, as in the production of /bib/ from which this vowel spectrum was computed, the relative amplitude of the harmonic around 1000 Hz is expected to be fairly low; it is not emphasized by the presence of a nasal resonance. In this particular case, the A1 – P1 amplitude difference is approximately 30 dB, a value reported by Chen (1995) to be consistent with vowels produced in oral consonant environments (i.e., vowels that are non-nasalized). When a vowel is nasalized in a CVC such as /bib/, the acoustic effects on A1 and P1 are predictable from the acoustic theory of nasalization: the amplitude of the first oral formant, A1, decreases because of the effects of increased energy loss as well as the presence of antiresonances in the spectrum, and the amplitude of the harmonic close to the region of the second nasal resonance, P1, increases because it is emphasized by the nasal resonance. The effect of VPI on the A1 – P1 index is to *reduce* its value, relative to the "normal" values of A1 – P1.

Now imagine that researchers have collected normative data on the A1 – P1 difference in CVC syllables where C = oral consonants, and they express this as $(A1 - P1)_{oral}$. Consider this data collection effort to result in average $(A1 - P1)_{oral}$ values (the values will differ somewhat across vowels, and possibly across oral consonants having different places of articulation) that can be used as a standard against which to acoustically evaluate a client's VP port control. Clients with suspected VPI produce the same CVC syllables used to develop the $(A1 - P1)_{oral}$ norms, resulting in an $(A1 - P1)_{nasal}$ index that can be compared to the normative values obtained from speakers without VPI. The index $(A1 - P1)_{oral} - (A1 - P1)_{nasal}$ approximates a value of "zero" when a client produces the CVC syllable with a closed VP port, because the two amplitude differences $(A1 - P1)_{oral} - (A1 - P1)_{nasal}$ are the same; when one is subtracted from the other, the result is zero. More specifically, if these are $(A1 - P1)_{oral}$ norms, and a particular individual who does not have VPI produces a CVC where C = a non-nasal obstruent, the $(A1 - P1)_{oral}$ norms – $(A1 - P1)_{oral}$ for a particular production should be close to "zero." As a vowel is increasingly nasalized in the CVC form and the $(A1 - P1)_{nasal}$ value becomes smaller, the index, $(A1 - P1)_{oral} - (A1 - P1)_{nasal}$ grows *larger*.

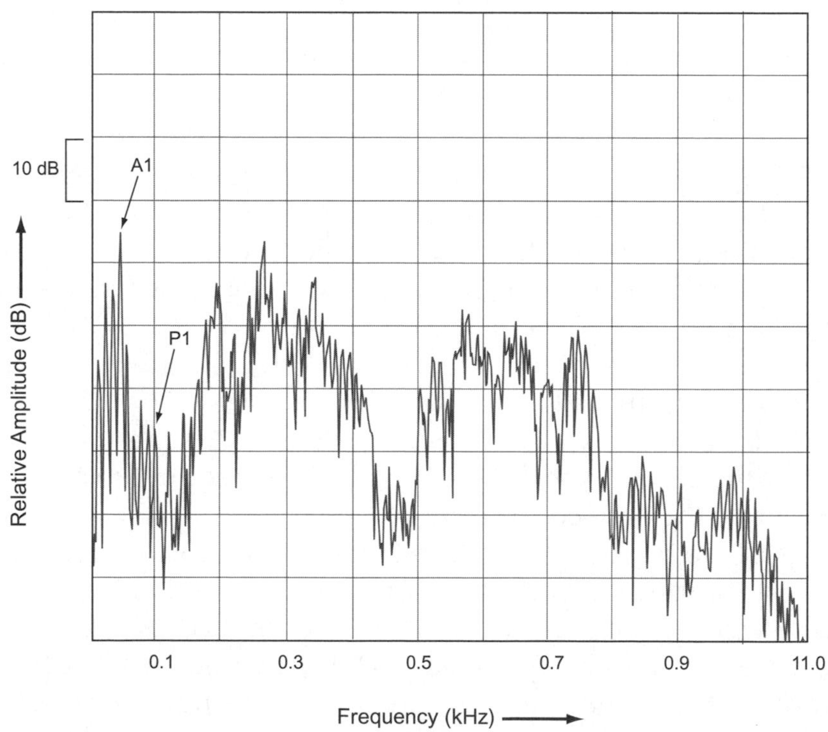

11–13

F2 and F3, as coordinates in an F2–F3 graph, are most likely to differentiate among the semivowels (see Figure 11–19 in the textbook, p. 552). F1 of the constriction interval is not useful in distinguishing among the semivowels because the value is very similar for /ɹ, l, w, j/.

11-14

All semivowels have rapid and extensive formant transitions into and out of their constriction intervals; these formant transitions reflect rapidly changing vocal tract configurations.

11-15

The spectrogram shows the nonsibilants (labeled "NS" in the spectrogram below) and sibilants (labeled "S"). The nonsibilants /θ/ and /f/ are distinguished from the sibilants /s/, /ʃ/, and /z/ primarily by their respective intensities; the nonsibilants are considerably less intense (as inferred by their lighter tracings) than the sibilants. The location(s) of primary frequency peaks for each of these fricatives can be estimated from the spectrograms by finding the locations within the fricative segments where the trace is darkest. For example, the nonsibilant /θ/ has its most intense energy between about 4.0 and 8.0 kHz, with possible peaks around 6.5 kHz and 7.5 kHz (note darkened areas around those frequencies). The sibilant /s/ has intense energy from 3.0 to 8.0 kHz, with what appears to be greatest energy between 3.5 to 4.0 kHz. The nonsibilant /f/ has energy extending from roughly 2.0 to 9.0 kHz, with regions of greatest energy between 6.0 to 8.0 kHz. The sibilant /ʃ/ has intense energy from 1.5 to 8.0 kHz, with areas of relatively intense energy around 2.5, 3.5, and between 5.0 and 6.0 kHz. Finally, the sibilant /z/ (which appears to be completely devoiced in this production, except for a few glottal pulses at the very end of the frication noise, just before the following vowel) has intense energy from roughly 3.0 to 8.0 kHz, with the most intense frequency region around 3.5 kHz.

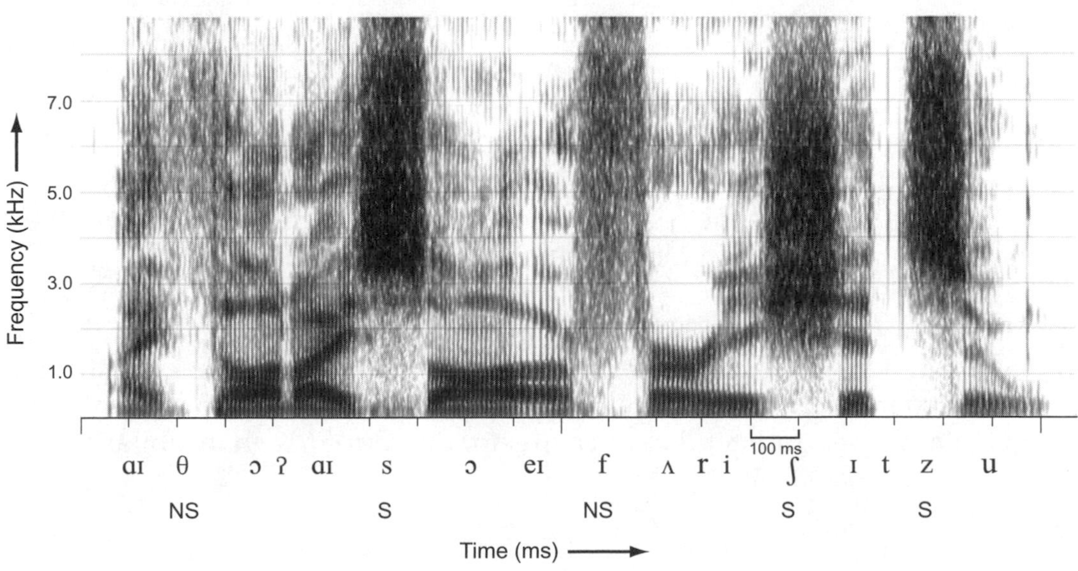

11–16

The table below shows the correct answers

Spectrum Description		
Fricative with sharp peak	Kurtosis =	positive
Vowel	Skewness =	positive
Nasal murmur	Skewness =	positive
/p/ burst	Skewness =	positive or close to zero
/f/	Kurtosis =	negative
/r/	Skewness =	positive

Explanation: In general, any "peaky" spectrum has kurtosis values in excess of the reference peakiness of the normal distribution, which has a spectral moments value of "zero." Therefore, a fricative with a sharp peak is likely to have a positive value of kurtosis. Any sound whose energy is concentrated in lower frequencies has a skewness value that is positive (lots of energy toward the low part of the distribution), with a long "tail" toward the high values of the distribution. This applies to spectra for vowels, nasals, and rhotics (note they all have "positive" skewness). A /p/ burst may have positive skewness (most energy in low frequencies) or skewness close to zero (if energy is spread more or less equally across the spectrum; see text). Finally, an /f/ spectrum tends to be flat and nonpeaky, which is associated with negative values of kurtosis (less peaked than the "normal" distribution).

11–17

(a) The value of M1, the "mean" of the spectrum, for lingual fricatives (such as /s/ or /ʃ/) is typically determined by the size of the cavity in front of the constriction; the larger the cavity, the lower the resonant frequency, and therefore the lower the mean of the frequencies (M1) within the frequency-analysis band.

(b) M2, or the variance of the spectrum (the dispersion of the energy within the energy band under analysis), will be greater for flatter, as compared to peakier, spectra. Nonsibilants such as /θ/ and /f/ tend to have flatter spectra than sibilants /s/ and /ʃ/. Nonsibilants therefore tend to have greater values of M2 than sibilants.

11-18

Voiceless fricatives, like other voiceless obstruents, are produced with the laryngeal devoicing gesture (LDG), a relatively slow opening-closing gesture of the vocal folds. This gesture is controlled by active muscular forces. The LDG separates the vocal folds and in doing so, prevents them from vibrating, an important component of voiceless consonants. The onset of the LDG is timed to coincide with the onset of supraglottal constriction for fricatives, and the duration of the typical LDG is approximately 120 to 150 ms. If the supraglottal constriction is released prior to the completion of the LDG, there is a substantial interval of aspiration. Because such aspiration is a common characteristic of English voiceless *stops*, the presence of aspiration during production of a voiceless fricative whose supraglottal constriction is released too soon, relative to completion of the LDG, could result in the fricative having substantial aspiration and being perceived as a voiceless stop. The fricative constriction is maintained for about 120 to 150 ms (or sometimes a little longer) to "match" the duration of the LDG and avoid this potential confusion. In this sense, the duration of voiceless fricatives is determined by laryngeal articulatory events.

11-19

Spectrographically, /h/ has a noise interval, typically of relatively weak intensity. Within the noise interval, there are likely to be formant-like areas (darkened regions) "lined up" with the formants of surrounding vowels. Also, there is likely to be very weak or no energy in the region of F1 of the surrounding vowels during the /h/ interval; energy at that frequency location is absorbed in the trachea. Finally, some /h/ sounds have a mix of noise energy and weak voicing energy.

11-20

There are several articulatory changes that can modify the VOT as shown in Figure 11–28 in the textbook. Below is a reproduction and elaboration of that figure to illustrate these changes and how they affect VOT. In the top trace glottal activity is shown for a VCV where C = voiceless stop, as discussed in the textbook. Example 1 of "Timing of Stop Closure" shows the original physiologic events, where the onset of the supraglottal closure for the stop is synchronized with the onset of the LDG. This synchrony point is indicated by the long, dashed vertical line at the left side of the figure. In this original example, the time interval between the release of the supraglottal gesture (right edge of rectangle showing the duration of the supraglottal closure) and the end of the LDG (beginning of vocal fold vibration, indicated by the long dashed vertical line on the right-hand side of the figure) is the VOT. Examples 2 and 3 show how dysynchronies between the onsets of the LDG and supraglottal closure can affect the value of VOT. Example 2 shows the onset of the supraglottal closure *leading* (ahead of, in time) the onset of the LDG, with exactly the same closure duration and LDG magnitude and duration as in Example 1.

In this case, the VOT is longer than in Example 1. The only event that has changed is the lack of synchrony between the onsets of the two events. Example 3 is a similar example of dysynchrony, but in this case the onset of the supraglottal closure *lags* the onset of the LDG. With no change in the closure duration or the LDG, this dysynchrony results in a shorter VOT. Examples 4 and 5 illustrate how changes in the supraglottal closure duration, with all other events held constant (including the synchrony of LDG and supraglottal closure onsets), can affect the VOT value. In Example 4, a longer closure duration results in a shorter VOT, and in Example 5, a shorter closure duration results in a longer VOT, with everything else constant. Finally, the dashed LDG, when compared to the solid-line LDG, shows how a reduction in the magnitude of the LDG (which may occur in cases of laryngeal muscular weakness, particularly of the muscle that opens the vocal folds [posterior cricoarytenoid] for the LDG) can result in a shorter VOT. The smaller opening means that the vocal folds return to the phonation-ready position earlier, allowing the vocal folds to initiate vibration earlier, which shortens the VOT when all other events are held constant. These examples show that inferences from acoustically measured VOT to underlying physiologic events are complex!

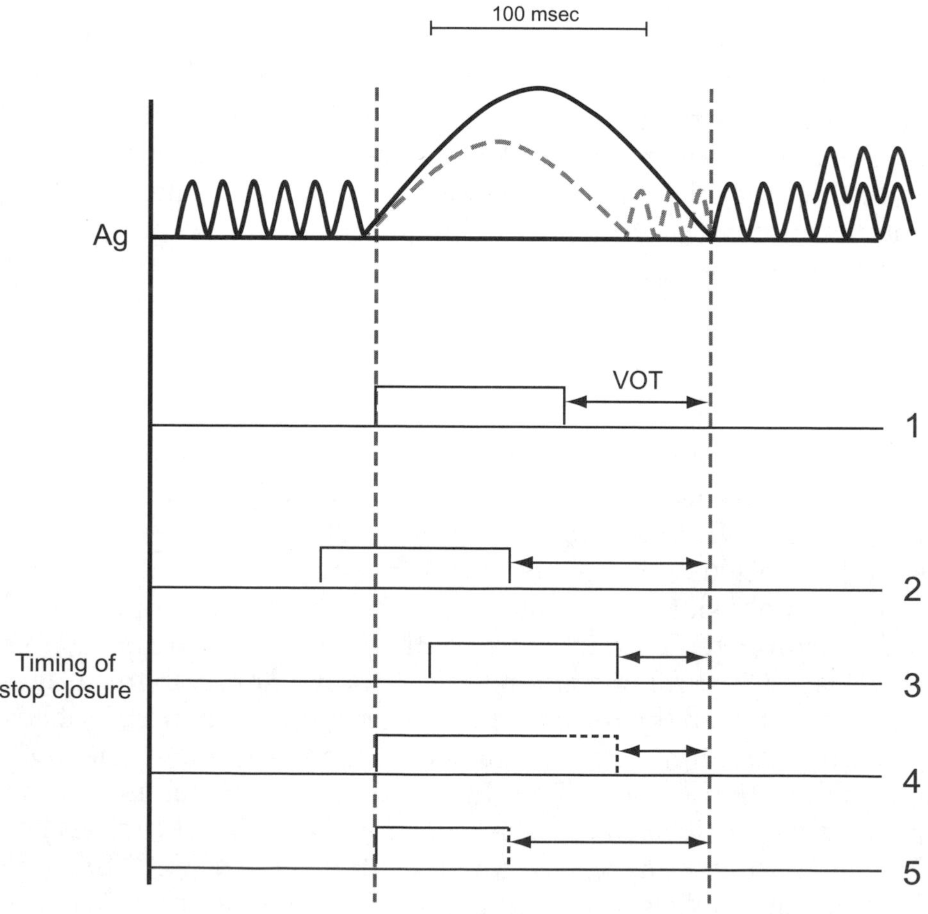

11-21

(a) Positive VOTs are recorded when the first glottal pulse occurs *after* the stop release (i.e., the stop burst); negative VOT's are recorded when the first glottal pulse occurs *prior* to the stop release.

(b) Most VOTs of singleton (unclustered) voiceless stops are in the so-called, "long-lag range," meaning, the first glottal pulse occurs at least 25 ms after the stop release, in contrast to many voiced stops in American English which are produced in the short-lag range: between 0 and +20 ms (some voiced stops are produced with voicing "lead": VOT having negative values). When voiceless stops are produced in s + stop clusters, the VOT of the stop is typically in the short-lag range, like English voiced stops. Even so, when listeners are asked about the voicing status of voiceless stops in s + stop clusters, they label them as voiceless.

11-22

A spectral template is a spectral shape (the pattern of amplitudes over a specified range of frequencies) that is thought to capture the consistent features of a burst spectrum associated with a particular place of articulation. Spectral templates are like "ideal" spectra for the different stop places of articulation and capture the essential features of a place-specific spectrum even with changing phonetic contexts, changing speakers, and changing speaking styles (e.g., causal vs. formal). Spectral templates for stop place of articulation were developed from short-duration spectra computed from a time interval extending roughly 25 ms from the stop burst into the frication interval.

11-23

The labeled spectrograms below show that for the top-row pair, the VCV's are /ɛtʃɛ/ and /ɛtɛ/; the bottom shows /ɛdɛ/ and /ɛdʒɛ/. The affricate in each pair is easily identified by its much longer frication interval: the relatively intense interval of aperiodic energy following the burst. Note also the slightly shorter closure duration for the affricate, as compared to its singleton companion.

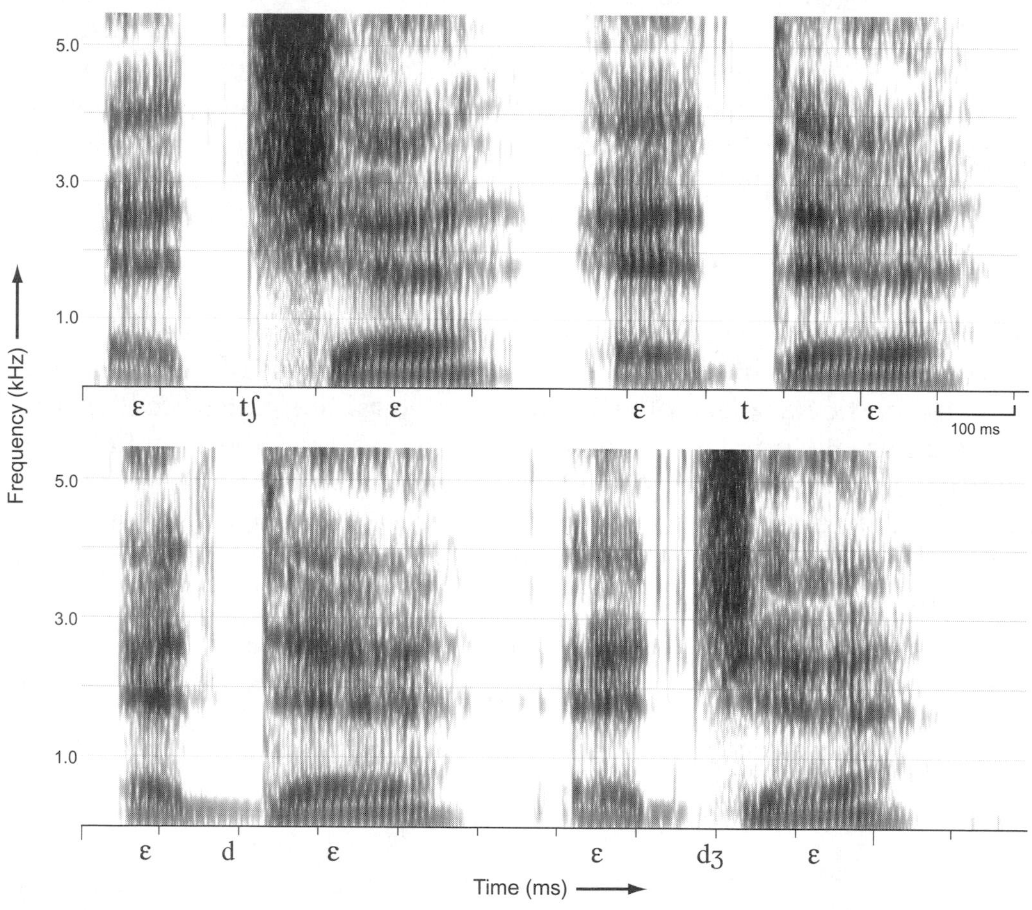

11-24

(a) F0 contours for declarative utterances typically have their peak values near the beginning of the utterance (often the first or second content word), with slowly falling values for the rest of the utterance and either a sharp drop at the end or a steady value or slight rise (see [b]).

(b) Speakers create a rapidly declining F0 at the end of utterances to signal that they are finished speaking, and either raise their F0 slightly at the end or do not allow the F0 values to fall rapidly to signal their intent to continue speaking.

11-25

The F0 contour of the top spectrogram is relatively flat (unchanging as a function of time). In contrast, the F0 contour of the bottom spectrogram has relatively large changes as a function of time, and the big, sweeping change on the word "love" suggests that this word was produced with a great deal of emphasis. Stated in another way, it appears as if in the bottom spectrogram the speaker really means it!

CHAPTER 12

12-1

The pattern-playback machine, an early speech synthesizer, required a scientist to paint spectrographic patterns on a clear sheet of plastic. When the painted pattern was illuminated by a light source as the plastic sheet was conveyed across the instrument by a moving surface, the patterns of light reflection from the dark versus light-painted areas were converted to sound. The painted patterns were simplified versions of actual spectrograms for syllables such as /bɑ/, /dɑ/, and /gɑ/. Many listeners heard these simplified representations of spectrographic patterns as the syllables the painted patterns were meant to represent (in other words, as /bɑ/, /dɑ/, and /gɑ/, or any other syllable pattern that was painted). This "proved" that the machine could synthesize speech patterns, and allowed scientists to make very small changes in the painted patterns to determine how these changes related to the perception of stop place of articulation, vowel identity, and other phonetic events.

12-2

The continuum of signals created on the pattern-playback machine was a series of two-formant stimuli, varying from the ideal /b/ configuration, to the /d/ configuration, and finally to the /g/ configuration. In the early identification experiments, the scientists had shown that an F2 transition starting frequency around 700 Hz gave the best /b/ responses, at 1800 Hz the best /d/ responses, and around 3000 Hz the best /g/ responses. These initial experiments led the scientists to believe that the F2 transition starting frequency was the critical cue to identifying place of articulation for stops. A *continuum* of stimuli was created by painting patterns that varied the F2 transition starting frequency in 50-Hz steps, from the ideal /b/ through the ideal /d/, and finishing at the ideal /g/ (e.g., starting frequencies of 700 Hz, 750 Hz, 800 Hz, etc.). The scientists were able to create this continuum of F2 starting frequencies because they had complete control over the painted patterns.

12-3

In an *identification* experiment, listeners hear a series of stimuli and are required to provide a label for each stimulus. The labels are typically restricted to a small group of possible responses. In the original Haskins Labs identification experiments, listeners heard the stimuli from the continuum of F2 starting frequencies and were required to label each stimulus as /b/, /d/, or /g/. This is sometimes called a forced-choiced identification (or labeling) experiment, because the listeners had no other option than the three choices noted above. The identification experiment determines which stimuli belong within a category and which belong to different categories. In a *discrimination* experiment, listeners are presented with two stimuli, either from within one of the categories determined by the identification experiment, or one each from different categories determined by the identification experiment. If the identification experiment has truly revealed stimuli that are heard categorically, listeners should not be able to discriminate pairs of stimuli chosen from *within* a category determined by the identification experiment. When members of a stimulus pair are chosen from different categories established by the identification experiment, they should be discriminated with very high accuracy, even when the stimulus pair is chosen to "straddle" a category boundary. The discrimination experiment is so critical to the interpretation of categorical perception because the identification experiment forces listeners to use a label (i.e., a place of articulation), and the appearance of categorical perception functions may result simply because of the restriction of available labels. If the discrimination experiment reveals chance discrimination ability when a stimulus pair is chosen from within a category, but high discrimination ability when members of the stimulus pair are chosen from either side of a category boundary, even when the physical difference between the stimulus pairs are the same for within- versus across-boundary pairs, the categorical perception demonstrated in the identification experiment is thought to be proven.

12-4

Scientists at Haskins Labs performed perceptual experiments in which they demonstrated that the perception of a single, stop place of articulation (such as the perception of /d/) was related to many different acoustic patterns. More specifically, when synthesized stimuli were generated with the pattern-playback device, a variety of starting frequencies and directions (rising or falling) for F2 transitions were shown to be associated with the perception of a given place of articulation. This acoustic variation was observed, as an example, when the /d/ was paired with different vowels. The scientists reasoned that if a wide variety of acoustic signals cued the same percept, listeners were unlikely to remember all these patterns as reliable cues to the stop place of articulation. Rather, listeners depended on some other, more stable perceptual process to make decisions concerning place of articulation. The Haskins Labs scientists looked to the articulation of the stop as the stable cue to place of articulation. A motor theory of speech perception was deemed necessary because the place of articulation for a stop consonant remained constant across a variety of vowel contexts, even as the acoustic patterns differed across the varying vowel contexts. Listeners transformed the acoustic signal, via a species-specific, "automatic" module in the brain, into this stable articulatory representation; speech was perceived by reference to the articulation that produced it.

12-5

Because the motor theory of speech perception, both in the original and revised form, claimed that a species-specific, human mechanism was used to perceive speech, and, in particular, was responsible for the categorical perception of stop place of articulation, scientists were interested to know how animals responded to the stimuli used in the human experiments on categorical perception. The reasoning for the animal experiments is very simple. If animals had categorical perception functions for synthetic speech stimuli like those observed in humans, the categorical functions observed in humans could not be taken as "proof" that speech perception was limited by speech production (humans perceived place of articulation categorically because they produced the places categorically: this is the hypothesized link between the perception and production mechanisms in the motor theory). Animals were shown to perceive place of articulation categorically, in much the same way as humans; because animals do not articulate stop consonants, their categorical perception of stop place of articulation was inconsistent with the hypothesized species-specific link between speech production and perception. The similar perception of speech signals by animals and humans suggested another theoretical view of speech perception: that it was based on information in the acoustic signal (or at least partially based on this information), and did not require special mechanisms to process the signal. Animals such as chinchillas and birds, who have auditory mechanisms similar to those of humans, show speech perception behavior similar to that of humans because they are using similar auditory mechanisms. "Auditory theories" of speech perception claim that the information in the speech acoustic signal is sufficient to support speech perception —there is no need to hypothesize special mechanisms in humans for the decoding of speech signals.

12-6

The "duplex" in "duplex perception" is the simultaneous percept of a single component of a speech signal in both the hypothesized "speech mode" and "general auditory mode." In other words, one part of a speech signal elicits, simultaneously, a phonetic percept and a nonphonetic percept. In the duplex perception experiments, a brief F3 transition was shown to cue place of articulation for a stop consonant while also producing an impression of a rising or falling whistle (the rise or fall depending on the direction of the transition). This "duplex" perception was thought to prove the engagement, in response to a speech signal, of a species-specific, dedicated brain module for the perception of speech. In these experiments, the manipulation of the speech signal showed that an *isolated* F3 transition was heard as a nonphonetic "chirp" (a pitch glide). On the other hand, when a synthesized signal lacking only this F3 transition (i.e., with correct vowel formants, and intact F1 and F2 transitions) was presented to listeners, many heard the signal as a poor version of a stop-vowel syllable, as if the stop had an ambiguous place of articulation. The presentation of the F3 transition "piece" in one ear and the remainder of the signal in the other ear resulted in the percept of a clear stop-vowel syllable, with an unambiguous place of articulation, *plus the "chirp."* The F3 transition appeared to be doing double duty: as part of a speech signal that engaged the special speech mode of perception to elicit the clear percept of a stop consonant, and as a signal analyzed by "general" auditory mechanisms to elicit the percept of a "chirp."

The duplex evidence for a species-specific (human) mechanism for speech perception is compromised to a significant degree by the experimental evidence showing duplex perception for nonspeech signals, such as the sound of a slamming door. When the spectrum of a slamming door is separated into a lower and upper frequency region, the two signals are heard differently when presented separately: the lower spectrum signal is heard as a dull thud, the upper spectrum signal as a shaking can of rice or jangling keys. When these two signals are presented under duplex perception conditions, however, the perceptual impression is a simultaneous "good" slamming door and shaking can of rice! This duplex percept from a single signal, whose spectral characteristics have been separated in much the same way as the F3 transition was separated from the stop-vowel syllable, seems to imply—based on the logic used in the speech duplex experiment—that the brain has a special module for perceiving the sound of slamming doors. And of course that is not reasonable.

12-7

(a) These /k/ burst spectra are displayed over a frequency range of 0 to 11 kHz. All three of the spectra have increasing energy in the low frequencies up to a peak, which is the strongest energy component in each spectrum. From that peak in the spectrum, all three spectra have slowly decreasing energy with increasing frequency. Thus, the shapes of these three spectra are similar, with a fairly rapid increase in energy to a major peak, followed by slowly decreasing energy across the remainder of the frequency range. One could describe each spectrum as having a central peak surrounded by lesser energy on either side of that peak.

(b) The differences in the spectra are that one has the peak at a much lower frequency than the other two (the left-most spectrum just below 2.0 kHz, and the middle and right-hand spectra at 3.0 kHz), and the details of "secondary" peaks (especially those at the higher frequencies) vary quite a bit across the three spectra.

(c) Spectral similarities and differences for spectra derived from the same sound, such as the /k/ burst of these three spectra, have had an important influence on theories of speech perception. For example, the *detailed* differences in the spectra, such as the frequency differences for the major peak and the differences in secondary peak locations, have been argued by some scientists as showing that the acoustic characteristics of speech sounds are too variable across contexts to support an "auditory theory" of speech perception. An auditory theory is one in which the listener depends on stable information in the speech signal to make reliable identifications of incoming speech sounds. If this information is too variable, a listener cannot use the acoustic signal as a reliable source of speech sound identity. This is essentially the argument for a motor theory of speech perception. Other scientists, however, have argued for attention to the *gross* characteristics of speech spectra such as the three /k/ burst spectra shown here, not the detailed differences discussed above. In this view, all three of these /k/ burst spectra have the same shape, that is, a central peak surrounded by lesser energy below and above the frequency of this peak. This gross shape, according to this view, is sufficiently stable across phonetic contexts, speakers, speaking styles, and other sources of speech variation to permit listeners to use the acoustic information reliably as an indicator of /k/ (or /g/, depending on other cues such as VOT) articulation.

This view is consistent with an auditory theory of speech perception, and is thought to eliminate the need for specialized mechanisms for the perception of human speech.

12-8

The "trading relations" phenomenon is often taken as support for a motor theory of speech perception, and more specifically for the revised motor theory. The revised motor theory claims that the special speech perception module in the brain of humans is designed to transform components of the speech acoustic signal into the underlying articulatory gestures that produced the signal. Because articulatory gestures are produced over time, their acoustic effects are distributed over time. Listeners appear to perceive speech by taking the acoustic information across a time interval, rather than at a single point in time, and integrating it by means of the specialized speech perception mechanism to yield an output corresponding to the articulatory gesture most likely to have produced the acoustic information within the time interval. This was illustrated in Figures 12–9 and 12–10 (pp. 606–607) in the textbook. Researchers showed that the perceptual effect of one "piece" of a speech acoustic signal can be offset by manipulating a nearby but separate piece of the speech acoustic signal. In other words, different combinations of adjacent or nearly adjacent acoustic events can cue perception of the same phonetic event. For some scientists it seems unreasonable for humans to know all potential combinations of speech acoustic events that can cue the many phonetic percepts in the sound system of any language. It seems more reasonable for a speech perception mechanism to integrate the acoustic cues and determine the gesture that produced them.

The spectrogram included with Question 12–8 is reproduced below with additional information to illustrate how these two speech signals can be used to demonstrate trading relations. The ovals superimposed on the frication noises indicate the regions where the aperiodic energy is most intense. When the /s/ precedes /i/, this region is around 5.0 kHz; but when the /s/ precedes /u/, the most intense frication energy is around 3.0 kHz. The shift in the region of most intense energy for these two /s/ sounds is the result of the differing articulatory, and therefore spectral characteristics of the following vowels. The /i/ has spread lips and therefore a relatively short vocal cavity in front of the lingua-alveolar fricative constriction; in the case of /u/, which is likely to involve a certain degree of lip extension (for rounding), the cavity is longer and larger. These cavity differences are reflected in the higher F2 of /i/ (around 2.2 kHz at the vowel midpoint in the spectrogram below), as compared to the F2 of /u/ (around 1.0 kHz at the vowel midpoint). Because these vowel articulatory differences are coarticulated with the /s/ production, the vowel-related spectral differences are seen in the frication noise as well, as indicated by the ovals on the two frication noises.

Now imagine an experiment in which an /s/ frication noise is synthesized with its greatest energy *midway* between the ones shown in the spectrogram (i.e., at 4.0 kHz). Then imagine the vowel being synthesized with an F2 midway between the F2s of the two vowels /i/ and /u/ (for the vowels below, an F2 halfway between them is roughly 1.6 kHz). If an /s/ + vowel signal with these midway frication noise peaks and vowel F2s is presented to listeners who are told to choose either /si/ or /su/, there is a strong likelihood that the "ambiguous" speech signals will yield ambiguous responses (perfect ambiguity has 50% of the responses /si/, 50% /su/). Now we change the /s/ frication noise to a slightly higher frequency, say 4.5 kHz, but leave the vowel at the F2 midway point (1.6 kHz) described above. What happens? More listeners will respond with /si/, because the integrated cues of frication noise peak energy and vowel F2 are biased toward the high-front vowel context (because of the higher resonant frequency of the /s/ spectrum). Now comes the interesting part. This new bias toward /si/ can be offset by decreasing the F2 of the vowel, from the midway value of 1.6 kHz, in the direction of the /u/ F2. A 50-50%, "perfect" ambiguity for this signal can be re-established for a signal that is different from the original ambiguous signal. The spectral characteristics of the /s/ noise can be traded against the F2 of the following vowel to produce this equivalent effect. Scientists who supported the revised motor theory argued that this was a form of proof that the s + vowel gesture was perceived by integrating the syllable-sized acoustic information, not by correlating specific (and fixed, or invariant) acoustic cues to specific segments.

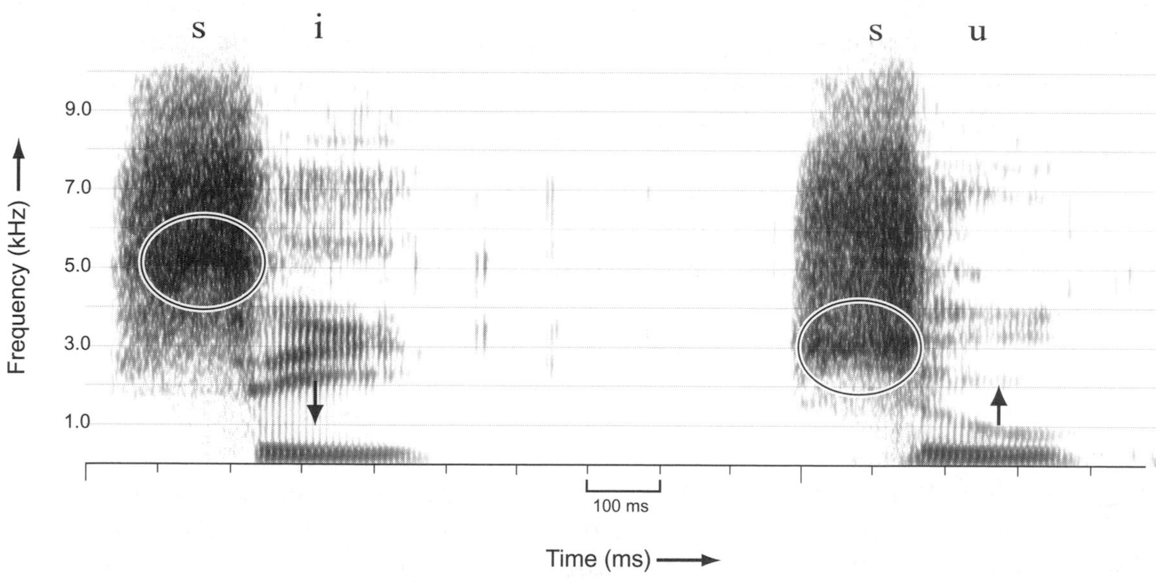

12-9

An auditory theory of speech perception is reasonable because even with all the acoustic variability in a given speech sound, a core consistency across phonetic contexts, speakers, and so forth may still be found if a scientist looks at the speech signal in the right place or in the right way (or both). In other words, a scientist's definition of "variability" determines the likelihood that an auditory theory of speech perception can reasonably explain how people perceive speech. If a scientist requires the acoustic characteristics of a speech sound to have a *detailed consistency* across all the variables that may change a speech signal, a stable characteristic for the speech sound will not be found. However, if some of the detailed variations are ignored and a broader consistency is found, an auditory theory of speech perception may be reasonable. This is the approach taken by Blumstein and Stevens (1979) in their study of the acoustic characteristics of stop bursts. First, these scientists looked for consistency where the Haskins scientists had not looked. Blumstein and Stevens examined stop burst spectra, whereas the Haskins scientists had only examined formant transition patterns (see explanation in the textbook). Second, Blumstein and Stevens treated the stop burst spectrum as an overall shape, rather than paying attention to the many details of a speech spectrum (See also Question and Answer 12–7). Finally, the degree to which a speech spectrum, or any acoustic characteristic of a speech sound, must be absolutely constant across contexts, speakers, and so forth depends on a perspective concerning the extent to which speech perception is a matter of identifying a sequence of sounds and then putting them together to form words. A view of speech perception that depends heavily on such bottom-up processing, in which precise analyses of incoming speech segments are critical to determining the meaning of the incoming message, does require a fairly rigid stability in the acoustic characteristics of speech sounds. However, there is good evidence that speech perception makes use of top-down processes, in which various language perception processes (knowledge of topic, preceding words, etc.) are used to clarify the incoming signal. It is as if the listener is constantly formulating hypotheses concerning the identity of the incoming words, based on his or her knowledge of everything relevant to the communication situation. Under these circumstances, where some ambiguity in the acoustic signal can be resolved by these top-down processes, absolute constancy of the acoustic characteristics of particular speech sounds is clearly not required.

12–10

In the figure below, two *y*-axes are shown. The left-hand *y*-axis shows percentage identification of /b/ when listeners are given the response options of /b/ versus /d/, and the right-hand *y*-axis shows the percentage of "different" responses when two of the stimuli along the *x*-axis are presented to listeners in pairs and the task is to say whether the two stimuli are the "same" or "different." Imagine the stimulus numbers along the *x*-axis to correspond to a series of signals, varied by small and equal steps across the stimulus series, whose acoustic characteristics are known to be relevant to the /b-d/ distinction. The identification function (solid line) shows that stimuli 1–5 are labeled /b/ 100% of the time they are presented; between stimuli 6 and 7 there is a very sharp decline in the function; and for stimuli 7–14 there are 0% /b/ identifications. This is a classic categorical perception identification function, where one sequence of stimuli (in this case, 1–5) elicits only one response (/b/, in this case) up to a certain point in the sequence or continuum where a sharp drop in identification occurs over two stimuli (between 6 and 7). The succeeding stimuli along the continuum (7–14) yield a completely different identification (in this hypothetical case, most likely /d/). The identification function only "proves" categorical perception if a discrimination task demonstrates that the "same-different" judgment produces chance behavior (average of 50% correct) when two stimuli are chosen from *within* a category determined from the identification experiment (e.g., stimuli 2 and 4 in the figure below), but nearly perfect discrimination ("different" responses) when the stimuli are chosen from either side of a category boundary (such as stimuli 5 and 7 in the figure). The figure shows a case where the discrimination data, plotted as the dashed line, do not support the categorical function implied by the identification function. Note the discrimination performance peaks *within* the /b/ category determined in the identification experiment; note also the absence of a clear peak in discrimination performance *across* the category boundary.

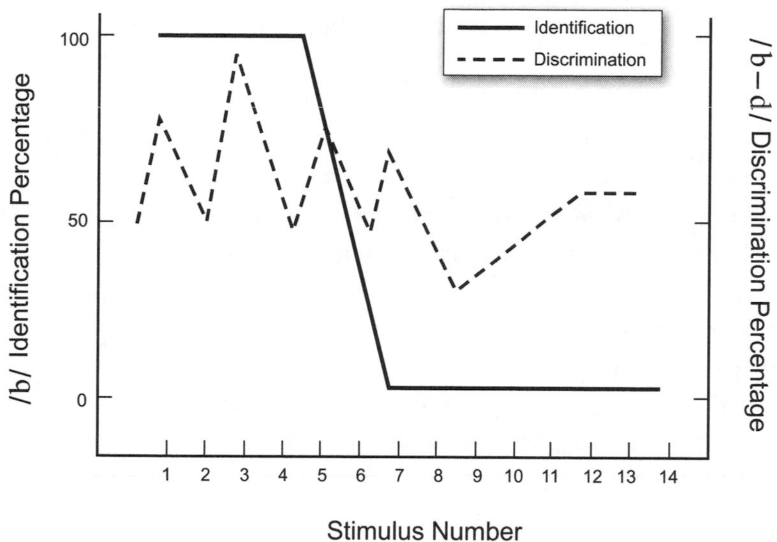

Following is a graph of discrimination data that would support the finding of categorical perception implied by the identification data.

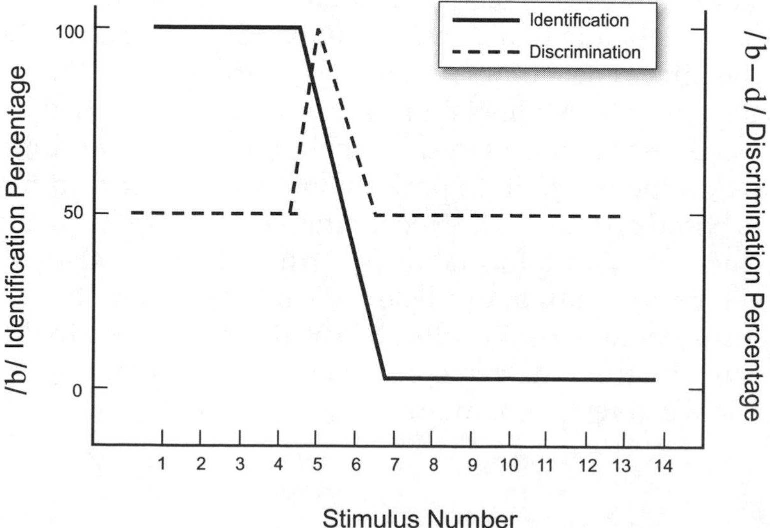

12-11

Data on categorical perception were interpreted as evidence of a match between speech perception and production processes by the Haskins scientists—you perceived place of articulation categorically because you could only produce categorical differences in place of articulation. This was then used to argue for a human-specific mechanism for the perception of speech (i.e., the motor theory). However, when it was demonstrated that animals perceived place of articulation categorically as well, the "proof" for a human-specific mechanism for the perception of speech became less convincing.

12-12

An auditory theory of speech perception requires a listener to analyze the incoming signal, extract its "stable" characteristics by means of some (as of yet) unspecified cognitive operations, and presumably match these to a stored set of acoustic-phonetic templates. These templates have presumably been developed over time by listening to a lot of speech. Direct realism attempts to eliminate all this analysis of the acoustic waveform and the learning of such templates by claiming that speech gestures are perceived directly, without the need for cognitive operations. In this sense, the proponents of direct realism regard this theory of speech perception as "simpler" than auditory theories of speech perception.

12-13

The most straightforward answer to this question is that listeners, when perceiving speech, seem to be sensitive to much more than just word representations. For example, nonphonemic information, including allophonic variation and speaker identity, seems to have an influence on the perception of speech. Neither of these factors typically is associated with the abstract, phonemic representation of words. As discussed in the textbook, a clear example of the importance of nonphonemic information in the perception of speech is found in the study by Mullenix, Pisoni, and Martin (1989), who showed that word recognition was poorer when a word list including words produced by a variety of talkers was compared to the recognition performance from a list read by a single talker. If speech perception is based strictly on the recognition of words via an abstract phonemic representation in which all other information is "stripped away," the word /spitʃ/ should have exactly the same representation in a listener 's mind, regardless of who the speaker is or what his or her dialect may be. Results such as those reported by Mullenix et al. suggest that more is involved in the perception of speech than an ultimate destination of an abstract, phonemic word representation.

12-14

Speech intelligibility testing originally was developed to evaluate the goodness of transmission (communication) systems. These evaluations consider the sender (e.g., a talker) to be normal and "constant," and employ listeners with normal hearing, while varying the characteristics of a transmission system. These variations may include amount of noise in the system, the bandwidth of the transmission (which frequencies are allowed to pass energy, which frequencies are not), the overall energy in the system, and so forth. Speech intelligibility also may be used to evaluate the speech reception abilities of listeners when the sender and transmission system are "good" and held constant. An example of this would be an evaluation of how a hearing loss affects a listener 's ability to hear a standard set of normally spoken words as transmitted through a "normal" system (or, through a system with varying degrees of noise, if one is interested in the interaction between listener problems and transmission problems). Finally, speech intelligibility is used to evaluate the ability of a talker to be understood through a good transmission system and with normal-hearing listeners. The intelligibility score can then be used as an index of the severity of speech involvement.

CHAPTER 13

13-1

a. Oral cavity
b. Upper esophageal sphincter
c. Lower esophageal sphincter
d. Pyloric sphincter
e. Small intestine
f. Stomach
g. Diaphragm
h. Esophagus
i. Pharyngeal cavity

13-2

(a) striated; smooth; smooth

(b) cricopharyngeus; middle constrictor

(c) smooth

(d) higher; slower

(e) higher

(f) The contents of the stomach (food and/or liquid) could flow back (reflux) into the esophagus.

13-3

(a) __c__ The velopharynx closes.

__a__ A solid bolus is masticated.

__d__ The bolus moves by peristalsis.

__c__ The constrictor muscles contract sequentially.

__c__ The upper esophageal sphincter begins to open.

__a__ A liquid bolus is contained in the anterior oral cavity.

__b__ The velum begins to elevate.

__b__ The bolus moves toward the pharynx.

__c__ The larynx elevates and closes.

__d__ The bolus enters the upper esophageal sphincter.

__c__ The epiglottis moves backward and downward.

__a__ The back of the tongue elevates to separate the oral cavity from the pharyngeal cavity.

(b) *Deglutition* includes all phases of swallowing (oral preparatory, oral transport, pharyngeal transport, and esophageal transport). Technically, the term *swallowing* includes only the pharyngeal transport phase, but it is often used to refer to the all phases of deglutition.

(c) A *bolus* is the mass of solid substance (food) or volume of liquid to be swallowed.

(d) *Apnea* is the cessation of breathing.

(e) Pharyngeal transport phase

(f) The oral preparatory phase usually lasts about 1 second for a liquid bolus, but can last as long as 20 seconds for a solid bolus, depending how long it is chewed.

(g) less than 0.5 second

(h) less than 0.5 second

(i) 8 to 20 seconds

(j) Yes

A good example of overlap is during the eating of food, when part of the substance is chewed and moves into the pharyngeal area while the rest of the substance is being chewed.

13-4

(a) 1 second

(b) expire

(c) The flow of expired air may help to move any food or liquid away from the lower airways to help prevent aspiration.

(d) True

(e) slightly larger than the resting expiratory level

13-5

(a) V (trigeminal)

VII (facial)

IX (glossopharyngeal)

X (vagus)

XI (accessory)

XII (hypoglossal)

(b) C1–8 (cervical 1–8)

T1–12 (thoracic 1–12)

L1–2 (lumbar 1–2)

(c) cranial nerve X (vagus)

(d) autonomic

(e) oral preparatory and oral transport; pharyngeal transport and esophageal transport

13-6

(a) more time; higher forces

(b) True

(c) thinner; larger

(d) Yes

(e) False

(f) During sequential swallows (in contrast to single swallows):

overall movement times for individual swallows are shorter;

certain movements may occur simultaneously;

the hyolaryngeal complex does not fall back to the resting level after each swallow;

successive boluses often merge in the epiglottic valleculae before the pharyngeal transport phase is triggered;

laryngeal penetration is more common;

inspirations following the apneic interval are more common;

esophageal peristalsis is lower in force and frequency.

(g) You can voluntarily increase the pressure exerted during the swallow by using more effort.

(h) True

13-7

(a) False (it occurs before birth)

(b) both forward and backward (horizontal) movements of the tongue and large vertical movements of the mandible

(c) False

(d) False

(e) 6 months of age

(f) slower

(g) False

13–8

(a) modified barium swallow study.

(b) False

(c) Oral preparatory phase
Oral transport phase
Pharyngeal transport phase
Esophageal transport phase

(d) radiologist (or radiology technician); speech-language pathologist

(e) *Laryngeal penetration* occurs when food or liquid moves into the laryngeal vestibule (but stays above the vocal folds).

(f) *Aspiration* occurs when food or liquid travels below the vocal folds.

(g) videofluorscopy.
flexible endoscopy.

(h) flexible endoscopic evaluation of swallowing (FEES).

(i) pressure

13–9

(a) *Dysphagia* means disordered swallowing (or, more accurately, disordered deglutition).

(b) One example is phagophobia (fear of swallowing). Another example is feeling a "lump in the throat" with no apparent organic cause.

(c) Yes

A glossectomy could cause a swallowing disorder because the tongue is a critical player in the oral preparatory and oral transport phases of swallowing. A glossectomy is surgical removal of part or all of this critical structure.

(d) Bilateral paralysis of the facial muscles could make it difficult to adduct the lips, causing the oral preparatory phase to be more difficult to execute.

Removal of a vocal fold might leave the lower airways unprotected and increase the chance of aspiration.

A stroke in the brainstem could cause impairment of various cranial nerves that are important to swallowing, thereby resulting in problems with essentially every phase of swallowing (with the possible exception of the esophageal transport phase).

Chronic obstructive pulmonary disease can cause a variety of problems, one of which is dyspnea (breathing discomfort). An abnormally strong drive to breathe can make it difficult to breath-hold during the pharyngeal transport phase of swallowing and can increase the risk of aspiration, especially if an inspiration immediately follows a swallow.

(e) oropharyngeal

(f) gastroenterologist

(g) occupational

References

Blumstein, S., & Stevens, K. (1979). Acoustic invariance in speech production: Evidence from measurements of the spectral characteristics of stop consonants. *Journal of the Acoustical Society of America, 66,* 1001–1017.

Chen, M. (1995). Acoustic parameters of nasalized vowels in hearing-impaired and normal-hearing speakers. *Journal of the Acoustical Society of America, 98,* 2443–2453.

Hillenbrand, J., Getty, L., Clark, M., & Wheeler, K. (1995). Acoustic characteristics of American English vowels. *Journal of the Acoustical Society of America, 97,* 3099–3111.

Hixon, T., & Hoit, J. (2005). *Evaluation and management of speech breathing disorders.* Tucson, AZ: Redington Brown.

Hixon, T., Hawley, J., & Wilson (1982). An around-the-house device for the clinical measurement of respiratory driving pressure: A note on making simple even simpler. *Journal of Speech and Hearing Disorders, 47,* 13–15.

Hixon, T., Weismer, G., & Hoit, J. (2014). *Preclinical speech science: Anatomy, physiology, acoustics, perception* (2nd ed.). San Diego, CA: Plural.

Hoit, J., & Hixon, T. (1987). Age and speech breathing. *Journal of Speech and Hearing Research, 30,* 351–366.

Lee, S., Potamianos, A., & Narayanan, S. (1999). Acoustics of children's speech: Developmental changes of temporal and spectral parameters. *Journal of the Acoustical Society of America, 105,* 1455–1468.

Mullenix, J., Pisoni, D., & Martin, C. (1989). Some effects of talker variability on spoken word recognition. *Journal of the Acoustical Society of America, 85,* 365–378.

Quanjer, P., Tammeling, G., Cotes, J., Pedersen, O., Peslin, R., & Yernault, J-C. (1993). Lung volumes and forced ventilatory flows. *European Respiratory Journal, 6*(Suppl. 16), 5–40.

Stevens, K., & House, A. (1955). Development of a quantitative description of vowel articulation. *Journal of the Acoustical Society of America, 27,* 484–493.

Stevens, K., & House, A. (1963). Perturbation of vowel articulations by consonantal context: An acoustical study. *Journal of Speech and Hearing Research, 6,* 111–128.